THE EVOLUTION OF CHINESE FILIALITY

This unique book brings a fresh interdisciplinary approach to the analysis of ancient Chinese history, creating a historical model for the emergence of cultural mainstays by applying recent dramatic findings in the fields of neuroscience and cultural evolution.

The centrality in Chinese culture of a deep reverence for the lives of preceding generations, filial piety, is conventionally attributed to Confucius (551–479 B.C.), who viewed hierarchical family relations as foundational for social order. Here, Porter argues that Confucian conceptions of filiality themselves evolved from a systemized set of behaviors and thoughts, a mental structure, which descended from a specific Neolithic mindset, and that this psychological structure was contoured by particular emotional conditions experienced by China's earliest farmers. Using case study analysis from Neolithic sky observers to the dynastic cultures of the Shang and Western Zhou, the book shows how filial piety evolved as a structure of feeling, a legacy of a cultural predisposition toward particular moods and emotions that were inherited from the ancestral past. Porter also brings new urgency to the topic of ecological grief, linking the distress central to the evolution of the filial structure to its catalyst in an environmental crisis.

With a blended multidisciplinary approach combining social neuroscience, cultural evolution, cognitive archaeology, and historical analysis, this book is ideal for students and researchers in neuropsychology, religion, and Chinese culture and history.

Deborah Lynn Porter is Professor of Global Studies at the Jackson School of International Studies. Her interdisciplinary research on the impact of shameful secrets on cultural production spans a wide swath of time and geography, including Early China, and fifteenth- and sixteenth-century Western Europe, Russia, and Korea.

THE EVOLUTION OF CHINESE FILIALITY

Insights from the Neurosciences

Deborah Lynn Porter

Routledge
Taylor & Francis Group
NEW YORK AND LONDON

Cover credit: Turtle graphs in oracle-bone inscriptions. After Yang Xiaoneng (2000). Ed. Reflections of Early China: Decor, Pictographs, and Pictorial Inscriptions. (University of Washington, 114, Fig. 251).

First published 2022
by Routledge
605 Third Avenue, New York, NY 10158

and by Routledge
2 Park Square, Milton Park, Abingdon, Oxon, OX14 4RN

Routledge is an imprint of the Taylor & Francis Group, an informa business

Library of Congress Cataloguing-in-Publication Data
A catalog record for this title has been requested

ISBN: 978-1-032-10398-3 (hbk)
ISBN: 978-1-032-10396-9 (pbk)
ISBN: 978-1-003-21513-4 (ebk)

DOI: 10.4324/9781003215134

Typeset in Bembo
by MPS Limited, Dehradun

抛砖引玉

CONTENTS

FIGURES

TABLE

PREFACE

This book tells a story about the discomfort of social isolation and the evolution of mechanisms to transcend this social pain. Initially, my intellectual intentions were historical. I trained my lens on Chinese culture, which boasts a contiguous, nine-thousand-year material record, to investigate the transgenerational transmission of mechanisms that evolved to modulate the social pain caused by shame. But the global pandemic has shed light on the broader and contemporary relevance of the findings. If this book stimulates a dialogue that heightens understanding of our current conditions and the ways it triggers and generates behaviors, it will be an unanticipated but welcome outcome.

A serendipitous exposure to the application of neuroscience findings to cultural and psychological analysis catalyzed my ability to imagine the story's arc, which unfolds in the following account. The company of the brilliant scholars who work in that field, and in related fields of evolutionary cognitive science, social, and behavioral psychology, and of course Early China, transformed my isolated conditions over the past two years into a richly fulfilling period. I humbly express gratitude. I cannot predict the reception of this interdisciplinary effort, but I am clear about occupying the position of the proverbial Chinese poet who construes himself as a "brick thrower," lobbying his lyrical "blocks" in the hope of eliciting refined jade responses.

Extraordinary support from the University of Washington Library, during the time when in person access to sources was prohibited, also deserves warm acknowledgment. Thanks too to Bart Wright who untangled a skein of different maps to produce two that help illustrate the story. Alex Howard's enthusiasm for the project and the gracious support provided by Routledge's Psychology editors and staff truly enhanced the process of completing the book and preparing the manuscript. Tamara Morgan and Peter Miller provided timely support to ensure the story kept its heart, which meant making it as accessible as possible to a wide readership.

Deborah Lynn Porter
Seattle, WA
August 16, 2021

1

INTRODUCTION

It is an exciting time to be a student of Early China (8000-221 B.C.). Not only have archaeological discoveries consistently refined our understanding of the way humans transitioned from hunter-gatherer to sedentary life habits, but the methods and techniques applied to extrapolate information about pre-historic and early historic behavior are increasingly sophisticated. The recent publication of two encyclopedia devoted to the field testifies to growing interest beyond the confines of area studies specialists.[1] Furthermore, interdisciplinary research findings have encouraged reconsideration of some regnant assumptions about the origins of Chinese culture.

This book rides on the wave of these smart reassessments. Even as I acknowledge wide local variances among artifactual expression, I use the term "China" as a convention to refer to shared behavioral attributes among Neolithic and Bronze Age populations who inhabited geographical spaces that were later associated with Chinese state-like societies.[2] The notion that "inter-regional interactions result[ed] in the creation of a shared cultural language" is a foundational premise of this study. Gideon Shelach-Lavi suggests that this process "catalyzed the need for demonstrations of local identities."[3] If so, the endemic dynamic implies that local expressive forms performed translative or mediatory work, they filtered the shared cultural language to suit local needs and belief systems.

1 Goldin (2018); Childs-Johnson (2021).
2 Goldin (2018); Shelach-Lavie (2018). See also Liu (2005); Liu and Chen (2012); Shelach-Lavi (2015) for similar articulations of China's cultural origins.
3 Shelach-Lavi (2018, 32).

DOI: 10.4324/9781003215134-1

For example, this book argues that one defining feature of the shared cultural language generated by Neolithic interaction is its relationship with normative astro-calendrical knowledge. Although local ecological realities—including pre-existing belief systems—shaped the mediation process, the shared cultural information that drove the various expressions can nonetheless be discerned. Roel Stercx has shown that ancient agrarian epistemology was "concerned with the issue of when to engage in agricultural activities, rather than how to farm... [focusing on t]he issue of timing, sowing and harvesting, selecting the right crops according to the seasons."[4] Different ecological conditions would account for variance, while the growth of populations and settlement size tacitly point to the agricultural advantages provided by shared astro-calendrically-based agrarian assumptions.

The claim is based on evidence drawn from three types of sources: 1) the archaeological record; 2) a corpus of texts transmitted from the Han Dynasty (202 B.C.-220 A.D.); 3) the paleographical record, comprising texts inscribed in or written on materials such as turtle plastrons, bronze ritual vessels, bamboo strips, and silk. Recent paleographic findings have affirmed the accuracy of transmitted literature.[5] At the same time, epigraphic analysis has yielded examples of differences among the Chinese graphs used to transcribe the same passage in transmitted and newly recovered textual traditions.[6] The discrepancies arose from the homophonous relationship between graphs that were used as "loan" words to substitute for each other. Sometimes, when the loan words' own semantic ranges do not converge, questions over which word was originally intended arise. As we shall see, the answers to such questions may hold serious implications for interpretation.

At this time Neolithic cultural remains lack evidence of written language. There is dubiety in methodologies that project back on to this time a first millennium historiographical sensibility, although they are not uncommon in Early China scholarship. One rationale for the recalcitrance of this intellectual propensity is a historical perspective regarding the existence of three ancient dynasties, the Xia (1953?-1576? B.C.), Shang (1576?-1046 B.C.), and (Western) Zhou (1046-771 B.C.), the founders of which were memorialized as the fount of normative cultural values. This entrenched historical assumption is longstanding: it appeared in the renowned historical treatise called *The Grand Scribe's Records* (*Shiji*) composed by the Han dynasty historian Sima Qian (145-86 B.C.).[7] Because the list of Shang ancestors preserved in his "Basic Annals of the

4 Stercx (2018, 303).
5 This is especially the case with the canonical or "classical" (*jing*) texts, such as the *Book of Poetry* (*Shijing*) the *Book of Documents* (*Shujing*) and the *Book of Changes* (*Yijing*). Differences in organization of the latter text will be discussed below. For an account of recent excavations and paleographic methods, see Shaughnessy (2019, 35–41).
6 Shaughnessy (2019).
7 Bagley (2018, 67ff.).

Yin [Shang]" (Yin benji) was validated by the discovery of Shang dynasty written materials, it was seen to obviate the question of whether or not a dynastic-level sociopolitical unit that identified as Xia in fact preceded the Shang. This assuredness has oriented the target of Chinese archaeological work, not to mention interpretation of its findings.[8]

Nonetheless, there is growing consensus that the archaeological record portrays a sociopolitical landscape that clearly does not reflect condensation of power in ways that anticipate Shang royal behavior at the end of the second millennium B.C.[9] The predetermined historical framework premised on the conception of a Xia dynasty is not necessary to trace the emergence of dynastic polities. As we shall see in Chapter 4, the remains of early Shang city-settlement sites reflect an extended process of political development and cultural refinement. It was not until Shang royalty settled at Anyang, Henan Province, that political behavior exemplifies behavior characteristic of centralized control.

While first millennia B.C. imaginaries of rulers whose reigns were projected back into pre-historic time are inappropriate to explain the archaeological record, there is much of value in some of the transmitted texts. I refer especially to preserved historical records that reflect a preoccupation with astronomical issues of agrarian timing and techniques for ensuring activities accord to the seasons. Because references to the recurring seasonal appearances of stellar configurations can be corroborated or invalidated on the basis of contemporary astronomical calculations, I treat some first millennium texts that record the reliance on the achronycal appearance (after sunset) of a determined cluster of stars to initiate agrarian activities as archaeoastronomical data.

David Pankenier's groundbreaking research on the astronomical underpinnings of Chinese cosmopolitical thought also established a methodological precedent of searching the skies for historical data.[10] I follow suit though my aim is not to refine dynastic chronology but rather to demonstrate the intimate degree to which ancient Chinese brains were shaped by their engagement with celestial relational objects. The evidence I adduce attests to the incontrovertible role played by astronomical observations in the evolution of Chinese culture.

8 Cf. Grimberg (2019). For another interpretation of Xia, see the perspective advanced by Allan (1984, 2007), who argues that the story about the Xia was a fiction woven and then perpetuated by Shang and Zhou rulers.

9 Chen (2019) provides a chronological account of the vicissitudes of the debates.

10 Pankenier (2013) is the best and most comprehensive articulation of his findings and their implications for understanding Early Chinese cosmopolitical thought and the behavior it determined. Pankenier's discovery of a rare five-planet conjunction that occurred in 1059 B.C. has been generally accepted as coinciding, if not catalyzing, the Zhou overthrow of the Shang. For dissenting perspective see Keenan (2002, 2007), and Panenkenier's rebuttal (2007).

At its most basic level, cultural evolution correlates to the expansion of brain processes in order to accommodate changing social, emotional, and psychological realities. Evolutionary cognitive scholars agree that the long process of transitioning from hunter-gatherer existence to full-fledged agricultural subsistence wrought significant changes in human cognition and interpersonal psychology. These changes were catalyzed by membership in an interdependent group's settlement life. Cognitive expansion and integration facilitated the identification of interdependent normative behavior, adherence to which stimulated collective processes of self-fashioning and identity formation. The expression of this identity, culture, took a symbolic form that was transmissible. Shelach-Lavi claims that these symbolic systems lie at the crux of cultural attributes and qualities that emerged in and then extended beyond the Neolithic to influence Chinese dynastic culture.[11]

The application of social science perspectives to the analysis of archaeological cultures has led some researchers to theorize the sociopolitical, economic, and religious behaviors that might have catalyzed them. Much attention has been directed to the integrative dynamic that characterized interactions among Neolithic regional cultures.[12] The present study investigates the phenomena of cultural integration from a neuropsychological angle. It applies to the analysis of ancient Chinese history the dramatic findings in recent research that links neuroscience and cultural evolution.[13] This approach, sometimes referred to as "cultural neuroscience" (CN) emerged in the wake of discoveries of cultural "variations in the neural substrates of human cognition."[14]

A recent review of the field's evolution and intellectual findings sums up the investigative aim: cultural neuroscience seeks to account for "how implicit and explicit patterns of beliefs, values, meanings and practices in specific sociocultural contexts shape the neural mechanisms underlying human cognition, emotion and behavior."[15] The contiguity of Chinese cultural behavior over seven millennia makes it an exemplary data source for testing the idea that the root of cultural institutions and their preservation over time lie in the emotional experiences of our prehistoric ancestors. My lens focuses on the unique social and ecological conditions in Neolithic China that shaped relevant neuropsychological processes.

11 (2018, 24).
12 Ibid. We discuss this in more detail in Chapter 4.
13 Smail (2007).
14 Han et al. (2013, 336); Chiao et al. (2016) discuss the "cultural neuroscience of pain and empathy," which has been shown to be contoured by cultural group membership; Downey (2015, 43) discusses "human echolocation," that is, "the degree to which human senses are trainable, especially given appropriate feedback and social support." We shall see how perceptions and pain intersected consequent to particular ecological conditions experienced by Early Neolithic farmers.
15 Han et al. (2013, 335).

This basic assumption is distinct from other studies of the Neolithic mind that advance human neurology as a foundation for projecting cultural forms. I do not subscribe to the idea that since humans share the same brain structure it tends to reason that similarities among (Neolithic) symbolic forms derive from established neural networks and processes. Nor do I engage with the scholarship that links cultural semantics to the notion of a shaman, whose capacity for transcendence is assumed without proper archaeological evidence to support it.[16] While alcohol remains in Neolithic mortuary contexts indicate that fermentation may have functioned to trigger altered states of consciousness, I found no other evidence to support the idea that the altered dimension itself was the source of religious and figurative representation.[17] If pressed to use the word "hard-wired," which I'm glad I'm not, I would rush to add that the hard-wiring of relevance to my study is not psychotropic-induced altered states of consciousness, but rather the cultural dimensions of the relationship between emotional experiences and the brain systems recruited to mediate their impact.

To clarify, the neuropsychological model I advance is not confined to the role played by hallucinogens as the sole conduit for the development of symbolic expression. Nonetheless, insomuch as it argues that Neolithic responses to a collectively experienced ecological loss influenced the development of group cognition and representative symbolic systems, my approach is open to critiques of "neurological determinism."[18] Although this critique was directed to reliance on a neuropsychologically-based "trance model," which I too reject as too narrow, I do link the production of archaeologically observable forms to the impact of brain processes on the development of Neolithic cognitive attentional proclivities.[19] Moreover, I suggest that these neuropsychologically forged tendencies account for the attitudes pressed within representative ideas and forms that evolved from them.[20]

That said, this book's culturally deterministic line of argument does not suffer from the tautology reflected in the argument about Neolithic mindsets and altered states, which cites imagistic cosmological tropes as proof and product of (shamans) achieving altered states. Rather, archaeological and archaeoastronomical evidence are marshaled to reconstruct a semiotic network of symbolic meaning organized around collectively valued (and scientifically verifiable) ecological knowledge. Thus, deployed to explain an implicit causality informing the development of Chinese cultural forms, the neuropsychological model accommodates variance in the shifting conditions within which shared

16 Pearce and Lewis-Williams (2005).
17 McGovern et al. (2004); Liu (2021).
18 Helvenston and Bahn (2005); Pearce and Lewis-Williams (2005, 11) deny their model engages in neurological determinism.
19 Malafouris (2010).
20 Geertz (2010).

(ecologically related) cultural assumptions were filtered and manifested. The book's unifying theory seeks to explain the complex dynamic between symbolic expression and evolving aspects of collectively lived existence. The analysis is situated within cultural factors that can be demonstrated to have been experienced. While many of the elements are not novel the attempt to integrate them into a long-term diachronic dimension is.

Removing the idea of a shaman, or at least the notion that such a figure is key to tracing neuropsychological structures that were shaped by Neolithic experience, allows issues of psychological states and emotional experiences related to fear or loss to take center stage; I view them as agentive entities capable of shaping perceptions, symbolic expression, which culminate in cultural production where collective existential memory and materiality intersect.[21] The mental structure that evolved was a result of interactions between humans, socially organized as interdependent groups, and their Neolithic ecology at the earliest stages of year-round settlement life.

We can accept the premise of a neurologically generated "culturally specific expression" without arguing for a pre-existing embodied mind that was triggered into expression through Neolithic media.[22] The line of logic borne from this interdisciplinary approach yields a fresh historical model for explaining the emergence of Chinese cultural mainstays. It also makes this historical record of human behavior accessible to neuroscientists and scholars of evolutionary cognition. Stimulating collaborative work among these experts and those of Chinese and other ancient cultures is this book's driving aim.

An Alternate Theory

A short comparative discussion of a recent book by anthropologist Li Min, *Social Memory and State Formation in China,* who also advances a unifying theory to "move beyond regional variations in archaeological remains to discuss broad patterns of social change," further adumbrates the intellectual aims of this study.[23] Li seeks to explain the emergence of a social memory about the three dynasties, Xia, Shang, and Zhou. He claims that this historical conception can be traced to the rise of Late Neolithic political centers in two distinct regions, the Jinnan Basin and the Luoyang Basin. Li's diachronic, long-view approach, based on the archaeological record, permits him to trace "dynamic shifts in cultural concepts,

21 Malafouris (2010). See Gutchess and Huff (2015) discuss the literature on the "cognitive biases and strategies that can shape memory." Especially relevant is the association between "increased attention to field and context and focus on functional relationships" which are characteristics of biases seen among subjects socialized in Chinese speaking societies.

22 Scarre (2007, 226).

23 Li (2018, 23).

categories and techniques that crosscut seemingly natural boundaries."[24] On this evidence, Li argues that Neolithic social memories and identities were woven into a narrative in response to "dynamic relations between the physical and cultural landscapes."[25]

Li's account delineates the shift "from a plural to a singular narrative of political and religious authority."[26] He relies on an ancient (originally oral) story structure built around the legendary Great Yu, a cultural hero renowned for his feats of hydraulic prowess in controlling a catastrophic flood. Using a first millennium account of the hero's "flood-control odyssey" as a "master narrative of the book" Li argues the story of Yu's division of the landscape into nine-sections "represent[s] a legacy of religious responses to the climatological and ecological crisis of the late third millennium BCE."[27] Li ties the "given moment" of these conditions to the emergence of a spatial ideology that ultimately shaped cosmopolitical schemas and Late Neolithic and early Bronze Age Chinese cultural behavior. For example, Li explains the practice of "time-mapping ceremonies closely associated with defining the location of axis mundi,"[28] as reflective of the "[o]ngoing construction of place and collective memory that occurred through carefully orchestrated and meaning-laden earthen and stone depositional practices."[29]

The Evolution of Chinese Filiality independently arrives at a similar historical conclusion drawn by Li, namely that the Yu cosmovision was incompatible with the Zhou notion of an axis mundi. Oddly, the evidence I adduce to discern this cultural condition implicitly questions the historical validity of Li's claim that an identifiable historical ecological crisis generated the production of a Yu story structure. This book, like Li's, demonstrates a process whereby collective imaginary objectivation of different nucleo-peripheral relations merged to form a shared memory and concomitant political identities. Nonetheless, I argue the cultural roots of this evolutionary phenomenon antedate the second millennium by more than four thousand years.

The historical issues raised by Li's analysis have been addressed in a recent study that warns against making facile correlations between paleoclimatic research and archaeological findings. The reason for the caution is that many studies ignore differences is scale metrics. Critiquing a plethora of scholarship motivated to link historical flooding events to the Yu story cycle (and some that extend this to the foundation of the Xia dynasty, which Li to his credit, does not), the authors argue that climatological related events operate on a temporal framework

24 Ibid.
25 Ibid. (22).
26 Ibid. (27).
27 Ibid.
28 Ibid. (414–417; 479, 455).
29 Ibid. (47).

that cannot be easily reduced to timelines of cultural evolution.[30] Once this imposed, potentially inaccurate, historical construct is removed, the question that still remains is why would such a story emerge and do the components of the story offer a key to unlocking the answer?

Twenty-five years ago I wrote a book about this; its title, *From Deluge to Discourse: Myth, History and the Generation of Chinese Fiction*, clearly articulates the study's process-tracing orientation.[31] The book argued that the Yu story cycle should be understood as a response to a catastrophic experience. I claimed that the inundation story was a metaphorical account of the astronomical events that triggered a profound sense of loss and confusion. Shifts in the spatiotemporal positions of stars used to determine the timing of agricultural activities were the "historical cause" of the flood described in Yu story structures, and my findings strongly suggest they lie at the origin of what Li identifies as "time-mapping" rituals related to Yu's flood controlling acts. The source of the flood metaphor, in my account, was the Milky Way, known to the Chinese as Sky River. This celestial waterway was perceived as a site of catastrophe because proximate celestial objects that served as calendrical harbingers failed to sustain their function. Succinctly, I argued that the Yu stories transmitted important ecological information relating to the passage and accounting of astro-calendrical time.

On this premise, I presented evidence to account for the astro-calendrical intentions conveyed by details of Yu's characterization in the flood story. For example, I explained the association between the hero and the number nine; his renowned technique for mediating flood crises; the philological roots of his name; and the reason why Yu is collectively remembered for his "limping gait." All of these were imagistic accounts of a collective memory involving the vicissitudes of human efforts to coordinate their agricultural and social behavior with seasonal transitions marked by the movements of the constellation known as Dragon (*long*), about which much will be said below. Li does not offer explanations for these features of Yu's characterization, although his study emphasizes the "nonary" dimension of Yu's legend, and the significance of Yu's limp for dancing rituals associated with his worship.

From Deluge to Discourse anticipated the psychosocial dimensions of Li's inquiry: he views narrative forms of cultural production as performing a mediating function in response to (psychological and ecological) crises. I demonstrated how interpolations of the Yu flood story lexicon into a travel account of a Western Zhou king pointed to a subtext of unexpressed grief, what I called the "founding silence" of the journey. The manifest content of the story: traveling; ecological observations; delineation of sequenced space; reflects a discourse generated by the need to refashion and adapt behavioral parameters triggered by a traumatic relational loss. Recognizing the great affective force of the Yu complex on

30 Jaffe et al. (2021).
31 Porter (1996).

representations and memories of the Western Zhou king uncovered its status as an expressive form used by society to tell itself about the way by which some situation came about and was maintained. Pursuing the conditions surrounding this loss, and asking why the effects of astro-calendrical realities would be experienced in terms of interpersonal and intrapsychic discomfort, I proposed that the contingencies of the cultural codes already in force when the Yu flood myths emerged exemplified a metapsychological situation: the processes by which obstacles to royal self-fashioning were transcended.

While the Yu flood stories do make an appearance in this book, they emerge only toward the end of the evolutionary story (in Chapter 5). Before that, I return to Sky River, the site implicated in the relationship between a king's silenced trauma and the Yu flood lexicon. With the benefit of archaeological evidence not available to me when I conducted the earlier research, I am able to reconstruct the deep history of the conditions leading to Yu worship. The book extrapolates an extraordinary long line of collective emotional contiguity that explains the emergence of Yu flood stories and its coevolved relationship with early Chinese royal self-construal and political self-fashioning.

The Conception of Confucian Filiality as a Launching Point

Paul Goldin has suggested that "asking what it means to be Chinese was always connected with asking what it means to be civilized."[32] The findings of this study generally concur with his insight. Nonetheless, the book insists that the status of being civilized was inextricable from astro-calendrically-based conceptions of proper deportment to ensure human behavior was "aligned" and in sync with seasonal time. I use a neuropsychological model to trace the evolution of this dimension of Chinese civilization in epigenetic terms. I identify the developmental trajectory of Chinese cultural evolution as determined by a neuro-emotional residuum of responses to specific identifiable aversive events.

I use the word "epigenetic" cautiously, aware that its application to human transgenerational inheritance is debated.[33] Recent findings of investigations into the "variation in the nervous system and its relationship to social behavior" offer different, evidence-based perspectives, even as the researchers concur that more evidence is needed.[34] While I submit that the story I uncover about Chinese

32 Goldin (2018, 5).

33 Horsthemke (2018).

34 See Jiang et al. (2019) who point to epigenetic evidence in contexts of childhood trauma. Recent studies on the monogamous prairie vole have shown the neurobiology of "brain-region specific receptor patterns" that "underl[ie] pair bonding and the selective attachments." Sadino and Donaldson (2018). Phelps et al. (2010) found that socially monogamous prairie voles demonstrated that "pronounced individual differences… in spatial memory and sexual fidelity than are areas known to regulate pair bonding directly."

cultural evolution may invite consideration that genetic variation in brain function was a source of the adaptive behavioral variations I identify, the thrust of my findings does not hinge on a literal understanding of the word.

Rather, I use it to call attention to the plasticity of cultural constructs, clusters of ideas, and affects that I construe as "cultural cells." These units or "cells" act like an epigenome, changing "with time and exposure to the environment."[35] Material culture found at the earliest sedentary site that was occupied year-round in China yields evidence of an archetypal "cultural genome" in which all the "cultural cells" operated "essentially identical[ly with] all cells" within the social organism. This "cultural genome" was "stable throughout the life-time" of the group members, indeed it was stable for the group for more than a millennium.[36]

In time, as has been detected in neurobiological findings of epigenome vulnerability tied to development stages, "alterations in gene expression patterns induced at these times may persist for long periods, influencing the phenotype of the adult."[37] Because this occurred at the early stages of Neolithic development, the alterations to the "cultural cells" that were made to adapt to new external conditions emerged to enhance the fitness value of specific behavioral traits. The endurability of cultural traits among the Neolithic and Bronze Age Chinese populations, as well as conspecifics, correlate with obstacles encountered by a group in the course of its cultural and developmental evolution. The relationship between this cultural genome and its variations are what I mean by "epigenetic" in this book.

One trait that emerges as defining in Chinese cultural behavior involves the neural correlates of self-perception or "self-construal." Self-construal is evaluated in terms of the degree to which thoughts of others' thoughts and experiences shape a subject's propensity to make decisions and act.[38] Broadly speaking, those for whom action choices do not rely on consideration of others' reactions are identified as "independent," while those whose choices were mediated by consideration of others were termed "interdependent."[39] It is important to note that these self-construal structures are not mutually exclusive but operate on a spectrum. Nonetheless, findings demonstrate that cultural norms can operate to "prime" a subject's inclination toward independence or interdependence in decision-making tasks.[40]

35 Gibney and Nolan (2010, 11). Sadino and Donaldson (2018).
36 Gibney and Nolan (11).
37 Ibid. (11).
38 Cross (2020).
39 Markus and Kitamaya (1991); Kitayama and Park (2010); Lee and Jeyaraj (2014); Gutchess and Huff (2015).
40 Lee and Jeyaraj (2014, 2): "multiple modes of self-construal exist in all individuals from any culture… and the use of priming enables temporary access to either an independent or interdependent self-construal, allowing the examination of either self-construal on behavior. See also Han and Ma (2015).

In this light, we may appreciate the salience of interdependence found among subjects raised in cultures whose social norms are generally described as "Confucian."[41] Because the fifth century philosopher Confucius is a figure commonly recognized, and because the ethical system attributed to his thought is also conceptualized as an agentive factor in the evolution of Chinese socialization patterns, Confucian concepts provide a compelling launching point for this book's neuropsychological line of inquiry. I focus on the ethical behavior known as filial piety, which encompasses the emotional dimension of reverence and respect for parents and lineage ancestors. Goldin identifies filiality as the first of "seven basic features of Chinese civilization that endured despite regional diversity and historical change."[42] It is not overstatement to say that filiality is the affective linchpin of Chinese interpersonal order so central in Chinese culture.

My starting point is what I perceive to be an implicit dissonance between the presumed positive valence of filial behavior in Confucius' ethical system, and the salience of shame and unmitigated grief that seems to saturate Confucius' imagination of a paradigmatic filial son. To answer the question as to the cause and meaning of such dissonance, I pursue these emotions as a prehistorical vector. The book's findings reveal Confucius' filial son's grief and shame to be an evolved structure of feeling, a legacy of a cultural predisposition toward particular moods and emotions that were inherited from the ancestral past. Although the formation of this culturally distinct neural representation of the self has been attributed to the shaping influence of Confucian filial norms themselves on Chinese child-rearing, the Neolithic evidence suggests a far earlier origin.

Mental structures shaped by Neolithic experience are linked to the Confucian mental image of filiality via emotional coherence: both were shaped by the distress of social separation. I trace the historical, neurological—i.e., "neurohistorical"—roots of filiality by identifying the formation of an emotionally conditioned neural substrate in response to a Neolithic experience of separation distress. Using this perspective to scrutinize Middle and Late Neolithic cultural behaviors opens a new vantage point from which to account for similarities and distinctions between cultural expressive forms.

The lens also permits a new view of Shang and Western Zhou royal behavior. To exemplify the potential of the heuristic I apply it to the enigmatic context of an archaeologically verifiable late middle Western Zhou social transformation, about which scant information is preserved in historical sources. The phenomenon, referred to as the "Western Zhou Ritual Reform" (hereafter Ritual Reform) serves as an excellent case study for a brain-based investigation of *felt*-history. Because the Zhou were socialized and acculturated via familial relationships with the Shang, the analysis treats the Ritual Reform as a product of

41 See for example, Li et al. (2006).
42 Goldin (2018: 5).

the complex and ongoing interaction between the Western Zhou royal family and the cultural niche they inhabited.

A Spiral Historical Line

The following sequence of five chapters begins and ends at the same spatio-temporal point: mid-point of the first millennium B.C., in the Central Plains, when Confucius' paradigmatic filial son first found expression. Together, with the three chapters sandwiched between, the order reflects my belief that cultural evolution was not a straight-line continuum. The book's looped structure reflects the spiral-like historical line that emerges in an emotionally anchored historical analysis. Each chapter breaks up the contiguous line into kernel experiences and responses, and then reformulates them along the deeper, historical lines of corresponding cultural expressive forms and thought patterns.

This order also highlights the recursive dimension of the neuropsychological processes that shaped Chinese shared culture. When exposed to emotional conditions evocative of a similar primary aversive experience, neural structures constructed in response to the primary aversive experiences were recruited and recapitulated (or scaffolded upon) in response. A history that traces cultural evolution in terms of recursive patterns generated by an archaic response to unpleasant deviant condition sheds light on the emotional sources of Chinese cultural history's unfolding. The chapters' varied foci represent the decisive historical implications of a neurohistorical approach.

Chapter 2 introduces the Confucian concept of filiality, situating it within specialized scholarship on Confucian thought. Most of this research focuses on the canonical text known as the Confucian *Analects* (*Lunyu*), which includes purportedly transcribed conversations held between the philosopher/teacher and his students.[43] It is in this text that snippets of conversations about filial behavior can be configured to reveal the paradigmatic image of a grief-stricken filial son. Neuroscientific scholarship, especially on the role emotions play in cognitive processing, is invoked to more concretely identify the behavior exhibited by the filial son as one involving "complicated grief," or ceaseless mourning. Reviewing the state of the field on neuropsychological explanations for the evolution of complicated grief and the behavioral patterns it fosters, the chapter establishes a foundation for the book's driving question: what neuropsychological conditions lie behind the salience of grief and shame that characterizes Confucius' paradigmatic filial son? In short, how did Confucian/Chinese filiality evolve?[44]

---

43 Hunter and Kern (2018).

44 Cf. Kitayama and Cohen (2007), where he poses ten questions that cultural and neurocultural psychologists should aim to answer. He insists consideration of the causal relationship to account for the differences attested in the neuroscience findings.

Chapter 3 initiates the investigation into what I identify as a primary (collective) experience of separation distress. I access this emotion via artifactual forms discovered in Wuyang, Henan Province, at an archaeological site called Jiahu culture. The discovery of the Jiahu settlement, which was continually occupied between 7000-5500 B.C., dramatically challenged the perspective that Chinese agriculture and culture originated in the Central Plains area, just south of the Yellow River, where some of China's oldest Neolithic cultures had been identified. Jiahu, located just north of the Huai River—the lower reaches of the Yellow River Valley—occupied a unique ecological niche. While they shared a tool repertoire indicative of early agrarian activity, and revealed habits that resembled northern settlements, the grain cultivator that supplemented the Jiahu settlement's nutrition needs was rice not millet.

Extensive and wide-ranging scholarship on recovered materials from the site yields a surprisingly vivid account of the lives lived by members of the interdependent group. The chapter zeroes in on the relationship between the unique prestige objects found in graves, Box Turtle shell sets, and what I hypothesize was seasonally organized agrarian behavior. The chapter links the archaeologically verified increase in population growth and increase in overall status of living that transpired between Phase I and Phase II of Jiahu occupation to the community's reliance on the appearance and disappearance of a celestial configuration. I argue that Jiahu farmers relied on the configuration as a proto-calendar for syncing agrarian acts with seasonal transformations. According to a fifth-century B.C. star-chart, this configuration was known as (fresh-water) Turtle (Corona Australis, CrA), which was located south of Sagittarius.[45]

Having established the fact of Turtle's relationship with the community, and contouring role regarding the emergence of collective norms, the chapter then explores the consequences to the collective psyche when, as a function of an astronomical fact, Turtle's seasonal timing slowly lagged. I explain that the experience of Turtle's apparent withdrawal from the vernal scene was experienced as an ecological loss. Moreover, I delineate how the unique conditions of the emotional experience, wherein Turtle remained visible albeit calendrically dysfunctional as a seasonal sign, had psychological consequences that influenced cognitive development, especially on the level of attention direction.[46] A preoccupation with observing, measuring, and identifying the

45 The star chart is called *Shen's Star Chart* (*Shi Shen Xingjing*). Sun and Kistemaker (1997) provide a detailed account of the text. See also Cullen (1996) for discussion of its relevance to early astronomical mathematics.

46 Van der Kolk (2015), advances the biological underpinnings of the way "the body keeps score" in response to traumatic experiences. We discuss this further in Chapter 2 below, especially the idea that the hippocampus is involved in preventing the development of memory, functioning instead to fragment and store the memory in bodily or sensory memory.

Pole Star is one cultural manifestation of the cognitive orientation that emerged in response to the loss.

Shame and grief triggered by Turtle's actions are implicated in the preoccupation with delimiting true north. These emotions, indicative of having experienced an aversive event, explain the appeal of behaviors that align and fix the built environment along the north-south axis. The chapter concludes by showing how the social impracticality of acknowledging the shame and grief required the experience be silenced in public discourse. These conditions then account for the way that Turtle's original astronomical intentions underwent a process of transformation in which traces of its original meaning were preserved as they were reformulated to symbolize a new cosmovision that was reflected in Middle Neolithic artifactual expressions.

Chapter 4 argues that the appearance circa 4000 B.C. of a bright star, Fire Star (Antares, α Scorpii), whose regular vernal and autumnal movements recapitulated Turtle's Early Neolithic calendrical function, catalyzed a positive emotional rejoinder to the separation distress. I connect increased agricultural production, among culturally disparate communities, to the establishment of a normative agrarian schedule regulated to sync with Fire Star's seasonal movements. Recognizing how this phenomenon would have been perceived by elites who sought to control the symbolic means of displaying the knowledge, as well as farmers, whose livelihoods depended on the timeliness of agrarian acts, suggests that astronomical literacy was an important component of the shared cultural knowledge.

The chapter traces the link between astro-calendrical knowledge, prestige status, and emerging conceptions of rulership. The connection between prestige and agrarian success becomes the background context for conceptions of sovereignty that emerged in response to yet another deviant astronomical event, this time involving the planets as well as constellations. Given the consistent preoccupation with celestial observations, it should not be surprising that the Chinese provide the only extant human record of two spectacular and dense planetary conjunctions in which all five planets visible with the naked eye occupied an extremely narrow bandwidth of the sky. The chapter discusses the implications of this new, external source of prestige conferral for an evolving psychology of kingship. Because we have paleographical data that reflects on the mentalities of subjects who lived during these eras, we are in a position to bring textual evidence to bear on our comprehension of the way an inherited neuropsychological structure evolved to adapt to new conditions.

Chapter 5 provides a case study of a Western Zhou cultural phenomenon whose emergence is considered enigmatic due to the lack of written materials to explain it. I view the fact of the record's lacuna as a clue that the conditions surrounding the Ritual Reform can be explained in terms of a psychic structure forged by the interaction between an archaic neural substrate and the ecological realities that confronted the Zhou royal family. Much research has focused on the dramatic formal changes seen in the clear favoring of shapes and décor distinct from what preceded it in Western Zhou ritual expression. Similarly, the repertoire performed as part of the rituals, which reflected changes in ancestral sacrificial practice, has elicited specialized attention. The chapter diverges from this approach to first historicize the Ritual Reform as a cultural unit produced in response to a catastrophic royal death. Having established the psychological conditions of this loss, and the implications that the loss could be interpreted as a sign of the Zhou's slipping prestige, the chapter reveals the emotional basis of the Ritual Reform to resonate with the archaic neural substrate.

This correlation helps explain why the royal family turned toward the sky as a space to mediate the trauma. I argue that the Ritual Reform was first and foremost a calendrical reform. I add to the historical record archaeoastronomical discoveries that strongly underscore the Ritual Reform's contribution to the evolution of the Chinese zodiac. I link the invention of constellations, their identification, and how they fit in the larger scheme of the Ritual Reform to psychological symbolic operations that reveals the degree to which this celestial vision was instrumental for transcending complicated grief. Neuropsychologically motivated by conditions that threatened their prestige status, the Zhou recapitulated the ancient process of establishing new cardinal coordinates to create a new standard for a new cosmovision.

Just as the process of symbolization that transformed Turtle from an object contaminated by negative affect into an object associated with a broader positive vision that all but obviated Turtle's earlier career, so too did the calendrical reform expand the boundaries within which death and transformation could be conceived and publicly commemorated. I claim the Ritual Reform can be seen as a product borne from the specific psychosocial conditions that shaped a grandson's experience of complicated grief. Because it performed this mediating function, the astro-calendrical reforms became the model for Zhou's terrestrial rituals and institutions.

It was not just the royal Zhou family that found transcendence but the allies and aristocrats who assisted the Zhou and whom the Zhou relied on to perpetuate their claim to sovereignty. The chapter emphasizes the psychosocial effects on the royal retinue and others who were incorporated into the expanded Zhou ritual fold. I argue that membership in this select group was signaled by the term *xiaoyou*, "offering comrade." The combination of words conveys both vertical and horizontal vectors of connection to the Zhou community, whereas the latter flattens the vertical dimension. In both cases the terms point to the larger social transformations they represented. The group identity forged by such nomenclature and communal participation in seasonally coordinated ancestral sacrifices is an essential component of the evolution of Confucian ethical thought, especially filiality.

Chapter 6 returns to the era of Confucius in the wake of the foregoing analysis. Although the Ritual Reform was widely adhered to, the social solidarity it provided could not prevent the capital from being sacked, which forced the Zhou and their aristocrats to flee eastwards. Zhou prestige could not survive such fragmentation, even as it retained some nominal stature among the allies and aristocrats whose own control over regional estates eventually rivaled the Zhou. Because of the Zhou's shame, aristocratic families found it necessary to distance themselves as they also silenced the positive valence of membership in the *xiaoyou* group.

I suggest that these conditions triggered a form of suspended mourning among the *xiaoyou* population, for whom Confucius was a figurehead, this time over a lost idyll whose memory became retroactively clandestine. One symptom of this psychological state is an unconscious obligation to keep preserved, that is, concealed, an unspeakable experience. I propose that these psychological conditions explain the image of a paradigmatic filial son who represents the existential experience of suspended mourning that is required to fulfill the obligation. Confucius' filial son turns out to be an image of the king whose effort to mourn his grandfather was retroactively spurned.

The chapter goes on to link other generic expressions, such as ghost stories and accounts of extreme, self-mutilation, as articulative forms that evolved from the impact exerted on cultural evolution by the Ritual Reform. The chapter concludes with a psychological analysis of the political persona of the state of Qin, whose rise during the Eastern Zhou (771-221 B.C.) culminated in the establishment of the foundation of Chinese imperial rule. Because the Qin's own origins were connected to the era of the Ritual Reform, its evolving personality provides a striking opportunity to document the impact of the Reform on Chinese political mindsets and self-construal.

Cited Sources

Allan, S. (1984). The myth of the Xia Dynasty. *Journal of the Royal Asiatic Society, 116*(2), 242–256.

Allan, S. (2007). Erlitou and the formation of Chinese civilization: Toward a new paradigm. *The Journal of Asian Studies, 66*(2), 461–496.

Bagley, R. (2018). The Bronze Age before the Zhou Dynasty. In *Routledge handbook of early Chinese history* (pp. 61–83). Routledge.

Chen, M. Z. (2019). Faithful history or unreliable history: Three debates on the historicity of the Xia Dynasty. *Journal of Chinese Humanities, 5*(1), 78–104.

Chiao, J. Y., Cheon, B. K., Pornpattananangkul, N., Mrazek, A. J., & Blizinsky, K. D. (2013). Cultural neuroscience: Progress and promise. *Psychological Inquiry, 24*(1), 1–19.

Chiao, J. Y., Li, S. C., Seligman, R., & Turner, R. (Eds.). (2016). *The Oxford handbook of cultural neuroscience.* Oxford University Press.

Childs-Johnson, E. (Ed.) (2021). *Oxford handbook of early China.*

Cohen, D., & Kitayama, S. (2007). *Cultural psychology: This stanza and the next.*

Cross, S. E. (2020). Self-construal. In B.J. Carducci and C.S. Nave (Eds.), *The Wiley encyclopedia of personality and individual differences: Personality processes and individual differences* (pp. 381–386). Wiley.

Cullen, C. (1996). *Astronomy and mathematics in ancient China, TheZhou Bi Suan Jing'* (p. 255). Cambridge University Press.

Cullen, C. (2007). *Astronomy and mathematics in ancient China: The'Zhou Bi Suan Jing'* (No. 1). Cambridge University Press.

Downey, G. (2015). Sensory enculturation and neoroanthropology: The case of human echolocation. In J.Y. Chiao, S.-C. Li, R. Seligman, and R. Turner (Eds.), *Oxford handbook of cultural neuroscience*. Oxford.

Geertz, A. W. (2010). Brain, body and culture: A biocultural theory of religion. *Method & Theory in the Study of Religion, 22*(4), 304–321.

Gibney, E. R., & Nolan, C. M. (2010). Epigenetics and gene expression. *Heredity, 105*(1), 4–13.

Goldin, P. R. (Ed.). (2018). Introduction: What is early Chinese history?In *Routledge handbook of early Chinese history* (pp. 1–11). Routledge.

Grimberg, P. (2019). Nationalism and politics in Chinese archaeology. *Journal: Encyclopedia of Global Archaeology*, 1–11. doi: 10.1007/978-3-319-51726-1_3366-1

Gutchess, A. H., Huff, S. (2015). Cross-cultural differences in memory. In J. Y. Chiao, S.-C. Li, R. Seligman, and R. Turner (Eds.), *The Oxford handbook of cultural neuroscience*. Oxford.

Han, S., Northoff, G., Vogeley, K., Wexler, B. E., Kitayama, S., & Varnum, M. E. (2013). A cultural neuroscience approach to the biosocial nature of the human brain. *Annual Review of Psychology, 64*, 335–359.

Han, S. H. & Ma, Y. N. (2015). Cultural neuroscience studies of the self-reflection. In J. Y. Chiao, S.-C. Li, R. Seligman, and R. Turner (Eds.), *Oxford handbook of cultural neuroscience*. Oxford.

Helvenston, P. A., & Bahn, P. G. (2005). *Waking the trance fixed*. Wasteland Press.

Horsthemke, B. (2018). A critical view on transgenerational epigenetic inheritance in humans. *Nature Communications, 9*(1), 1–4.

Hunter, M., & Kern, M. (2018). *Confucius and the Analects revisited: new perspectives on composition, dating, and authorship*. Brill.

Jaffe, Y. Y., Castellano, L., Shelach-Lavi, G., & Campbell, R. B. (2021). Mismatches of scale in the application of paleoclimatic research to Chinese archaeology. *Quaternary Research, 99*, 14–33.

Jiang, S., Postovit, L., Cattaneo, A., Binder, E. B., & Aitchison, K. J. (2019). Epigenetic modifications in stress response genes associated with childhood trauma. *Frontiers in Psychiatry, 10*, 808.

Keenan, D. J. (2002). Astro-historiographic chronologies of early China are unfounded. *East Asian History, 23*(2002), 61–68.

Kitayama, S., & Cohen, D. (2007). *Handbook of culturalpsychology*. New York, NY: Guilford Press.

Kitayama, S., & Park, J. (2010). Cultural neuroscience of the self: Understanding the social grounding of the brain. *Social Cognitive and Affective Neuroscience, 5*(2–3), 111–129.

Lee, J. J. Y., & Jeyaraj, S. (2014). Effects of self-construal differences on cognitive dissonance examined by priming the independent and interdependent self. *SAGE Open, 4*(1), 2158244014521434.

Li, M. (2018). *Social memory and state formation in early China*. Cambridge University Press.

Li, H. Z., Zhang, Z., Bhatt, G., & Yum, Y. O. (2006). Rethinking culture and self-construal: China as a middle land. *The Journal of Social Psychology, 146*(5), 591–610.

Liu, L. (2005). *The Chinese neolithic: Trajectories to early states*. Cambridge University Press.
Liu, L. (2021). Communal drinking rituals and social formations in the Yellow River valley of Neolithic China. *Journal of Anthropological Archaeology*, *63*, 101310.
Liu, L., & Chen, X. (2012). *The archaeology of China: From the Late Paleolithic to the Early Bronze Age*. Cambridge University Press.
Malafouris, L. (2010). The brain–artefact interface (BAI): a challenge for archaeology and cultural neuroscience. *Social Cognitive and Affective Neuroscience*, *5*(2-3), 264–273.
Markus, H. R., & Kitayama, S. (1991). Culture and the self: Implications for cognition, emotion, and motivation. *Psychological Review*, *98*(2), 224.
McGovern, P. E., Zhang, J., Tang, J., Zhang, Z., Hall, G. R., Moreau, R. A., ... & Wang, C. (2004). Fermented beverages of pre-and proto-historic China. *Proceedings of the National Academy of Sciences*, *101*(51), 17593–17598.
Pankenier, D. W. (2007). Caveat lector: Comments on Douglas J. Keenan, 'Astro-historiographic chronologies of early China are unfounded'. *Journal of Astronomical History and Heritage*, *10*, 137–141.
Pearce, D., & Lewis-Williams (2005). *Inside the Neolithic mind*. London.
Phelps, S. M., Campbell, P., Zheng, D. J., & Ophir, A. G. (2010). Beating the boojum: Comparative approaches to the neurobiology of social behavior. *Neuropharmacology*, *58*(1), 17–28.
Phelps, S. M., Okhovat, M., & Berrio, A. (2017). Individual differences in social behavior and cortical vasopressin receptor: Genetics, epigenetics, and evolution. *Frontiers in Neuroscience*, *11*, 537.
Sadino, J. M., & Donaldson, Z. R. (2018). Prairie voles as a model for understanding the genetic and epigenetic regulation of attachment behaviors. *ACS Chemical Neuroscience*, *9*(8), 1939–1950.
Scarre, C. (2007). Review. David Lewis-Williams & David Pearce. *Inside the Neolithic mInd: Consciousness, Cosmos and the Realm of Gods*. 320 Pages. 75 illustrations, 29 colour plates. 2005: London: Thames & Hudson. *Antiquity*, *81*(311), 225–226.
Shaughnessy, E. (2019). *Chinese annals in the western observatory: an outline of western studies of Chinese unearthed documents* (Vol. 4). Walter de Gruyter GmbH & Co KG.
Shelach-Lavi, G. (2015). *The archaeology of early China*. Cambridge University Press.
Shelach-Lavi, G. (2018). Main issues in the study of the Chinese Neolithic Gideon Shelach-Lavimain issues in the Chinese Neolithic. In *Routledge handbook of early Chinese history* (pp. 15–38). Routledge.
Smail, D. L. (2007). *On deep history and the brain*. University of California Press.
Sterckx, R. (2018). Food and agriculture. In *Routledge handbook of early Chinese history* (pp. 300–318). Routledge.
Sun, X. C., & Kistemaker, J. (Eds.). (1997). *The Chinese sky during the Han: Constellating stars and society* (Vol. 38). Brill.
Van der Kolk, B. A. (2015). *The body keeps the score: Brain, mind, and body in the healing of trauma*. Penguin Books.

2

SEEKING A CHINESE FILIAL MIND MODULE

The idea that a deep history of cultural behavior can illuminate the interaction between our Neolithic ancestors' brains and their external environment animates this study. This chapter presents the conundrum whose resolution implores the book's investigatory orientation. It begins with a description of cultural behavior that found expression in a deep reverence for the lives of preceding generations, filiality (*xiao*). The centrality in Chinese culture of filial behavior is conventionally attributed to the thinker Confucius (551-479 B.C.), who viewed hierarchical family relations as foundational for social order during chaotic times.[1]

I construe Chinese filiality as a complex to the degree that it condenses what is understood culturally into identifiable behavior. Daniel Lord Smail argues that the orientation of behavioral tendencies hinges on the degree to which the collective nervous system was conditioned by interactions with the environment that were experienced as positive or negative.[2] He claims that the conditioning of the nervous system accounts for the establishment of cultural institutions and behaviors that are "extended over long expanses of space and time."[3]

I approach Chinese filiality as an evolved structure of feeling.[4] The book's central claim is that filiality evolved from a systemized set of behaviors and

1 Goldin (2017).
2 Smail (2007).
3 Fuller (2014, 100). Panksepp (1999 a, b) and Damasio (1999), suggest that emotional responses to external and internal stimuli are responsible for a pre-reflective core self, which is the basis of higher order cognitive functions and reflective awareness.
4 Smail (2007, 2014). Cf. Marks et al. (1995, xi), where they advocate that academic attention focus on understanding the "structure and experience of emotion in non-Western cultures."

DOI: 10.4324/9781003215134-2

thoughts, a mental structure, which descended from a specific Neolithic mindset. This psychological structure was contoured by particular emotional conditions experienced by China's earliest farmers. Before tracing the emotional roots of filiality back to the Neolithic, it is important to describe more precisely what I mean by "Confucian filiality."

To proclaim that this is an extremely well-studied topic is an understatement.[5] Most scholars agree that Confucius promoted hierarchical strategies for ordering the self, the family, and the state.[6] At the root of self-order is an affective system organized around the child-parent bond, denoted by the word "filial" (*xiao*).[7] Underlying Confucius' notion of filial children is the expectation that their behavior adheres to his proscribed idiom for self-management.[8] When scholars speak of Chinese filiality, they refer to this self-management grammar, and its imprint on the brains of people born into and raised by cultures organized by Confucian relational axioms.[9]

Neuroscientific Underpinnings

This chapter situates Confucian filiality within a neurological context of *felt*-history. Taking Confucius at his word that he "transmits but does not invent" (*shu er bu zuo*),[10] I ask about the emotional source of the portrait of a paradigmatic filial son that he transmits, which can be extrapolated from Confucius' sayings and descriptions of a filial son's actions. Some general neurological findings guide this chapter's line of inquiry.

First is that brain structure reflects evolutionary development. The most archaic part, the brainstem, is found in all animals. It plays a critical role in integrating neural network activity that modulates arousal, responses to sensations, autonomic functions, and motor control. It is also the source of the neurogenetic evolution of "our affective rather than our cognitive nature."[11] I heed Jaak Panksepp's warning to avoid conflating cognition and emotion, and find his

5 Goldin (2014; 2017); Radice (2017); Chan and Tan (2004).

6 Ivanhoe (2008).

7 For a comprehensive account of the word's use and evolution in early Chinese texts see Maye et al. (2002); see also Harry Hsin-I Hsiao; Jones (2008); Chan and Tan (2004).

8 Nichols (2013). See also Ke (2014).

9 Ebrey (2014, 4). See Ivanhoe (2000, 2008); Kinney (2017, 148–151). These self-management practices, known as "rituals" (*li*), derive from social "structures of meaning that help [people] interpret themselves and their relations to others.

10 *Lunyu* 7:1. All citations of transmitted texts refer to those included in The Chinese Text Project, which contains "accurate and accessible copies of ancient (in particular pre-Qin and Han dynasty) Chinese texts in an organized and searchable format." Complete with concordances linked to textual commentaries, the site is a helpful aid in the study and research of these texts.

11 Panksepp (2009, 231).

working definitions to be helpful parameters for the following discussion: "Cognitions can be defined as the processing of information entering the brain-mind through the sensory portals; affects are better defined as evaluative felt states of mind that reflect evolved internal brain functions that code survival issues."[12]

Recent neuroscience studies based on neuroimaging have more clearly delineated the foundational role played by the brainstem in emotion processing, which has deep implications for psychology and behavioral science researchers.[13] Especially relevant for this case study is the shaping power exerted by brainstem networks on the functioning of the evolutionarily newer regions, such as the neocortex layer. This is where mechanisms related to cognitive and linguistic acts are located. Research on the neurobiology of social emotions reveal that they "had more influence than the non-social, self-preservative emotions, such as anger and fear, providing a substrate for harmony and discord."[14] Panksepp theorizes that acoustic patterns generated by mother-offspring habits that prevented or assuaged separation distress reveal the "social biological foundations" of cognitive practices.[15]

This leads to the second general finding that guides this book's analysis: the idea that brainstem operations bind and encode all cogniutive and emotional information[16] Both Douglas Watt and Panksepp attribute to emotions a glue-like capacity, which holds together affective information to produce an affective state that exerts influence over executive cognitive functions. Panksepp has identified distinct affective systems, which he correlates with the neural circuitry of specific social behaviors.[17] Interactions between the higher order cognitive systems and the affective neural circuitry rooted in the human brainstem contributes to the evaluation of sensory information. The fixed-action pattern triggered in repeated responses together constitute a range of possible emotions.[18]

Panksepp's core findings suggest that a repeated pattern of associations between emotional triggers and responses provides a historical context for the emergence of specific behaviors.[19] Hominin cognitive systems, including the late emergence of language, were contoured by the brain's conditioned responses to past socioemotional conditions.[20] If we view language as the apotheosis of our species' trend toward progressive disambiguation in human

12 Ibid.
13 Ibid. See also Venkatraman et al. (2017).
14 Panksepp (2009, 229).
15 Ibid.
16 Watt (2007, 2012); Panksepp (2007).
17 Panksepp (1998).
18 Damasio (1999).
19 Van der Kolk (2015) delineates how some traumatic experiences can only be stored as somatic memory, which can lead to aversive behavior.
20 Panksepp (2004, 2012).

communication, as do somce evolutionary cognitive scientists, then we must acknowledge that specific emotional conditions triggered the need.[21] In this way, cultural behavior resulting from disambiguation processes may be approached as a residuum of the collective emotional experiences that triggered it in the first place.

The third general finding that informs my study relates to "the interplay and mutual constitution between neural and cultural forces," which influences psychological processes at both the behavioral and neural levels.[22] The results validate the idea that mental tasks accomplished by brain functions are not processed in any universal way; cultural differences reflect how culture operates at the level of the neuron.[23] The work of identifying the specific mechanisms that underlie the co-constitution of culture and personality has advanced significantly over the past decade. Findings confirm early observations that "cross-situational variability" exists. The results encourage efforts to trace the evolution of the affective-cognitive units that shaped cultural norms and values.[24]

Research that shows priming a subject with culturally relevant knowledge impacts processes that make knowledge available has shaped my understanding of what is being "brought to mind" when culturally relevant knowledge is used to prime a subject. The book's findings complement studies that construe "interdependence" and "independence" as behavioral indices of "cultural variation particularly between Westerners and East Asians." The neurological evidence, primarily variations in frequencies of brain responses to events measured with fMRI, ERP techniques, is compelling.[25] Researchers concluded that the variated behavior revealed distinctions between how subjects viewed themselves, their "self-construal." More specifically, the researchers

21 Donald (1993); Panksepp (2009, 229), links the emergence of propositional language to "proto-musical communications," which we will discuss in more depth in Chapter 3. Dunbar and Shultz (2007) provide a helpful literature review of the findings.

22 Chiao and Ambady (2007, 239–240). Cf. Kitayama and Uskul (2011), who propose a model of neuro-culture interaction in which the brain serves as a crucial site conditioned by the effects of cultural experience. Repeated practice and performance conditions neural connectivity to produce "embrained" results that are triggered by participation in cultural practices.

23 For helpful accounts of the intellectual aims driving the emerging field of neurocultural analysis see Chiao (2009, 2010); Han and Northoff (2009); Kitayama and Park (2010); Han et al. (2013). Cf. cultural transmission theory, which asserts that culture is best understood as information stored in brains and conveyed horizontally, at one time, or vertically, across generations. Boyd and Richerson (1988); Heinrich and Boyd (1998).

24 Mendoza-Denton and Mischel (2007); Kitayama et al. (2007, 139).

25 Chiao and Ambady (2007, 243). ERP refers to "event-related potential," it is the measured brain response to a specific sensory, cognitive, or motor event. fMRI, "functional magnetic resonance imaging," captures images of blood flow that occurs with brain activity.

posit that self-construal accounts for behaviors motivated by "collectivist" considerations, or "individualist" ones, which they also labeled "interdependent" or "independent" self-construal.[26]

Because I have found in Western cultures examples of the particular behavioral signature whose origins I claim can be reconstructed for China, including in Spain, Britain, Russia, and Korea, therefore I do *not* subscribe to any dogmatic understanding of this cultural distinction.[27] That said, evidence that points to selective pressure exerted by Confucian ethical axioms on self-construal habits and Chinese social behavior implores an explanation that can account for the longevity and centrality of these priming conditions for East Asian subjects twenty-five hundred years later.[28]

Chinese filiality is consistently invoked as a priming condition that heightens interdependent predispositions.[29] Interdependence refers to a self-construal in which the individual is defined by their relationship to others,[30] its formation is viewed as a culturally distinct neural representation of the self. In Chapter 3, I lay out the deep history of the emotional conditions that shaped the formation of a collective interdependent mental concept of the self. For now it is important to emphasize that neuroscience research acknowledges an inextricable link between interdependent mindsets and Confucian filial norms.

For example, studies link a disposition toward specific inhibitory behaviors to interdependent self-construal.[31] These key features have been shown to derive from a heightened sensitivity to situational context, and a heightened sensitivity to contextually deviant events.[32] One recent finding links interdependent mental structures to the brain's capacity to down-regulate emotional arousal when stimulated by situational contexts. Markers of emotional arousal in Chinese subjects' brains reduced when subjects carried out a task to suppress an emotion triggered by an unpleasant picture.[33]

26 Oyserman and Lee (2007, 263); Lee and Jeyaraj (2014).

27 Porter (2018). Cf. Hong et al. (2007, 340), who claim that "all individuals are capable of representing multiple cultures in their minds and switching between representations of cultures."

28 Chiao and Blizinsky (2010, 535) advance evidence for "culture-gene coevolution of individualism-collectivism and the serotonin transporter gene." They surmise that "heightened selective attention and increased amygdala response to negative information," features of collectivist subjectify, evolved because it conferred "varying degrees of advantage or disadvantage to individuals." The following analysis looks carefully at the "functional utility" of this "endephenoytpe."

29 Kitayama and Park (2010).

30 Kraus and Kitayama (2019).

31 Grecucci et al. (2015).

32 Kraus and Kitayama (2019).

33 Ibid.

There is no doubt that ideas about human self-management attributed to Confucius are the mainspring of the filial complex. From a neuroaffective perspective, Confucian filiality takes shape in an offspring's emotional responses to interactions with parents (primary caretakers). Confucianism assumes a positive valence imbued these interactions, which conditioned the down-regulation of emotional arousal in particular ways when external conditions require it to. This pattern of forming new stable synapses between neurons accounts for the quasi-biological dimension of filiality as both a mental and an embodied practice.[34]

From an evolutionary point of view, filiality is an exaptive trait, which means that although it evolved for the adaptive reason of biological survival, it then became used for another, culturally determined, one.[35] Ryan Nichols, who has investigated the cognitive roots of Chinese filiality, points to the strategic implications for family survival conferred by Confucius' view that family relations are most advantageous for its members and society at large when organized hierarchically around the father. Nichols attributes the emergence and longevity of this cultural module to its capacity to solve "an evolutionary problem for parents."[36] He posits Confucianism as a cultural construct wrought by centuries of interstate conflicts, when aristocratic lineages struggled to survive the Western Zhou fall. Nichols suggests that Confucius' ideas on filiality and child rearing offered a cognitive survival strategy for preserving family lines. The efficacy of this strategy accounts for the normalization of his perspective of filial relations between children and parents in Chinese society.[37]

Nichols' analysis is accurate inasmuch as it describes the normative role ascribed to Confucius and a thought system that bore his name, but it does not explain the neuropsychological incongruity of such a positively charged interpersonal relationship and the emotional portrait of a filial son characterized by excessive distress in the wake of their deaths. A close investigation of the components that configure this portrait yields a deep-seated neuropsychological context. This is focused upon in the following section.

Confucius' Psychological Portrait of a Paradigmatic Filial Son

We access Confucius' ideas via conversations he carried out with his students, the memory and record of which were preserved in a twenty-chapter book called the *Analects*, (*Lunyu*), as well as other historical, philosophical, and ritual sources.[38]

34 Zhong, et al. (2008).
35 Nichols (2013).
36 Nichols (2013, 215). See also Nichols (2016).
37 Nichols (2013).
38 Hunter (2012); Stumpfeldt (2010).

The text of the *Analects* is so central for Chinese collective self-construal that it has been used as a substitute for the idea of China itself.[39] Questions surrounding the historicity of the *Analects*, which stem from processes related to the text's composition, as well as internal inconsistencies itself, have led to a consensus that it is a sedimented cultural object. The text reflects the variety of ways in which Confucius' speech was used and contoured by discrete local communities.[40] Debates about what precisely constitutes "Confucian thought" are current given the stratified dating of the text's components, and textual contradictions. Nevertheless, scholars agree that Confucius' training in the ritual procedures associated with the Western Zhou royal family was the basis of a cluster of social values transmitted by Confucius to his students. Confucius' authority and renown were primarily functions of his success as teacher and transmitter of Western Zhou ritual information.

Confucius' insistence that he "transmits and does not create," points to his self-construal as a pedagogue.[41] Both Lothar von Falkenhausen and Mark Csikszentmihalyi emphasize how the foundation of Confucius' knowledge was shaped by earlier experts on Western Zhou ritual performance. These authorities counseled regional leaders on how to deploy the rituals.[42] Known as Ruists (*Rujia*), the experts were intimately acquainted with the Western Zhou ritual system, and regional rulers, whose political power was increasing as it waned for the royal Zhou clan, desired the information to buttress their own claims to political legitimacy.[43] This intrinsic association would have made Ruist knowledge alluring to politically aspirant rulers because it was seen as holding important historical information that had immediate sociopolitical application.

39 For representative scholarship that focuses on textual dating issues see Lau (1992). Recently, Michael Hunter (2017) has argued the *Analects* to be a product of the Han dynasty, disavowing any pre-Qin attribution. Acknowledging the late compilation of the text, I follow Goldin's (2017) and Slingerland (2000), who argue that themes and concepts central to later Warring States discourses are absent in the *Analects*, thereby demonstrating a chronologically earlier dimension of the *Analects* content. For a direct refutation of this counter argument, see Hunter (2017, 315 n. 1). This book's interest is in the emotional structure embedded in an exemplary filial son's behavior as reflected in Confucius' speech and records of his behavior.

40 Radice (2017) identifies three important sources in addition to the *Analects*, that include references to Confucius and his discourses including ritual texts: *Records of Ritual* (*Li ji*); the *Elder Dai's Records of Ritual* (*DaDai Liji*); other collections of teachings, such as *Family Discussions of Confucius* (*Kongzi jiayu*); citations of Confucius' discourse in interpretive commentary to the Chinese classics, such as the *Zuo Commentary* (*Zuo zhuan*) to the *Springs and Autumns* annals. In another study Radice (2021) approaches filial death rituals as performance events. Archaeological discoveries made over the last decades have also yielded texts that both expand and refine our understanding of the corpus.

41 See Puett (2002a; 2002b), for a deep exegesis of the word I translate "create" (*zuo*).

42 Von Falkenhausen (2006, 398); Csikszentmihalyi (2020).

43 For the sociopolitical underpinnings of Confucian thought see Hall and Ames (1987, 156–176); Pines (2002, 94–104; 209–210); von Falkenhausen (2006, 4–11).

Confucius' distaste for the ill use of ritual for political gain reflects awareness of the broad propensity among rulers of his time to do just that. His negative judgment of rulers who deploy Western Zhou rituals simply as a means to perform political power evokes his implicit rejection of rulers who rely on ancestral sacrifice as a sole organizing principle for establishing and sustaining social and political order. Confucius famously commented that "As for [ancestral] spirits, best to respect [them] while maintaining a distance" (*jing er yuan zhi*).[44] His discernment is often taken as evidence of a humanistic turn in Chinese thinking about sociopolitical organization, away from the Western Zhou supernatural context of sacrificial offerings, and especially away from the association that sacrificial offerings lead to beneficent bestowals in response.[45]

Many scholars construe the shift as representative of the transformations undergoing in the Eastern Zhou (772-221 B.C.) sociopolitical landscape. As the name of the era indicates, this landscape was shaped by the catastrophic collapse of the Western Zhou dynasty (1046-772 B.C.), when the royal court was forced to migrate because it could not protect itself from attacks launched by northwestern polities at the Zhou periphery. Although the royal family eventually reestablished their court in Luoyang, Henan, their loss of political and social rank in the aftermath of the migration drained the social value of ancestral sacrifice practices premised on the superiority of their clan status. In the meantime, other conduits for signaling status and rank emerged.[46] As such, Confucius' statement can be seen to tacitly reflect on the practice's loss of social currency and prestige.

While this rationale has merits, the lack of references in Confucius' discourse about to precise historical conditions that catalyzed the devaluation of ritual performances he decries warrants further explanation. In other words, if the rituals he claims will signal and therefore manage social order are to be prized for their efficacy during the [Western] Zhou, he provides no explanation for why they came to be discarded and disregarded. Rather, a consistent fuzziness surrounds the historicity ascribed to the rituals Confucius advocated were essential for balanced social organization.

For example, a reader of the *Analects* might assume that Confucius the Ruist's expertise involved rituals performed at the beginning of the Western Zhou given his

44 *Lunyu* 11:12. Cf. Brooks and Brooks (1998, 158) who claim Confucius rejects the "belief in the unseen world on which the validity of sacrifice rests"; and Ivanhoe (2003, 95), where he claims that Confucius' is not interested in spirits because he was "primarily concerned with understanding what place death and our reactions to it play in a well-ordered life."

45 Von Falkenahusen (2006, 2) argues that Confucius and his followers intellectualized "the ritual institutions of the Western Zhou, removing them from their original time-specific and class-specific frame of reference, and extracting from them a set of human values universally applicable to all polities and to future ages"; Cook (2009).

46 Pines (2002; 2017); Cook (2009).

frequent mention of the dynastic founders and their royal siblings.[47] But this is not the case. Rather, the ritual system intimately known by Confucius was the product of a dramatic and comprehensive social transformation that occurred during the late middle Western Zhou.[48] We will return to detail this transformative event, what Jessica Rawson calls the "Western Zhou Ritual Reform," in Chapters 4 and 5 below.[49] Our focus now will settle on the fact of historical ambiguity in Confucius' discussion of Western Zhou rituals. When read in tandem with his dictum that "proclaims his desire not to speak," and his contention that this "preference [for silence] does not prevent transmission to later generations," his position evokes a social "ambivalence" over the origins of state institutions and power.[50]

I see the textual lacunae regarding the Ritual Reform and Confucius' ambivalence as phenomena akin to his shunning of spirits. For this reason, despite his disavowal of spiritual concerns as necessary for sociopolitical order, his advocacy for spatial dissociation from spirits contrastively intimates an unarticulated emotional tension. Neuropsychological studies of avoidant behavior point to its evolutionarily adaptive function, borne from the need to mitigate social distress. This raises the possibility that the distress conditions Confucius prefers to avoid may be linked to the reason that information about the Ritual Reform was occluded.[51]

These ambiguous conditions related to how the Western Zhou collapse and the royal family's loss of prestige and status was memorialized. In spite of the absence of references to the Western Zhou demise in Confucius' speech, it is possible to extrapoloate from the over-determined silences a pattern whose contours point to a traumatic collective loss about which social knowledge was, for reasons yet to be determined, precluded from sociolinguistic exchange. Confucius does speak about loss. From his accounts of his own loss-induced distress, and proscriptions for how to behave in the face of relational loss, we can extrapolate a neuropsychological condition that undergirds his ideal of a filial son.

Analect 17.21 recounts a conversation between Confucius and his student Zai Wo, in which the Master suggests that the degree of suffering experienced by a

---

47 See *Lunyu* 9.5 for a reference to the Western Zhou founder King Wen (Wenwang), and 8.20 for reference to King Wu (Wuwang), who completed the Shang overthrow. Confucius invokes King Wu's brother, the Duke of Zhou (Zhou Gong) four times: 1.5; 8.11; 11.17; 18.10.

48 Von Falkenhausen (2006). A ritual text "Ritual Records" (*Liji*) probably composed contains proscriptive accounts of ritual regulations that scholars agree is a mythicized rendering of Western Zhou Ritual Reform practices. The text's scope and level of detail have been analyzed as a ritual metalanguage, which encodes memories of ritual mechanisms. For dating and compositional issues of the text see Loewe (1993).

For a recent exploration into the function of the text in legitimizing dynastic power, see Tang (2020).

49 Kraus and Kitayama (2019).

50 Puett (2002, 48).

51 Kraus and Kitayama (2019).

grieving child over the loss of a parent is a key index for exemplary filial piety.[52] Zai Wo queries Confucius as to why the latter proscribes a three-year mourning period for deceased parents, when a full year of mourning seems long enough,[53] and he invokes the impracticality of prolonged withdrawal from ritual observances for the successful maintenance of social institutions as evidence.[54]

Confucius responds that a [paradigmatically filial son, as embodied in the] "cultivated man" (*junzi*) would not, within three years "experience delectability when eating good food, nor feel pleased when hearing music, nor feel at ease when comfortably lodged."[55] Later, after Zai Wo departs, Confucius critiques what he viewed as Zai Wo's premature appetitive inclinations as marks of a void of benevolence. He justifies his assessment with a transactional account of the affective dynamic at the core of child-parent bonds: "It is not till a child is three years old that it is allowed to leave the arms of its parents. [It is for this reason that] the three-year mourning is universally observed. Did [Zai Wo] not also receive three-year's affection from his parents?"[56]

The word "filial" does not appear in this account but the reference to parental nurturing reveals it to be a "classic endorsement of filial devotion in the *Analects*. It is also one of the most controversial parts of the text."[57] Some cite the passage to argue that filial piety is a primary emotional bond,[58] but Radice observes that although there is certainly an emotional component for Confucius' understanding of filial piety, "it is also noteworthy that 'love' or 'affection' toward one's parents is rarely, if ever, mentioned explicitly in the *Analects*."[59] Indeed, rather

52 *Lunyu*. See Liu (2003) for a discussion of this Analect.

53 Slingerland (2003, 5) points out in his commentary on *Lunyu* 1.11 that the three-year period is usually understood as into the third year, or twenty-five months. Since it is not till a child is three of years of age that it can be less dependent on parents due to language acquisition, it is possible that Confucius really did mean three years is the appropriate duration for mourning. Cf. *Lunyu* 4.20 "The Master said 'He who has within three years not altered the path of his father's intention, is someone who can be called filial." See also Wang (2011).

54 Liu (2006) points out how this Analect is narratively and structurally more complex, and rhetorically more determined than most other discourses. Chapter 17, where it appears, has long been viewed with suspicion as representing a later strata of the text's content (Brooks and Brooks (1998). The implication is that chronologically late was tantamount to historically inauthentic as a representation of Confucius the man's thought. However, notwithstanding the stylistic distinction, because an earlier set of *Analects* represent Confucius himself as exhibiting grief characterized by a similar degree of excessiveness, albeit in response to the loss of a beloved student, the latter account reinforces the idea that for Confucius inconsolable and extended suffering are components of the grief and mourning process for parents.

55 *Lunyu*.

56 Fung (1952, 63) points to the dialogues rhetorical objective to provide "a rational basis to a social institution."

57 Radice (2017, 192).

58 For example, Liu (2003); Rosemont and Ames (2008, 2009).

59 Radice (2017, 191).

than affection, in *Analect* 2.6, Confucius invokes distress (*you*) as a definitive feature of filiality:"Meng Wubo asked about filiality. The Master said: 'As for parents, it is only distress that they may fall ill.'"[60]

The absence of affection as a component of parent-child bonding assumes greater significance when considered alongside the repeated link between filiality, grief, and mourning. While "it is reasonable to assume that grief in mourning rituals certainly involves some kind of love,"[61] the intensity of suffering that Confucius assumes a paradigmatically filial son will experience is tantamount to a complete prohibition of outward engagement with the environment. Indeed, the *Analects* refers to the vicarious draining of Confucius own appetitive incentives when exposed to affective conditions involving the loss of an attachment relationship, even if he did not know the bereaved.[62]

Why Confucius would posit that a child's response to a parent's death would take the form of a complete appetitive shutdown is a motivating question for this study's line of inquiry. Recent scholarship on grief in the *Analects* has deepened our understanding of Confucius' perspective on grief, and mourning, the latter generally understood in the literature as a reconstructive response to the "facticity of loss."[63] Mathew Foust views "Confucius' behavior toward those in mourning, to be indicative of his disposition toward those in grief,"[64] while, following Amy Olberding, Michael Radice argues that Confucius' concerted attention toward the emotional experience of grief should be understood as playing a role in a "kind of performer-observer relationship in filial ritual behavior."[65]

Radice asserts that Confucius' focus on the significance of reception in regard to filial piety is evident in the latter's consistent insistence that observations of people's speech and countenances (*yan, se*) are a key resource for acting in ritually appropriate ways.[66] Foust and Olberding view Confucius' attitude toward mourning as strategic insomuch as it models a technique for enduring the grief. Olberding argues that even if Confucius' excessive grief represents "failed mourning," it nonetheless tacitly articulates "a program amenable" to the task of transforming death into a space that permits the bereaved to dwell as it prepares to relinquish the dead.[67] Although Olberding and others have recognized

60 Radice (2017, 192).
61 Foust (2009).
62 Radice (2017, 192).
63 Foust (2009, 350).
64 Olberding (1997, 30; 2004, 2008); Seachris (2008).
65 Foust (2009, 350).
66 Radice (2017, 191).
67 Ibid. points to *Analect* 13.20 as an example of the significance of audience reception regarding whether a set of behaviors may be regarded as exemplarily filial: "(those whose) clan praises them as filial, and whose fellow villagers praise as respectful to elders."

Confucius' conception of prolonged mourning as eccentric, no one has suggested that the behavior invites another diagnosis.

Confucius shows disregard for the body of a bereaved subject in his expectation of the latter to live in complete retraction from all libidinal attachments for over two years, as if a corpse. Although practical and governing realities frequently made it impossible for sons to fulfill this obligation, something Confucius himself acknowledged,[68] this portrait of praiseworthy filial piety nonetheless became a cultural mainstay in texts reporting on extraordinarily pious children. Keith Knapp and Donald Holzman call attention to a persistent focus on "obsessive," "exaggerated," or "bizarre" actions in representations of Eastern Zhou, Han, and medieval filial practices, especially some that are particularly extreme in the degree of "self-sacrifice" and "self-abnegation" displayed.[69] Holzman interprets the "fanaticism" manifested in this behavior as a quasi-religious expression of devotion.[70] Benjamin Schwartz surmises that the "sentiments of gratitude and self-abnegation that dominate the prolonged mourning rites for parents may be considered the ultimate basis of that power of yielding on which all *li* [propriety] are based."[71]

To wit, here is a fourth century B.C. critique of Confucius' paradigmatic filial behavior:

> As for the [Confucian] methods for managing mourning, what are they? It is said that the mourner should wail and sob incessantly so that sound is produced in uneven intervals [as if choking]; wear sackcloth and hemp stained with tears. They should live in a mourning hut with a straw mat for a bed and a clod of earth for a pillow. They should also mutually follow [the obligation] to keep others from eating so as to appear starving, and wear thin clothes so as to be cold. [This behavior] renders their appearance gaunt and decrepit, their countenance, sallow and dark, their eyes and ears insensitive, not sharp, and their hands and feet would be without strength such that they cannot be used. It is also said, in respect to the production of mourning [rites] by high officers, that they must have support to be able to rise and a cane to be able to walk, and in this way, carry out their duties for three years.[72]

---

68 Olberding (2008, 137).

69 Analect 17.12 Although he nonetheless claims that an absence of virtue, suggested by a reduction in mourning time, would be more destructive to society.

70 Knapp (2005, 2); Holzman (1998, 188).

71 Holzman (1998, 185).

72 The criticism was voiced by the philosopher Mozi (470-391 B.C.) Defoort (2016, 20) identifies the chapter in which it appears as part of a group of "oppositional expressions" that reflect an activist spirit in concretely depicting an opponents' flaws. See Mozi, "Jiezangxia". Translation modifies that of Legge provided along with the original text.

Knapp argues that such extreme representations reflect efforts by patriarchs to use this structure of representation to preserve a "politically fragmented world."[73] Like Nichols, the findings of both Knapp and Holzman are sensitive to the complexity of the sociohistorical conditions that contributed to the apparent normative value of these representations. Nonetheless, the hyperbolic rhetoric of such accounts, and the fact that they were viewed with apparent unease both by intellectuals and officials—reflected in the inconsistency of their assessments of such extreme practices,[74] raises questions about the nature of the link between prolonged mourning and filial emotion.

Confucius' logic claiming three-year child development processes as the pretext for his proscribed period of prolonged grief appears to have been taken at face value by scholars of Confucian thought, regardless of how his excessive mourning proscription was assessed. I am less persuaded by the logic, especially in light of the absence of references to childhood affection noted above. Moreover, Olderding's diagnosis of Confucius' "failed mourning" in the case of his student's early demise, suggests the same diagnosis is applicable to Confucius' paradigmatic filial son. While Olderding elegantly and clinically lays out the affective conditions that triggered Confucius' failed mourning, similar narrative details that explain why filial children should experience this too when their parents die have yet to be identified.

If a narrative account that explains why a paradigmatic filial child should experience prolonged mourning is missing, Mozi, Olderding, and Foust's attention to the performative dimension of mourning rites, not to mention the rituals' association with status and rank, provides a basis from which to begin an investigation that can answer the question. The notion that mourning rites are public, so that the sincerity of the bereaved can be scrutinized, begets the question of who precisely is the target audience. Why would the sincerity of the bereaved be questioned in the first place? It is not clear who questions the bereaved's sincerity, is it the members of society who observe the performance of the rites? Or, the lost parent? These questions reveal confusion over the source activating the affective conditions that lie at the heart of a Confucian filial disposition.

From a neuropsychiatric perspective, Confucius' ideal of filial bereavement is one of "complicated grief" (CG), a state of mind in which grief over a loss persists as an intrusive feature of everyday life beyond eighteen months. CG is considered maladaptive because it represents the incapacity of the brain to accommodate the reality of the loss.[75] Like readers of Confucius, scholars of CG are also challenged

73 Knapp (2005, 188).

74 Ibid.

75 *Lunyu,* 2.8 "Zi Xia asked about filiality. The Master said: as for the countenance, it is difficult, as for the filial nowadays, it refers to the capacity to feed and nurture to the extent the dogs and horses can all be fed and nurtured this behavior extends to dogs and horses, both are able to feed and nourish. Without reverence, what can be used to distinguish between the two types of support?"

to account for the source. The following section synthesizes the findings of recent scholarship that investigate this neuropsychological phenomenon.

Complicated Grief Theory

In Jaak Panksepp's overarching taxonomy of human emotion, sadness and shame are secondary to a primary affective system organized by PANIC/GRIEF.[76] This system emerged as a response to "maternal separation-distress,"[77] but the system evolved to respond to the distress of social separation more generally. Watt and Panksepp propose that "shut down mechanisms" activated by sadness and grief were selected to terminate separation distress, including that caused by the loss of social rank.[78] Research using fMRI imaging has shown how the intensity of grief pain decreases over time among some people who suffered the loss of an attachment relationship. Neurological evidence for the dissipation of grief manifests as the reduction of brain activation over time when the subject is presented with cues related to the deceased.[79] However, no similar reduction occurred in others also suffering from profound grief.

The presence of opiates responsible for dulling social (as well as physiological) pain in subjects whose grief had diminished eighteen months post-loss, suggests that the reduction of pain is a necessary component for shifting brain attention away from the lost object toward SEEKING/EXPECTANCY behavior. This affective system "drives explorative and approach behaviors, sustains goal-directed activity, promotes anticipatory cognitions, and evokes feelings of positive excitement which control reward-learning."[80] A shift toward SEEKING facilitates a gradual process of detachment from the lost object as attention is directed outward.

> Bereaved persons decouple outdated stimulus-reward associations while allowing the memory of the deceased loved one to live on. Such detachment plays an important role in the resolution of bereavement, as it may allow the bereaved person to reframe the memories of the deceased in terms of a past physical and current spiritual relationship without the ongoing pain of grief and loss.[81]

Peter Freed asks why prolonged grief would occur when we know the brain has the "capacity to rapidly dampen strong negative emotions." Why do shutdown mechanisms activated by a separation distress episode fail to self-limit or terminate

---

76 Freed et al. (2009).
77 Panksepp (2004).
78 Watt and Panksepp (2009).
79 Ibid.
80 Stroeb and Schut (1999).
81 Alcaro and Panksepp (2011, 1); Panksepp and Watt (2011b).

and thus preclude brain mechanisms from resuming its SEEKING/EXPECTA-NCY disposition?[82]

The question as to what might obstruct the brain's reconfiguration process is of interest to prominent scholars who study grief.[83] Freed suggests an intrapsychic source for complicated grief. Observing how CG is pathological to the extent that it is a symptom of the brain's inability to terminate/suppress sadness, he posits that CG "sadness is an internally generated punishment."[84] Unfortunately he stops short of explaining why such punishment would be warranted. Serendipitously, Confucius' image of a filial son afflicted by CG yields a possible source for the punishment: shame. Recognizing that the filial son's ceaseless grief is organized by shame aversive strategies opens a fresh vantage point from which to resolve this question.

I refer to the Confucian imperative that a filial son avoids causing shame to the family, which has drawn extensive scholarly attention.[85] In this regard, *Analect* 13.18 has long attracted interest from researchers for the way it encapsulates a lineage survival strategy: Confucius condemns the acts of a son who publicly bore witness to the authorities about his father's theft. Dismissing the implication that the son warranted praise for his "straight [e.g., corrective]" (*zhi*) behavior, Confucius invokes the sociolinguistic conditions of his own upbringing: "[As for] the *dang* [social unit] I come from, those who are 'straight' are quite different. Fathers conceal for their sons; sons conceal for their fathers. 'Straightness' is to be found in such behavior."[86]

There is dissention among interpretations of this Analect, devolving on whether Confucius' statement conveys a general opinion about "straight," understood in the sense of "upright," behavior or one situationally contextualized by the need to resolve a conflict of values.[87] These interpretive variances rest in part on how scholars understand the implicit logic of Confucius' comment. Does

82 Freed (2009, 66).
83 Freed and Mann (2007, 32).
84 Freed (2009, 66). Watt and Panksepp (2009, 10) propose that withdrawal also helps terminate risky or damaging dominance conflicts.
85 Lobb et al (2010) provide a helpful review of CG studies that streamlines the often inconsistent definitions used by researchers. They estimate that between 10% and 20% of the population experiences this form of bereavement. For a lucid account of neuropsychiatric contributions to psychoanalytical therapy see Carroll (2018).
86 Translation modifies that of James Legge, renowned linguist and missionary, who was one of the earliest Western scholars to translate the Chinese Classics. Legge's translation of the *Lunyu* is presented alongside the original Chinese on the Chinese Text Project site.
87 *Lunyu, 13:18*. Scholars of Confucian thought have noted tensions implicit in a view of social order that apparently prioritizes preserving family integrity over state efforts to order and manage society. These conflicts, according to some, reflected an inherent incompatibility between two organizational entities notwithstanding their analogous hierarchical structures. From this perspective, some critiqued Confucian visions of bringing order to chaos as inapt for application to realpolitik.

it reflect a minimization of theft because the object was merely a sheep, so not serious enough to report a father to state authorities? Or, again, situationally, did Confucius mean to imply that there are other times and places and means to privately, as opposed to publicly, call attention to transgressions?[88]

Ryan Nichols views the dominance of shame in Confucian concepts of filiality as a function of its cognitive roots. "[C]ivil and political authorities in the Confucian diaspora have employed the social utility of shame" to the extent that it became "uniquely encoded in pedagogy and in parent-child interaction" in East Asia.[89] The popular *Canon of Filiality* (*Xiaojing*) ostensibly composed by Confucius' student but actually compiled during the third century B.C., mandates that a filial child will not cause disgrace (*ru*) to befall parents; this is echoed in other contemporaneous texts, which list not shaming one's family as one of the most important criterion for filial behavior.[90] Encoded in filiality is a concern to preserve one's family's reputation.

Drawing on the work of Edward Lieber, Nichols claims shame is a practice "intended to heighten children's sensitivity to the emotional and behavioral cues in Chinese social contexts."[91]

> When to feel shame, how to feel shame and when to apply shame to others is subject to unique amounts of social training, despite the presence of evolved capacities for shame experience. Historical China's longstanding hierarchical social structure, its collectivism and its emphasis on social roles have contributed to the formation of a social environment in which one can feel more varieties of shame as a result of a greater number of causes than anywhere in the world. Such finely grained uses of the sense of shame must be produced through cultural learning. Developing a sense of shame allows Chinese children to be sensitive to the perceptions of others and thereby avoid future behaviors that would bring shame or embarrassment to the family.[92]

Michael Radice identifies concealment as one technique for managing impressions. Noting how Confucius' disapproval is triggered not by the son's passivity in simply not reporting, he argues that "Confucius prescribes going a step further: to conceal or cover up for his father requires a deliberate act of deception on the part of the son. It is not sufficient to be a passive bystander."[93] Radice sees

88 Wang (2011).
89 Qiu (1995).
90 Nichols (2015, 270).
91 See for example the "Emotive Response" (*ganying*) chapter of the *Classic of Filial Piety*, *Xiaojing zhushu* (1980, 2559), the *Record of* Rites, (*Liji zhushu* 1980, 1234). See also Ikezawa (1994), for an in-depth discussion of the compilation, composition, and philosophy of the *Xiaojing*.
92 Nichols (2015, 274–275); Lieber (2006, 145).
93 Ibid.

concealment behavior as a filial performance style, whose rhetorical objective was "not a matter of expressing intentions directly to spectators, so much as concealing from public view a certain part of oneself—in this case, the knowledge that one's father committed a crime. There is still a relationship between the son and those who observe him, and this form of style deliberately limits information to the public."[94]

Neurological evidence attests to the validity of Radice's insight. Refining Panksepp's list of affective systems Toronchuk and Ellis propose the addition of a new affective system: "POWER/dominance," which involved emotions related to "rank, status, submission."[95] In particular, they claim that neural mechanisms related to experiences of shame and grief evolved to regulate conflicts over social status, because a "well-functioning" hierarchical social structure strengthened survival advantage for individuals and the group. Thus, behaviors activated by emotions belonging to the POWER/dominance system were selected to contain excessive behavior and ensure a social equilibrium that can be perpetuated.[96]

Physiological signaling of shame, such as blushing and palpitations, are triggered autonomically, demonstrating that this expression of submission is deeply wired in our brains.[97] Animal behavior suggests that shame evolved as a submission signal to reduce aggression.[98] Submission involves cognizance of one's status and standing within a group. Shame is the neural product of emotional and cognitive engineering: the pain of the threat of social exclusion due to transgression of dominance hierarchies selected for avoidant behavior, wherein shame's negative affect functions as a mechanism to deescalate social conflict.

Several comments in the *Analects* suggest that Confucius understood how affective awareness of one's sense of belonging was necessary for survival in an environment regulated by displays of dominance or submission.[99] One of the most famous, a response to a "question asking about filiality" (*wen xiao*), identifies a tension between performing filial obligations even in the face of conflicting embodied signals. Ryan Nichols points to a Confucian precept ostensibly articulated by his student, Zi Lu, who recalls his teacher's encouragement to pay attention to changes "in 'facial coloration'... Blushing and sweating signal inauthentic behavior, knowledge which the disciple of Confucianism is to use to his advantage. Savvy Confucians expertly perceive when people's social rank has been reduced, and train in advanced techniques of impression management."[100]

94 Radice (2017, 192).
95 Ibid.
96 Ellis and Toronchuk (2013, 2, 4 *et passim*).
97 Ibid. (7, 12).
98 Sorel (2019).
99 Watt and Panksepp (2009).
100 Price (1967).

These techniques highlight the parental role in emotional and cognitive development at the onset of a child's life. It is well attested in literature that reciprocal interaction between child and caregiver during early life, which requires "shared attention," is a fundamental experience that contributes to the ontogeny of self-concepts and shapes the neuronal context that regulates responses to social affiliation and separation.[101] Some have argued that this communication provided emotional motivation for the development of language, while others have claimed that through this communication, the child acquires its own version of a moral code and builds it into an intrapsychic moral complex.[102]

Scholarship on the Confucian Self

Among scholarship looking to extrapolate from Confucian texts general principles of the self, there is consensus that its constitutive nature is "interconnected and communal" as well as "porous," in terms of "the boundaries" that are seen to exist between an individual and others."[103] David Wong contends that Confucian notions of the self reject "the idea that one belongs to oneself alone."[104] The self's porous quality recalls the interdependent disposition of Chinese mindsets identified in contemporary studies of filial subjects' brains. Ni Peimin's study of Confucian moral teachings suggests that a Confucian self is a self that undergoes constant moral refinement, implying an inner plasticity that leads, with disciplined attention, to a self-disposition wherein all speech and acts will be socially appropriate.[105]

Debates about whether these moral teachings comprise a Confucian ethics, and if so, whether the ethics pertain to virtues or roles, reflect different perspectives on the concept of a Confucian inner life: Ivanhoe, who stands in the ethics are virtues position, critiques the idea that a Confucian self lacks a center of agency, that it is the sum of an interrelated role-bearing performance of various social role obligations.[106] Rosemont, whose position emphasizes that Confucian selves are "interrelated role bearing persons," supports it with repeated references in Confucian sources to "role standardization around specific duties," such as filiality.[107]

---

101 Nichols (2015, 267), citing Csikszentmihalyi (2004, 135). Like Nichols, I appreciate Czikszentmihalyi's literal translation for how it accentuates the embodied dimension of affective experience as a social signal.

102 Schore (2003).

103 Panksepp (1999); Smetana and Killen (2008).

104 Ing (2019, 371).

105 Wong (2011).

106 Ni (2008).

107 Ivanhoe (2008). See also Song (2020).

Michael Ing argues that a narrow scholarly focus on the interrelatedness of the core self has led to a misconception, namely the idea that the Chinese self operates only to ensure that harmony is the result of social interactions.[108] This "harmonizing theory," according to Ing, inadvertently occludes how "Confucian treatments of moral conflicts" have much to say about the "mixed emotions and difficulties of the [social] conflicts" that the harmonizing self was expected to resolve. Ing claims that Confucian self-construal bears traces of a mindset made vulnerable by affective conditions.

The situations challenge the integrity of a self, such as when "one's actions cannot fulfill" two moral actions that have competing values" (*xing bu liang quan*). Because the self is "partially constituted by relationships," and because the self is realized by the way moral acts enable it, "value conflicts and unfortunate situations" impede the maintenance of social bonds, thus rendering vulnerable the status of an interdependent self.[109] Ing suggests that Confucian values derive from the distillation of unfortunate situations, such as conditions in which every possible act is tantamount to severing one of two equally valued social bonds. This insight into the salience of loss in the emotional conditions that triggered the production of Confucian values renders more precisely the informational aim of the *Analects* content: it comprises a manual for transcending these conflicts.

Ing argues that Confucian conceptions of self imply a cognizance that one cannot attend to all relevant values. He cites for validation the salience of "tragic" accounts of people who were unable to transcend the conflicts that are marbled throughout Eastern Zhou historical texts.[110] Therein, selves constricted by allegiances to values rendered conflictual by situational contexts exemplify the tragic consequences for an inner life organized by interrelated role bearing people. Ing's thesis brings to the fore an emotional backdrop that nuances our understanding of the origins of Confucian value norms.

Michael Puett has also proposed that Confucian education implies transmitting responses to dispositions, "certain situations in the past."[111] Underlying the encouragement to rehearse or "reenact" previous responses is the behavioralist assumption that the emotional impact of a fragmented world would trigger responses to mediate it. In other words, Confucius' ethics assume behavioral conditioning will follow from recapitulations of responses to emotional destabilization.[112] Significantly, Puett asserts that these emotional conditions drove the formation of the Chinese canon as well; he argues that a repertoire consisting of rituals, verse and cultural narratives emerged as repositories of refined responses to

108 Rosemont (2015, 51). See also Jie (2013).
109 Ing (2017).
110 Ibid.
111 Ibid.
112 Puett (2006, 29–34). See also idem., (2019) for an extended theorization of this insight.

emotional experiences. In short, the ritual repertoire functioned as a tool for navigating the psychological terrain of emotionally destabilizing experiences.[113]

Scholarship that views Confucianism as the source of Chinese "collectivistic" values that prioritize "social harmony, conformity, and adherence to group norms" emphasizes traits for which neurological correlates have been identified among interdependent mental structures.[114] Compelling evidence is seen in the simultaneous activation of brain information processes related to information about the self and mother among subjects raised in East Asian societies. This merging of processes contrasts the consistent separation of brain regions among Western subjects who were asked the same emotionally salient questions.[115] Brian Kraus and Shinobu Kitayama hypothesize that the "purported link between the interdependent self-construal and emotion suppression may be culture-bound."[116]

The problem of precisely what neural apparatus is responsible for instantiating codes and moral complexes remains recalcitrant to elucidation, even as the field increasingly calls for theoretical frameworks that can explain neuroscience findings in terms of psychological organization and functioning. Bessel A. Van der Kolk's findings that traumatic experiences exert influence on neural processes that regulate information distribution and memory construction, offers a helpful framework for explaining the etiology of dissociative phenomena.[117] He presents a review of scholarship that finds the impact of trauma on physical and psychological development, concluding that "[t]rauma results in a fundamental reorganization of the way mind and brain manage perceptions. It changes not only how we think and what we think about, but also our very capacity to think."[118]

The link between dissociative symptoms and the storage of trauma-related information in somatic memory attests to the brain's capacity to spontaneously control and organize responses. The responses to traumatic experience unfold on both physical and emotional levels in daily life. This is the case for adults who experience trauma and for children as well. Indeed, Van der Kolk emphasizes how the repetition of behavioral patterns resulting from childhood trauma

---

113 Ibid. (30).

114 Ibid. (34).

115 Zhu et al. (2007); Markus and Kitayama (2010); Kitayama and Park (2010). Zhu and his colleagues asked native Chinese and Western participants to decide whether a given trait adjective described themselves (self condition), their mother (mother condition), or an unrelated other (other condition), or if the adjective was pleasant or unpleasant (semantic condition).

116 Zhu et al. (2007).

117 Kraus and Kitayama (2019).

118 Van der Kolk (2015). Dr. Van der Kolk's work aims toward providing treatment modalities based on his findings.

evinces the varied modalities by which memories for those who experienced trauma function.

The following section will bring to the conversation related concepts theorized by the Hungarian-French psychoanalysts, Nicolas Abraham and Maria Torok. Their concepts, which together comprise a metapsychology of secrets, extend the implications of Van der Kolk's findings about neural memory strategies aimed to diffuse the overwhelming impact of unsayable experience. While Van der Kolk identifies how traumatic experience speaks in a dissociated manner through somatic memory, Abraham and Torok theorize the existence of a traumatic memory storage area within the psyche's topography as well. This memory structure does not preclude coexistence with the somatic memories identified by Van der Kolk, but it does provide a more detailed rationale for the basis of the evaluative decisions that shape distribution of trauma related information in the first place. Finally, their theories bridge the domains of evolution, psychology, social behavior, and neural functioning that drive this book's investigative angle.

Bridging the Disciplinary Divide between Neuroscience and Psychoanalytical Theory

Significantly, Abraham and Torok's theorization shares an intellectual source of inspiration with British psychoanalyst John Bowlby, whose work is consistently cited as seminal for the affective neurological understanding of complicated grief discussed previously. Bowlby brought clinical evidence to bear on the claim that attachment is a governing human instinct, and asserted its centrality in conceptualizations of a "core-self." Moreover, Bowlby made "attachment theory" a cornerstone of a model of psychoanalysis distinct from Sigmund Freud's psychosexual approach toward human development.[119] Bowlby theorized that children's affective responses to detachment from the mother brings problems of separation anxiety to the forefront of potential sources of psychiatric disorders. He linked despair over separation to depression, grief, and mourning; and he linked detachment resulting from despair to psychic mechanisms of defense, claiming the posture belies an anxious attachment.[120]

Bowlby's focus on the autonomous motivational aspect of attachment was inspired by the animal research of Hungarian psychoanalyst Imre Hermann, who concluded that the life-long drive for attachment is a descendant of "Clinging" behavior observed among anthropoid apes.[121] Hermann claimed that the perpetuation of clinging behavior in human life beyond childhood was because the

119 Ibid. (21).
120 Bowlby (1979).
121 Ibid. Cf. Van der Kolk knew Bowlby personally and cites him regarding the etiology of attachment disorders (2015, 111–113).

"human baby in relation to his instinctual tendency is prematurely disconnected from mother's body."[122] For this reason, a human's "Going in search" instinct (auf-die Suche-gehen)," (a psychoanalytical precursor of Panksepp's SEEKING), is tempered by the instinct to cling to the mother's body.

Hermann concluded that "Clinging" is an organizing psychic principle and the source of a core-self constituted by the early experience of "dual unity" between infant and mother.[123] Understanding how the clinging relationship represents a paradigm for a whole series of object relations opened the way to identify emotions related to distress and subsequent anxiety as primarily responses to social disconnection. Hermann noted that attachment, along with hunger and sexuality, ensured the perpetuation of social relationships.[124]

Nicolas Abraham and Maria Torok, independent of Bowlby, also developed the psychoanalytical implications of Hermann's "Clinging instinct," or "filial instinct," in its French translation (*l'instinct filial*), after they emigrated to France. They incorporated Hermann's understanding of the dynamic between "Clinging" and "Searching" instincts into a metapsychology whose tenets bridge the theoretical gap decried by scholars committed to explaining the conditions that would preclude a brain from transitioning from sadness to SEEKING, the defining characteristic of CG. Their theories account for the affective conditions that trigger brain mechanisms to facilitate or obstruct psychic reorganization in the face of a traumatic loss. Implicitly, they offer an explanation for the failure of synaptic networks to accommodate "reality."

Abraham and Torok proposed a theory of human consciousness in order to elucidate a phenomenology of the mind that could account for the way intrapsychic conflicts impinge on the communication between basic affective systems and higher-level brain functions.[125] Conceptualized over a period of years spanning the 1950s-1970s, their metapsychology anticipated a neuroaffective theory of mind. In addition, it provides the conceptual tools for extrapolating from neuro-mental operations, a "core-self."

Abraham, who was a Ph.D. student in phenomenology at the Sorbonne during the 1950s while he also practiced as a psychoanalytical clinician, dismissed the regnant phenomenological assumption that "consciousness is directly transparent to itself."[126] Rather, he advanced a psychoanalytical concept of the unconscious to theorize the relationship between the world and the psyche. In the words of Nicolas Rand, the primary translator of Abraham and Torok's theoretical work, "[i]f, for the phenomenologist, the world exists only in

122 Vikár. (1985). Kächele (2009).
123 Kächele (2009, 421). Marinelli and Mayer (2016).
124 Kächele (2009); Marinelli and Mayer (2016).
125 Kächele (2009, 422b).
126 Cf. Panksepp and Watt (2011), where they present formidable evidence for the existence of a neural "affective consciousness."

relation to a sense-giving consciousness, for Abraham, the psychoanalyst, the sense of both the world and consciousness itself resides in a transphenomenological realm, beyond the reach of direct apprehension, in the unconscious, for example."[127]

> Leaving behind the Freudian domain of psychopathology and the description of unconscious mental processes, Abraham effectively generalizes the idea of symptom, positing beyond all phenomena an analyzable sphere that motivates their individual existence, giving them their specific underlying sense. Abraham makes this methodological leap because he sees the most productive conceptual originality of Freudian psychoanalysis in the structure of the symptom as a telltale memory trace of latent or unavailable promptings and traumas. In keeping with this principle, Abraham suggests further that the world and the psyche are the result of catastrophes whose fragmented remnants survive in the phenomena they engender... While phenomenology contributes the idea of the world's fundamental link to a sense-giving agent, the scope of Freudian psychoanalysis is enlarged. It is now called upon to investigate apparently inaccessible sources of meaning and thereby, ultimately to read in all areas of animate and inanimate existence the symptom-like genesis of being.[128]

Abraham's phenomenology defined consciousness as a function of responses to threats experienced by a subject. More specifically, he theorized that reality should be understood as the metapsychological state of affairs that required a response in the form of a topographic shift in psychic processing habits. The shift or transformation is demanded in order to accommodate new experiential information. He posited a "natural" inclination in processing mechanisms toward expansion (akin to processes of synaptogenesis), which he conceived as a function of Hermann's "Searching" instinct. At the same time, he observed how the principle of expansion and accommodation also served to preserve an internal systematic integrity, or core-self.

Abraham construed linguistic processes as an analog of biological digestion, words function as enzymes breaking down the emotional components of an experience so that the psyche can reorganize itself and accommodate it as part of

---

127 Abraham and Torok (1994, 6).

128 Ibid. Cf. Neuroscience studies that have shown the existence of disparate memory storage systems for experiences whose conditions produced a negative or positive impact. The dominance of negativity bias in human behavior is also reflected in data that show merely recounting a negative experience that occurred earlier increased complex neural activation. See Vaish et al. (2008); Kiley Hamlin et al. (2010). These findings recall Michael Ing's observations about the affective etiology of Confucian ethics, a perspective that is commensurate with evidence for the outsize influential role played by neural networks related to negative experiences on behavior.

the core-self.[129] A core-self is the product of digested experiences; digested experiences are experiences that have been converted into words.

> This view disallows the idea that the so-called "real" world is a transparent, intentional, and objective correlate of subjective lived experience—an idea that, according to Abraham, discounts the role of the unconscious in shaping and informing conscious experience. Abraham maintains that "reality" is experience that demands to be accommodated; it is experience that agitates the psyche toward the process of psychic expansion that Nicholas Rand calls self-fashioning. Self-fashioning is a system of assimilation and adaptation that continues throughout life, and which Abraham understood to be the organizing or sense-making principle of the psyche.[130]

Brain research on the neural correlates of consciousness have found evidence that corroborates and deepens Abraham's insights.[131] Georg Northoff's notion that spatiotemporal schemata endemic to brain processes are ultimately extended outward toward "self-expansion" resonates with Abraham's conception of the orientation of the psyche's organizing principle.[132] Cognitive scientist Merlin Donald also calls attention to the adaptive, expansive and accommodating, nature of the brain's "conscious capacity."[133] Donald attributes human's evolving conscious capacity to the emergence of modern language and attendant "cognitive pyrotechnics."[134] He frames the evolutionary function of consciousness as a response to the "deceiving" nature of the "surface appearance" of symbol-using cultures, which "hide their secrets from all but the most curious and attentive mind." He does not include consideration of whether psychoemotional conditions might account for culture's deceptive character.

If consciousness functioned as a "powerful intellectual guide" to pierce through the otherwise impenetrable veneer of cultural patterns, Abraham and Torok's theories implore that we foreground the emotional contexts that catalyzed the production of a symbolic (cultural) system that was not "immediately present in perception." Their theorization of the relationship between consciousness and language helps contextualize why symbolic

129 Ibid.

130 Rashkin (1995); Cf. Panksepp (2010) who discusses the affective properties of hunger and normal satiety. Northoff (2016, 197, 201) discusses neurological evidence for the spatiotemporal alignment of brain and the stomach processes.

131 Porter (2018).

132 See for example, Block (2005); Tononi and Koch (2008); Sui et al. (2013); Northoff (2016).

133 Northoff (2016, 207ff).

134 Cf. notion of maturation and evolution proposed by Konner (2007).

systems/culture "showers the observer with blizzards of encrypted messages."[135] Although the clinicians accepted Hermann's concept of a relational dual unity between mother and child, they rejected the idea that the human psyche's natural inclination orients toward remaining or returning to that state of bounded (un)consciousness.

Instead, Abraham and Torok argue that human development is constituted by a "constant process of differentiation or 'division from a more primary union': the mother."[136] While they do not deploy the terminology of neurochemicals, they do offer a logic of human development that accounts for the positive pleasurable experience of expansion and differentiation, which they assert is intrinsic to psychic functioning.[137] A paradigm of this affective logic

> is found right after birth in the infant's experience of an "empty mouth." The absence of the maternal object (the breast) leads to crying and howling, and these eventually give way to speech addressed to the mother as a partial replacement for absent satisfactions of the mouth. Ultimately, the mother's presence itself is replaced by words. The absence of objects and the empty mouth are transformed into words; at last, even the experiences related to words are converted into other words. So the wants of the original oral vacancy are remedied by being turned into verbal relationships with the speaking community at large. [Assimilating] a desire, a grief, a situation means channeling them through language into a communion of empty mouths... The passage from food to language in the mouth presupposes the successful replacement of the object's presence with the self's cognizance of its absence.[138]

Just as the emergence of language in human cognitive development is associated with the structural expansion of the brain, Abraham and Torok construe language acquisition as the ephiphenomenal event that triggers expansion processes in a human child's psyche. They claim this social developmental milestone marks a child's transition from existing in an undifferentiated state within the mother's conscious and unconscious worlds. The mechanism for psychic expansion is triggered upon a child's "magical discovery" of the word when she "detaches the mother's words—what Abraham and Torok call the

135 Ibid. (36).
136 Ibid. (35).
137 Rashkin (1995) points out the intellectual genealogy of this conceptualization: Abraham draws "on Sandor Ferenczi's theory of 'bio-analysis' and by Imre Hermann's notion of 'filial instinct.'"
138 (1995, 360).

'pieces-of-the-mother' [*bouts-de-mére*—from her person and uses them to designate" her own experiences:[139]

> Every child's emergence as an individual is distinctive, constituted by repressions of uniquely charged pieces-of-the-mother, each bearing affects specifically related to the singular circumstances and psychic traumas of the mother's life. Moreover, since every mother is also the child of another mother, she must herself be understood as always already carrying the contents of another's unconscious. This is why Abraham and Torok refer to the[ir theory of] dual unity as the "genealogical concept par excellence"... We are all the psychic products of our infinitely regressive family histories. We all recapitulate, in our individual, ontogenetic work of being, the phylogeny of our ancestor's sagas, all the while expanding these sagas with the stuff of our own lives.[140]

While there is debate in language acquisition research over whether the process is achieved via "critical periods (CPs) in development during which the system is most responsive to environmental input," Abraham's conception of the mental transformation accomplished with that first articulation of a word aligns with neuroscientific findings, especially those that "provide a mechanistic explanation of CPs, with the balance between excitatory and inhibitory processes establishing the onset and molecular brakes establishing the offset of windows of plasticity."[141] More to the point, Abraham provide a concrete response to the question of "what processes open them [CPs], keep them open, close them, and allow them to be reopened."[142]

According to Abraham and Torok, the ability to process experience into language derives from a process of mastery, which "depends for a crucial developmental period on the linguistic surround provided by parents, and the parents' own past experiences, conscious or not, will have imparted an affective charge to their speech and so to the words that they offer their children. Thus, Abraham and Torok argue, psychic organization is not only a dynamic response to a subject's predictable lived experience but also a conceptual structure that is passed down in families."[143] The clinicians assert

139 Rashkin (1992, 34). Cf. the notion of psychotherapy as a "talking cure," premised on the idea that psychic relief is derived through linguistic action and interaction between a patient and therapist. Abraham and Torok's metapsychological framework provides the operative specifics of why language use is therapeutic; see also Marx et al. (2017).

140 Rashkin (1992, 17).

141 Werker and Hensch (2015).

142 Ibid.

143 Porter (2018, 3).

> that when the words necessary to name a child's experience are overly laden with affect or content that is unavailable or unwelcome to the parent's awareness, the words that the child needs may be (consciously or unconsciously) withheld, or transmitted to the child with an affective burden that is beyond the child's capacity to process. The child may or may not consciously perceive the parent's discomfort, but in either case the necessary linguistic tools are not made available. The processing and naming of the child's experience fail, and a void is left in their stead. In this way the unconscious linguistic distortions and repressions embodied in the parent's speech are reconstructed in the child's. Abraham believed that traumatic experience interrupts or overwhelms a person's capacity to process it into language, leaving behind fragments of personal history of which the person can neither think nor speak. Inaccessible to awareness, they remain present in the person's psyche and language only as an absence. Yet they do remain present, and in their absence may be felt, seen, and passed on to linguistic heirs.[144]

Implicit in this account is the belief that *absence may be analyzed as a construct having a definable way of generating meaning and identity.*[145] This concept too finds resonance with neuroscientific findings that document the brain's sensitivity to absence. Brain structures connected to the management of threat detection, such as the amygdala, demonstrate heightened sensitivity to the body's expression of fear when there is an absence of object stimuli or conflicting stimuli signals that do not match expectations and thereby hampers positive expression reinforcement.[146]

Similar conclusions are advanced in studies that measure brain responses to "violations of regularities in the auditory scene."[147] The ambiguity produced by an absence of matches activates an attentional bias that favors environmental sources of threatening information. Studies reveal that conflicting signals occur in the absence of social signals that could reinforce expectations, suggesting the

---

144 Porter (2018, 4).

145 This idea, that the linguistic surround colors how people process and name experience, is of course not novel to Abraham and Torok; indeed it was a premise of Halbwachs' understanding of collective memory, Halbwachs (1992). Cf. Tal (1996) who shows how individual trauma narratives seep into the idiom of larger realms of social circulation.

146 Cf. The theory proposed by Georg Northoff (2009, 85), in which he posits a theory to explain coded neuronal activity changes, based on the brain's unconscious awareness of differences between its "intrinsic resting-state activity level and the stimulus-induced activity changes that is coded in the brain's actual activity level."

147 Phelps et al. (2001); Phelps et al. (2005), both investigate the neural links between language and fear conditioning, especially the role played by the amygdala. One significant finding is that these links operate on the preconscious perceptual analysis of emotional stimuli, which regulates attention.

reliance of the amygdala on "social signals to rapidly and flexibly learn threatening and rewarding associations."[148] Infant brains are sensitive to complex phonological rules;[149] a neonate can extract phonetic information from a wide physical variation included in speech.[150]

The existence of two archaic pathways that stream auditory information to the frontal lobe has been seen as an indication of the centrality of auditory experience for language emergence.[151] Studies based on fMRI, EEG, and other measurement mechanisms have shown that each pathway performs a distinct linguistic function. The auditory ventral stream governs sound recognition, involving processes that discern the "what" of the sound. The other, the auditory dorsal stream, functions to discern the locative source or "where" of the sound.[152] The latter processing stream is also implicated in speech production, speech repetition. Evolutionary scientists have posited that the multiplicity of functions and processes that transpire in the auditory dorsal stream represents an early stage of the brain's cognitive evolution.[153]

Theories that account for the evolution of heightened sensitivity to discerning "where" information have focused on separation distress as a paradigmatic affective context.[154] Studies argue that language emerged from the institutionalization of interpersonal bonds forged by contact calls made by mothers to reassure infants of their proximity or to report location in cases of separation. The theory suggests that the contact calls underwent a process of evolution, with the accrual of intonations that were used to disambiguate alarm from safe contact calls.[155] This evolutionary account contextualizes the role played by the auditory dorsal system in encoding phonological memory—from the names of objects, to intonations modulated with affective intentions, to speech repetition and lip reading.

Research on prosody, those speech elements that operate independently alongside phonetic information (such as vowels and consonants), deepens these implications. These speech elements, such as tone, stress, pitch, and rhythm, to name a few, are features not only of human communicative behavior but also of nonhuman primates, pointing to an evolutionary function. Prosody in humans is frequently linked to the emotional state of the speaker; it conveys information not necessarily encoded in other linguistic processes but important for survival.[156] The fact that neural networks become selectively tuned to sound violations in the linguistic surround, to the degree that such tuning in turn leads to more refined

148 Kujala and Risto (2010).
149 Hooker et al. (2006).
150 Sun et al. (2015).
151 Dehaene-Lambertz and Pena (2001); Bristow et al. (2009).
152 Rauschecker (2012).
153 Ibid.
154 Cohen et al. (2004).
155 Ibid.; Panksepp (2009); Poliva (2016).
156 Panksepp (2009); Poliva (2015, 2016).

responses to changes in that linguistic environment, aligns with the notion that subtle emotional charges carried by words in the mother's idiom would be registered.[157] It is this network of sounds and neural responses that comprises the seed of psychic activity.[158]

Ultimately, the brain's capacity to "form memory representations of the relationships between the elements of the auditory input," establishes a structure that informs linguistic processes.[159] Investigations that measure emotional interference caused by absences of matches in informational management reveal how it inhibits the speed with which cognitive tasks, such as naming a color word, are executed.[160] Words associated with neutral or negative emotions produce distinctive effects on cognitive processing operations.[161] Research on taboo words reveals they inhibit lexical-decision performance. Hearing or speaking taboo words activates the amygdala, therefore eliciting slower response times in lexical-decision performance than neutral words.[162]

This evidence suggests that "emotion interacts with a number of lexical, semantic and syntactic features in different brain regions and timings."[163] The inhibitive effect on cognitive processes exerted by a word's emotional charge recalls Abraham and Torok's theory that obstacles to converting an experience into words emerge when their unconscious emotional charge threatens in the same way that taboo words do.[164] They posit an intrinsic "tabooness" due to their association with an experience that for some reason had to be denied expression. These charged words, although absent from a subject's idiomatic expression, nonetheless contour her lexicon by virtue of the avoidant strategies established to exclude the word(s) from social circulation.[165]

Research on the emotional consequences of using euphemisms, words or phrases understood to mean the same thing as their negatively charged counterparts,[166]

157 Panksepp (2009); Ackermann et al. (2014).
158 Paavilainen et al. (2007); Panksepp (2009).
159 Kuhl et al. (1992); Maye et al. (2002).
160 Kujala and Näätänen (2010). Paavilainen et al. (2007).
161 Cf. the hypothesized "emotional Stroop effect," which claims the delay is manifested when the emotional relevance of a word to a subject inhibits the speed with which she can name the color word associated with it. MacLeod (1991); for a critique of the hypothesis, see Frings et al. (2010).
162 Studies have shown that words suffused with negative affect, such as "cancer" and "kill," elicit stronger responses than neutral words, see Dinn and Harris. (2000).
163 Severens et al. (2012); Sulpizio et al. (2019).
164 Hinojosa et al. (2020, 813); Espuny et al. (2018); Vergallito et al. (2019).
165 Ibid. Cf. similar neuroscience findings related to stigmatized words, Derks et al. (2008).
166 Cf. the theory that primary emotional systems "mediate the core nature of the selection criteria guiding the refinement of synaptic connections to provide the emotional palette that guides individual brain development… this mechanism ultimately influences learning, cognitive and social development" (Ellis & Torunchuk, 2013, 3). See also Heilman (1997), Han and Northoff (2008).

reinforce these links. Studies have found that euphemism functions to "protect speakers from undesired emotional arousal."[167] The effect of this protection implies a direct link between word forms and emotion. Empirical data on heightened autonomic responses to swear words also reflects a form of verbal conditioning in which the phonological form of the word links directly with an emotional response.

Abraham and Torok would suggest that this conditioning is shaped by the unique circumstances and psychic traumas of the mother's life, perceived by a child through unconscious discernment of acoustic patterns in her speech. Lexical fragments or symbols cryptically intone a dimension of concealed affect. As mentioned above, these patterns are inscribed in the child's speech patterns as well. Unconscious discrimination is also a feature in operational mechanisms related to word learning.[168] Early word learning processes index the degree to which irrelevant associations between words and objects have been suppressed, so that neural links are pruned.[169]

From an evolutionary perspective, the psyche/brain's ability to unconsciously identify emotional charges carried by a mother's words enabled a child to avoid and even segregate emotionally contaminated words from her own speech and consciousness.

> Psychic repression… would have great power in sociocultural environments where issues of inclusion or exclusion were at stake. The capacity of the psyche to displace words contaminated by unutterable… experience into lexical and phonetic fragments suggests that such expressive linguistic hiding benefited human continuity…. [unconscious] repression may have developed as a "fast and frugal"… way of compacting dangerous facts and feelings into safe little packets at a time in human linguistic and cognitive evolution when new social and environmental demands for cooperation were increasing the need for economical information transmission. The survival benefits of cooperation thus shaped linguistic behavior to ensure that language continues the conditions that maintain it.[170]

As a mechanism for repression, language operates like genetic material inasmuch as the mother's idiom shapes how her offspring interacts with and adapts to the environment. This conception nuances cognitive scientist Merlin Donald's thesis that human minds are hybrid minds forged by "cognitive "operational systems."[171] Conceptualizing the phenomenon of human speech as a fragment or

167 Bowers and Pleydell-Pearce (2011).
168 Ibid.
169 Mathews and MacLeod (1985); Merriman et al. (1989); McMurray et al. (2012); Taxitari et al. (2019); Borovsky, A. and Fernald, A. (2013).
170 Porter (2018, 230).
171 Donald (2000, 23).

"vestige of [intragroup] psychic conflicts experienced in the early stages of human self-fashioning,"[172] brings to the fore language's status as a symptom of and medium for transcending psychic distress induced by conflicting psychosocial positions. The next section investigates the implications of this position for understanding the etiology of the CG manifested in Confucius' ideal filial son.

Why Obstacles to Linguistic Processing Occur in Grief

Abraham and Torok theorize that blockages to processes that convert experiences into words are caused by intrapsychic conflicts. Drawing from an analysis of the behavior of the titular character in the 1987 Danish film, *Babette's Feast*, directed by Gabriel Axel, will help concretize the clinicians conception of suspended mourning as an "obstacle to self-fashioning."[173] Esther Rashkin deploys Abraham and Torok's understanding of psychic operations to interpret Babette's actions as stemming from a blockage to the conversion of her traumatic loss into words. The reason language was unavailable to function as an enzyme and process her loss is because it involved an intrapsychic conflict.

The conflict derived from tensions between two types of loss experienced by Babette: one involved the loss of her social status as a gastronomical artist celebrated by the aristocratic class. The other involved the loss of her beloved husband and son at the hands of the same aristocrats whose opinions were so central for her self-construal.[174] Grieving her losses was complicated by the conflictual nature of her attachments.

Rashkin's reading claims that the film allegorizes what happens in the face of this type of conflict. Babette's withdrawal from social intercourse and SEEKING activities is caused by the conditions in which, unable to mourn either lost object without negating the other, *the words necessary to initiate psychic digestive processes were suspended.*

Babette's pain, as the feast trope intimates, was ultimately named and digested. As the trope also indicates, the feast contents point to the words capable of effecting the transformation. Transcendence required the creation of a symbolic language to "speak" of loss. In the case of Babette, she eventually was able to speak of her loss through the language of her gastronomical prowess: the names of specialty dishes for which she was renowned. Rashkin deconstructs the internal dynamics of the menu's s nomenclature, noting their "magical" effect in stimulating communal expression reminiscent of the moment during

172 Porter (2018, 231). Cf. Ellis and Toronchuk (2013) who theorize that "emotional systems evolved due to their efficacy with regard to changing behavioral patterns… after processes of selection the resulting systems were those that enhanced survival within a group, which carried benefits of food, safety, learning, and eventually culture."

173 Rashkin (1995); Porter (2018, 42).

174 The film is based on a short story by renowned author Karen Blixen (pen name Isaac Dinisen), see Blixen (1958).

early language acquisition stages, when a child first uses a word to indicate something that is absent.

The magic lies in the efficacy of the words that name the food to be physically ingested to ensure figurative digestion as well. Thus, the champagne "Veuve de Clicquot," includes the word "widow" (*veuve*), an indirect self-reference to Babette's present social status. Similarly, the name of the meal's pièce de résistance, "Caille en sarcophage," literally "[burying the] quail in the coffin," tacitly "speaks" of burying her "little quail," a common French term of endearment for loved ones. The dishes metaphorically demonstrate the "need to bury the dead in such a way that they can be psychically devoured and digested and hence transformed into a tomb or memorial to their own disappearance," in order for mourning to begin.[175]

The conversion of the absence of loved ones into the language of food became a way to "speak" of her loss with others. This link between meal preparation and mourning may help explain the ubiquity of eating objects in burial practices in hominin social life:[176] When contextualized in terms of psychic functioning and organization, the similarities between food and burial preparation, not to mention the inclusion of eating or cooking vessels in burial spaces, raise the possibility that the positive psychotropic effect of burying, commemorating, and thereby naming the dead is a driving force of human mourning practices. Their capacity to speak of loss reduces its concomitant pain and initiates unhindered reorganization necessary to assimilate the experience.[177]

CG may involve a disorder of naming. While Babette's gastronomical language reveals the infinite variety of means through which grief can be expressed to transcend suspended mourning, for certain subjects, even these portals for speech are prohibited. Abraham and Torok observed this type of blockage in patients whose speech was at times delivered as if the words were shrouded by an enigma too dense to be deciphered by known forms of listening.[178] Furthermore, they found linguistic expression in these patients' speech involved the invention of particular forms of obfuscation. In other words, "the patients obscured beyond recognition the linguistic elements that might reveal" the source of their psychic suffering. Stymied by the inefficacy of Freudian therapy to explain this behavior, the clinicians hypothesized that breakdowns of signification may in fact be "markers of crucial experiences of which" their patients were "not consciously aware."[179]

---

175 Rashkin (1995, 364).
176 Rashkin (2008, 36).
177 Ekengren (2013); Pettit (2010).
178 Rashkin (1992, 33).
179 Porter (2018, 8) Cf, Van der Kolk (2015, 40–44) describes some dissociative patterns he has observed that resonate with: those times when symptoms have no obvious indexical relationship to a traumatic event. He uses the word "haunted" to describe the sensation of this dissociative experience that seems to return a subject into the physical and sensory dimensions of the traumatic event.

To explain what would cause their patients to make themselves linguistically unintelligible, Abraham and Torok theorized that in addition to a topographical split wrought by the brain's reorganization to accommodate human's use of language, there is another mechanism of repression, termed "preservative repression" (*refoulement conservateur*). Preservative repression works to conceal a lived shameful experience from conscious awareness. The clinicians make a sharp distinction between the dynamic nature of the former repression and the non-dynamic preservative repression.[180] To be clear, the shameful, psychically in-assimilable experience that is secreted

> is not primarily a hushed up fact, a covert plot, a private feeling, or confidential knowledge kept from others. "Secret" is not synonymous with "hidden," "unknown," or "latent," even in the Freudian sense of a person's unconscious or repressed desires, apt to reappear only in opaque, symptomatic compromise formations. In Abraham and Torok's sense, the secret is a *trauma* [emphasis added] whose very occurrence and devastating emotional consequences are entombed and thereby consigned to internal silence, albeit unwittingly, by the sufferers themselves.[181]

The linguistic mechanisms that preserve the unspeakable shameful trauma distort words related to the shameful trauma so as to perpetuate their concealment. Concealment is accomplished through operations of lexical displacement. Chains or networks of linguistic deferment, via homophones and synonyms, ensure that the psychically occluded traumatic experience remains secreted. The incongruence in their patients' speech required the clinicians to reconstruct the concealed shameful experience via an "anasemic or 'backward' reading" strategy. Identifying fragmented linguistic patterns that are produced by breakdowns in the processes of psychic assimilation is the first step toward reconstructing the shameful event that disrupted the function of other mechanisms that work in concert to unify a conscious self. For example,

> imagine a story about mail delivery, in which the word "post" never appears—not in postal, not in postman, not in post office. Why and how should this be?… it is because the writer is profoundly uncomfortable with the word "pillar," which is associated with some terrible episode in his past—a theft… or we ourselves might even imagine a death. The word "pillar" is thus prohibited from consciousness along with all its synonyms, the word "post" being one of them. Even though "post" in this story would connote mail and not columns, its affective contamination is

180 Rashkin (1992, 28).
181 Porter (2018, 6). Cf. Van der Kolk's finding that each bodily or mental register of traumatic experience can be separated from each other in consciousness.

> sufficient to forbid it in its own form, and the hypothetical writer is forced away from it and to associated but uncontaminated words like the "letters, dispatches, stamps, parcels."

These uncontaminated words are "the 'words that hide,' the cryptonyms of the secret word 'pillar.' Each one carries secreted within it, through a process of lexical and phonetic encrypting … the word that cannot be said."[182]

Abraham and Torok surmised that the linguistic mechanisms aimed toward rendering their patients' speech illegible were either the result of preservative repression enacted because of a subject's lived unspeakable shame; or were vestigial structures of deferment related to an ancestors' shameful experience, which were transmitted and unwittingly inherited by offspring and their descendants via the linguistic surrounds of family lines. This intrapsychic phenomenon—in which an ancestor's shameful experience exerts an "invisible" psychic presence on the child's development, brings to the fore an implicit group dynamic: it "holds the individual in a group dynamic" constituted by unspoken and unconscious risk-avoidant lexical rules that regulate spoken expression.[183] This formation recalls the interdependent mindset that we have seen is an endemic Chinese cultural trait.

Preservative repression mechanisms operate differently than the mechanism "known as the return of the repressed." In the case of a preserved shameful secret, "[what] returns to haunt" is what *an other* could not say, not one's own words or experiences. Abraham and Torok call the shameful secret a "phantom" to denote how, like folkloric ghosts, it represents the visitation on a descendant of a dead person's unsettling psychic disruptions, and their unconscious negative influence. The haunting experience of these "visitations" is triggered when normal assimilative processes threaten to activate a contaminated word.

Abraham and Torok view the relationship between a subject and the ancestor whose shame he is obligated to preserve as a diseased "dual unity." Unlike healthy "dual unity" in which gradual differentiation from the mother is supported to the degree that a child is capable of successful assimilating her own lived experiences, the diseased form holds the child with the parent in an unspoken pact to preserve the secret intact.[184] The presence of the concealed drama exerts disruptive influence on the psyche of a child whose self-fashioning processes must submit to an unconsciously inherited linguistic regimen organized by deferment patterns to preserve an ancestor's shameful experience. The ancestor's unspeakable drama "lies buried yet alive" in the descendant.[185]

182 Abraham and Torok (1994, 99).
183 Rashkin (2008, 95).
184 Abraham and Torok (1994, 173).
185 Ibid (104).

The notion that ancestral shameful experiences, and the linguistic distortions they enact, may endure over generations, yields an alternative entry into the mindset of Confucius' paradigmatic filial son. Abraham and Torok's conceptual tools can help explain historical, social, and cultural phenomena as catalyzed by crises that have been experienced as shameful. The following chapter looks to the archaeological record for clues that might account for the evolution of the salience of two affective genealogies, shame and grief, which entwined and fed off each other to produce a cultural defining mindset in China.

The evidence suggests it has much to tell us about Neolithic neuropsychological self-fashioning processes. I disinter from the record a structure of feeling that is core to the filial. My analysis will teach us to view Confucius' putative father, the paradigmatic filial child's lost object, as a figuration of a phantom who, like a guard, is vigilant in its efforts to prevent a son's psyche from reorganizing to accommodate the new reality of a profound loss. We will see why being filial means preserving a shameful secret, which means preserving the status-quo of a mindset.[186]

The idea that an ancestor and descendant may be bound by an unconscious prior contract to conceal a shared secret opens a new portal for reconsidering how the portraits of two filial sons, a concealer and a mourner, painted in the *Analects'*, delineate an affective filial logic. The reason why a son should observe closely his father's acts when alive, and then model them for three years after his death, is to reassure the father's ghost of his mastery of the family's idiom of concealment.[187] Just as a child takes three years to acquire language, so too must a son learn to navigate life, *sans pére*, with an innate grasp of the lineage's idiosyncratic linguistic mechanisms for concealing contaminated words. When the child has mastered the lineage's idiom, what his family says about him and what others say about him will not differ; this is the case of Min Ziqian, whose filiality, manifested by the alignment of inner and outer words, earned Confucius' praise.[188]

The idea of an unconscious but enforceable (through phantom returns) pact between ancestors and descendants also resolves the implicit contradiction between Confucius' proscription that the filial son be consumed by sincere emotion when performing mourning rituals and his promulgation of concealment techniques as necessary tools for the filial son. Both evoke Michael Ing's conception of an anxiety pervading Confucian concerns that internal emotions and external behavior match. The "cognate relationship between the graph of the word *xiao* and [the word] 'education' (*jiao*)," reinforces these links. The lexical overlaps

186 Rashkin (2008, 94).

187 Cf. Chan and Tan (2004) suggests that the father figure is a symbol of tradition, making filiality less about obedience to one's immediate father, and more about respect for the length of ritual precedent.

188 *Lunyu*, 1.11.

articulate "the substance of Confucian education as the serious responsibility of each generation to transmit the culture that they have inherited,"[189] Confucius' fastidious care with speech so that it does "not outpace or conceal the *reality* of the speaker's character" (emphasis mine),[190] resonates with his injunction that a son's mourning rituals aim toward complete libidinal withdrawal; both find coherence in light of a mind structured by preservative repression.[191]

In sum, Abraham and Torok's assumption that consciousness is a function of psychic catastrophes nuances Van der Kolk's insight that "the body keeps score" of "traumatic experiences." We shall see that the clinicians' theorizations suggest that some somatic symptoms may be "read" linguistically as symbolic clues that hint at why a traumatic fragment of memory is most recalcitrant to transformation, that is, to being named, digested and psychically accommodated. Most important is the fact that the threat posed by the traumatic experience—shame—resulted from implicit prohibitions against placing awareness of the crisis within a subject's social emotional existence.

Chapter 3 pursues the idea that the neuropsychological and intrapsychic aspects extrapolated from Confucius' image of an ideal filial son have deep evolutionary roots that can be reconstructed from the evidentiary record. It traces the hypothesized "structure of feeling" intrinsic to the filial son's behavior back to specific historical conditions involving an obstacle to memorializing an unspeakable loss. Once reconstructed, the archaic emotional context is also revealed to be a vector for transmitting unspeakable, but crucially important, cultural information.

Cited Sources

Abraham, N., & Torok, M. (1994). *The shell and the kernel: Renewals of psychoanalysis* (*Vol. 1*). University of Chicago Press.

Ackermann, H., Hage S. R., & Ziegler, W. (2014). Brain mechanisms of acoustic communication in humans and nonhuman primates: An evolutionary perspective. *Behavioral and Brain Sciences*, *37*(6), 529–546.

Alcaro, A., & Panksepp, J. (2011). The SEEKING mind: primal neuro-affective substrates for appetitive incentive states and their pathological dynamics in addictions and depression. *Neuroscience & Biobehavioral Reviews*, *35*(9), 1805–1820.

Axel, Gabriel. (1988). *Babette's feast*. Nordisk Film.

Blixen, K. (1958). *Anecdotes of destiny and ehrengard*. Random House.

Borovsky, A. & Fernald, A. (2013). Fast mapping, slow learning: Disambiguation of novel word–object mappings in relation to vocabulary learning at 18, 24, and 30 months. *Cognition*, 126(1), 39–53.

189 *Lunyu*, 11.4; see also Knapp (2008).
190 Rosemont and Ames (2009, 133).
191 Loy (2014).

Bowlby, J. (1979). The Bowlby-Ainsworth attachment theory. *Behavioral and Brain Sciences, 2*(4), 637–638.

Bowers, J. S., & Pleydell-Pearce, C. W. (2005). Verbal conditioning, euphemisms, and linguistic relativity. *PLoS One*, 6(7), e22341.

Boyd, R., & Richerson, P. J. (1988). *Culture and the evolutionary process*. University of Chicago Press.

Bristow, D., Dehaene-Lambertz, G., Mattout, J., Soares, C., Gliga, T., Baillet, S., & Mangin, J.F. (2009). Hearing faces: How the infant brain matches the face it sees with the speech it hears. *Journal of Cognitive Neuroscience, 21*(5), 905–921.

Brooks, E. B., & Brooks, A. T. (1998). *The original analects: Sayings of Confucius and his successors*. Columbia University Press.

Carroll, R. (2018). "At the border between chaos and order": What psychotherapy and neuroscience have in common. In *Revolutionary connections* (pp. 191–211). Routledge.

Chan, A. K. L. & Tan, S. H. (Eds.) (2004). *Filial piety in Chinese thought and history*. London: RoutledgeCurzon.

Chiao, J. Y. (2009). Cultural neuroscience: A once and future discipline. *Progress in Brain Research, 178*, 287–304.

Chiao, J. Y. (2010). At the frontier of cultural neuroscience: Introduction to the special issue. *Social Cognitive and Affective Neuroscience, 52*(2-3), 109–110.

Chiao, J. Y., & Ambady, N. (2007). Cultural neuroscience: Parsing universality and diversity across levels of analysis. In S. Kitayama & D. Cohen (Eds.), *Handbook of cultural psychology* (pp. 237–254). The Guilford Press.

Chiao, J. Y., & Blizinsky, K. D. (2010). Culture–gene coevolution of individualism–collectivism and the serotonin transporter gene. *Proceedings of the Royal Society B: Biological Sciences, 277*(1681), 529–537.

Chiao, J. Y., Li, S. C., Seligman, R., & Turner, R. (Eds.). (2016). *The Oxford handbook of cultural neuroscience*. Oxford University Press.

Cohen, Y. E., Russ, B. E., Gifford, G. W., 3rd, Kiringoda, R., & MacLean, K. A. (2004). Selectivity for the spatial and nonspatial attributes of auditory stimuli in the ventrolateral prefrontal cortex. *The Journal of Neuroscience: The Official Journal of the Society for Neuroscience, 24*(50), 11307–11316.

Csikszentmihalyi, M. (2004). *Material virtue: Ethics and the body in early China*. Brill.

Damasio, A. R. (1999). *The feeling of what happens: Body and emotion in the making of consciousness*. Houghton Mifflin Harcourt.

Defoort, C. (2016). The gradual growth of the Mohist Core philosophy: Tracing fixed formulations in the Mozi. *Monumenta Serica, 64*(1), 1–22.

Dehaene-Lambertz, G., & Pena, M. (2001). Electrophysiological evidence for automatic phonetic processing in neonates. *Cognitive Neuroscience and Neuropsychology Neuroreport, 12*, 3155–3158.

Derks, B., Inzlicht, M., & Kang, S. (2008). The neuroscience of stigma and stereotype threat. *Group Processes & Intergroup Relations, 11*(2), 163–181.

Dinn, W., & Harris, C. L. (2000). Neurocognitive function in antisocial personality disorder. *Psychiatry Research, 97*, 173–190.

Donald, M. (1993). Human cognitive evolution: What we were, what we are becoming. *Social Research, 60*, 143–170.

Donald, M. (2000). The central role of culture in cognitive evolution: A reflection on the myth of the isolated mind. In L. Nucci (Ed.), *Culture, thought, and development* (pp. 19–38). Lawrence Erlbaum Associates.

Downey, G. (2016). Sensory enculturation and neuroanthropology: The case of human echolocation. In Joan Y. Chiao, Shu-Chen Li, Rebecca Seligman, and Robert Turner (Eds.), *The Oxford handbook of cultural neuroscience* (pp. 41–55). Oxford University Press.

Dunbar, R. I. & Shultz, S. (2007). Evolution in the social brain. *Science, 317*(5843), 1344–1347.

Ebrey, P. B. (2014). *Confucianism and family rituals in imperial China: A social history of writing about rites*. Princeton University Press.

Ellis, G. F. R., & Toronchuk, J. A. (2013). Affective neuronal selection: The nature of the primordial emotion systems. *Frontiers in Psychology, 3*, 589.

Ekengren, F. (2013). Contextualizing grave goods. In Liv Nilsson Stutz and Sarah Tarlow (Eds.), *Oxford online handbook of the archaeology of death and burial*. Oxford University Press.

Espuny, J., Jiménez-Ortega, L., Casado, P., Fondevila, S., Muñoz, F., Hernández-Gutiérrez, D., & Martín-Loeches, M. (2018). Event-related brain potential correlates of words' emotional valence irrespective of arousal and type of task. *Neuroscience Letters, 670*, 83–88.

Foust, M. A. (2009). Grief and mourning in Confucius's analects. *Journal of Chinese Philosophy, 36*(2), 348–358.

Freed, P. J., & Mann J. J. (2007). Sadness and loss: Toward a neurobiopsychosocial model. *American Journal of Psychiatry, 164*(1), 28–34.

Freed, P. J., Yanagihara, T. K., Hirsch, J., & Mann, J. J. (2009). Neural mechanisms of grief regulation. *Biological Psychiatry, 66*(1), 33–40.

Frings, C., Englert, J., Wentura, D., & Bermeitinger, C. (2010). Decomposing the emotional Stroop effect. *Quarterly Journal of Experimental Psychology, 1*(1), 42–49.

Fuller, S. (2014). Neuroscience, neurohistory, and the history of science: A tale of two brain images. *Isis, 105*(1), 100–109.

Fung, Y. L. (1952). Derk Bodde trans.*A history of Chinese philosophy. Vol. 1: Period of the philosophers (from the beginnings to circa 100 BC)*. Princeton University Press.

Fung, H. (1999). Becoming a moral child: The socialization of shame among young Chinese children. *Ethos, 27*(2), 180–209.

Goldin, P. R. (Ed.). (2017). *A concise companion to Confucius*. John Wiley & Sons.

Grecucci, A., Theuninck, A., Frederickson, J., & Job, R. (2015). Mechanisms of social emotion regulation: From neuroscience to psychotherapy. *Emotion Regulation: Processes, Cognitive Effects and Social Consequences, 57*, 84.

Guo, Q.M. (2010). Ru-Mo liangjia zhi "xiao," "sang" yu "ai" de qubie he zhenglun. *Zhexue yanjiu, 1*(4-55), 128–129.

Halbwachs, M. (1992). *On collective memory*. University of Chicago Press.

Hall, D. L., & Ames, R. T. (1987). *Thinking through confucius*. Suny Press.

Han, S., Northoff, G., Vogeley, K., Wexler, B. E., Kitayama, S., & Varnum, M. E. (2013). A cultural neuroscience approach to the biosocial nature of the human brain. *Annual Review of Psychology, 64*, 335–359.

Han, S., & Northoff, G. (2008). Culture-sensitive neural substrates of human cognition: A transcultural neuroimaging approach. *Nature Reviews Neuroscience, 9*(8), 646–654.

Han, S., & Northoff, G. (2009). Understanding the self: A cultural neuroscience approach. *Progress in Brain Research,Cultural Neuroscience: Cultural Influences on Brain Function, 178*, 203–212.

Heinrich, J., & Boyd, R. (1998). The evolution of conformist transmission and the emergence of between-group differences. *Evolution and Human Behavior, 19*, 215–241.

Heilman, K. (1997). Review. The neurobiology of emotional experience. *Journal of Neuropsychiatry and Clinical Neurosciences. 9*(3), 439–448.

Hinojosa, J. A., Moreno, E. M., & Ferré, P. (2020). Affective neurolinguistics: towards a framework for reconciling language and emotion. *Language, Cognition and Neuroscience, 35*(7), 813–839.

Holzman, D. (1998). The place of filial piety in ancient China. *Journal of the American Oriental Society*, 185–199.

Hong, Y., Wan, C., No, S., Chiu, C. (2007). Multicultural identities. In S. Kitayama and D. Cohen (Eds.), *Handbook of cultural psychology* (pp. 323–345). New York: Guilford.

Hooker, C. I., Germine, L.T., Knight, R. T. & D'esposito, M. (2006). Amygdala response to facial expressions reflects emotional learning. *Journal of Neuroscience, 23*(5), 8915.

Hsiao, H. H. I. (1979). Concepts of Hsiao (filial piety) in the classic of poetry and the classic of documents. *Zhongguo wenhua yanjiusuo xuebao*, 10, 425–445.

Hunter, M. (2017) *Confucius beyond the analects*. Brill.

Ikezawa, M. (1994). The philosophy of filiality in ancient China: Ideological development of ancestor worship in the Zhanguo period (Doctoral dissertation, University of British Columbia).

Ing, M. (2017). *The vulnerability of integrity in early confucian thought*. Oxford University Press.

Ing, M. D. K. (2019). Sages, integrity, and the paradox of vulnerability: Reply to Chung, McLeod, and Seok. *Res Philosophica, 96*, 401–408.

Ivanhoe, P. J. (2000). *Confucian moral self cultivation*. Hackett Publishing.

Ivanhoe, P. J. (2003). Death and dying in the analects. In Weiming Tu and Mary Evelyn Tucker (Eds.), *Confucian spirituality* (pp. 1–220). Crossroad Pub. Company.

Ivanhoe, P. J., Chandler, M., & Littlejohn, R. (2008). The shade of Confucius: Social roles, ethical theory, and the self. *Polishing the Chinese Mirror: Essays in honor of Henry Rosemont, Jr*, 34–49.

Jie, Fang. (2013). Cong "Lunyü" Zhong de "chi" kan Zhongguo zhexue de zilu jingshen. *Shehukexuejia, 2*, 22–24, 32.

Kächele, H. (2009). A Hungarian precursor of attachment theory: Ferenczi's Successor, Imre Hermann. *American Imago, 66*(4), 419–426.

Ke, R. (2014). Xiaodao—yi zhong ziran zhuyi de jiieshi. *Kexue jishu zhexue yanjiu, 31*(5), 98–106.

Kiley Hamlin, J., Wynn, K., & Bloom, P. (2010). Three-month-olds show a negativity bias in their social evaluations. *Developmental Science, 13*(6), 923–929.

Kinney, A. B. (2017). *Women in the analects. A concise companion to Confucius*, 148–163.

Kitayama, S., & Cohen, D. (Eds.). (2007). *Handbook of cultural psychology*. New York.

Kitayama, S. , Duffy, S., & Uchida, Y. (2007). *Self as cultural mode of being. Handbook of cultural psychology*, 136–174.

Kitayama, S., & Park, J. (2010). Cultural neuroscience of the self: Understanding the social grounding of the brain. *Social Cognitive and Affective Neuroscience, 5*(2–3), 111–129.

Kitayama, S., & Uskul, A. K. (2011). Culture, mind, and the brain: Current evidence and future directions. *Annual Review of Psychology, 62*, 419–449.

Knapp, K. N. (2005). *Selfless offspring*. University of Hawaii Press.

Knapp, K. N. (2008). Learning Confucianism through filial sons, loyal retainers, and chaste wives. In Jeffrey L. Richey (Ed.), *Teaching Confucianism, 39*. doi: 10.1093/acprof:oso/9780195311600.003.0004

Konner, M. (2010). Evolutionary foundations of cultural psychology. *Handbook of cultural psychology*, 77.

Kraus, B., & Kitayama, S. (2019). Interdependent self-construal predicts emotion suppression in Asian Americans: An electro-cortical investigation. *Biological Psychology, 146*, 107733.

Kujala, T., & Näätänen, R. (2010). The adaptive brain: A neurophysiological perspective. *Progress in Neurobiology 91*(1), 55–67.

Kuhl, P. K., Williams, K. A., Lacerda, F., Stevens, K. N., & Lindblom, B. (1992). Linguistic experience alters phonetic perception in infants by 6 months of age. *Science, 255*(5044), 606–608.

LaBar, K. S., Phelps, E. A. (1998). Arousal-mediated memory consolidation: Role of the medial temporal lobe in humans. *Psychological Science, 9*, 527–540.

Lau, D. C. (1979). *The analects*. UK: Penguin.

Lee, J. J. Y., & Jeyaraj, S. (2014). Effects of self-construal differences on cognitive dissonance examined by priming the independent and interdependent self. *SAGE Open, 4*(1), 2158244014521434.

Li, J., Wang, L., & Fischer, K. (2004). The organisation of Chinese shame concepts? *Cognition and Emotion, 18*(6), 767–797.

Lieber, E., Fung, H., & Leung, P. W. L. (2006). Chinese child-rearing beliefs: Key dimensions and contributions to the development of culture-appropriate assessment. *Asian Journal of Social Psychology, 9*(2), 140–147.

Liu, Q. P. (2003). Filiality versus sociality and individuality: On Confucianism as "consanguinitism". *Philosophy East and West*, 234–250.

Lobb, E. A., Kristjanson, L. J., Aoun, S. M., Monterosso, L., Halkett, G. K. B., & Davies, A. (2010). Predictors of complicated grief: A systematic review of empirical studies. *Death Studies, 34*(8), 673–698. doi: 10.1080/07481187.2010.496686. PMID: 24482845.

Loewe, M. (1993). Early Chinese texts. *A bibliographical guide, Berkeley*.

Loy, H. C. (2014). Language and ethics in the analects. In A. Olberding (Ed.), *Dao companion to the analects* (pp. 137–158). Springer.

MacLeod, C. M. (1991). Half a century of research on the Stroop Effect: An integrative review. *Psychological Bulletin, 109*(2), 163–203.

Marinelli, L., & Mayer, A. (2016). The receding animal: Theorizing anxiety and attachment in psychoanalysis from Freud to Imre Hermann. *Science in Context, 29*(1), 55–76.

Marks, J., Ames, R. T., & Solomon, R. C. (Eds.). (1995). *Emotions in asian thought: A dialogue in comparative philosophy, with a discussion by robert C. solomon*. SUNY Press.

Markus, H. R., & Kitayama, S. (2010). Cultures and selves: A cycle of mutual constitution. *Perspectives on psychological science, 5*(4), 420–430.

Marx, C., Benecke, C. & Gumz, A. (2017). Talking cure models: A framework of analysis. *Frontiers in Psychology, 8*, 1589.

Mathews, A., & MacLeod, C. (1985). Discrimination of threat cues without awareness in anxiety states. *Journal of Abnormal Psychology, 95*, 131–138.

Maye, J., Werker, J. F., & Gerken, L. (2002). Infant sensitivity to distributional information can affect phonetic discrimination. *Cognition 82*(3), B101–111.

McMurray, B., Horst, J. S. & Samuelson, L. K. (2012). Word learning emerges from the interaction of online referent selection and slow associative learning. *Psychology Review, 119*(4), 831–877.

Méndez-Montoya, A. F. (2012). *The theology of food: Eating and the Eucharist.* John Wiley & Sons.

Mendoza-Denton, R., & Mischel, W. (2007). Integrating system approaches to culture and personality: The cultural cognitive-affective processing system.

Merriman, W., Bowman, L. & MacWhinney (1989). The mutual exclusivity bias in children's word learning. *Monographs of the Society for Research in Child Development, 54*(3/4), 1–129.

Michael, D. K. (2019). Précis to *The Vulnerability of Integrity in Early Confucian Thought. Res Philosophica, 93*(3), 369–372.

Ni, P. (2008). Do not take Confucians as Kantians: Comments on Liu Qingping's interpretation of Confucian teachings. *Dao*, 7(1), 45–49.

Nichols, R. (2015). Early Confucianism is a system for social-functional influence and probably does not represent a normative ethical theory. *Dao, 14*(4), 499–520.

Nichols, R. (2016). A sense of shame among the virtues. *Journal of Moral Education, 45*(2), 166–178.

Northoff, G. (2009, January). How can neuroscience support phenomenological and psychotherapeutic understanding of psychosis. *Psychosis-Psychological Social and Integrative Approaches, 1*, S26.

Northoff, G. (2016). Is the self a higher-order or fundamental function of the brain? The "basis model of self-specificity" and its encoding by the brain's spontaneous activity. *Cognitive Neuroscience*, 7(1–4), 203–222.

Olberding, A. (1997). Mourning, memory, and identity: A comparative study of the constitution of the self in grief. *International Philosophical Quarterly, 37*(1), 29–44.

Olberding, A. (2004). The consummation of sorrow: An analysis of Confucius' grief for Yan Hui. *Philosophy East and West, 53*(3), 279–301.

Olberding, A. (2008). Dreaming of the Duke of Zhou: Exemplarism and the analects. doi: 10.1111/j.1540-6253.2008.00508.x

Olberding, A. (Ed.). (2013a). *Dao companion to the analects* (*Vol. 4*). Springer Science & Business Media.

Olberding, A. (2013b). *Moral exemplars in the Analects: The good person is that* (*Vol. 15*). Routledge.

Oyserman, D., & Lee, S. W. S. (2007). Priming "culture": Culture as situated cognition. In S. Kitayama and D. Cohen (Eds.), *Handbook of cultural psychology* (pp. 255–279). The Guilford Press.

Panksepp, J. (1998). The periconscious substrates of consciousness: Affective states and the evolutionary origins of the self. *Journal of Consciousness Studies, 5*(5–6), 566–582.

Panksepp, J. (1999). Emotions as viewed by psychoanalysis and neuroscience: An exercise in consilience. *Neuropsychoanalysis, 1*(1), 15–38.

Panksepp, J. (2004). *Affective neuroscience: The foundations of human and animal emotions.* Oxford University Press.

Panksepp, J. (2007). Emotional feelings originate below the neocortex: Toward a neurobiology of the soul. *Behavioral and Brain Sciences, 30*(1), 101–103.

Panksepp, J. (2009). The emotional antecedents to the evolution of music and language. *Musicae Scientiae, 13*(2_suppl), 229–259.

Panksepp, J. (2010). Affective neuroscience of the emotional BrainMind: Evolutionary perspectives and implications for understanding depression. *Dialogues in Clinical Neuroscience, 12*(4), 533.

Panksepp, J., & Watt, D. (2011). Why does depression hurt? Ancestral primary-process separation-distress (PANIC/GRIEF) and diminished brain reward (SEEKING) processes in the genesis of depressive affect. *Psychiatry: Interpersonal & Biological Processes, 74*(1), 5–13.

Panksepp, J., & Watt, D. (2011). What is basic about basic emotions? Lasting lessons from affective neuroscience. *Emotion Review, 3*(4), 387–396.

Paavilainen, P., Arajärvi, P., & Takegata, R. (2007). Preattentive detection of nonsalient contingencies between auditory features. *Neuroreport, 18*(2), 159–163.

Pettit, P. B. (2010). *The palaeolithic origins of human burial.* Routledge.

Phelps, E, O'Connor, K. J., Gatenby, C., Gore, J., Grillon, C. & Davis, M. (2001). Activation of the left amygdala to a cognitive representation of fear. *Nature Neuroscience, 4*, 437–441.

Phelps, E, O'Connor, K. J., Gatenby, C., Gore, J., Grillon, C. & Davis, M. (2005). The interaction of emotion and cognition: The relation between the human amygdala and cognitive awareness. *The New Unconscious*, 61–76. doi: 10.1093/acprof:oso/9780195307696.001.0001

Pines, Y. (2002). *Foundations of Confucian thought.* University of Hawaii Press.

Poliva, O. (2015). From where to what: a neuroanatomically based evolutionary model of the emergence of speech in humans. *F1000Research, 4*. doi: 10.12688/f1000research.6175.3

Poliva, O. (2016). From mimicry to language: A neuroanatomically based evolutionary model of the emergence of vocal language. *Frontiers in Neuroscience, 10*, 307.

Porter, D. L. (2018). *Collective trauma and the psychology of secrets in transnational film.* Routledge.

Price, J. S. (1967). Hypothesis: The dominance hierarchy and the evolution of mental illness. *Lancet, 2*, 243–246.

Puett, M. J. (2002). *The ambivalence of creation: Debates concerning innovation and artifice in early China.* Stanford University Press.

Puett, M. J. (2006). Innovation as ritualization: The fractured cosmology of early China. *Cardozo Law Review, 28*, 23.

Puett, M. J. (2019). Life, domesticated and undomesticated: Ghosts, sacrifice, and the efficacy of ritual practice in early China. *HAU: Journal of Ethnographic Theory, 9*(2), 439–460.

Qiu, Z. L. (1995). Bu xiao zhi xiao: Sui Tang yilai geguliaoqin xianxiang de shehuishi chutan. *Xin shixue, 6*(1), 49–94.

Radice, T. (2017). Confucius and filial piety. In Goldin, P.R. (Ed.), *A concise companion to Confucius.* John Wiley and Sons, 185–207.

Radice, T. (2021). A dramaturgy of death: Performing (and spectating) filial piety in early China. *Zhongguo lishi xuekan*, 1–24.

Rashkin, E. (1992). For a new psychoanalytic criticism: The works of Abraham and Torok. *Family Secrets and the Psychoanalysis of Narrative*, 13–48.

Rashkin, E. (1995). A Recipe for Mourning: Isak Dinesen's "Babette's Feast." *Style, 29*(3), 356–374.

Rashkin, E. (2008). *Unspeakable secrets and the psychoanalysis of culture.* Suny Press.

Rashkin, E. (2009). Unmourned dead, filtered history, and the screening of anti-Semitism in Kieślowskis "A short film about killing". *American Imago*, 311–342.

Rashkin, E. (2014). *Family secrets and the psychoanalysis of narrative.* Princeton University Press.

Rauschecker, J. P. (2012). Ventral and dorsal streams in the evolution of speech and language. *Frontiers in evolutionary neuroscience, 4*, 7.

Rosemont, H., & Ames, R. T. (2009). *The Chinese classic of family reverence: A philosophical translation of the Xiaojing*. University of Hawaii Press.

Rosemont Jr, H. (2015). *Against individualism: A Confucian rethinking of the foundations of morality, politics, family, and religion*. Lexington Books.

Schore, A. N. (2003). *Affect regulation and the repair of the self (norton series on interpersonal neurobiology) (Vol. 2)*. WW Norton & Company.

Schwartz, B. I. (1985). *The world of thought in ancient China*. Harvard University Press.

Seachris, J. (2008). Yan Hui's death as a threat to Confucius' expression of virtue: A further look at the Master's Grief. *Asian Philosophy, 18*(2), 105–122.

Severens, E., Kühn, S., Hartsuiker, R. J., & Brass, M. (2012). Functional mechanisms involved in the internal inhibition of taboo words. *Social Cognitive and Affective Neuroscience*, 7(4), 431–435.

Shun, K. L. (2004). Conception of the person in early Confucian thought. In Shun *Confucian ethics: A comparative study of self, autonomy, and community* (pp. 183–199). Cambridge University Press.

Slingerland, E. (2000). Why philosophy is not "extra" in understanding the Analects. *Philosophy East and West, 50*(1), 137–141.

Slingerland, E. (2003). *Analects: With selections from traditional commentaries*. Hackett Publishing.

Smail, D. L. (2007). *On deep history and the brain*. University of California Press.

Smail, D. L. (2014). Neurohistory in action: Hoarding and the human past. *Isis, 105*(1), 110–122.

Smetana, J. G., & Killen, M. (2008). Moral cognition, emotions, and neuroscience: An integrative developmental view. *International Journal of Developmental Science, 2*(3), 324–339.

Song, Y. H. (2020). zhong Kongzi de ziwo guan. *Linyi daxue xuebao, 3*, 63–70.

Sorel, E. (2019). The social brain: Wired to connect and belong. *World Social Psychiatry, 1*(1), 23.

Stroeb M, & Schut H. (1999): The dual process model of coping with bereavement: Rationale and description. *Death Studies, 23*, 197–224.

Stumpfeldt, H. (2010). Thinking Beyond the "Sayings:" Comments about sources concerning the life and teachings of Confucius (551–479). *Oriens Extremus, 49*, 3–27.

Sui, J., P. Rotshtein, & G.W. Humphreys. (2013). Coupling social attention to the self forms a network for personal significance. *Proceedings of the National Academy of Sciences 110*(19), 7607–7612.

Sulpizio, S., Toti, M., Del Maschio, N., Costa, A., Fedeli, D., Job, R., & Abutalebi, J. (2019). Are you really cursing? Neural processing of taboo words in native and foreign language. *Brain and Language, 194*, 84–92.

Sun, Y., Giavazzi, M., Adda-Decker, M., Barbosa, L. S., Kouider, S., Bachoud-Lévi, A. C., Jacquemot, C., & Peperkamp, S. (2015). Complex linguistic rules modulate early auditory brain responses. *Brain and Language, 149*, 55–65.

Tal, K. (1996). *Worlds of hurt: Reading the literatures of trauma* (No. 95). Cambridge University Press.

Tang, Q. (2020). *Ritual civilization and mythological coding: Cultural interpretation of Li Ji*. Springer Nature.

Taxitari, L., Twomey, K., Westermann, G., & Mani, M. (2019). The Limits of Infants' Early Word Learning. *Language and Learning and Development, 16*, 1–21.

Thompson, S. U. R. (2012). On (not) eating the dead: A reader's digest of a 'Chinese' funerary taboo. In K. Latham, S. Thompson, and J. Klein (Eds.), Consuming China: Approaches to cultural change in contemporary China (pp. 131–159). Routledge.

Tian, S. L. (2019). zhong Kongzi de ziwo yanshuo yu jiaoyu qidi. *Zhida Xuebao, 4*, 65–71.

Tononi, G., & Koch, C. (2008). The neural correlates of consciousness: An update. *Annals of the New York Academy of Sciences, 1124*, 239–261.

Vaish, A., Grossmann, T., & Woodward, A. (2008). Not all emotions are created equal: The negativity bias in social-emotional development. *Psychological Bulletin, 134*(3), 383.

Van der Kolk, B. A. (2015). *The body keeps the score: Brain, mind, and body in the healing of trauma*. Penguin Books.

Venkatraman, A., Edlow, B. L., & Immordino-Yang, M. H. (2017). The Brainstem in Emotion: A Review. *Frontiers in Neuroanatomy, 11*, 15.

Vergallito, A., Petilli, M. A., Cattaneo, L., & Marelli, M. (2019). Somatic and visceral effects of word valence, arousal and concreteness in a continuum lexical space. *Scientific Reports, 9*. doi: 10.1038/s41598-019-56382-2

Vikár, György. (1985). Obituary. Imre Hermann, 1889–1984. *International Journal of Psycho-Analysis, 66*, 111.

Von Falkenhausen, L. (2006). Chinese society in the age of Confucius (1000-250 BC): The archaeological evidence (Vol. 2). ISD LLC. Csikszentmihalyi, Mark, "Confucius", The Stanford Encyclopedia of Philosophy (Summer 2020 Edition), Ed.: Edward N. Zalta.

Wang, H. (2011). Piety and individuality through a convoluted path of rightness: Exploring the Confucian art of moral discretion via Analects 13.18. *Asian Philosophy, 21*(4), 395–418.

Watt, D. F. (1999). Consciousness and emotion: review of Jaak Panksepp's 'Affective Neuroscience'. *Journal of Consciousness Studies, 6*(6–7),191–200.

Watt, D. F. (2007). Affirmative-action for the brainstem in the neuroscience of consciousness: The zeitgeist of the brainstem as a "dumb arousal" system. *Behavioral and Brain Sciences, 30*(1), 108–110.

Watt, D. F. (2012). Theoretical challenges in the conceptualization of motivation in neuroscience: Implications for the bridging of neuroscience and psychoanalysis. *From the couch to the lab: Trends in psychodynamic neuroscience*(pp. 85–108).

Watt, D. F., & Panksepp, J. (2009). Depression: An evolutionarily conserved mechanism to terminate separation distress? A review of aminergic, peptidergic, and neural network perspectives. *Neuropsychoanalysis, 11*(1), 7–51.

Werker, J. F., & Hensch, T. K. (2015). Critical periods in speech perception: new directions. *Annual Review of Psychology, 66*, 173–196.

Wong, D. (2011). Confucian political philosophy. In G. Klosko (Ed.), *The Oxford handbook of the history of political philosophy*. Oxford University Press.

Wong, D. B. (2019). In Michael DK Ing (Ed.), The vulnerability of integrity in early China. *Dao, 18*(4), 641–646.

Wong, D. B. (2019). *The vulnerability of integrity in early confucian thought*. Oxford University Press.

Xiaojing, . (1980). *Shisanjing zhushu*. Zhonghua.

Zhang, L. (2019). Kongzi de xiaodao sixiang yu 'Lunyü' sang, yu qi yi ye, ning qi' de lijie. *Hubei Gongcheng Xueyuan Xuebao, 39* (1), 5–8.

Zhao, Xun. (2016). Kongzi de 'sannian uw gai yu fu zhi dao' de hanyi daodi shi shenmo? *Jiamusi zhiye xueyuan xuebao*, *6*, 101.

Zhong, J., Wang, A., Qian, M., Zhang, L., Gao, J., Yang, J., & Chen, P. (2008). Shame, personality, and social anxiety symptoms in Chinese and American nonclinical samples: A cross-cultural study. *Depression and Anxiety*, *25*, 449–460.

Zhu, Y., Zhang, L., Fan, J., & Han, S. (2007). Neural basis of cultural influence on self-representation. *Neuroimage*, *34*(3), 1310–1316.

3

THE EVOLUTION OF A CHINESE CULTURAL NERVOUS SYSTEM

The central claim advanced in this chapter is that a systemized set of Chinese behaviors and thoughts, a mental structure, descended from a specific Neolithic mindset (8000-2000 B.C.)[1] This psychological structure was contoured by particular emotional conditions experienced by China's earliest farmers. I begin with the premise that the archaeologically evidenced "preoccupation with north-south alignment, reflected in the Neolithic built environment—extending to walls, palaces, tombs, common burials and even storage pits,"[2] may be construed in terms of conditioned aversive behavior. Cardinal alignment seeks to enclose and lodge the self in community within clear and fixed situational boundaries. This spatial dimension of self-construal evokes the mental structure that neuropsychologists have categorized as interdependent. As we saw in Chapter 2, interdependence refers to a mindset in which the individual is defined by her relationship to others. Although the formation of this culturally distinct neural representation of the self has been attributed to the shaping influence of Confucian filial norms on Chinese child rearing, the Neolithic evidence suggests a far earlier origin.

The cognitive ability of middle Neolithic farmers to execute north-south alignment has received much scholarly attention.[3] David Pankenier draws on a plethora of sources to delineate a Neolithic preoccupation with alignment. He identifies evidence that links "good harvests and relief from natural disasters" to

1 See Chang (1999); Liu (2004); Yang (2004); Jiao (2007); Flad and Chen (2013); Underhill (2013); Liu and Chen (2012); Shelach (2006, 2016); for excellent overviews and specific studies of Neolithic culture.

2 Pankenier (2013, 118). See also Pankenier (2004, 2009).

3 Ibid., (91).

DOI: 10.4324/9781003215134-3

the forces associated with the cardinal directions (the Four Quarters), the Big Dipper, and celestial North Pole, "from which cosmic control appeared to emanate." Pankenier argues that the "absence of a distinctive Pole Star" created challenges for establishing "axial orientation of monumental architecture in the landscape." This insight about challenges caused by the lack of a pole star leads him to claim that the "career of the celestial Pole from the Neolithic through the Bronze Age [ca. 1,600-256 B.C.]"[4] is essential background context for understanding how a preoccupation with alignment shaped the criteria associated with emerging concepts of charismatic leadership. For example, Pankenier links the centrality of the concept of a "Supernal Lord," called Di in Shang Dynasty (1953-1046 B.C.) political and religious discourse to the dynastic founders' success in identifying a usable Pole Star.[5]

We have an opportunity in Chapter 4 to unpack more carefully the link between the visual experience of an empty celestial Pole and the evolution of Shang political authority and royal charisma. Our attention now first focuses on the possibility that sensitivity to the absence of the Pole Star was itself preconditioned by an earlier, Neolithic experience of celestial absences. This chapter seeks to demonstrate how the emotion associated with the precedent was expressed in the cognitive turn toward cardinal alignment as a collective survival strategy. I focus on the particularity of the emotional conditions that generated and contoured neural circuits underlying these cognitive advances.[6] Following insights from neuroscientists, I hypothesize that the link between separation distress-induced pain is key to understanding why a preoccupation with north-south alignment would emerge as a defining Neolithic cultural behavior. I suggest that the cognitive turn functioned to regulate unspeakable grief by "orienting attention" away from an aversive event and its affect. Once this was accomplished, rituals for "regulating performance goal states, the processing of the same actions" served to orient group attention toward the (new) goals.[7]

The Case of the Early Neolithic Jiahu

The remains of early Neolithic Jiahu culture discovered in 1962 in Wuyang County, Henan Province, and excavated in different stages between 1983 and 1987, yield evidence to reconstruct the conditions of distress that catalyzed attention to the celestial Pole (Figure 3.1).[8] The settlement was continuously

4 Ibid., (96).
5 Pankenier (2004, 2009, 2013).
6 LeDoux (2000).
7 Hobson et al. (2018, 269).
8 Henan Provincial Institute of Cultural Relics and Archaeology (1999) provides the Jiahu coordinates: 113°40′ E, 33°36′ N); for informative accounts of the excavation process and findings, see Zhang and Cui (2013), but also Smith and Lee (2008); Underhill (2013); for incisive related analysis.

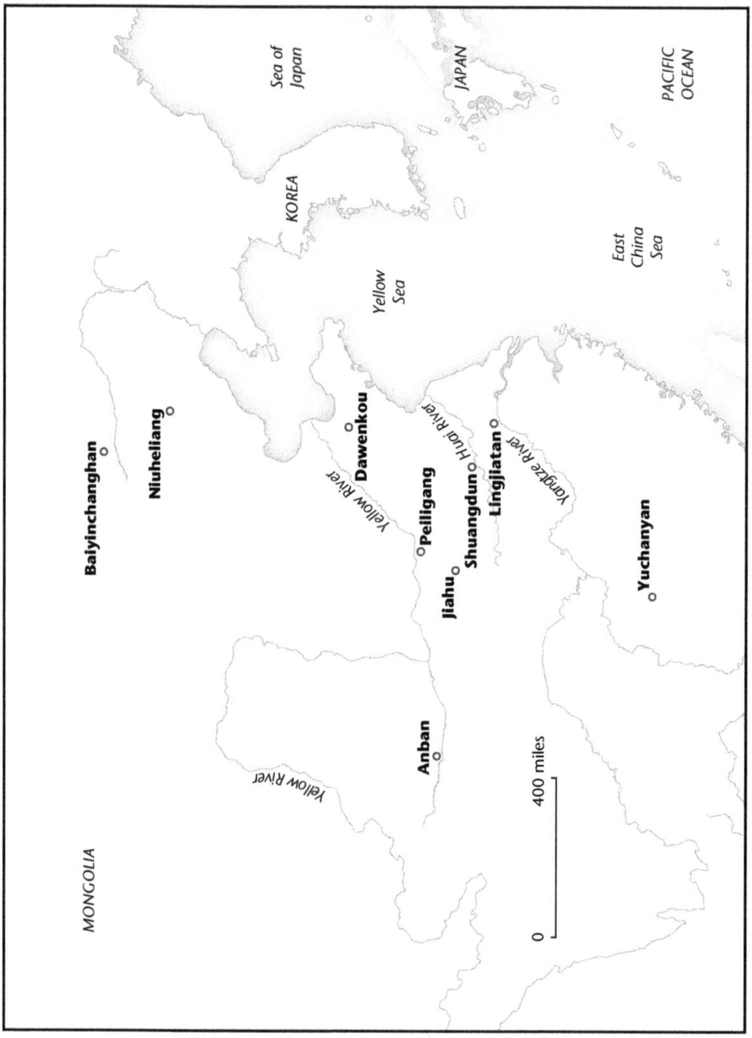

FIGURE 3.1 Map of important archaeological sites mentioned in this chapter.

occupied for a millennium and a half (7000-5500 B.C.), with stratification showing evidence of three broad Phases that endured for five hundred years each.[9] Each of these periods were also divided into three phases as well.

The settlement occupied a total area of 55,000 square meters; 2,700 square meters were excavated.[10] Evidence points to population growth, reflected in the settlement's spatial expansion (including the construction of a moat on the southeastern border), and a marked increase in Jiahu occupants' attention to spatial planning between Phase I and II (7000-6000 B.C.).[11] Zhang and Cui claim that "social-cultural development almost reached its zenith during the second phase, and it rose a little more during the third phase (6000-5500 B.C.) before declining."[12] Moats have been understood as material expressions of a group's solidarity within established spatial parameters. Its construction later in the settlement's occupation intimates a sense of solidarity that developed over the settlement's long occupation.

Zhang and Cui assert that a clear line from less to more spatial planning is evident in the settlement remains that span all three phases. Clusters of round houses, an early Neolithic norm, were found, sometimes in relation to bigger constructed spaces. The archaeologists hypothesize that this form of spatial organization reflects a diversifying social economy that emerged in response to the growth trends between Phases I and II. They conclude that at the culture's height there were three levels of organization: "clan, family, and the household."[13]

The observed developmental trends lend themselves to an investigation of the evolution of psychosocial adaptations to settlement life. Not only do the artifacts body forth a rich and sophisticated social and symbolic life, but the bodies themselves suggest that Jiahu was a "good place for humans to live"![14] There is consensus that population growth due was due in part to the emergence of new subsistence techniques and division of labor.[15] An analysis of tools found in graves of three contemporary cemeteries raises the possibility that kinship groups formed units responsible for managing specific activities important to settlement subsistence. One cemetery yielded mainly farming implements whereas the other two were rich with hunting and fishing tools.[16] Whether this points to a burgeoning system of economic specialization is unclear, nonetheless there is clear

9 Dates following Zhang and Cui (2013, 194).
10 Ibid. (194).
11 Ibid.
12 Ibid. (202).
13 Ibid. (201). Shelach (2006, 319) suggests that northeast Chinese settlement patterns of socioeconomic development was different from communities located further south, which were "more closely integrated and practiced inter-household cooperation."
14 Ibid. (194).
15 Ibid. (198).
16 Liu and Chen (2012, 146).

evidence that farming activities came to occupy a growing percentage of the toolkits recovered from the three phases. Whereas only 6.8% of tools recovered from Phase I comprised agricultural tools, by Phase II they accounted for 53.4% of the tools recovered.[17]

Archaeobotanical studies have found that rice cultivation played an important if not dominant role in Jiahu enrichment.[18] This chapter argues that although the proportion of the settlement's enrichment made by rice cultivation was limited to begin with, its growing centrality to food production, evinced in the data that demonstrates social and cultural development, warrants deeper consideration.[19] I propose that rice domestication contributions to settlement subsistence grew when ancient seasonal habits and traditions of hunter-gatherers were adapted and applied to rice cultivation.[20] Recognizing how Jiahu domesticators' increasing control over their domesticate would have driven social and cultural behaviors allows us to see how agriculture enriched Jiahu settlement life far beyond its caloric contribution to the subsistence diet.[21]

Jiahu Rice Cultivation

Many scholars point to specific and unusual ecological conditions that might account for the emergence and longevity of the Jiahu settlement.[22] Situated on the boundary between the rice and millet agriculture regions, Jiahu culture played a very "significant formative role in the development of rice."[23] Warmer climes in the Huai River Valley may have favored rice cultivation.[24] The possibility that Jiahu rice cultivation efforts derived from the northward expansion of ancient settlements further south in the Yangtze Valley is a compelling thesis.[25] That such an expansion would have carried with it "an existing knowledge of pottery production and rice cultivation," could explain "why such a high percentage of morphologically domesticated rice occurred initially" in Jiahu.[26] The south to

---

17 Ibid.
18 Ibid.
19 Wu et al. (2014).
20 Larson et al. (2014).
21 In addition to the actual work of tilling and reaping, which required the fashioning of lithic tools for farming and grinding, it increased the need for pottery to store harvests and ferment wine. That kilns were found by houses and not placed elsewhere in the settlement reflects the degree to which familial units were the basis of subsistence related production (Ibid).
22 Zhang and Cui (2013, 198).
23 Chi and Hung (2013, 61).
24 Ibid.; Zhang and Cui (2013, 198).
25 Zhang and Cui (2013, 206); Chi and Hung (2013). Liu et al. (2007); Zheng et al. (2016, 7), describe how rice had unique economic significance, inferred by the northward movement of the plant during the Jiahu occupation.
26 Chi and Hung (2013, 57). See also Molina et al. (2011).

north progression of plant domestication information may also be relevant to the relationship between the Jiahu and early Neolithic sites that are identified with Peiligang culture. Zhang and Cui note that immigration frequency increased over the span of the cultural site's occupation.[27] As we shall see below, Li Xinwei's attributes the transmission of jade representations of cosmological motifs in spatially disparate cultures to northward migrations up the eastern coast.[28]

While Jiahu was not the earliest site to yield charred rice remains,[29] Jiahu rice differs morphologically from its wild progenitors found in earlier sites such as Shangshan, and the older remains recovered at Yuchanyan cave (16,300 B.C.), even as this evidence bore traces of "human intervention" (Figure 2.1).[30] Recovered carbonized rice grains at Jiahu reveal that wild rice was not the primary rice consumed by its residents.[31] Rather they ate the domesticated *Oryza sativa* (subsp. *Japonica*).[32] As mentioned above, data gathered from measurements of grain sizes reveal clear evidence of increasing size between cultural Phases I and II.[33] Another study that compared morphological domesticated rice spikelets recovered at Jiahu and those at a later, northern cultural site known as Baligang, found an advanced rate of change in the progress of rice domestication that occurred during Jiahu settlement occupation.[34] Zhang and Cui conclude that "compared to hunting and gathering, agriculture increased the carrying capacity of the land."[35]

The material evidence for Jiahu domestication practices reflects on the way human cognitive capacities for goal-directed action were shaped by earlier interactions with early wild rice. Liu et al. cite Oka and Morishima's 1971 "experiment of planning and harvesting wild rice," which demonstrates how "after only five generations" of "using knives" to harvest, "the rice sample showed an increase in width and spikelet number and a reduction in the rate of seed shedding." The rapidity with which rice's morphological change was controlled

27 Zhang and Cui (2013, 207).
28 Li (2004, 71). For more on the Hongshan jade industry and related religious and implications see Childs-Johnson, (1991); Guo (1995).
29 Liu et al. (2007, 1061).
30 Ibid. (1061–1066); Cohen (2011); Zheng et al. (2016). Cohen et al. (2019) link pottery remains recovered at the Yuchanyan cave to seasonal occupation. As we shall see, seasonality emerges as a determinant of Jiahu social organization and culture.
31 Chen et al. (1995). Liu and Chen (2012, 123–198), discuss the evidence showing early domestication of plants and animals, as well as evidence that points to sedentism and food production in the early Neolithic (7000-5000 B.C.). Li (1998, 2009); Xie (2002); An et al. (2004, 2005, 2006); Hou et al. (2010) have focused on an east west transmission paradigm focusing on links between Majiayao (5300-4300 B.C.) and Qijia (4200-3800 B.C.) cultural periods on the Western Loess Plateau.
32 Chi and Hung (2013).
33 Ibid. See also Liu et al. (2007, 2009).
34 Chi and Hung (2013, 48).
35 Zhang and Cui (2013, 2017).

as a "result of selection for non-shedding genes," suggests that the Paleolithic "rice provided the basis upon which people could have selected for those cultigen types and shifted the balance of the rice population."[36]

The preference for dry-grinding cereal processing in Jiahu intimates how the subsistence technique of rice domestication affected group enrichment beyond the settlement. Li et al. studied use-wear manifested on grinding tools, which were predominant in Jiahu tool assemblages. Their analysis finds that the larger (increased) grain size of the cultivated rice would have made it suitable for dry-grinding processes.[37] Moreover, the authors suggest that the rice flour produced by dry-grinding would have enhanced the high mobility required by a settlement that relies on mixed subsistence strategies to survive.[38] Reinforced by geological data that reveals raw materials used for tool production came from a distance ranging from twenty-four to fifty kilometers, the authors infer that rice flour would have been "fundamental" to the Jiahu community as an "easily portable" foodstuff.[39] Production of flour may have supported the necessary mobility and autonomy required of the hunter-gatherers. When we add to this the nutritional value of dry flour, we can appreciate how rice cultivation would have been valued as an integral part of Jiahu subsistence strategies.

Although grinding stones were used to process many other foodstuffs such as nuts, its importance for crop production suggests that grinding technology may have been transferred early in the Neolithic. The discovery in Peiligang cultural remains of a footed stone grinding slab marked by the same manufacture and style features seen in one recovered in a Houli culture (6550-5500 B.C.) site located in Inner Mongolia, offers an idea of how cultivation related techniques may have migrated from the middle Yellow River Valley Peiligang site to the northeastern cultural site.[40] Significantly, turtle shells—an identifying feature of Jiahu culture—were discovered in Hauli tombs.[41]

Archaeobotanical studies are providing increased evidence to refine our understanding of the process and timing in the domestication of *japonica* cultivars. The findings emphasize that changes leading to the increase of grain size may

36 Liu et al. (2007, 1061).
37 Li et al. (2019).
38 Ibid. (942).
39 This estimate of distances traveled to access game correlates with distances that have been calculated for Jiahu's lithic supply. Zhang and Cui (2013, 205) note that soft lithics (slate, shale, and schist) used to produce shovels, sickles, and knifes were retrieved from as far as 25 to 40 km away from the site.
40 Wang (2013, 390).
41 Ibid. (407). Larrivé-Bass (2015, 153) cites the discovery of "a stone turtle found at Shangzai [Hemudu culture (5050-3050]... and jade turtles found inside Hongshan culture (4,500-3,000 BCE)" as evidence of the warmer climes that supported the animal's northern presence during the Neolithic, though as we shall see below Liu (2007b) attributes the salience of chelonian forms in those cultures as a function of a particular cosmology that had become associated with elite power.

have been a function of efforts to inhibit wild-type rice growth. The tremendous expansion in growing regions of cultivated rice as far north as 31° latitude is attributed to the acceleration of germination processes that were shaped by a genetic shift in rice growth and flowering traits. Because the plant can recognize the seasonal changes of day length to determine flowering time, and members of a population will flower synchronously, it was capable of acquiring cold-tolerance traits. The increase seen in Jiahu grain size over a thousand years is the result of manipulating this gene to control the flowering-time of cultivars.[42] While sensitivity to seasonality was a matter of survival for hunter-gatherers, what Jiahu domestication success indicates is the application of this cognitive knowledge to sedentary food production practices.[43]

Fuller et al. surmise that effects of cultivation success resulting from seasonally determined changes made to seed dispersal and harvesting methods were likely "dramatic."[44] This positive result would have justified perpetuating intensified attention to domestication efforts as a reliable new subsistence technique. Whereas wild rice harvesting required dehusking and winnowing tasks after harvest, rice domestication required preparing land, seed dispersal, and threshing before harvests. The decision to invest resources to perpetuate this behavior reinforces the idea that it was valued for its contribution to settlement enrichment.

Seasonally organized rice cultivation would have shaped human adaptation to settlement life as the accumulation of domestication knowledge played a more dominant role in the operation of an incipient social economy. Preservation and transmission of the knowledge would have been important for continued benefits, which enhanced group solidarity. The following section situates Jiahu group identity and mortuary behavior within the perceptual and cognitive trends that were shaped by Jiahu farmers' multisensory relationship with seasonality.[45] I liken this relationship to that between a mother and an infant: repeated seasonal changes over time promoted development of a responsive neural substrate for season-specific agricultural behavior.[46]

Specifically, I interpret a unique prestige object found in Jiahu graves as a sign pointing to the value of seasonality and related agricultural knowledge in Jiahu society. The items, sets of turtle carapaces and plastrons that were polished and manipulated to form box-like objects, are considered highly prestigious. Recognizing the seasonal meaning that imbued the turtle ensembles with prestige

42 Izawa (2007).
43 Shim and Jang (2020).
44 Fuller et al. (2017, 319).
45 Fuller and Allaby (2018).
46 Cf. Mircea Eliade, who suggests that celestial dynamics bring to awareness structurally coherent meanings in the sense that sky is a legible script to be read and interpreted hermeneutically (1969, 62ff). This will be address in more detail in the following chapter.

value provides insight into how the shell sets promoted and protected an "ecological inheritance." The turtle shells played a special communicative role as a symbol of the interplay between humans, plants, and animals in rice domestication efforts.

The Symbolic Intent of Jiahu Turtle Prestige Objects

Twenty-three Jiahu graves, out of three hundred and forty-nine that were excavated, contained turtle shells. The number of sets found in graves ranged between one and eight. More than fifty shell sets were recovered at Jiahu.[47] Because the shells reveal evidence of added craft work, and because they were intentionally placed around the corpse, once even in the place of a missing skull, it is clear that the objects were highly valued.[48] Their distribution among graves and phases was random, underscoring the predominant egalitarian social organization seen in early Neolithic cultures where grain domestication was one of a variety of subsistence strategies.[49]

The turtles found in Jiahu tombs belonged to a fresh water species *Cuora flavomarginata* (*bie*).[50] This chelonian genus is also called the Box Turtle because its plastron is so closely connected to its carapace by ligaments that its movement is constrained.[51] Another physical feature, namely the "golden rim" on the margins of the carapace which encloses all the carapace markings, also distinguished the genus.[52] This spatial design mirrored the region's landscape, which had evolved to "a largely enclosed, wetland system." We have seen how this newly established freshwater marsh environment was identified as a condition that made the northern boundary of the Huai River Valley a "habitat favorable to rice domestication. The early Neolithic farmers took the opportunity presented

47 Ye and Zhang (1994, 32). Fan and Zhang (2008b); Scholars distinguish between those turtle plastron and carapaces that were buried intact from the multiple fragments of the same species found in waste pits, which they construe as refuse generated by eating the animals.

48 Smith and Lee (2008).

49 Ibid.

50 Studies of chelonian evolution trace the trajectory of the genus *Cuora* from the Late Miocene through the middle and late Pleistocene, up to the Neolithic. In terms of distribution, scholars agree that historically *Cuora flavomarginata* lived along the eastern Yangtze River and its tributaries. See Parham et al. (2004).

51 Ota et al. (2009, 035.1–035.10). This genus is different from the species whose "bony lateral extensions [are] present on the plastron found at an Erligang cultural site (1600-1400 B.C.). See Henan Provincial Institute of Cultural Relics and Archaeology (1999); Larrivé-Bass, (2015, 220n. 74). For a description and analysis of the Erligang state see Liu and Chen (2012, 278–289).

52 Another appellation for the genus is "the yellow edged turtle with closed shells" (*huangyuan bike gui*).

to them and started rice cultivation in locations where freshwater wetland systems were established."[53]

That *Cuora flavomarginata* was a source of meat is evidenced by the presence of fragmented shells in ash pits, alongside other waste.[54] These broken shells differ from the turtle objects found in tombs, which preserved both plastron and carapace to form an encasement, in which polished pebbles were placed.[55] In addition to being associated with burial practices, Zhang and Cui also cite "evidence for ritual activity with turtle shells in habitation contexts as well." For example, preserved ensemble was found placed in a house foundation, "in the bottom of a posthole, underneath an earthen wall. The turtle's head faced west, the same direction as the door. It appears that the turtle had been placed there before the wall was built."[56] They conclude that placement of the turtle in the house foundation was a spiritual act. The discovery of residue from alcoholic fermentation on the inner walls of potsherds found in domestic contexts, and the likelihood that the beverage was "served to the dead during the inhumation," suggests that the turtle's semiotic power was enhanced by psychotropic effects.[57]

Efforts to explain the turtle shell symbolism have yielded robust discussions.[58] For example, some construe the fact that pebbles were encased by the two shells as pointing to a musical function, like a rattle.[59] This interpretive gesture receives support from the fact that flutes with five, six, seven, and eight holes, made out of the bones from the wing of a red-crowned crane (*Grus japonensis*), were also recovered as grave prestige objects.[60]

In addition to the possible musical dimension of the turtle shells' symbolism,[61] the presence of a forked-shaped bone object and finely crafted bone needles within close proximity of the turtle boxes has also yielded a range of interpretations.[62] For example, some hypothesize that the encasement might have served as a medicinal bag of sorts,[63] which many ascribe to shamanistic activities that the deceased presumably undertook when alive.[64] Others view the turtle shells as representative of devotional intentions directed toward spirits whose

---

53 Zong et al. (2012, 1). See also Wang et al. (2010).
54 Ye and Zhang (1994). See also, Fan and Zhang (2008a); idem., (2008b).
55 Ibid., Fan and Zhang (2008a).
56 Zhang and Cui (2013, 208).
57 McGovern et al. (2004); Smith and Lee (208, 258); Liu (2021); Fang (2021).
58 Ibid. See also Fan and Zhang (2008a, 2008b); Smith and Lee (2008).
59 Fan and Zhang (2008a).
60 Zhang et al. (2004).
61 Fan and Zhang (2008a).
62 Henan Provincial Institute of Cultural Relics and Archaeology (1999, Plates 39, 40); Smith and Lee (2008).
63 Fan and Zhang (2008b).
64 Fan and Zhang (2008b); Ye and Zhang (1994).

existence was a feature of religious beliefs. The shells' meaning derives from their capacity to signal communication between humans and the spirit world.[65]

The findings of a rigorous cluster analysis of the spatial and temporal distribution of turtle sets in Jiahu graves, (among individual and collective, primary, and secondary burials), warn against easy assumptions about social status and its relation to the obvious high value of prestige objects.[66] The data shows that the deceased subjects suffered from pathologies resulting from a dearth of animal protein. These data problematize the idea that high status would have meant access to more protein food sources.[67] Because some corpse bones where turtle sets were not present indicate a diet with more meat than less, Smith and Lee conclude that prestige in Jiahu society did not derive solely from birth into conditions of an enriched food supply.

Jiahu Prestige Status

Status psychology literature suggests that status related behavior evolved from pressures on human sociality exerted by humans' need for reciprocal support.[68] Tomasella et al. theorize how permanent settlement enhanced the degree to which individuals "had a direct interest in the well-being of their partners."[69] The selection favored social incentives to sustain cooperation in order to preserve group interdependence. The benefits of cooperation motivated adaptations. For example, cognitive capacities were recruited to attend to others' behavior and adjusting.[70]

Interdependent group life required a coordination of individual neurological, emotional, and psychological development in relation to social others. This heightened sensitivity to each other's behavioral predictability. Group standards that helped discriminate an individual's predictability emerged as a social mechanism for promoting conformity to cooperative behavior.[71] Social knowledge about an individual's conformist behavior became a valuable asset because it solidified the potential to be included in cooperative ventures. Social knowledge about someone's failure to conform could threaten efforts to engage in reciprocal relationships, leading to social isolation.

Matt Rossano argues that ritualized behaviors evolved in response to these conditions; rituals "reliably signal an intentional mental state giving credibility to verbal expressions while emotionally binding people to each other and

65 Fan and Zhang (2008a, 2008b).
66 Smith and Lee (2008, 270–274) for gendered analysis; for primary and secondary burial data, see 277–280).
67 Ibid. (283–284).
68 Richerson et al. (2016); Boyd and Richerson (2020).
69 Tomasello et al. (2012, 673). See also Levinson and Enfield (2020).
70 Sznycer (2019).
71 Ibid.

group-based values." He calls attention to rituals' function as mechanisms that imbue words and actions with "credibility." This is why rituals, and the symbolic systems they fostered, evolved, to facilitate the "transmission of social norms vertically from parent to offspring, while adult community rituals [were] a primary mechanism by which norms [were] reinforced horizontally within the community."[72]

Prestige status evolved from these interdependent group conditions. Prestige status is distinguished from dominance status, which is a function of prowess and hierarchal structures. Prestige status is "horizontally" structured, and evolves less from fear and submission than as a motivational system for norm conformity that relies on the neurochemical rewards consequent to positive social attention.[73] The parts of the brain integrally involved in social cognition have been consistently implicated in neuroimaging studies of status-based consequences for social attention. Findings have shown that the apperception of someone conferred with prestige status is itself rewarding, "especially when the high-status individual who is perceived reflects favorably on the perceiver (e.g., an ingroup member or a favorable social comparison)."[74]

In this light, Jiahu prestige objects tell us something about the role public scrutiny of behavior played in the process of conferring status. Studies in which subjects were "subliminally primed with religious" or "legal or moral" concepts exemplify how primes "unconsciously trigger cognitive mechanisms sensitive to the potential for judgmental public scrutiny."[75] Because prestige is granted by others, the capacity for perceivers to recognize the prestige that was conferred

---

72 Rossano (2012, 529). See also Watson-Jones and Legare (2016, 42ff), whose cognitive and functional approach to ritual reveals it to be a "socially stipulated group convention." Most relevant to the discussion at hand is the "combination of causal opacity and social stipulation [that] inhibits individual-level innovation." They conclude that this "makes rituals ideally suited to high-fidelity cultural transmission over time." Hobson et al. (2018, 363–266), offer a neuropsychological framework for understanding the regulatory function of rituals in human life. They identify the mechanisms underlying ritual's regulation of "emotions, performance goal states, social connection," ascribing them to "bottom-up" or "top-down" processes. Lang (2019) argues for an evolutionary approach to the psychology of rituals in order to identify the mechanism that "underlie[s the] effects of collective rituals on trust based cooperation." His study shares with this one the position that "socio-ecological pressures" are responsible for the emergence of rituals, and the belief that these selective pressures on collective action account for the "role rituals played in response to these pressures" (243).

73 Fessler (2004, 241); De Hooge et al. (2010); Cheng et al. (2010), Cheng et al. (2013). Cheng et al. (2014) have proposed two main pathways to status attainment in humans: dominance and prestige.

74 Koski et al. (2015).

75 Rossano (2012, 541).

presupposed a knowledge of the domain on which the evaluation of social status was based.[76]

The ability to understand others' assessments of one's worth also became crucial to evaluating one's position in an evolving social order. These cognitive capacities reflect the degree to which norms that enhanced behavioral predictability may have been valued by the settlement inhabitants. While prestige signaling externalized qualities of the deceased that warranted the conferral of prestige, it also reflects on a deep-seated inclination to think of others' assessments of oneself.[77] Prestige status implicitly marks one's actions as having been watched and judged as worthy (for their prosocial contribution) by "powerful others."[78]

The link between music and prestige suggests that musical talent or performance might have enhanced public assessment which led to the accrual of prestige. The instruments, especially the flutes, are assumed by many scholars to have belonged to the deceased.[79] One can imagine how the rhythm produced by a Box Turtle rattle and the harmonies of melodious flutes would have elicited emotional empathy and contagion.[80] Neuroscientific studies of "the brain on music" have shown how the phenomenon elicits prosocial responses from those exposed to it.[81] Moreover, music was an apt conduit for transmitting social affiliation cues, which would have heightened a sense of affiliation and well-being among participants.[82] Attachment-based opioid releases would also have enhanced a feeling of community cohesion and "euphoria, certainty and belongingness."[83] Mortuary behavior that reinforced attachment bonds would also have triggered the release of opiates, "producing psychobiological synchrony within the group" of mourners.[84] Repeated exposure to these experiences would have established feedback loops that determined how subjectivity was molded through interrelations forged by musically contoured social networks.

This section has developed the idea that prestige conferral was a prosocial behavior aimed toward enhancing interdependent social cohesion through mechanisms that emphasize public self-consciousness. The following section investigates the source of the Box Turtle ensembles' prestige. It focuses attention on the shell ensembles' seasonal associations. From this perspective, the objects reveal how value and prestige in the settlement derived from the manner by which Jiahu

76 Mattan et al. (2017).
77 Ibid.
78 Rossano (2012, 541).
79 Smith and Lee (2008, 285).
80 Panksepp (2009, 237) speculates that "a drum was the first cultural musical instrument of our species" based on ethological evidence of animal drumming when emotionally aroused. The function of the percussive rattles may have descended along these lines.
81 Granot (2017). See also Levitin (2008).
82 Granot (2017); Panksepp (2009); Fritz and Koelsch (2008).
83 Hatfield et al. (2014).
84 Frecska and Kulcsar (1989, 72).

inhabitants attuned their social and cultural behavior to synchronize with patterns observed in the external world.[85]

The Box Turtle and Seasonality

A detailed description of the carapace's unique markings is a good starting point to begin an account of the evolution of the turtle's prestige. Based on an exemplary set of thirteen sets of shells discovered in grave M363, Ye and Zhang describe and comment on the Box Turtle's carapace markings. They pay particular attention to the geometric layout of the design formed by the shapes of the carapace's scutes—the horny plates that protect the shell from harm.[86] For example, the archaeologists note how the first scute over the vertebrae is pentagonal, while the second third and fourth are hexagonal, projecting slightly backwards. They also describe how the vertebral shield forms a trapezoid with a narrow front and a wide rear, and how the first, second, third, and fourth scutes, on both the left and right of the vertebrae, are rectangular. As for the edge plate scutes, they were marked by small rectangular shapes. They conclude with the observation that the totality (*yiban*) of the carapace is indicated by the rib area (costal) scutes which are marked with a concentric circular design (*huiwen*). The four pairs on each side of the round carapace represented an enclosed environment[87] (Figure 3.2).

The abundance of geometric shapes that distinguish the Box Turtle's carapace markings must have been meaningful to the Jiahu hunter-gatherers, who had inherited from their forebears geometric knowledge. Whether it was applied to the construction of dwellings, or the alignment of graves, Jiahu remains reveal much about the mathematical skills necessary for complex planning and measurement.[88] The fact that the turtle's carapace, its natural abode, externalized and stored geometric figures that "run automatically in the brain,"[89] would have been appreciated as an externalization of internalized knowledge. Representations dating to the Paleolithic have shown that a "good knowledge of geometric figures and measuring methods can be assumed on the basis of archaeological findings dating to 15,000 B.C."[90]

In addition to externalizing geometric knowledge, the Box Turtle would have been an object of increasing intention to hunter-gatherers in the region who were adapting to ecological conditions shaped by the warming process of the

85 Legare and Wen (2014).
86 Ibid. (33–34).
87 Ye and Zhang (1994, 33).
88 For Jiahu spatial organization see Zhang and Cui (2013).
89 Rappenglück (2020).
90 Ibid. Cf. Gao et al. (2004), who discuss evidence of concept marking one elephant tusks found in Xinglongdong Cave in the Three Gorges Region in South China.

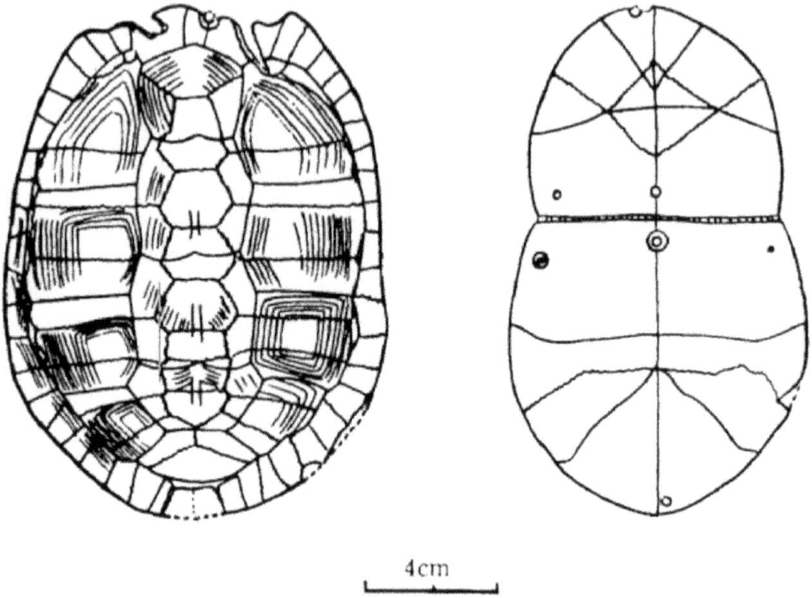

FIGURE 3.2 Drawing of carapace and plastron of a *Cuora flavomarginata* turtle recovered at the Jiahu site. *Source*: Ye and Zhang (1994, 33).

early Holocene. Tools and fish bones recovered at the Guanzhou Site located in the western part of the Jianghan Plain suggest that the formation of lakes and marshes had created a new ecological niche that opened up possibilities to include new food sources into subsistence strategies.[91] The ecological changes account for an increasing emphasis on utilizing aquatic resources. Similar conclusions about adaptation strategies were made on the basis of evidence found in a tool assemblage found at a lower Paleolithic site at Lingfengdong in Fujian province.[92] Lithic evidence in the form of new tools for cutting and scraping fish and other aquatic animals, and the fact that they were produced by an emergent technique called "ridged hammer bipolar flaking" (RHBF), reinforce the hypothesis that they are the products of adapting to a new hydrous ecology.[93]

The slow-moving and protein-rich *Cuora* genus was among the chelonian fare available for Paleolithic hunter-gatherer consumption.[94] Moreover, adaptations to aquatic food source accessibility would have led to observations about aquatic animal behavior, which reflects obvious seasonal utilization.[95] Cave figurations

91 Gao et al. (2008); Liu et al. (2020).
92 Li et al. (2001).
93 Liu et al. (2020).
94 Rhodin et al. (2015). See also Parham et al. (2004) for a discussion of the genus in China during the Paleolithic and older eras.
95 Parkington (2001).

document how animal habits conveyed knowledge about time and space that affected human conceptualizations. Scholars have posited that the emergence of a cognitive mathematical syntax that exceeded the "logical, arithmetical geometric and navigational skills" observed in animals had occurred by the Achuelean era, between 1.76 million to 150,000 years ago.[96] Based on these conditions, it is not unrealistic to hypothesize that a tradition of ecological knowledge related to the Box Turtle's habits and unique markings may have behavioral antecedents in the forbears of Jiahu hunter-gatherers.

The idea of an ecological niche that supported intensification of food procurement is appropriate for understanding how knowledge related to the seasonal habits of aquatic animal may have contoured the symbolic significance of the Jiahu Box Turtle's prestige. For example, the seasonality of the Box Turtle's mating and hibernation activities would have been important for aquatic food procurement planning. Attention to seasonal habits would have yielded information about the chelonian's courtship and copulation practices, which require males and females to entwine tails so that mating can occur.[97]

Such externalized mutuality resonates with the birdsong duets performed by mating red-crowned cranes whose bones were made into flutes. The flutes reveal a sophisticated sense of tonal scales capable of producing an interplay of "male" and "female" (*xiongci*) voices.[98] This sound production quality suggests its source of inspiration was the dramatic mating duet that male and female red-crowned cranes engage in every summer. The salience of seasonal associations that link flutes and Box Turtle ensembles encourages further investigation into the potential that other seasonal associations are also embedded in the prestige object's signaling intentions.

I propose that if the prestige symbolism speaks to an emotional contribution made by the deceased to collective enrichment and cohesion, it also points to the deceased's possession of ecological knowledge. In the case of the Box Turtle, this knowledge was astronomical and was related to rice domestication efforts. My claim is that the conferral of prestige is tantamount to promoting the preservation of an ecological inheritance important to interdependent group survival. This vantage point deepens the implications of Smith and Lee's finding that prestige status was not determined by social status factors related to early childhood protein access but rather to merit accrued through life experience.[99]

I argue that although the Box Turtles' seasonal associations were a source of their prestige, it was their relevance to rice cultivation and an emerging control over seasonally manipulated flowering time that made them so important to Jiahu subsistence and, ultimately, settlement status. The implication of this cluster of

96 Rappenglück (2012).
97 Ota et al. (2009, 035.5).
98 Rao (1999, 35).
99 Liu (2004, 78, 128, 155 et passim); Smith and Lee (2008, 270, 282).

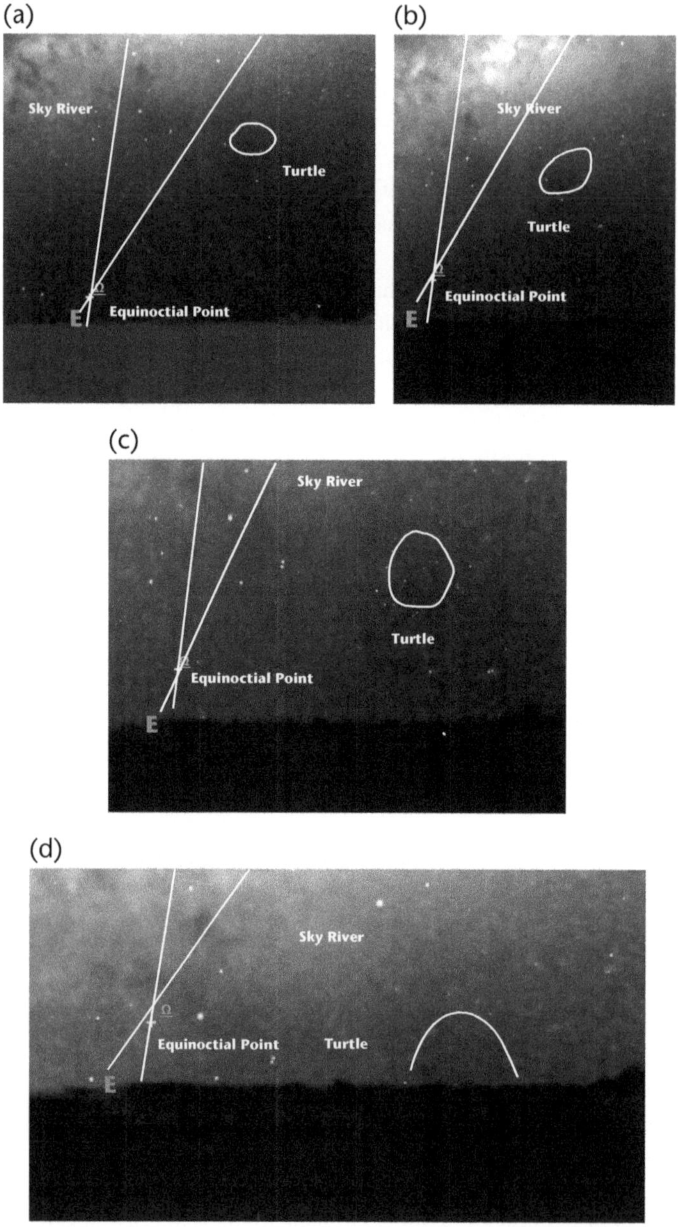

FIGURE 3.3 (a)-(d): The Vernal Career of Turtle 7000; 6500; 6000; 5500 B.C. *Source*: Redrawn from screenshot based on Stellarium, an open source software.

associations becomes clearer when considered with the calendrical role played by astronomical entities whose appearance in the night sky at the advent of each season were viewed as harbingers. I submit that the round stellar configuration, known to the Chinese as Turtle (*bie*), known as Corona Australis to the West, played this role for the Jiahu occupants, and that it was the basis for an evolving rice cultivation system.

In 7000 B.C., Turtle appeared above the eastern horizon after the sun dipped below it on the west for several weeks before the arrival of the spring equinox. The constellation occupied a place on the southern bank of the Milky Way, known to the Chinese as Sky River (*Tianhe*). This spatial perception was likely the source of the constellation's name, which means "fresh water" chelonians, like the Box Turtle.[100] I contend that the link between Turtle's spatiotemporal presence is also related to the extraordinary advances seen in rice domestication techniques that occurred over the span of Phases I and II (7000-6000 B.C.).

Moreover, although Turtle was part of the vernal scene for close to a millennium, its seasonal signaling function shifted from first announcing the arrival of spring, that is, appearing before the arrival of the spring equinox; to appearing above the horizon right at the equinox. This span of time correlates to the increase in grave wealth that occurred between Jiahu's Phase I and Phase II. Turtle's temporal lag, manifested spatially as an eastward slippage, was the effect of a phenomenon known as the precession of the equinoxes, a fundamental fact of astronomy.[101] Eventually precession rendered Turtle's seasonal role obsolete so that by the spring equinox in 5500 B.C., the end date of Jiahu culture, Turtle had not even risen over the horizon (Figure 3.3(a–d)). In short, Turtle's calendrical career aligned with the rise and fall of the Jiahu settlement.

Turtle Figuration and Ecological Inheritance

The Jiahu settlement's close to one-thousand-year relationship with Turtle broadened the scope of the animal's association with important ecological information. Semiotically, the Box Turtle ensembles functioned as perceptual cues indicating spatiotemporal association.[102] A cultural logic can be traced starting with the "savvy" use of the shells as "signifiers." Sandrine Larrivé-Bass argues that Chinese Neolithic figuration production derives from "material-representation synergies" that determined the representational quest of figure-makers. Craftsmen relied on the "constancy of physical attributes exhibited by both the substances they knew from handling and the animals and humans they sought to represent. These consistent and dependable factors facilitated figuration through

100 Porter (1996).
101 Ibid.
102 Rossano (2010, S89).

formal and material approximations."[103] Drawing from studies of how the brain integrates touch along with visual and auditory perception, she views this tactile familiarity as a source of the "cognitive dynamics" driving the development of figuration techniques.

Larrivé-Bass argues that Neolithic figuration is the product of processes that integrate the interactions between sensory stimuli and perception.[104] It is her invocation of the phenomenon known as *pareidolia*, which involves the projection of mental images onto forms, that is most relevant to the conditions that gave rise to the link between Box Turtles and Turtle.[105] The material-bound cultural logic that drove the projection of the Box Turtle on to the celestial landscape was determined by its ovoid figure and its habits in marshy environment. The likelihood that the perception of the Milky Way as a river antedates the imagining of Turtle is attested in the cross-cultural universality and antiquity of Milky Way tropes that view it as a path.[106] The point is that a multisensory ecological familiarity with the surroundings allowed for the experience of imaginative perception and projection of the Box Turtle's image onto the natural circular form made by a cluster of stars. This phenomenon transformed the celestial space occupied by Turtle into a "legible zoomorphic figure."[107]

Neuroscience studies on the phenomenon of pareidolia explain how extended exposure to the "pareidolia turtle" would have conditioned a specific direction of attention. One study in which subjects were given "repeated exposure to 'pareidolia faces'" revealed that the repetition "cause[d] a systematic bias in the perception of where human [subjects'] faces are looking." This consequence was described as a function of "overlapping sensory mechanisms… that are recruited to extract specific social content from human faces."[108] A similar process may have unfolded once the celestial Turtle was identified and then collectively "seen." Repeated exposure to Turtle in the spacetime of

103 Larrivé-Bass (2015, 246). See also Guthrie (1993). Cf. Pankenier (2013, 189).

104 Ibid. (242), citing Zhang and Cui (2013, 5), claims that the "Jiahu Site in the Huai River Area," exemplifies how refined attention to a material-function synergy had become by the Neolithic period. Hard substances like quartzite, quartz sandstone, and diorite served to craft anvils and hammerstones; rough substances like sandstone served to make pestles and grinding stones; slate served to produce thinner tools such as knives, sickles, and shovels; flint served to craft scrapers and crystal to make drilling tools."

105 Ibid.

106 Rappenglück (2018). Among myth motifs the concept of the Milky Way as a path for the deceased, or for the setting sun, is one of the oldest. Investigations of Milky Way nomenclature reveal the salience of aqueous metaphors; conceptualizations of the path as a river are distributed throughout the world, see also Thuillard et al. (2018).

107 Larrivé-Bass (2015, 243).

108 Palmer and Clifford (2020, 1001).

spring would have caused a systematic bias generated by the recruitment of overlapping sensory mechanisms.[109]

Recalling that genetic adaptations that occurred in *japonica* domestication advanced human capacities to gain control over the flowering-time of cultivars, we can imagine that Turtle's role as a basis for predictions would have endeared it to the interdependent group that occupied Jiahu. A reliable calendar that helped predict cultivation yields based on observations of increases in grain size, would have in turn promoted the intensification of domestication efforts. Moreover, evidence suggests that better control over yields and grain size growth was matched by an increase in grave wealth over the course of a millennium. In sum, the integration of seasonal information that had been crucial for hunter-gatherers' food procurement strategies into sedentary conditions exemplifies the neural integrative capacities driving accommodation to conditions of permanent settlement life.[110]

Repeated attentional direction to the synchrony between the duration of Turtle's visibility in the sky over the year and the seasonality of Box Turtle mating and hibernation patterns would have enhanced an already familiar bond between chelonians and humans. From its vernal ascendance over the eastern horizon after dusk to its autumnal disappearance from the western night sky, Turtle's presence was reliable and predictable. Internalization of this knowledge would have built on existing neuromodules related to social dimensions of spatial orientation and time factoring. Behavior conditioned by social knowledge about Turtle would have shaped the emergence and transmission of traditions that consciously externalized it as a collective norm.[111]

The transition from a mobile to a sedentary life organized by seasonality transformed the Jiahu inhabitants into "ecosystem engineers." Repeated efforts to integrate and orient themselves to evolving settlement life included Turtle. Turtle was part of a landscape that Jiahu farmers partnered with to sustain subsistence. The deep-seated attachment to Turtle is critical for understanding the logic that links the affective experience of Turtle's unpredictable lag to the adaptative behavior marked by a preoccupation with north-south alignment. This context raises the possibility that the orientation of the Jiahu graves, which were aligned on an east-west axis, with heads of the deceased facing west,[112] may be related to the cardinal location of Turtle's nightly descent between the spring and autumnal

109 Cf. Mircea Eliade (1959, 86ff, 107) where he discusses symbols as cryptic signals that became an important informing resource that can be deciphered to specify the space and time parameters of an ontological world order.

110 Fuller and Allaby (2018, 279).

111 Marshack et al. (1979). Hu et al. (2006). Bar-Yosef (1998, 143); discusses the transition from mobile to sedentary life in terms of a Neolithic revolution.

112 Smith and Lee (2008, 254). Analysis of the graves' spatial organization reveals a tendency to expand westward when additional deceased remains were added to a collective grave, such that secondary burials were placed west of primary interment (277).

equinoxes. Because after autumn, Turtle resides below the horizon, invisible, until its vernal return, the space associated with Turtle's departure may have been associated to the absence of dead relations as well. The location of Turtle's departure may have been associated with the absence of dead relations.

Regardless if the rationale driving Jiahu grave cardinal alignment stems from Turtle's movements, "definite efficacies" were manifested by aligning cultivation activities within the spatiotemporal nexus of planting and harvesting.[113] The efficacies explain how Turtle's presence emerged to organize the Jiahu world into a meaningful, consistent and dynamic framework of social interactions. The calendar functioned as a "cosmovision" in the way it "integrate[d] and orientate [d] the human lifeworld within changing natural ecospheres."[114] As the Box Turtle rattles intimate, Turtle established and maintained order and rhythm for Jiahu residents' interaction with the settlement's environmental conditions especially regarding rice production. Turtle provided a holistic conceptualization of a "world edifice." To paraphrase Michael Rappenglück, Turtle "helped man make the [Jiahu settlement] world homely."[115] The symbolic language constituted by Box Turtle sets evoked this cosmovision and made the ecological inheritance more understandable and thus memorable.

The appearance of inscribed markings on some of the turtle sets that resemble the written form of the numbers six and eight found in the earliest extant evidence of written Chinese dating to 1500 B.C., suggests a link between the objects and numeracy associated with calendrical knowledge.[116] If interpretations of the incised graphs as numbers are valid, it would be particularly suggestive in light of the Box Turtle's characteristic markings, which include *eight* scutes marked by concentric circles, as well as the prominence of *hexagonal* markings along the vertebrae's axis. Inscriptions that may denote other numbers, such as one, two, and ten, were found as well. The range of numbers of pebbles found encased in Box Turtle shell sets has also been linked to possible lunation counts, but no pattern can be discerned from the number of pebbles included in the many sets.[117]

While more conclusive evidence is needed to establish the graphs' meanings, it is clear that the Box Turtle shells, prestige derives from their association with a ritual behavior that aimed to preserve ecological information. Studies on the selective influence exerted by ritual on human development suggest that those surrounding the Box Turtle may have aimed toward maintaining proximity to Turtle. We saw above how some have theorized that as hominid groups became larger, mothers began to interact with infants in "'turn taking' bouts" of ritualized

---

113 Rappenglück (2013, 389).
114 Ibid. (387).
115 Ibid.
116 Li et al. (2003).
117 See for example the salience of numerals in archaic Sumerian, Sampson (1985, 60–61); Mikulska (2014).

social interaction.[118] These ritual practices catalyzed expansions in working memory capacity, which is linked to the evolution of human musicality and language. Social selection pressure accounts for why these rituals evolved to promote group solidarity and inhibit aggression.[119]

I hypothesize that Box Turtle related rituals reflect an extension of the dynamics of proximity maintenance between mother and child. Social rituals that promoted proximity to Turtle would have enhanced integration into a group environment that relied increasingly on grain cultivation for subsistence. The percussive yet soothing effect of rattles, conventionally a baby's first toy, conjures an affective context of mother-child ritualized social interactions. This affective context nuances the implied aim of these prestige objects, to display proximity to Turtle, and the status and power to maintain the proximity for the benefit of the group.

On the basis of mortuary evidence, proximity maintenance was also a driving consideration in Jiahu burial practice. Smith and Lee note the extraordinary degree of intentionality required to dig burial pits that overlapped and cut into previously dug pits. They suggest that such clustering was an expression of Jiahu interdependent mindsets. Group members strove to maintain a close-knit proximity in death as in life. The practice of "placing the dead of shared social relations next to each other," reinforced the idea that maintaining proximity to the deceased projected "an image of a collective group" and thereby promoted "group solidarity."[120] Jiahu burial practices "minimized the social identities of the individual dead and magnified them as members of the group."[121]

The behavioral preconditions established by an attachment to Turtle must be fully appreciated if we are to understand the neuropsychological impact caused by Turtle's eventual obsolescence as an effective seasonal sign, which disrupted the bond. The Box Turtle burial contexts reveal how (mortuary) rituals and symbolic objects generated a sense of group identity and boundaries. This had social as well as epistemological implications. I argue that a Turtle-based calendar induced psychological and neural modifications of consciousness that catalyzed the integration of interactions with Turtle across all levels of the brain. In other words, the relational bond with Turtle mediated the evolution of behavioral, emotional, and cognitive processes.

The Box Turtle's visual form represents the mentation of Turtle-regulated behavior. The ensembles portray Turtle's influence on the evolution of Jiahu behavioral norms: they merged with those of Turtle. The relationship was one of mutual interdependence, a model of cooperative behavior that contributed to the group's benefit. These associations find reinforcement in the communicative

118 Rossano (2012, 532).
119 Rossano (2010, 4, 30–36).
120 Smith and Lee (2008, 277–278).
121 Ibid. (277)

implications suggested by an incision on a Box Turtle plastron recovered from a Jiahu grave, which scholars have noted looks like an "eye."[122] Larrivé-Bass notes that "the placement of the eye on the right section of the plastron is remarkable because it appears slightly off the median of the plastron's vertical line, as would a right eye on a human face. Could it be that someone at Jiahu perceived a plastron as a featureless human head and felt compelled, in part, to materialize the experience by adding an eye?"[123]

Regardless if it is valid to interpret the incised graph as the word "eye," its spatial placement gives rise to this perception. Perhaps the yellow ring that encompasses the geometric shapes found on the Box Turtle's carapace scutes is the source of the formal synergy between turtle and human heads seen in later Neolithic expressions.[124] The fact that the incised plastron was one of eight Box Turtle sets placed in the space where the deceased's skull would have been, implicitly links the space of human mentation to the shells (Figure 3.4).

It may be that the formal synergy between the "folds in fused joints of the skull bones" and turtle scutes was a source of inspiration for this arrangement.[125] But there are other possibilities as well. One stems from the ancient use of the body or parts to represent a schema for transferring important cultural information.[126] The relationship between skulls and Box Turtle shells intimates that both operated in a metaphoric system of self-representation. The schema linking the skull to Box Turtle sets, and the coincidence of the number eight, the same number of scutes with whorl marking that encompass the other geometric forms on the carapace, can be construed as a template for integrating the sensory domains of felt experience as a function of the bond with Turtle. The tomb where the headless skeleton was found, M344, belonged to Phase II, the period when the Jiahu inhabitants were most enriched. The number of prestige objects furnished communicates that the deceased was a leader, a "head" of a group whose prestige derived from his maintenance of the symbolic system.

The next section theorizes the separation distress experienced by Jiahu cultivators in the face of Turtle's astro-calendrical deviance. I draw on research that investigates climate change induced grief in contemporary contexts to elucidate how Jiahu residents would have experienced Turtle's withdrawal. Integrating this with neuropsychological studies on responses to emotionally aversive events, I claim that the mutualistic relationship between them and Turtle, borne from the

122 Henan sheng wenwu yanjiu suo (1999, 984–981; Plates 41.1, 47.1). Reproduced in Larrivé-Bass (2015, 398, Figures 4.28, 4.29).
123 Larrivé-Bass (2015, 219–220).
124 Ibid. (220–223).
125 Major (1993, 69).
126 Smith and Lee (2008, 244) comment on the use of body elements as a metaphoric system related to social memory.

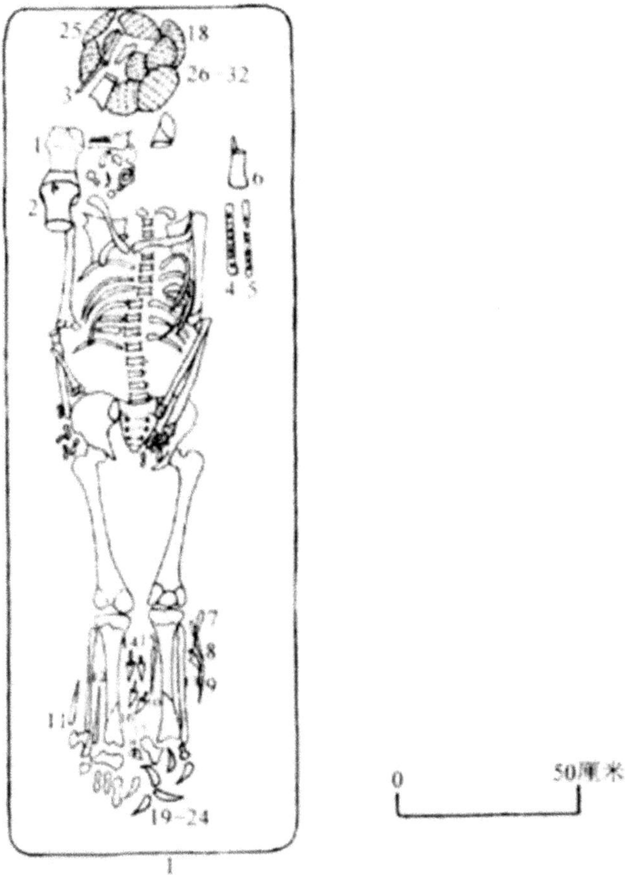

FIGURE 3.4 Drawing of eight Box Turtle sets placed in location of absent skull in tomb M344. *Source*: Wuyang Jiahu (1999, Figure 18. 26–32).

coupling of human and natural systems over the course of a millennium, was so deep that it limited "opportunities to leave the partnership."[127]

Moreover, shame experienced in the wake of Turtle's distancing, created obstacles to placing awareness of this crisis within the socioemotional conditions of Jiahu existence. This emotional denial is a precursor for the structure of feeling whose vector we will follow up to Confucius' paradigmatic filial son. For now, it is enough to see how such denial explains why even though Turtle's calendrical obsolescence would have been noted by agricultural practitioners during Phase III, evidence, albeit reduced, shows that Box Turtles still were used to signal the

127 Zeder (2015, 3192).

conferral of prestige. The following section approaches this phenomenon from the neuropsychological perspective of ecological loss.

Turtle's Obsolescence and Ecological Loss

The cultural remains from Phase III tell a story of diminished enrichment that I attribute to the obsolescence of Turtle's calendrical function. While agriculture subsistence continued even without Turtle's timely presence, this section investigates the neuropsychological implications of this experience. Its starting premise is that an interdependent self-construal, and its reliance on shame aversive behavior, created obstacles for placing awareness of the crisis front and center; the community's socioemotional conditions all but preculded it.[128] I advance an explanation for this mentality, drawing on a body of work that studies human responses to ecological loss. I suggest that these socioemotional conditions effectively suspended group mourning processes related to the loss of Turtle as a reliable member of the community were delayed.

Keeping in mind the observable spatial relationships between Turtle and other celestial entities in the vernal scene helps contextualize the reaction to Turtle's withdrawal from it. Although Northoff rejects the notion of "psychic properties or processes" his theorization that the brain's "spontaneous activity and its temporal structure align themselves to the temporal structure of the body" is borne out by my reading of the Jiahhu evidence.[129] While he refrains from engaging with the ontological implications of his model of the basic neuronal and phenomenal "units of existence and reality," I pursue them with the help of Abraham and Torok's conceptual tools.

My contention is that if Jiahu cultural features can be characterized by the specific spatiotemporal conditions I have delineated above, and if Jiahu bodies were aligned to Turtle's temporal movements, then deviance in Turtle's behavior would have challenged the validity of the "units of existence and reality." The following chapter shows how this emotional and cognitive crisis generated new "units" of spatiotemporal reality, even as they scaffolded on Jiahu neuronal architecture to reconceive it. The Jiahu context raises questions about neuronal fixity in the relationship between consciousness and spatiotemporal perception.[130]

---

128 Abraham and Torok (1994, 5, 14).

129 Northoff (2018, 188). He claims that "structure and relation as basic units of existence and reality are not psychic or mental by themselves."

130 In a publication that theorizes the neurological basis of schizophrenic symptoms, Northoff (2018, 87) presents evidence of "spatiotemporal discontinuity." I will return to the important implications of this finding for my analysis of a vaunted cultural object in Chapter 5 below. Here I propose that a similar discontinuity accounts for the cognitive turn to the Pole star area. This implies that the schizophrenic pathology is on the extreme end of a spectrum of spatiotemporal "dis-ease." Cf. Wheatley (1971, 414), who argues that the ancient Chinese conceptualized "an intimate parallelism between the mathematically expressible regimes of the heavens and the biologically determined rhythms of life on earth."

Giulia Piccaluga's account of the role played by calendars in the evolution of religious behaviors claims the universality of calendars in ancient cultures is an acknowledgement of the "periodicity of the world." She notes that "one concept that proves to be constant across the most varied cultural contexts and the most diverse calendrical forms and manifestations [is] that time is of interest not in and of itself and as a simple fact of nature, but only as a dimension of life that can be submitted to cultural control."[131] Calendars were originally ciphers that operated at the interface between empirical observation and human cultural time, and therefore lent themselves to sociocultural organization. Piccaluga contends that, conceptually, calendars "assert the priority of the unqualifiedly cultural essence of time over the mere natural fact of time."[132] If we concede validity to this insight, then attachment to a Turtle-based calendar even in the face of its temporal dysfunction makes sense. In turn, this emotional logic might also operate to bind an embrained and embodied spatiotemporality to consciousness.

Neuropsychologists who study mental disorganization observable in adult grief attribute it to the loss of regulatory functions previously experienced during the course of a long relationship.[133] Recent studies on the impact of climate change induced distress have noted the "long-term emotional consequences of anticipated or actual environmental changes, with ecological grief as a prime example."[134] Although this scholarship predominantly situates the experience of mourning the loss of ecosystems and landscapes within the context of contemporary climate change, Turtle's unpredicted slippage encourages a similar approach. Reinforcement for this approach can be found relationship between Turtle and Sky River: as Turtle slipped eastward, Sky River assumed the former's spatiotemporal position. Such encroachment lent itself to being read as cosmic flooding and Turtle's calendrical deviance was seen as resulting from it. This disaster trope conveys the shock and dissonance experienced by those for whom Turtle was an idyll, a figure that centered group identity.

Scholarly findings on climate change induced grief among Indigenous populations show that those whose livelihood "rely most closely on the land and land-based activities" suffered in particular. The research helps us conceptualize how Turtle's inevitable obsolescence could have been experienced as an "intangible harm." Cunsolo and Ellis' studies on Indigenous Peoples and farmers focus on the specificity of traits manifested in expressions of grief caused by "ecological loss." This grief is associated both with the physical ecological loss, but *also* "the loss of environmental knowledge and grief associated with anticipated future losses."[135]

131 Piccaluga (2005, 1352).
132 Ibid. (1353).
133 Hofer (1984, 191); Shear and Shair (2005).
134 Comtesse et al (2021, 734).
135 Cunsolo and Ellis (2018, 276). See also Savo et al. (2016).

These insights intersect with those of scholars who adopt an environmental connectedness perspective.[136] This approach offers a "multidisciplinary consideration of how biological selection and cultural learning may have interacted during human evolution to support human affiliation with nonhuman nature via specific place attachment."[137] The concept of connectedness views place as endemic to personality constructs. Attachment to places derives in part from their centrality in constructions of individual and collective identity.[138] Strong emotional bonds with places are inextricably linked to strong social ties.[139] Ecological loss relativizes environmental knowledge and this disrupts "personal and cultural identities that are constructed in relation to features and knowledge of the physical environment."[140] Severance of attachment bonds, or the threat of disruption, are linked to the salience of separation distress in responses to ecological loss.[141]

The long duration of Turtle's withdrawal, moreover, created conditions related to a particular loss type known as ambiguous loss.[142] This type of loss is one "that occurs when a loved one is physically present, but psychologically absent." Because Turtle remained in the sky, but no longer served the same role, mourning was "put on hold," with no possibility of "closure."[143] This emotional experience has been theorized in terms of connectedness and "place attachment," a concept that draws on Bowlby's "attachment theory," discussed in Chapter 2.[144] Recent research has shown a link between place attachment and interpersonal attachment.[145] Shared features include efforts at "proximity-maintenance, safe haven, secure base, and separation distress," even as we acknowledge the different means by which these features may be expressed.[146]

Contemporary studies of ecological loss show that intense yearning motivated environmental behavior aimed at proximity-maintenance.[147] The psychological resistance and disruption triggered by ecological loss is linked to obsessive psychic focus on the loss and its consequences, which give rise to "sadness, bitterness, deep anxiety, guilt, and even shame about... lifestyle choices."[148] Findings in studies of ecological-induced anxiety triggered by the

136 Beery and Wolf-Watz (2014, 204).
137 Beery et al. (2015, 8839).
138 Cunsolo et al. (2012), Cunsolo and Landman (2017).
139 Raymond et al. (2010, 218).
140 Cunsolo and Ellis (2018, 277).
141 Fullilove (2020).
142 Boss (2010).
143 Boss (2006, 4). Boss cites dementia in a parent or loved one as an example of what could cause ambiguous loss (163).
144 Manzo and Devine-Wright (2014).
145 Lewicka (2011).
146 Scannell et. al. (2020, 46). Cf. Rossano (2012).
147 Comtesse et al. (2021, 736).
148 Ibid.

anticipation of future situations are helpful for understanding how Turtle's withdrawal would have shaped cognitive restructuring to mediate "excessive feelings of guilt/responsibility for the loss."[149] The pervasive sense that an ecological loss might have been prevented if a subject's behavior was different among those who experience the phenomenon explains why avoidance motivation would emerge as a guiding principle for adaptive behavior.

As we saw in Chapter 2, most scholars agree the neuropsychological origins of shame lie in human reliance on mutual aid for survival.[150] Research on the evolution of human cooperation has refined our understanding of the psychosocial conditions that would have favored shame as an adaptation that promoted prosocial, conformist behavior.[151] Avoiding social isolation would have been a paramount determinant in the evolution of behavioral norms. Findings that point to neural and structural correlates of interdependent self-construal provide a basis for thinking about how Jiahu's culture would have predisposed its occupants to respond to Turtle's behavior in (culturally) specific ways.[152] Studies show that the construal of the self as interdependent shaped neural pathways and mediated psychological processes. Interdependent mindsets functioned as a mechanism for processing cultural tasks. Mu et al. find that among Chinese subjects "social norm violations are detected at the neurobiological level… illustrating culture-specific neural substrates underlying detecting norm violations."[153] This explains why the emotion of shame would have been so salient in the wake of the ecological loss.

In light of the growing empirical literature that finds consensus regarding the cultural influences on neural responses and neural structure, the case of Jiahu, culture offers an opportunity to look more closely at the suite of cognitive and affective processes that were recruited in the wake of Turtle's ambiguous death.[154] I suggest that the aversive event stimulated processes that generated memory biases.[155] fMRI-based studies have uncovered an anatomical neural signature in humans that accounts for central autonomic and cognitive responses to fear;[156] I propose that perception of Turtle's removal from the vernal scene catalyzed a fear network related dominated by shame aversion; this determined the selection of cognitive procedures that could modulate and integrate the

149 Clark and Beck (2010).
150 Sznycer et al. (2018).
151 Gilbert (2003); Cheng et al. (2010); Cheng et al. (2013); Steckler and Tracy (2014); Henrich and Muthukrishna (2021).
152 Cohen and Hoshino-Browne (2007); Hitokoto et al. (2016); Kitayama et al (2017); Kitayama et al. (2019).
153 Mu et al. (2015).
154 Haberstroh et al. (2002) posit that self-construal mediates and explains the effects of culture on a wide variety of behavior. See also Nisbett et al. (2001).
155 Cheng et al. (2010). See also Van Bockstaele et al.(2014) on fear and attentional bias.
156 Fullana et al. (2016).

aversive environmental stimuli into an emotional defense response.[157] A memory network generated by a Turtle-based interdependent self-construal would have influenced the "cognitive system by way of projections to 'arousal' centers" that shape perceptions and motivate actions.[158]

The system placed specific demands on learning, attentional, and cognitive evaluation processes. Negative biases perpetuated anticipatory anxiety or "instructed fear."[159] Aversive responses to spatial contexts is attested in neurological findings. fMRI imaging has shown that negatively affective biases are augmented in processes related to fear conditioned *spatial memory* formation.[160] Contextual fear conditioning of rats revealed that the rat encodes stimulus features that are recruited for integration in the processing of spatial memory. These include visuospatial and acoustic information.[161] The fact that an aversive memory of the event is retained and accessed when the rat is placed back in the aversive space even in the absence of the original stimulus implicates place as an emotional as well as a conceptual experience. A similarly structured fear network may have evolved in response to the ambiguous conditions surrounding Turtle's lag.

Neural activity in the hippocampus, the brain system that plays a critical role connecting sensations to emotional responses and spatial navigation, would have been central to the formation of memories concerning Turtle.[162] Hippocampal-dependent learning is linked to contextual fear conditioning which involves memory. Vulnerability to heightened contingency awareness caused by continued exposure to a place that elicits aversive reactions would have triggered chronic cognitive attention to spatial relationships between humans and celestial entities. This in turn heightened sensitivity to situational context, and contextually deviant events. These sensitivities have been identified by neuroscientists as key features of interdependent self-construal.[163]

While the neurocortical correlates of interdependent self-construal are only just beginning to be understood, we discussed in the previous chapter that there are some findings that emphasize culture as a determining factor that shapes responses to social-evaluative threat. For example, interdependent self-construal is implicated in a psychoneurological condition known as "fear of isolation" (FOI), a form of social

157 Fellous and Ledoux (2005).

158 Ibid. (79).

159 Mechias et al. (2010). Gutchess and Huff (2016, 159) note that East Asians resolved conflicts in categorical and relational associations "... by engaging attentional networks, denoted by frontoparietal activity."

160 Fanselow (2000).

161 Ibid.

162 Ibid. See also Black et al. (1977); McDonald and White (2013).

163 Gutchess and Huff (2016) cite studies that showed "repetition of object–background pairs... induced adaptation in hippocampal regions associated with the binding of [emotional and cognitive] information together."

anxiety. Results produced from investigations of subjects with East Asian cultural backgrounds have shown that "exposure to an image of a watching face is sufficient to automatically evoke a social-evaluative threat."[164] Interdependent self-construal is also linked to the highly aversive "awareness that others know that one has failed to meet a minimum standard for social acceptability."[165]

The heightened perception and experience of self-threat associated with interdependent self-construal extended to more general reasoning about relationships among items in the world. It seems plausible that the affective impact of ambiguous loss determined a preference for observing the stable circumpolar stars as an adaptive strategy, which in turn generated the idea that proximity with true north would serve as a harm-avoidant strategy. Behavior that prioritized the flexible adaptation to astronomical stimuli would have been selected to regulate the social pain of distress. It would also have stimulated cognitive development with regard to discerning the source of the power responsible for the ambiguous loss.

By 3,000 B.C., archaeological evidence reveals that chronic cognitive attention to the celestial Pole had yielded a mental representation of the Pole Star as a seat of power that operated as a pivot around which celestial bodies revolved.[166] I construe the cognitive advances that permitted humans to align themselves with such precision along a north-south axis as a fragment of a more complete scene. If we follow Nicolas Abraham and Maria Torok's view that psychic operations aim to effect "gradual self-transformation in the face of interior and exterior changes in the psychological emotional relational landscape," then it is imaginable how the shame and confusion resulting from conditions of ambiguous loss would be an obstacle to the harmonious progress of self-fashioning and expansion. Whereas Turtle originally enriched Jiahu self-fashioning, it came to disturb it.

Intensified attention to gathering information about the celestial Pole evolved as a means to transcend the psychic discomfort. Turning attention to the north had the effect of diluting attention on the east, where Turtle had been a consistent participant in Jiahu spring activities. Turtle's vernal role ws thus camouflaged, focus on the celestial Pole served to shelter from view the shameful moment that hindered the ability to predict and control time for agricultural production. Over time, the cognitive advancements generated by the need to modulate the anxiety gave way to a new form of expression. The symbolism marked the transcendence over blocked mourning and renewal of the gradual process of psychical readjustment and expansion.

The following and last section of this chapter traces the trajectory of renewal from the dissolution of the Jiahu site as a result of flooding in 5500 B.C., to the emergence of a cosmology premised on chelonian physiology. Ritual turtle-

164 Park and Kitayama (2014, 201). See also Monfries and Kafer (1994); Kocovski and Endler (2000).
165 Fessler (2004, 231).
166 Pankenier (2013, 141–142).

shaped jade objects have been linked to other Middle Neolithic symbols that scholars claim had astronomical, mathematical and religious associations. Building on the significant scholarship that ascribes to the turtle form a complex cosmovision, I approach these links from a fresh angle, suggesting the cosmology be construed as a symptom or memory trace that reflects on the (cultural) mechanisms of successful transcendence in the wake of suspended mourning.

Culture as Adaptation

There is archaeological evidence to support the hypothesis that the Jiahu's relationship with Turtle was known by contemporaries of Jiahu residents. Out of the fourteen human bones that were tested for evidence of "prehistoric migration," five attested to the phenomenon. Zhang and Cui posit that "population flow" grew to be extensive between Phases I and III.[167] The existence of a cross-regional trade of prestige objects that revealed a consistent presence of turtle shells and turtle iconography in early to late Neolithic cultures is another example of interaction. Here we will delve deeper into the implications of the regional distribution of turtle symbols for understanding the process driving the transformation of Turtle-as-vernal-sign into a turtle-as-natural-model-of-the-universe. In this transformation lies the mechanism for transcendence and renewal.

Scholarship on figuration agrees that the production of two- and three-dimensional representations was a sense-making response to natural and social environments. Some argue that a figurative impulse evolved in response to the need for increased methods to externalize important group information.[168] Regional and local factors were thus primary influences on the emergence of symbolic iconographic systems. Given these conditions, the consistency of the high valence imbued in turtle iconography across spatial and temporal boundaries may be construed as objectified echoes of the Jiahu Turtle's former glory.

Li Liu opines that turtle shells recovered at early Neolithic Peiligang cultural sites (6400-4500 B.C.) in the Central Yellow River Valley, extending north to middle Neolithic Yangshao (5050-3050) culture, and then east (and southeast) late Neolithic Hongshang (4500-3000 B.C.), and Liangzhu (3400-2250 B.C.) cultures, was due to the animal's association with ritual practices related to cosmological knowledge.[169] By the fourth millennium B.C., chelonian forms of cultural expression was a shared feature among settlements in the Liao River Valley, the lower Yangtze River and Yellow River Valley cultures.[170]

167 Zhang and Cui (2013).
168 Larrivé-Bass (2015).
169 Liu (2007).
170 Liu (2007).

The fact that turtle figuration appeared in cultures, such as Hongshan, where it was not consumed, at least according to the record of local fauna excavated at the site, offers compelling negative evidence of its sacred associations.[171] The turtle was not by any means the only sacred animal represented, but along with birds, it represented an ancient strata of cosmological world views. Whereas the bird is almost universally understood to symbolize the sun, the convex shape of the turtle's domed carapace, together with the flat ventral shape of the plastron, encapsulated a cosmovision of Sky and earth.[172] The turtle's feet were conceptualized as cardinal pillars that fixed the two shells so that they would not move. The figures evoke the tight proximity of the Jiahu Box Turtle shells, which emphasized the constrained box-like movement of the turtles due to the way ligaments held the shells together.

The apparent standardization of turtle forms reflects how the iconography supports "well-established belief systems."[173] For example, at the Lingjiatan (3500-3300 B.C.) cultural site in Hanshan, Anhui, a turtle comprised two pieces of jade with a plaque placed between its shells draws attention to the liminal space between Sky and earth. On the plaque, moreover, "a complex geometrical design showing an octagonal star at the center" was incised, which scholars have suggested represented the sun or the polestar. An octagonal star also appears carved on the chest of a jade bird recovered from Lingjiatan remains.[174]

The number eight recalls the number of Box Turtle scutes that encompass the entirety of the geometric designs on its carapace. Those scutes bore whorl-like markings, which also have a long pedigree in Neolithic figuration. Many scholars interpret the whorl signs as representing stars.[175] Li Liu has argued that these sophisticated artifacts were used in rituals premised on a belief system concerning "the form of the universe," and "the movement of celestial bodies," which were central for determining bountiful harvests.[176] He claims that jade figurations of turtles represents the merger of a fourth millennium B.C. bird cult iconographic system seen in clay figures. From this merger evolved a new symbolic assemblage that concerned the shape of the cosmos, symbolized by the form of the turtle as well as other objects whose communicative message employs the language of a domed Sky and square earth.[177]

In addition to jade figures, the turtle, especially the Box Turtle genus, is intimated in other prestigious objects. For example, 118 shell pieces recovered from tombs M7 and M8 at the Hongshan cultural strata of remains found at Baiyinchanghan site, reflects an extraordinary effort to represent chelonian scutes. The bi-valve shell pieces, which were originally strung together, were crafted

171 Liu (2007, 274); Guo (1995; 1997).
172 Allan (1991); Major (1993); Li et al. (2003, 171–173).
173 Liu (2007b, 277).
174 Ibid.
175 Ibid. (279).
176 Ibid.
177 Ibid.

into "an irregular hexagon whose surface exhibits uneven and at times excentered concentric circles." Sandrine Larrivé-Bass suggests that the task of "maintaining the naturally concentric surface ribbing centered within the polygonal frame) indicates that their value had more to do with their natural surface configurations than with their bi-valve shape," extending "beyond mere beauty." She concludes that the "irregular hexagonal shape of each piece, the concentric ribbing present on their surface," suggests that the shell ensemble "formed a body ornament whose composition likely recalled that of scutes on a turtle carapace."[178]

The discovery of a turtle plastron in Anban, a Yangshao (5050-3050 B.C.) cultural site in Shaanxi, invokes the unique physiology of the Box Turtle's plastron "without a posterior notch. [The figure] reproduces the visible seams on this genus' plastron's surface: a median vertical line; a horizontal line; two lines projecting downward from the median at 45 degree angles (forming an inverted V); and the rhombus-shaped entoplastron visible on the bony surface of a plastron once scutes are removed."[179] At the same time that the lines reproduce those of a *Cuora flavomarginata's* bony plastron, they also "form the silhouette of a stick figure shown *en face* with open arms and split legs" (Figure 3.5).[180] This relationship between human body representations and turtle plastrons recalls the incision of an (eye) graph on the Jiahu plastron. Both gestures rely on the Box Turtle's physiological features to link human heads with turtle plastrons.

We have seen that the roots of the turtle iconography and its embedded cosmovision lay in the Box Turtle's physiology. The reliance on the animal's ovality for communicating the concept of Sky in cosmology recapitulated the original neurocognitive event that led to the production of a Turtle-based spacetime. This repetition encourages us to view both neurocognitive events as linked. The first event was catalyzed by the expansion of cognitive capacities to integrate ancient ecological knowledge into newly evolved sedentary subsistence practices; the turtle's shape and watery environs was projected on to a celestial space. The second event was borne from unresolved grief over the loss of the cosmovision established by the first event.

The connection between the two events reveals something about the process of transcending suspended mourning. Studies have shown how regeneration in the peripheral nervous system recapitulates features of development and growth, even as they expand upon them to facilitate accommodation of new internal and external conditions of being.[181] Whereas the earlier event projected the turtle's shape and watery environs on to a celestial space, the second event relies on the ovoid form to focus attention on the turtle's central keel, its vertebrae, and plastron markings. Put another way, the second event disambiguates the meaning of the circle. The specificity of the new focus all but conceals Turtle's relationship with the earlier cosmovision.

178 Larrivé-Bass (2015, 153).
179 Ibid. (401 Figures 4.35; 4.36).
180 Ibid.
181 Rossi et al. (2007); Bosse et al. (2006).

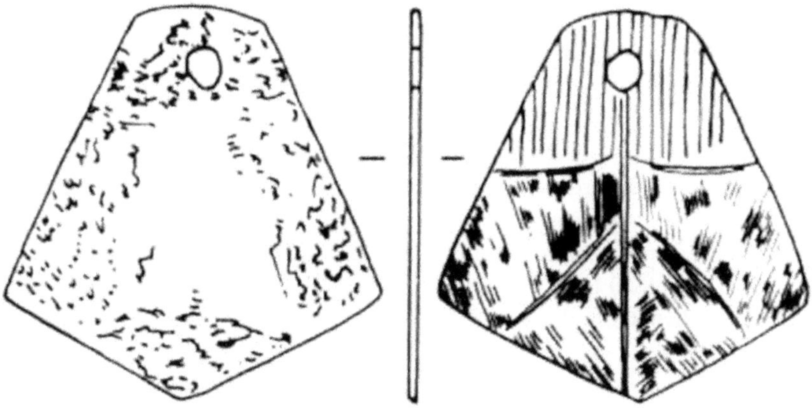

FIGURE 3.5 Turtle plastron with incised stick-figure found at Anban, Shaanxi Province Yangshao culture site. *Source*: Larrivé-Bass (2015 401, Figure 4.35).

The narrowing of focus to physiological markings made the animal legible in a different way than Turtle. This explains why it became a suitable vehicle for camouflaging Turtle's previous association with the vernal equinox. Significantly, the disambiguation process dismantled the discursive boundaries that precluded harmonious self-fashioning due to the ambiguity of the loss. The tendency toward precision parallels the turn toward the celestial Pole as a potential source for transcending the conditions that made it impractical to mourn Turtle's obsolescence. The transformation of Turtle into a turtle was the symbolic means by which the former could finally be named and memorialized as a prestigious symbol of social knowledge.

The turtle-based cosmology is product of Neolithic self-fashioning processes; it is a product of the transcendence over blocked self-fashioning. While a preoccupation with the celestial Pole first yielded the tools, techniques and knowledge characterized by the turtle's form, its underlying epistemology builds on antecedent biological, social, and culturally acquired structures that fed into an ancient expressive system organized around Turtle. Adaptations resulting from the modulation of a range of capabilities, including attention, representation, memory, learning, and behavior are the true "authors" of the cosmology. While the foregoing discussion cited figural evidence that indicates the emergence of the cosmovision and its mergence with other local and ancient traditions occurred during the fourth millennium B.C., figurations found at a fifth millennium B.C. cultural site reveal antecedent and intense interests in formal schemes that represent the spatial relationship between vertical lines and spherical realms. These are the very qualities of the turtle's plastron that rendered the turtle into an apt cosmological model.

The site, situated in the lower Huai River Valley in Anhui province, is identified by archaeologists as the Bengbu Shuangdun culture (5300-5100).[182] A chelonian figure is suggested by a dish that was recovered, which is raised from ground on four legs. The dish has a "lightly flaring rim from which extends a turtle-like head—devoid of carapace."[183] The figure may reflect the growing significance of the plastron as a source of knowledge about spatial relationships. Shuangdun has been proposed as a successor to Jiahu. Studies of grain remnants at the site show that rice was the dominant crop utilized at the Shangdun site between 5300 and 4800 B.C.[184] Evidence that shows broomcorn millet utilization has led to the hypothesis that it was an imported cereal crop, reinforcing the idea that Shangdun was a site of cross-regional interaction.[185]

The site is renowned for the large proportion of symbols recovered in the remains, as well as the level of technical, conceptual, and spatial sophistication exemplified in the craftsman's work.[186] The symbols were incised into the usually circular surface of pottery feet. The site is also intriguing for its lack of housing, which raises the question as to why so much inscribed pottery was found.[187] The discovery of two rammed-earth platforms whose size could accommodate public gatherings, has led some scholars to suggest that the site was used for collective events, but not as a permanently inhabited settlement. This hypothesis is given credence by the evidence of the symbolic system that reflect wide cross-cultural interactions.[188]

A recent rigorous analysis of the patterns driving symbol composition uncovered a formal grammar for producing meaning in the glyphs.[189] The findings reveal a communicative emphasis on signifying the concept of a central core. For example axial perspectives, concentric circles, cross-hatching signs, all draw attention to the center.[190] In addition, the symbols reflect keen exploration of forms that represent "separation" (*fenli*) and "gathering" (*zuhe*); this resonates with the emotional experience of separation distress and the cognitive strategies to maintain proximity in order to modulate it.[191] The salience of motifs that emphasized interconnections among spatially related components also tacitly speak of efforts to account for a sundered bond, as do the frequent representations of the cardinal directions through different angles.[192] The analysis concludes that

182 Anhui Provincial Institute of Cultural Relics and Archaeology and Museum of Bengbu City (2008). See Lee (2008) for an English account of the excavation report and symbol images.
183 Larrivé-Bass (2015, 65, 349, Figure 1.79).
184 Luo et al. (2019). Cohen (2011).
185 Luo et al. (2019).
186 Zhang and Fang (2005); Huang and Sun (2011).
187 Luo et al. (2019).
188 Cohen (2011).
189 Huang and Sun (2011).
190 Ibid. (58–59). See also 65, Figures 36–37; 45).
191 Ibid. (58).
192 Ibid. (57).

the formal rules that organize the representational systems adhere to a disambiguation process that reflect a proclivity toward central convergence.[193]

Li Xinwei links this orientation, and especially the eight-pointed star, to astronomical knowledge about the celestial Pole.[194] His systematic analysis suggests that octagonal patterns and forms that represent knots were correlated with the movement of the polestar. He shows how the motifs of crisscrosses, polygonal stars, as well as the knot reflect the concept of a "motion hub" (*tianti xuanzhuan*).[195] Accordingly, whorl like concentric circles—like the scute markings that frame the Box Turtle carapace—symbolize rotations that help center the celestial pole, while representations of pointy roofs symbolize the polestar.

The connection between pointy roofs, the pole star, and turtle carapace forms is important. Scholars of Early China will note my reticence to use the appellation "Canopy Sky" (*gaitian*) to refer to the turtle-based cosmology. Although this nomenclature is commonly—and understandably—attributed to the mode of thought represented by the chelonian carapace imagery, I refrain from using it even as I fully endorse the astronomical and cosmological intentions ascribed by scholars to the turtle symbols' embedded meaning.[196] The fact that we simply have no linguistic evidence to indubitably link the artifact to this label—itself an artifact from first millennia B.C. texts—is one reason for caution. But even more compelling, as Chapter 5 reveals, is the fact that before the conceptual locution *gaitian* emerged, the Western Zhou had established an astro-calendrical system whose metaphoric premise was, to be precise, the construction of a pointy-roofed structure in Sky. The lexicon of that system, including the words "base," "axis," "crossbeam," and "pointy roof" suggests itself as the true source of the nomenclature "Canopy Sky."

Once this is clear, and once, as I demonstrate in Chapter 6, it is understood how the Western Zhou system was implicated by the Zhou royal family's shameful loss of status after 771 B.C., we can understand why the ancient turtle form would be (unconsciously) recruited, (once again) to function as a reliable cipher that keeps at bay awareness of a relational crisis. The process raises questions about the psychosocioemotional conditions of Western Zhou existence. What would make it possible and perhaps warrant turtle's recruitment? These issues will be addressed in Chapters 5 and 6.

Shuangdun culture has been hailed for filling in gaps in the evolutionary history of Chinese Neolithic culture. Acknowledging the cross-regional spectrum of perspectives represented in the symbols should not obscure the possibility that Jiahu's fate may have been a preconditioning factor of an overall shared interest in spatial representation that characterizes the symbols. When

193 Ibid. (61).
194 Li (2020).
195 Ibid.
196 Cullen (1993) provides a seminal discussion.

Jiahu occupants were forced to migrate out of the settlement, rendered uninhabitable due to flooding, they carried their experiences to other settlements in the area. Given the endurance of the settlement and the prestige that was likely conferred to it by neighboring settlements, we can imagine how information about Jiahu's demise would have been of keen interest to neighboring settlements if not those farther away.

The longevity and relatively large size of the settlement strongly support the idea that these factors endowed the settlement with prestige. If the layout of the middle-late phase exerted a "pulse of development," then this pulse exerted a generative influence on both local cultures, located in the upper Huai River Valley,[197] and, on an interregional cultural level as well. Evidence that reinforces Jiahu's influential scope can be seen in the fact that turtle shells, the unique Jiahu prestige item, became a consistently traded prestige object during the Neolithic, not to mention the source of inspiration of much early figuration.[198]

In a regional analysis of early Neolithic cultural sites, David Joel Cohen finds that shared pottery shapes, stone tool kits, mortuary practices, and evidence of early grain domestication activities, all bespeak of interaction among settlements. Jiahu's location at the northern reaches of Lower Yangzi River/Huai Valley region, close to "interdigitating tributaries of the Huai River system," linked Neolithic contemporaneous cultures, such as Peiligang (6000-5400 B.C.), to other clusters within the Yangtze River system, including the earlier cultures of Pengtoushan (8,000-6400 B.C.) in the Middle Yangtze region and Shangshan (8,000-6500 B.C.) in the southeastern Lower Yangtze River region.[199] Cohen views the network of tributaries as a probable catalyst for interregional interactions and social networks that drove cultural development, especially grain domestication evolution, in parallel ways.[200]

Acknowledging the prestige of the culture in the context of early Neolithic interregional interactions allows us to trace how an emotional event experienced by Jiahu occupants would have been "cognitively distributed" along the same channels taken by agricultural techniques and prestige objects.[201] When I speak of an evolved Neolithic neural substrate, it is premised on these conditions. Li Xinwei finds that interest in the celestial Pole among many Neolithic cultures in the late fifth and fourth millennia B.C. is a structural feature of Neolithic religion. He points to the eight-pointed star as clear evidence that astronomical knowledge about the celestial Pole was the kernel of religious beliefs that were organized around access to this information.[202]

197 Ibid. (195).
198 Larrivé-Bass (2015).
199 Cohen (2011, S274).
200 Ibid. (S281). See also Zhu (2013, 186); Zhang and Cui (2013, 206).
201 Zhang and Cui (2013, 206).
202 Li (2020).

Li suggests such symbols, along with octagonal patterns and forms that represent knots were correlated with the movement of the Pole Star. Motifs of crisscrosses, polygonal stars, and the knot represented a "motion hub" (*tianti xuanzhuan zhitai*).[203] Accordingly, whorl like concentric circles—like the scute markings that frame the Box Turtle carapace—symbolized rotations that center the celestial pole. Representations of pointy roofs symbolized the Pole Star, located at the apex of Sky's canopy.[204] This symbolic discourse became a foundation for asserting and maintaining power over settlements whose populations were expanding due to enhanced predictive capacities resulting from the astronomical knowledge encased in the cosmology.

Li claims that the ritual activity involving cosmologically related prestige objects was carried out to project access to a suprasensible power. Access to that power was related to the capacity to predict and produce harvests to support expanding settlements. Knowledge that could assist with calendrical predictions became an important asset for emerging forms of leadership and social organization. Li traces a genealogy of religious evolution from evidence of social organization observed at Lingjiatan and Hongshan cultural sites. He claims that the foundation of power and wealth evidenced in late Neolithic Liangzhu cultural remains (3400-2250 B.C.) is the product of a merger between Liangjiatan and Hongshan religious practice and ideations.[205] He argues that the primary mechanism for this sociopolitical evolutionary trajectory was the valence of knowledge about the Pole Star.

Besides the turtle and bird and pig, which Li identifies as the central zoomorphic figures related to celestial Pole-based cosmologies, Li views frequently seen late Neolithic ritual objects, such as the round-within-a-square shaped *cong*, and the circular *bi*, as elegant epigenetic descendants of the square and round spatial motifs represented in Shuangdun. He cites the fact that Pole Star symbols were frequently inscribed on pottery as an indication that the cosmologies they represented were widely known, not just among the elite. This accounts for why the cosmology became a useful strategy for social organization.[206]

If we accept Nicolas Abraham's premise that emotional catastrophes are the source of phenomenological consciousness, and understand symbolic expression as a symptom of a threat posed to social emotional existence, then we may see in the spatial preoccupation communicated by Shuangdun symbols as a "telltale memory

203 Ibid.

204 Ibid.

205 Ibid. Liu et al. (2019) argue that jade rituals were deployed to enhance collective identity, which served to solidify centralized sociopolitical organization.

206 Li (2020). Cf. Green (1993), who argues that late Neolithic jade bi ritual objects represented a spindle whorl model of the world, which resonates with knot-related cosmologies, and Teng (2000) for the potential astronomical significance of *bi*. See also Pankenier (2015), for an extended analysis of the weaving trope in cosmo-political thought.

trace of latent or unavailable promptings."[207] Reading the Shuangdun symbols as embedding within them a crisis of disorientation permits us to view them as a product of the memory that emanated from a collective process of transcendence. The collectively construed grammar that organized spatial representation sought to portray wholeness and convergence, anticipating the communicative aims of the new turtle cosmovision. As we shall see in the following chapters, preoccupation with alignments with true north emerged, like the Shuangdun symbols, like chelonian-based cosmology, to "fix the fit" between a changed ecology and interdependent group identity. This pattern of fixing, which promotes conformist behavior in terms of cardinal alignment, evolved into an important behavioral trait that shaped Neolithic and Bronze Age state behavior.

References

Abraham, N., & Torok, M. (1994). *The shell and the kernel: Renewals of psychoanalysis* (Vol. 1). University of Chicago Press.

Allan, S. (1991). *The shape of the turtle: Myth, art, and cosmos in early China.* SUNY Press.

An, C., Feng, Z., & Tang, L. (2004). Environmental change and cultural response between 8000 and 4000 cal. yr BP in the western Loess Plateau, northwest China. *Journal of Quaternary Science: Published for the Quaternary Research Association, 19*(6), 529–535.

An, C.-B., Feng, Z. D., & Barton, L. (2006). Dry or humid? Mid-Holocene humidity changes in arid and semi-arid China. *Quaternary Science Reviews, 25*(3–4), 351–361.

An, C., Tang, L., Barton, L., & Chen, F. H. (2005). Climate change and cultural response around 4000 cal yr BP in the western part of Chinese Loess Plateau. *Quaternary Research, 63*(3), 347–352.

An, Z. S. (2017). Fangwei zunchong yuanyuan kao. Shehuikexue Zhanxian, 95–103.

Anhui Provincial Institute of Cultural Relics and Archaeology and Museum of Bengbu City. (2008). *Bengbu Shuangdun: xinshiqi shidai yizhi fajuebaogao.* Beijing: Kexuechubanshe.

Bar-Yosef, O. (1998). On the nature of transitions: The Middle to Upper Palaeolithic and the Neolithic Revolution. *Cambridge Archaeological Journal.* doi: 10.1017/S0959774300001815

Beery, T., Jönsson, K. I., & Elmberg, J. (2015). From environmental connectedness to sustainable futures: Topophilia and human affiliation with nature. *Sustainability,* 7(7), 8837–8854.

Beery, T. H., & Wolf-Watz, D. (2014). Nature to place: Rethinking the environmental connectedness perspective. *Journal of Environmental Psychology, 40,* 198–205.

Black, A. H., Nadel, L., & O'keefe, J. (1977). Hippocampal function in avoidance learning and punishment. *Psychological Bulletin, 84*(6), 1107.

Boss, P. (2006). *Loss, trauma, and resilience: Therapeutic work with ambiguous loss.* WW Norton & Company.

Boss, P. (2010). The trauma and complicated grief of ambiguous loss. *Pastoral Psychology, 59,* 137–145.

Bosse, F., Hasenpusch-Theil, K., Küry, P., & Müller, H. W. (2006). Gene expression

207 Abraham and Torok (1994, 5,14).

profiling reveals that peripheral nerve regeneration is a consequence of both novel injury-dependent and reactivated developmental processes. *Journal of Neurochemistry, 96*(5), 1441–1457.

Boyd, R., & Richerson, P. J. (2020). Culture and the evolution of the human social instincts. In S.C. Levinson and N.J. Enfield (Eds.), *Roots of human sociality: Culture, cognition and interaction* (pp. 453–477). Routledge.

Chang, K. C. (1999). China on the eve of the historical period. In Michael Loewe and Edward L. Shaughnessy (Eds.), *The Cambridge history of ancient China: From the origins of civilization to 221 B.C* (pp. 37–73). Cambridge University Press.

Chen, B. Z., Wang, X. K., & Zhang, J. Z. (1995). The finds and morphological study of carbonized rice in the Neolithic site at Jiahu in Wuyang County, Henan Province. *Chinese Journal of Rice Science, 9*(3), 129–134.

Cheng, J. T., Tracy, J. L., & Anderson, C. (2014). *The psychology of social status*. Springer.

Cheng, J. T., Tracy, J. L., Foulsham, T., Kingstone, A., & Henrich, J. (2013). Two ways to the top: evidence that dominance and prestige are distinct yet viable avenues to social rank and influence. *Journal of Personality and Social Psychology, 104*(1), 103.

Cheng, J. T., Tracy, J. L., & Henrich, J. (2010). Pride, personality, and the evolutionary foundations of human social status. *Evolution and Human Behavior, 31*(5), 334–347.

Chi, Z., & Hung, H. C. (2013). Jiahu 1: earliest farmers beyond the Yangtze River. *Antiquity, 87*(335), 46–63.

Chiao, J. Y., Li, S. C., Seligman, R., & Turner, R. (Eds.). (2016). *The Oxford handbook of cultural neuroscience*. Oxford University Press.

Childs-Johnson, E. (1991). Jades of the Hongshan culture: the dragon and fertility cult worship. *Arts Asiatiques, 46*, 82–95.

Clark, D. A., Beck, A. T. (2010). Cognitive theory and therapy of anxiety and depression: Convergence with neurobiological findings. *Trends in Cognitive Sciences, 14*(9), 418–424.

Cohen, D., & Hoshino-Browne, E. (2007). Culture and the structure of personal experience: Insider and outsider phenomenologies of the self and social world. *Advances in Experimental Social Psychology, 39*, 1–67.

Cohen, D. J. (2011). The beginnings of agriculture in China: A multiregional view. *Current Anthropology, 52*(S4), S273–S293.

Cohen, D. J., Bar-Yosef, O., Wu, X., Patania, I., & Goldberg, P. (2017). The emergence of pottery in China: Recent dating of two early pottery cave sites in South China. *Quaternary International, 441*, 36–48.

Comtesse, H., Ertl, V., Hengst, S., Rosner, R., Smid, G. (2021). Ecological Grief as a Response to Environmental Change: A Mental Health Risk or Functional Response? *International Journal of Environmental Research and Public Health, 18*(2), 734.

Cullen, C. (1993). A Chinese eratosthenes of the flat earth. Appendix A. In J. S. Major (Ed.), *Heaven and earth in early han thought*. State University of New York Press.

Cunsolo, A., & Ellis, N. R. (2018). Ecological grief as a mental health response to climate change-related loss. *Nature Climate Change, 8*, 275–281.

Cunsolo, A., & Landman, K. (Eds.). (2017). *Mourning nature: Hope at the heart of ecological loss and grief*. McGill-Queen's University Press, MQUP.

Cunsolo, W. A., Harper, S. L., Ford, J. D., Landman, K., Houle, K., Edge, V. L., & Rigolet Inuit Community Government. (2012). "From this place and of this place:" Climate change, sense of place, and health in Nunatsiavut, Canada. *Social Science & Medicine, 75*(3), 538–547.

De Hooge, I. E., Zeelenberg, M., & Breugelmans, S. M. (2010). Restore and protect motivations following shame. *Cognition and Emotion, 24*(1), 111–127.

Deng, Z. H., Qin, L., Gao, Y., Weisskopf, A. R., Chi, Z., & Fuller, D. Q. (2015). From early domesticated rice of the middle Yangtze Basin to millet, rice and wheat agriculture: Archaeobotanical macro-remains from Baligang, Nanyang Basin, Central China (6700–500 BC). *Public Library of Science One, 10*(10), e0139885.

Donald, M. (2001). *A mind so rare: The evolution of human consciousness.* WW Norton Company.

Donald, M. , Nucci, L. Saxe, G.B., & Turiel, E. (2000). The central role of culture in cognitive evolution: A reflection on the myth of the "isolated mind." In L. Nucci (Ed.), *Culture, thought, and development* (pp. 29–44). Psychology Press.

Durkalec D., Agata, F., Chris, S., Mark W., Sheldon, T. (2015). Climate change influences on environment as a determinant of Indigenous health: Relationships to place, sea ice, and health in an Inuit community. Social Science and Medicine, *136–137*, 17–26.

Eliade, M. (1959). Methodological remarks on the study of religious symbolism. In M. Eliade & J. M. Kitagawa (Eds.), *The history of religions: Essays in methodology.* University of Chicago Press.

Eliade, M. (1969, 1959). *The quest: History and meaning in religion.* University of Chicago Press.

Ellis, N., & Albrecht, G. (2017). Climate change threats to family farmers' sense of place and mental wellbeing: A case study from the Western Australian Wheatbelt. *Social Science and Medicine,* 175, 161–168.

Fan, F. F., & Zhang J. Z. (2008a). Cong shiqian yong guixianxiang kan Huanghuai, Jianghuai diqu de wenminghua Jincheng. *Zhongyuan Wen Wu, 4*, 29–35.

Fan, F. F., & Zhang J. Z. (2008b). Zhongguo shiqian guiwenhua yanjiu zonglun. *Huaxia Kaogu, 14*, 69–75.

Fang, Y. (2021). Liquor making and folk customs in Ancient China. In X. Jiang (Ed.), *A new phase of systematic development of scientific theories in China. History of science and technology in China* (pp. 175–203). Springer.

Fanselow, M. S. (2000). Contextual fear, gestalt memories, and the hippocampus. *Behavioural Brain Research, 110*(1-2), 73–81.

Fellous, J.-M., & Ledoux, J. E. (2005). *Toward Basic Principles for Emotional Processing: What the Fearful Brain Tells the Robot.* In J.-M. Fellous & M. A. Arbib (Eds.), *Who needs emotions?: The brain meets the robot.* Affective Science Series (p. 79–115). Oxford University Press.

Feng, S. (1990). Henan Puyang Xishuipo 45 hao mu de tianwenxue yanjiu. *Wenwu, 3*, 52–60.

Fessler, D. (2004). Shame in two cultures: Implications for evolutionary approaches. *Journal of Cognition and Culture, 4*(2), 207–262.

Flad, R. K., & Chen, P. C. (2013). *Ancient central China: Centers and peripheries along the yangzi river.* Cambridge University Press.

Frecska, E., & Kulcsar, Z. (1989). Social bonding in the modulation of the physiology of ritual trance. *Ethos, 17*(1), 70–87.

Fritz, T., & Koelsch, S. (2008). The role of semantic association and emotional contagion for the induction of emotion with music. *Behavioral and Brain Sciences, 31*(5), 579.

Fullana, M. A., Harrison, B. J., Soriano-Mas, C., Vervliet, B., Cardoner, N., Àvila-Parcet, A., & Radua, J. (2016). Neural signatures of human fear conditioning: an updated and extended meta-analysis of fMRI studies. *Molecular Psychiatry, 21*(4), 500–508.

Fuller, D. Q., & Allaby, R. (2018). Seed dispersal and crop domestication: shattering, germination and seasonality in evolution under cultivation. *Annual Plant Reviews Online, 38*, 238–295.

Fuller, D. Q., Lucas, L., & Boivin, N. (2017). Adapting crops, landscapes, and food choices: Patterns in the dispersal of domesticated plants across Eurasia. In N. Boivin, R. Crassard, and M. Petraglia (Eds.), *Human dispersal and species movement: From prehistory to the present* (pp. 304–331). Chicago: Cambridge University Press.

Fullilove, M. T. (2020). Revisiting "The Frayed Knot": What happens to place attachment in the context of serial forced displacement? In *Place Attachment: Advances in Theory, Methods and Applications*. doi: 10.4324/9780429274442-11

Gao, X., Huang, W., Xu, Z., Ma, Z., & Olsen, J. W. (2004). 120–150 ka human tooth and ivory engravings from Xinglongdong Cave, Three Gorges Region, South China. *Chinese Science Bulletin, 49*(2), 175–180.

Gao, X., Wei, Q., & Li, G. H. (2008). A report of the third excavation of the Ranjialukou Paleolithic site. *Acta Anthropologica Sinica, 27*(1), 1

Gilbert, P. (2003). Evolution, social roles, and the differences in shame and guilt. *Social Research: An International Quarterly, 70*(4), 1205–1230.

Granot, R. (2017). Music, pleasure, and social affiliation: Hormones and neurotransmitters. In R. Ashley and R. Timmers (Eds.), *The Routledge companion to music cognition* (pp. 101–111). Routledge.

Green, J. M. (1993). Unraveling the enigma of the Bi: The spindle whorl as the model of the ritual disk. *Asian Perspectives, 32*, 105–124.

Guo, D.S. (1995). Hongshan and related cultures. In S.M. Nelson (Ed.), *The archaeology of northeast China: Beyond the Great Wall*. Routledge.

Guo, D. S. (1997). Hongshan wenhua de 'weiyu weizang' yu Liaohe wenming qiyuan tezheng zairenshi. *Wenwu, 8*, 20–26.

Guthrie, S. E. (1993). *Faces in the clouds: A new theory of religion*. Oxford University Press.

Gutchess, A. H., & Huff, S. (2016). Cross-cultural differences in memory. In *The Oxford handbook of cultural neuroscience* (Vol. 155). Oxford University Press.

Haberstroh, S., Oyserman, D., Schwarz, N., Kühnen, U., & Ji, L. J. (2002). Is the interdependent self more sensitive to question context than the independent self? Self-construal and the observation of conversational norms. *Journal of Experimental Social Psychology, 38*(3), 323–329.

Hatfield, E., Bensman, L., Thornton, P. D., & Rapson, R. L. (2014). New perspectives on emotional contagion: A review of classic and recent research on facial mimicry and contagion. *Interpersona, 8*(2), 159–179.

Henan sheng wenwu kaogu yanjiusuo. (1999). *Wuyang Jiahhu*. 2 Vols. Beijing: Kexue chubanshe.

Henrich, J., & Muthukrishna, M. (2021). The origins and psychology of human cooperation. *Annual Review of Psychology, 72*, 207–240.

Hitokoto, H., Glazer, J., & Kitayama, S. (2016). Cultural shaping of neural responses: Feedback-related potentials vary with self-construal and face priming. *Psychophysiology, 53*(1), 52–63.

Hobson, N. M., Schroeder, J., Risen, J. L., Xygalatas, D., & Inzlicht, M. (2018). The psychology of rituals: An integrative review and process-based framework. *Personality and Social Psychology Review*, 22(3), 260–284.

Hofer, M. A. (1984). Relationships as regulators: A psychobiologic perspective on bereavement. *Psychosomatic Medicine, 46*(3), 183–197.

Hou, G.L., Xu, C.J., & Fan, Q.S. (2010). Three expansions of prehistoric humans towards northeast margin of Qinghai-Tibet Plateau and environmental change. *Dili xuebao (Acta Geographica Sinica), 65*(1), 65–72.

Hu, Y. W., Ambrose, S. H., Wang, C. S. (2006). Stable isotopic analysis of human bones from Jiahu site, Henan, China: Implications for the transition to agriculture. *Journal of Archaeological Science*, 33(9), 1319–1330.

Huang, R., Zhu, C., & Zheng, C. G. (2005). Anhui Huaihe liuyu quanxinshi huanjing yanbian dui xinshiqi yizhi fenbu de yingxiang. *Dili Xuebao, 60*(5), 742–750.

Huang, Y. P., & Sun, Y. Y. (2011) Shuangdun fuhao de goucheng fangshi yiji dui wenzi xingcheng de yingxiang. *Zhongguo Haiyang Daxue Xuebao, 1* (1), 56–61.

Izawa, T. (2007). Adaptation of flowering-time by natural and artificial selection in Arabidopsis and rice. *Journal of Experimental Botany, 58*(12), 3091–3097.

Jiao, T. Long. (2007). *The neolithic of southeast China: Cultural transformation and regional interaction on the coast.* Cambria Press.

Kim, K., & Markman, A. B. (2006). Differences in fear of isolation as an explanation of cultural differences: Evidence from memory and reasoning. *Journal of Experimental Social Psychology, 42*(3), 350–364.

Kitayama, S., Yanagisawa, K., Ito, A., Ueda, R., Uchida, Y., & Abe, N. (2017). Reduced orbitofrontal cortical volume is associated with interdependent self-construal. *Proceedings of the National Academy of Sciences, 114*(30), 7969–7974.

Kitayama, S., Varnum, M. E. W., & Salvador, C. E. (2019). Cultural neuroscience. In D. Cohen & S. Kitayama (Eds.), *Handbook of cultural psychology* (pp. 79–118). The Guilford Press.

Kocovski, N. L., & Endler, N. S. (2000). Social anxiety, self-regulation, and fear of negative evaluation. *European Journal of Personality, 14*(4), 347–358.

Koski, J. E., Xie, H., & Olson, I. R. (2015). Understanding social hierarchies: The neural and psychological foundations of status perception. *Social Neuroscience, 10*(5), 527–550.

Lang, M. (2019). The evolutionary paths to collective rituals: An interdisciplinary perspective on the origins and functions of the basic social act. *Archive for the Psychology of Religion, 41*(3), 224–252.

Larrivé-Bass, S. S. M. (2015). *Embodied materials: The emergence of figural imagery in prehistoric China* (Doctoral dissertation, Columbia University).

Larson, G., Piperno, D. R., Allaby, R. G., Purugganan, M. D., Andersson, L., Arroyo-Kalin, M., … & Fuller, D. Q. (2014). Current perspectives and the future of domestication studies. *Proceedings of the National Academy of Sciences, 111*(17), 6139–6146.

LeDoux, J. E. (2000). Emotion circuits in the brain. *Annual Review of Neuroscience, 23*(1), 155–184.

Lee, Y. K. (2008). Trans. The Neolithic Site at Shuangdun, Bengbu. *Chinese Archaeology, 1*, 92–126.

Legare, C. H., & Wen, N. (2014). The effects of ritual on the development of social group cognition. *International Society for the Study of Behavioral Development, 2*(66), 9–12.

Levinson, S. C., & Enfield, N. J. (Eds.). (2020). *Roots of human sociality: Culture, cognition and interaction.* Routledge.

Levitin, D. J. (2008). *The world in six songs: How the musical brain created human nature.* Penguin.

Lewicka, M. (2011). Place attachment: How far have we come in the last 40 years?. *Journal of Environmental Psychology, 31*(3), 207–230.

Li, J. J., Chen, Z. W., & Yu, S. F. (2001). Lingfengdong—Fujiansheng shouci faxian de jiushiqi shidai zaoqi yizhi. *Renleixue Sxuebao 4*(20), 247–255.

Li, X.W. (2004). Zhongguo shiqian yuqi fanying di yuzhouguan-jianlun Zhongguo dongbu shiqian fuza shehui de shangceng jiaoliuwang. *Dongnan wenhua, 3*(179), 65–72.

Li, W., Tsoraki, C., Lan, W., Yang, Y., Zhang, J., & van Gijn, A. (2019). Cereal processing technique inferred from use-wear analysis at the Neolithic site of Jiahu, Central China. *Journal of Archaeological Science: Reports, 23*, 939–945.

Li, X. Q., Harbottle, G., Zhang, J. Z., & Wang, C. S. (2003). The earliest writing? Sign use in the seventh millennium BC at Jiahu, Henan Province, China. *Antiquity*, 77(295), 31–44.

Li, X. W. (2020). Zhongguo shiqian taoqi tuxiang de fanying de "tianji" guannian. *Zhongyuan Wenwu, 3*, 81–93.

Liu, L., & Chen, X. (2012). *The archaeology of China: From the late Paleolithic to the early Bronze Age*. Cambridge University Press.

Liu, B., Qin, L., & Zhuang Y. J. (2019). Situating the Liangzhu Culture in late Neolithic China: An introduction. In B. Liu and L. Qin (Eds.), *Liangzhu culture* (pp. 1–17). Routledge.

Liu, L. (2004). *The chinese neolithic: Trajectories to early states*. Cambridge University Press.

Liu,L. (2007). Early figurations in China: Ideological, social and ecological implications. In C. Renfrew and I. Morley (Eds.), *Image and imagination: A global prehistory of figurative representation* (pp. 271–284). Cambridge: McDonald Institute for Archaeological Research, University of Cambridge.

Liu, L. (2021). Communal drinking rituals and social formations in the Yellow River valley of Neolithic China. *Journal of Anthropological Archaeology, 63*, 101310.

Liu, L., Lee, G. A., Jiang, L., & Zhang, J. (2007). Evidence for the early beginning (c. 9000 cal. BP) of rice domestication in China: a response. *The Holocene, 17*(8), 1059–1068.

Liu, R., Liu, H., & Chen, S. (2020). Alternative adaptation strategy during the Paleolithic–Neolithic transition: Potential use of aquatic resources in the Western Middle Yangtze Valley, China. *Quaternary, 3*(3), 28–45.

Luo, W. H., Gu, C. G., Yang, Y. Z., Zhang, D., Liang Z. H., Li, J. Huang, C. Q., & Zhang, J. Z. (2019). Phytoliths reveal the earliest interplay of rice and broomcorn millet at the site of Shuangdun (ca. 7.3–6.8 ka BP) in the middle Huai River valley, China. *Journal of Archaeological Science, 102*, 26–34.

Major, J. S. (1993). *Heaven and earth in early Han thought: Chapters three, four, and five of the Huainanzi*. SUNY Press.

Manzo, L. C. & Devine-Wright, P. (Eds.). (2014). *Place attachment: Advances in theory, method and applications*. Routledge.

Marshack, A., Bandi, H. G., Christensen, J., Gallus, A., Gunn, J., Johansen, A. B., … & Odak, O. (1979). Upper Paleolithic symbol systems of the Russian Plain: Cognitive and comparative analysis [and comments and reply]. *Current Anthropology, 20*(2), 271–311.

Mattan, B. D., Kubota, J. T., & Cloutier, J. (2017). How social status shapes person perception and evaluation: A social neuroscience perspective. *Perspectives on Psychological Science, 12*(3), 468–507.

McDonald, R. J., & White, N. M. (2013). A triple dissociation of memory systems: hippocampus, amygdala, and dorsal striatum. Behavioural Neuroscience, *107*(1), 3–22.

McGaugh, J. L. (2004). The amygdala modulates the consolidation of memories of emotionally arousing experiences. *Annual Review of Neuroscience, 27*, 1–28.

McGovern, P. E., Zhang, J., Tang, J., Zhang, Z., Hall, G. R., Moreau, R. A., … & Wang, C. (2004). Fermented beverages of pre-and proto-historic China. *Proceedings of the National Academy of Sciences, 101*(51), 17593–17598.

Mechias, M. L., Etkin, A., & Kalisch, R. (2010). A meta-analysis of instructed fear studies: Implications for conscious appraisal of threat. *Neuroimage, 49*(2), 1760–1768.

Mikulska, K. (2014). On numbers, tables and calendars: When writing appeared. *Contributions in New World Archeology*, 7, 47–72.

Molina, J., Sikora, M., Garud, N., Flowers, J. M., Rubinstein, S., Reynolds, A., … & Purugganan, M. D. (2011). Molecular evidence for a single evolutionary origin of domesticated rice. *Proceedings of the National Academy of Sciences, 108*(20), 8351–8356

Monfries, M. M., & Kafer, N. F. (1994). Private self-consciousness and fear of negative evaluation. *Journal of Psychology, 128*(4), 447.

Mu, Y., Kitayama, S., Han, S., & Gelfand, M. J. (2015). How culture gets embrained: Cultural differences in event-related potentials of social norm violations. *Proceedings of the National Academy of Sciences, 112*(50), 15348–15353.

Needham, J. (1970). *Science and civilisation in China, Vol. 3. Mathematics and the sciences of the heavens and the earth.* Cambridge: Cambridge University Press.

Nisbett, R. E., Peng, K., Choi, I., & Norenzayan, A. (2001). Culture and systems of thought: Holistic versus analytic cognition. *Psychological Review, 108*(2), 291.

Nisbett, R. E., Peng, K., Choi, I., & Norenzayan, A. (2008). Culture and systems of thought: Holistic versus analytic cognition. In J. Adler and L.J. Rips (Eds.), *Reasoning: Studies of human inference and its foundations* (pp.965–985). Cambridge.

Northoff, G. (2018). *The spontaneous brain: From the mind-body to the world-brain problem.* MIT Press.

Ota, H., Yashukawa, Y., Fu, J., & Chen, T.-H. (2009). Cuora flavomarginata (Gray 1863)—Yellow-Margined Box Turtle. In H. Ota, Y. Yashukawa, J. Fu, T.-H. Chen (Eds.), *Conservation on biology of freshwater turtles and tortoises: A compilation project of the IUCN/SSC tortoise and freshwater turtle specialist group* (pp. 035.1–035.10). Chelonian Research Monographs, no. 5. Chelonian Research Foundation.

Panksepp, J. (2009). The emotional antecedents to the evolution of music and language. *Musicae Scientiae, 13*(2_suppl), 229–259.

Pankenier, D. W. (2004). A brief history of Beiji 北極 (Northern Culmen), with an excursus on the origin of the character di 亲. *Journal of the American Oriental Society, 124*(2), 211–236.

Pankenier, D. W. (2005). Astronomy in early Chinese sources. In V. H. Mair, N. S. Steinhardt, and P. R. Goldin (Eds.), *Hawai 'i reader in traditional Chinese culture* (pp. 18–27). University of Hawaii Press.

Pankenier, D. W. (2009). Locating true north in Ancient China. *Cosmology Across Cultures, 409*, 128.

Pankenier, D. W. (2013). *Astrology and cosmology in early China: conforming earth to heaven.* Cambridge.

Pankenier, D. W. (2015). Weaving metaphors and cosmo-political thought in early China. *T'oung Pao, 101*(1-3), 1–34.

Palmer, C. J., & Clifford, C. W. (2020). Face pareidolia recruits mechanisms for detecting human social attention. *Psychological Science, 31*(8), 1001–1012.

Parham, J. F., Stuart, B. L., Bour, R., & Fritz, U. (2004). Evolutionary distinctiveness of the extinct Yunnan box turtle (Cuora yunnanensis) reealed by DNA from an old museum specimen. *Proceedings of the Royal Society of London. Series B: Biological Sciences, 271*(suppl_6), S391–S394.

Park, J., & Kitayama, S. (2014). Interdependent selves show face-induced facilitation of error processing: cultural neuroscience of self-threat. *Social Cognitive and Affective Neuroscience, 9*(2), 201–208.

Parkington, J. (2001). Presidential address: Mobility, seasonality and southern African hunter-gatherers. *The South African Archaeological Bulletin, 56*(173/174), 1–7.

Piccaluga, G. (2005). Calendars: An overview. In L. Jones (Ed.), *Encyclopedia of religion.* (Vol. 3. 2nd ed). Gale.

Rao, Z. Y. (1999). Lun gui wei shuimu ji youguan wenti. *Wenwu*, 10, 35–37.

Rappenglück, M. A. (2012). Stone age people controlling time and space: Evidences for measuring instruments and methods in earlier prehistory and the roots of mathematics, astronomy, and metrology. *Scientific Cosmopolitanism and Local Cultures: Religions, Ideologies, Societies*, 164–165.

Rappenglück, M. A. (2013). Palaeolithic stargazers and todays astro maniacs-methodological concepts of cultural astronomy focused on case studies of earlier prehistory. *DRU [TVO Antropologov Slovenije Slovene Anthropological Society]*, 85.

Rappenglück, M. A. (2013). The housing of the world: The significance of cosmographic concepts for habitation. *Nexus Network Journal, 5*(3), 387–422.

Rappenglück M. A. (2018). The world tree: Categorisation and reading of an archaic cosmographic concept. *Journal of Skyscape Archaeology, 3*(2), 253–267.

Raymond, C. M., Brown, G., Weber, Delene. (2010). The measurement of place attachment: Personal, community, and environmental connections. *Journal of Environmental Psychology, 30*(4), 422–434.

Richerson, P., Baldini, R., Bell, A. V., Demps, K., Frost, K., Hillis, V., … & Zefferman, M. (2016). Cultural group selection plays an essential role in explaining human cooperation: A sketch of the evidence. *Behavioral and Brain Sciences, 39*, E30.

Rhodin, A. G., Thomson, S., Georgalis, G., Karl, H. V., Danilov, I. G., Takahashi, A., … & van Dijk, P. P. (2015). Turtles and tortoises of the world during the rise and global spread of humanity: first checklist and review of extinct Pleistocene and Holocene chelonians. doi: 10.3854/crm.5.000e.fossil.checklist.v1.2015

Rossano, M. J. (2007). Supernaturalizing social life. *Human Nature, 18*(3), 272–294.

Rossano, M. J. (2009). Ritual behaviour and the origins of modern cognition. *Cambridge Archaeological Journal, 19*(2), 243–256.

Rossano, M. J. (2010). Making friends, making tools, and making symbols. *Current Anthropology, 51*(S1), S89–S98.

Rossano, M. J. (2012). The essential role of ritual in the transmission and reinforcement of social norms. *Psychological Bulletin, 138*(3), 529–549.

Rossi, F., Gianola, S., & Corvetti, L. (2007). Regulation of intrinsic neuronal properties for axon growth and regeneration. *Progress in Neurobiology, 81*(1), 1–28.

Sampson, G. (1985). *Writing systems.* London, UK: Hutchinson.

Savo, V., Lepofsky, D., Benner, J. P., Kohfeld, K. E., Bailey, J., & Lertzman, K. (2016). Observations of climate change among subsistence-oriented communities around the world. *Nature Climate Change, 6*(5), 462–473.

Scannell, L., Gifford, R., & Sarich, C. (2020). Parallels between interpersonal and place attachment: An update. In Lynne C. Manzo and P. Devine-Wright (Eds.), *Place attachment: Advances in theory, methods and applications* (p. 45). Routledge.

Shear, K., Shair, H. (2005). Attachment, loss, and complicated grief. *Developmental Psychobiology: The Journal of the International Society for Developmental Psychobiology*, *47*(3), 253–267.

Shelach, G. (2006). *Leadership strategies, economic activity, and interregional interaction: social complexity in northeast China*. Springer Science & Business Media.

Shelach, G. (2016). *Prehistoric societies on the northern frontiers of China: archaeological perspectives on identity formation and economic change during the first millennium BCE*. Routledge.

Shim, J. S., & Jang, G. (2020). Environmental signal-dependent regulation of flowering time in rice. *International Journal of Molecular Sciences*, *21*(17), 6155.

Smith, B. L., & Lee, Y. K. (2008). Mortuary treatment, pathology, and social relations of the Jiahu community. *Asian Perspectives*, *47*, 242–298.

Sosi, R., Wildman, W., & McNamara, P. (2013). On the naturalness of religion. *Religion, Brain & Behavior*, 3, 89–90.

Steckler, C. M., & Tracy, J. L. (2014). The emotional underpinnings of social status. In J.T. Cheng (Ed.), *The psychology of social status* (pp. 201–224). Springer.

Sznycer, D. (2019). Forms and functions of the self-conscious emotions. *Trends in Cognitive Sciences*, *23*(2), 143–157.

Sznycer, D., Tooby, J., Cosmides, L., Porat, R., Shalvi, S., & Halperin E. (2016). Shame closely tracks the threat of devaluation by others, even across cultures. *Procedings from the national Academy of Scienes of the United States of America PNAS March 8*, 113 (10) 2625–2630.

Sznycer, D., Xygalatas, D., Agey, E., Alami, S., An, X. F., Ananyeva, K. I., … & Tooby, J. (2018). Cross-cultural invariances in the architecture of shame. *Proceedings of the National Academy of Sciences*, *115*(39), 9702–9707.

Teng, S. P. (2000). The original significance of bi disks: Insights based on Liangzhu jade bi with incised symbolic motifs. *Journal of East Asian Archaeology*, *2*(1), 165–194.

Thuillard, M., Le Quellec, J. L., d'Huy, J., & Berezkin, Y. (2018). A large-scale study of world myths. *Trames: A Journal of the Humanities and Social Sciences*, *22*(4), A1–A44.

Tomasello, M., Melis, A. P., Tennie, C., Wyman, E., Herrmann, E., Gilby, I. C., … & Herrmann, E. (2012). Two key steps in the evolution of human cooperation: The interdependence hypothesis. *Current Anthropology*, *53*(6), 673–692.

Tseng, L. Y. (2011). *Picturing heaven in Early China* (Vol. 336). Harvard University Press.

Underhill, A. (2013). Introduction: Investigating the development and nature of complex societies in Ancient China. In A. P. Underhill (Ed.), *A companion to Chinese archaeology*. Oxford University Press.

Van Bockstaele, B., Verschuere, B., Tibboel, H., De Houwer, J., Crombez, G., & Koster, E.H.W. (2014). A review of current evidence for the causal impact of attentional bias on fear and anxiety. *Psychological Bulletin*, *140*(3), 682.

Wang, F. (2013). The Houli and Beixin Cultures. In A.P. Underhill (Ed.), *A companion to Chinese archaeology* (pp. 389–410). Oxford University Press.

Wang, W. M., Ding, J. L., Shu, J. W., & Chen, W. (2010). Exploration of early rice farming in China. *Quaternary International*, *227*(1), 22–28.

Watson-Jones, R. E., & Legare, C. H. (2016). The social functions of group rituals. *Current Directions in Psychological Science*, *25*(1), 42–46.

Wheatley, P. (1971). *The pivot of the four quarters: A preliminary enquiry into the origins and character of the ancient Chinese city*. Aldine Publishing Company.

Wu, Y., Jiang, L., Zheng, Y., Wang, C., & Zhao, Z. (2014). Morphological trend analysis of rice phytolith during the early Neolithic in the Lower Yangtze. *Journal of Archaeological Science, 49*, 326–331.

Xibeidaxue wenbuxueyuan. 2000. *Fufeng Anban yizhifajue baogao*. Kexue chubanshe.

Yang, X. N. (2004). New perspectives on China's past. *Chinese archaeology in the twentieth century*. Volume 2. *Major archaeological discoveries in twentieth-century China*. Yale University Press.

Ye, X. K., & Zhang, J. Z. (1994). Wuyang Jiahu yizhizhong de guibie lei. *Renleixue xuebao. 13* (1), 32–39.

Zeder, M. A. (2015). Core questions in domestication research. *Proceedings of the National Academy of Sciences, 112*(11), 3191–3198.

Zhang J. Z., & Cui Q. L. (2013). The Jiahu Site in the Huai River Area. In A.P. Underhill (Ed.), *A companion to Chinese archaeology* (pp. 194–212). Oxford University Press.

Zhang, J. Z., Xiao, X. H., & Lee, Y. K. (2004). The early development of music. Analysis of the Jiahu bone flutes. *Antiquity, 78*(302), 769–778.

Zhang, L., & Fang, Y. (2006). Shuangdun yizhi yu shuangdun wenhua zheji. *Jianghuai wenshi, 6*, 160–169.

Zheng, Y., Crawford, G. W., Jiang, L., & Chen, X. (2016). Rice domestication revealed by reduced shattering of archaeological rice from the Lower Yangtze valley. *Scientific Reports, 6*(1), 1–9.

Zhu, Y.P. (2013). The early Neolithic in the Central Yellow River Valley, c. 7000–4000 BC. In A.P. Underhill (Ed.), *Companion to Chinese archaeology* (pp. 171–193). Hoboken, NJ:Wiley-Blackwell.

Zong, Y. Q., Wang, Z., Innes, J. B., & Chen, Z. (2012). Holocene environmental change and Neolithic rice agriculture in the lower Yangtze region of China: A review. *The Holocene, 22*(6), 623–635.

4

ECOLOGICAL INHERITANCE, PRESTIGE, AND THE EVOLUTION OF A CHINESE LEADERSHIP MINDSET

This chapter extends the idea that the interaction between humans and Turtle established a neuro substrate, a founding architecture that shaped Neolithic cultural development. I zero in on the degree to which celestial observations became a system for distributing symbolic cognition. More specifically, the relationship with Turtle became an "integral part of [culture's] replicative machinery."[1] Turtle culture was a "storehouse of crucial replicative information for certain aspects of [a] collective cognitive matrix."[2] It was necessary to reproduce cognitive systems horizontally and vertically among social groups (Figure 4.1).

Memory repositories of Turtle culture that were vertically transmitted included literacy codes and structures necessary for it to operate as a "collective aspect of cognition."[3] The culture that emerged from the relationship with Turtle established a blueprint for cultural transmission. This blueprint was configured by a particular complex of symbolic systems related to celestial legibility: neural structures emerged from areas of the brain that were appropriated by the demands of "reading" Sky. Specific synapses strengthened by such experiences of reading, made it possible for cultural descendants "to interact with and use the cognitive instruments" and thereby continue to engage in a celestially legible culture.[4]

The construction of early calendars always implied some theoretic development, in the sense that implicit models were being built on the basis of astronomical events. We saw how Box Turtle symbols represented the fruits of systematic and selective observation, seasonal coding, visual storage of ecological

1 Donald (2000, 20).
2 Ibid.
3 Ibid. (22).
4 Ibid.

DOI: 10.4324/9781003215134-4

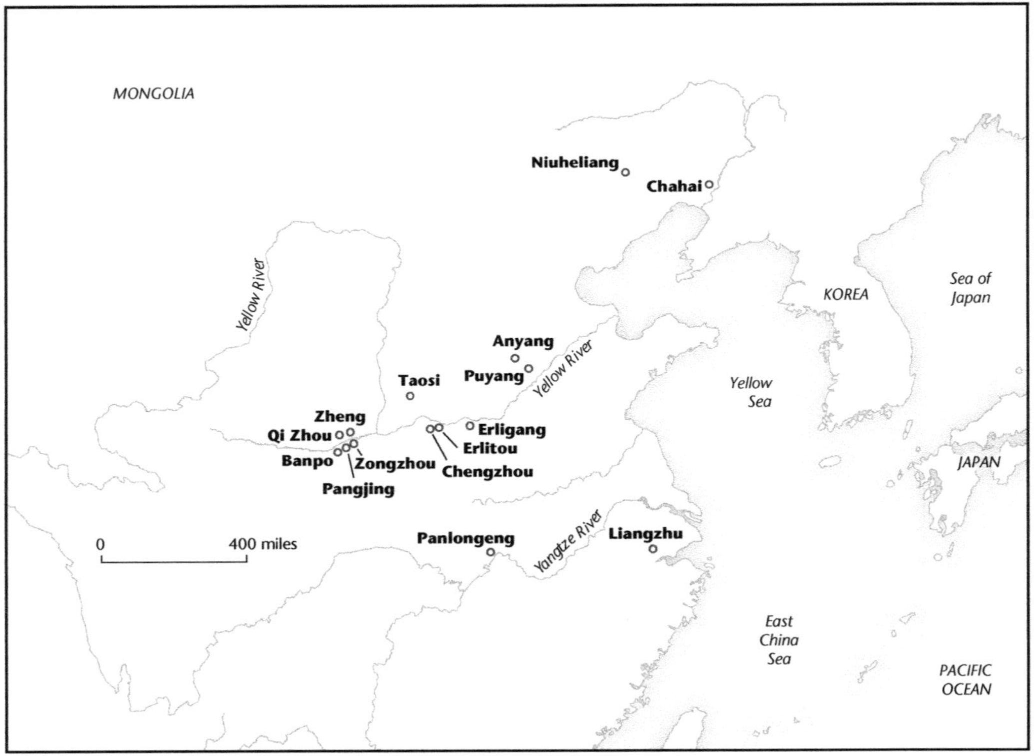

FIGURE 4.1 Map of important archaeological sites and locations mentioned in Chapters 4 and 5

information; and the extrapolation from it of regularities which support the formulation of predictions.[5]

My understanding of celestial legibility is shaped by the findings of recent studies that investigate the behavioral markers and neural selectivity patterns related to expert processing of faces. The brain's capacity for "fine, subordinate-level discrimination between highly similar objects (e.g., faces of two siblings or between two fingerprints)" is due to its ability to extract "configural information of faces as a whole rather than as a collection of individual face features."[6] This capacity for "holistic" processing results from "perceptual expertise," Expertise is conditioned by repeated experiences of refinement, and "a history of learned attention to diagnostic parts."[7] During the "acquisition of expertise, holistic processing develops as an optimal way to fulfill the demand of fine discrimination."[8]

Holistic processes are also indicated in celestial reading. Neurological studies have shown how holistic processes for discriminating faces have correlates in processes related to visual word recognition. While Turtle, and other celestial zoomorphs to be discussed immediately, are not words, nonetheless, they do carry semantic meaning. The meaning can be "read" thanks to the brain's efficient capacities to extract configural information of celestial regions as part of a whole scene rather than as made up of discrete objects. Neuroscientific studies on reading learning show changes in perceptions of letters (e.g., Turtle) once perceptual expertise was achieved; mastery facilitated a shift in attention from an individually focused system into a multi-component one.[9]

Similarly, recognition of the celestial sign Turtle, facilitated a shift in attention from an individually focused system into a multi-component, one including Turtle, Sky River, and, over time, other zoomorphic configurations. This system evolved into a process in which visual and conceptual systems interacted. Holistic reading operations were also involved with the distribution and retrieval of stored structures related to spatial memory. They exerted a formidable epigenetic role in the evolution of Chinese sociopolitical culture. I foreground the neurological underpinnings of celestial legibility because I want to highlight how they *encoded an obligation to attend to all object parts* (emphasis mine),[10] and even more to the point, how this endemic obligation was a key driver of Chinese cultural evolution.

The link between visual attention and memory processes plays a central role. Celestial perception was controlled by prior knowledge and an unconscious

5 Jiang et al. (2018) argue that cognitive control in the form of predictions are influenced by external cues as well as internal ones deriving from cognitive history.
6 Ventura et al. (2020, 2745). See also Ventura (2014); Wong et al. (2012).
7 Ventura et al. (2020, 2740).
8 Wong et al. (2012, 7). Cf. Ventura et al. (2020, 2739).
9 Richler et al. (2011).
10 Ventura et al. (2020, 2747).

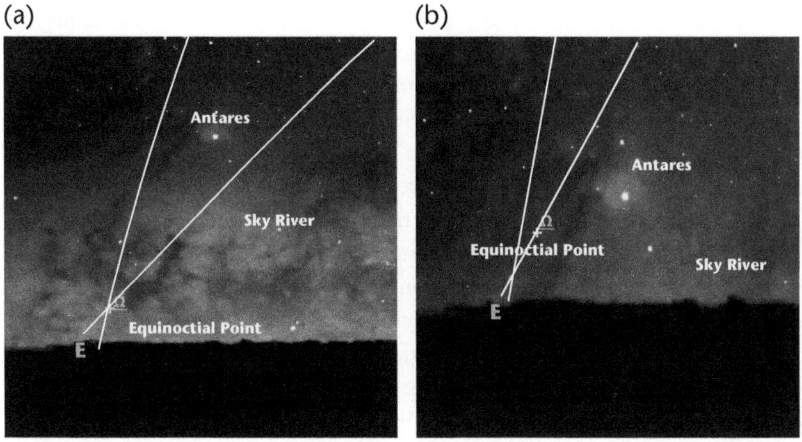

FIGURE 4.2 (a–b) Fire Star announcing imminent arrival of Spring, 4300 B.C., and its coincidence with the arrival of spring, 3200 B.C. Sky River magnified by 4x for emphasis

Source: Redrawn from screenshot based on Stellarium, an open source software.

affective evaluation, which influenced the active selection of (related) information at very early stages of cultural processing. This chapter identifies two instances of celestial perception that catalyzed the trajectory of cultural evolution. The observed phenomena were: the appearance, circa 4300 B.C., of a red supergiant star (Antares, Alpha Scorpii), aptly called the Fire Star (*huoxing*), which assumed Turtle's vernal harbinger role;[11] (Figure 4.2) and the rare close massing of the five planets visible with the naked eye (Mercury, Venus, Mars, Jupiter, Saturn) in 1059 B.C., respectively. The latter event was invoked to advance dynastic claims by the Western Zhou dynastic founders.[12] All events were attributed to suprasensible intentions of the Pole Star.

Integrating neuroscientific concepts to explain the iconicity of celestial configurations highlights the mechanism that explains why observations of these astronomical phenomena were historically fateful. Perception of the celestial phenomena cannot be separated from its pre-evaluation and filtering by social conditions, especially those surrounding Turtle. These factors had both a direct and an indirect influence on later observers' cognitive and affective evaluation of stellar configurations. As discussed in the previous chapter, the strength of the affective reaction (amygdala) triggered by the perceptual and conceptual deviance (hippocampus) created an obstacle to create a retrievable memory of the relational object; the socio-emotional need to first drain Turtle of contaminating seasonal

11 Porter (1996, 39); Cf. Pankenier (2013, 51). Feng (1990, 55).

12 Shang is a self-referential name, used to refer to their territory and capital as Great Settlement Shang (Da Yi Shang).

associations all the while preserving an affective veneration for it, was manifested in the emergence of a turtle-based cosmovision.

I construe this cosmology as a precursor for a neuroaesthetic interpretative code. Neuroscientific studies have affirmed the gestalt psychological pictorial theory advanced by Rudolf Arnheim in 1954. Findings that demonstrate how "seeing" is a function of constantly reviewing and correcting processes of perception, dovetail Arnheim's theory that "seeing" is not merely a function of recording of sensory impressions; instead, it is a "creative understanding of reality."[13] For this reason emotional conditions related to unpredictability and surprise are thus important factors that challenge visual perception.

Considering how the relationship with Turtle would have led to perceptions of celestial stimuli as imbued with strong valence (aversion and alignment), it is understandable why its status as a key image and catalyst for iconic coding was burned deeply into the cultural consciousness and memory of Neolithic China. Its influence on conceptions of celestial legibility became one of the most deeply ingrained parts of Chinese collective cultural memory.

A lens formed by the complementary integration of findings offered by neuroscientific, perceptual, cognitive, emotional, and sociopsychological scholarship, foregrounds the role played in Chinese cultural evolution by the presence of a pre-existing cultural mental architecture. When we remember how it is characterized by heightened attention to background context, heightened sensitivity to spatial deviance, not to mention risk aversive motivation, we are in a position to better understand the particular responses to the two phenomena I have identified as defining cultural forces in ancient China.

My point is not to reduce the complex phenomenon of cultural epigenesis to an astronomically determined teleology. Rather I aim to foreground a pattern of socioemotional conditions to nuance historical explanations for the evolution of sociopolitical behavior. I look at the psychological impact exerted by observations of celestial phenomena on cultural behavior. Because cultural constructs changed with each response, the line of evolution was never direct. Instead, what emerges is a spiral-shaped line of contiguity, defined by events and the co-evolved responses they triggered over time.

Thus, the coincidence of Fire Star's positionality, brilliance and regularity, with spring's arrival, stimulated emotional metabolization that would have scaffolded on memory and repicative mechanisms forged by psychoneurological responses to the time when Turtle's seasonal coincidence first came to consciousness: similar mental mechanisms were recruited to respond to similar environmental interactions.[14] The fact of this "shortcut" is manifested in a shared cultural language that reveals the relationship between Chinese Neolithic

13 Van de Cruys and Wagemans (2011).
14 Sosis (2009).

settlement occupants and this star to be "vestige" of a primary intersubjective relationship with Turtle.

As we shall see, the material culture recovered at two contemporaneous, yet geographically distinct, Middle Neolithic cultural centers, is salient with environmentally cued cultural expression. Both expressions reveal evidence of the development of beliefs and behaviors organized around maintaining proximity to Fire Star and the Pole Star, which evolved from earlier relational experiences with Turtle. Only once we consider the symbolic system's functional goal as a strategy for proximity maintenance can we begin to understand what drives the recurring coalescence of cognitive, emotional, and behavioral elements that make up the system.

Studies of ancient group organization have shown how iconic images were used to signal and project commitment to protecting the group. This may relate to the origins of celestial marker shapes, which externalized loyalty to the group it represented. Group leaders capable of regulating human activities to align with seasonal agricultural rhythms represented by the icons "achieved a net benefit and other status benefits available to trusted signalers."[15] Evolutionary cognitive scientist Richard Sosis suggests that such ritual and cultural mechanisms probably promoted in-group trust essential for channeling public prestige conferral. The rituals may have also operated as a social strategy to persuade the wealthy to "overcome [social] commitment problems."[16] He reasons that the "costliness of religious activities… belief, behavior (rituals), badges (such as religious attire) and bans (taboos)" enables them to serve as reliable and honest signals of group commitment. Only those who are committed to the group will be willing to incur the time, energetic, and opportunity costs" of consistent ritual performances."[17]

While deeply ingrained cognitive and emotional properties are the products of evolutionary history, differences in socioenvironmental input led to differential outcomes in real-life settings. The shift in conceptions of prestige from being an asset conferred by public scrutiny of a group member's contribution to the public good, to being an asset conferred to a lineage by an external, evaluative, suprasensible entity, is one such case. A study on second millennium B.C. cities located in the Central Plains finds that prestige conferral was still related to public good intentions manifested in wall and dike building. By the time early cities associated with Shang rule emerged, such as Zhengzhou and Panlongcheng, they began to exhibit a political economic model "centered on a kingship that was peripatetic within a royal demesne, moving between residences but also concentrating people and resources in a massive primate center."[18]

15 Sosis (2009, 351).
16 Ibid.
17 Ibid.
18 Campbell et al. (2021, 20).

The establishment of a concept of Shang royalty, indeed the concept of political legitimacy, has been ascribed to the intrasubjective relationship held between the Shang, the Pole Star deity, Di, and the dynasty's founders and subsequent rulers. The Zhou, who were acculturated by the former through political and familial socialization, emerge as a repository for the vertical transmission of an evolving cultural architecture. Written records—the earliest extant example of Chinese writing—recovered at the late Shang Central Plains capital at Anyang, Henan, provide incontrovertible evidence of centralized authority. The language, inscribed on turtle plastrons that had been prepared to use for pyromantic divination, recorded all or part of the divination process, which clearly reflect assumptions about royal power.

The ancient practice of applying a burning ember to an animal shell is well attested. The Shang are the first to prefer turtle plastrons, as opposed to cow scapula, and the first to prepare the plastrons for burning by carving a hollow (or two) along the plastron's axial line. This act suggests an interest in manipulating the response, manifested as cracks that jutted out horizontally from the axis.[19] Keightley and others surmise that the cracking sound was believed to represent "the voices or responses of those spirits and, in particular, their acceptance or rejection of the sacrifice."[20]

The mindset portrayed by the divination texts provides a portal for investigating the effects of the transmission of a functional collective architecture to that of individual minds and brains. Shang kings' psychology was inscribed in written records devoted to "fixing" and "aligning" proposed acts with sought and anticipated intentions of external evaluators. Similarly, the attitudes of early Western Zhou kings, whose anxious mindset we may infer from expressive bronze inscriptions, yield a vantage point from which to view Western Zhou royal cultural behavior as an epigenetic descendant of the Shang.

Fire Star, Dragon, and Alignment in Hongshan and Yangshao Culture Ceremonial Centers

This section advances the idea that an awareness of Fire Star's astro-calendrical regularity explains formal and thematic overlaps in Hongshan (4500–3000 B.C.) and Yangshao (5050-3050 B.C.) cultural expression. Inhabitants of both settlements, one located in the Liao River area of southeastern Inner Mongolia, northeastern Hebei, Liaoning and south central and western Jilin, and the other squarely within the Yellow River Central Plains, would have noted Fire Star's harbinger role toward the end of the fifth century. I contend that occupants of both sites relied on its increasing proximity to the vernal scene up to ca. 3200

19 For history of pyromantic divination see Flad et al. (2008). For manipulative possibilities see Song (2018).
20 Keightley (2006, 185).

B.C., to organize and manage agricultural activities and attendant sociopolitical events. Texts dating from the first millennium B.C. record the impact Fire Star exerted on social organization, analogizing its role to the invention of fire. Visibility of Antares' red hue, from its first appearance around the spring equinox, and its last at the autumn equinox, before it dipped below the western horizon, communicated important agrarian information. It demarcated the times when "fires should be brought out and brought in."[21]

I hypothesize that Fire Star's appearance stimulated specific distributed cognitive synapses that had been strengthened by repeated efforts to render space legible in the wake of Turtle's withdrawal. These synapses made it possible for cultural descendants "to interact with and use the cognitive instruments" to adapt to new conditions and cognitive awareness.[22] For example, the bright Fire Star was incorporated into a legible celestial zoomorph by virtue of the same neurocognitive process that produced a "pareidolia Turtle." Just as Box Turtle sets preserved and conveyed information about Turtle's celestial role, the same might be said of the "dragon tail" iconography, represented by a hooked curve, in Hongshan jade figuration. Scholarship that advances an astronomical interpretation for the symbolic significance of the jade objects have linked the "dragon tail" to the constellation Tail (Scorpius), which is situated in Sky River, north of Turtle.[23] It is impossible to discern when Fire Star was incorporated into the "legible zoomorphic space" to become Heart to the celestial Dragon's Tail, but like Turtle, Dragon had a terrestrial referent, the alligator (*Alligator sinensis*).[24]

This section argues that Fire Star's calendrical role is undertheorized in scholarship that acknowledges this period as one that witnessed increased agricultural production, subsequent population expansion, and the effects of this growth on cultural production, including channels for prestige conferral.[25] Recent scholarship shows an intensification and expansion of mixed agriculture based on the deployment of multiple crop structures within the Yangtze River valley. Intensification would have been a function of the capacity to predict yields, which would be more accurate when calculated on the basis of important astro-calendrical knowledge.[26] If "the environmental basis for agricultural [risk]

---

21 Pankenier (1981); Porter (1996, 40).
22 Donald (2000, 24).
23 See Feng Shi (1990a, 52–60, 69; and especially 1990b, 108–118). For a detailed discussion tying this graphic representation to subsequent cosmological conceptions and artifacts, see Li (1992, 3). Feng (1993, 9–17) has also studied the stone altars of the Hongshan culture dating from around 3000 BCE, concluding that they were used for sacrifices to a sky god and/or heavenly bodies such as the Sun and Moon; see also Tian (1998, 21–68).
24 Porter (1996, 55–56); Wu et al. (2019).
25 Shelach-Lavi (2018, 29–33); Pechenkina (2018, 49, 53).
26 Li et al. (2020). Drennan et al. (2020) note population growth that was new in Hongshan times.

strategies chosen by Neolithic farmers" is, as recent scholarship argues, essential for understanding why regional settlement and cultural development trajectories differed, this section argues that such distinctions should not obscure the possibility that a calendrical strategy for risk management may have operated in both contexts in different ways.[27]

Before continuing it is important to account for evidence of a mosaic figuration of what archaeologists have argued was the earliest representation of the alligator/dragon found at a fifth millennium B.C. stratum of Xinglongwa cultural remains at Chahai. The figure was discovered laid out at the center of a cemetery located in the southeastern end of the settlement at a place that was thought to have also served as an altar. The dating of the find antedates the spatiotemporal event I identify as catalyzing the formation of a shared cultural language, and the use of color variations at the site to communicate something about the form seems to anticipate Hongshan visual affordances.

While there is nothing that would mitigate against an earlier conceptualization of Tail—the determining feature of what is identified as a dragon, the long gap between the Chahai form and Middle Neolithic representations suggests the local idiom did not "catch" on till more than a millennium later. Chang and Sun's argument against interpreting the form as a dragon is also compelling. They argue that interpretations of the mosaic form should be guided by the prominent snake and toad motif found on pottery also recovered at the site. They claim these animals are ancient symbols for fertile reproductive organs. Claiming that the Chahai ritual site was a location for reproductive worship, the (snake) figure symbolized male fertility.[28]

The salience of shared celestial imagery reflected in prestige objects recovered at Hongshan and Yangshao cultural sites, notwithstanding the different risk buffering methods chosen by each farming population to protect their crops, exemplifies how distinct cultural styles emerged from the "spiraling intensification and expansion" of celestial iconography, and the social and cultural patterns they generated.[29] The distinct ecological conditions that confronted Hongshan and Yangshao culture farmers offer a potent context to begin this line of inquiry. Material evidence of settlement densities affirms that distinct social dynamics operating in the two cultures derived from ecological conditions that elicited different strategies to protect agricultural subsistence "from the dual risks of flooding and drought."[30] Whereas Yangshao settlements

27 Drennan et al. (2020, 8).
28 Chang and Sun (2017); see also Lü ((2018, 17) who details snake and toad traditions in ancient ethnographical accounts.
29 Drennan et al. (2020, 10).
30 Ibid. (4).

were large and densely populated, Hongshan cultural sites reflected "dispersed residence patterns, [the] absence of compact villages."[31]

The dearth of dense villages has been interpreted as an indication that "interdependence and cooperative action to cope with subsistence risk" was not necessary for the emergence of an effective agricultural system that could buttress a "pan-regional" ritual culture and ideology.[32] However, the public scale of the ceremonial architecture begs the question of what motivated and who engaged in these acts of environmental engineering in the absence of compact villages. Elizabeth Childs-Johnson and Zhang et al. observe that Hongshan ceremonial sites shared a range of features that required the mobilization of "substantial labour to build these constructions," not to mention the development of craft skills capable of producing the artifacts buried at the ritual center.[33]

Childs-Johnson makes a persuasive case for the existence of a Jade Age, by which she means the "significance of jade (primarily neophrite) to the identity of the East Asian Heartland during the late Neolithic period."[34] Her nuanced tracing of subtle yet recognizable relationships between Hongshan and Lingjiatan jade shapes and their implicit legacy on Liangzhu jade culture, notwithstanding the latter's distinct cultural style and content, anticipates my current interest. Although recently she has claimed that no "thoroughgoing cultural iconography that was incorporated into the historic period" was produced during this era, her earlier work on Hongshan jades all but identifies the Hongshan "dragon" shape as such an icon.[35] While she does not link the "curling," "C-shaped body" to Tail, she does connect it to the "hooked cloud" (*gouyun*) design, which she claims represents ancient interests in rain-bearing entities. Qiu et al. demonstrate how Tail/Dragon worship—with the use of clay dragons—was connected to rain prayers.[36]

Childs-Johnson concludes that there was equivalence between Shang dynasty graphic data denoting the word "dragon" and Hongshan artistic imagery.[37] I build off her observation that "Hongshan was one of the cultural influences that contributed to the historic tradition that came to define northern China in Shang times,"[38] by anchoring it within an astro-calendrical context. I argue that the legibility generated by the pareidolia-Dragon recapitulated an earlier psychological tendency to respond socially to nonhuman (stellar) objects. Conceptualized as an embodied agent, Dragon, like Turtle, interacted socially with those involved in crop production activity; their actions were synced seasonally. Dragon's movements were ascribed with properties,

31 Ibid. (1, 4, 8).
32 Ibid. (1, 8).
33 Childs-Johnson (2021b, 103); Zhang et al. (2013, 5).
34 Childs-Johnson (1991,2021b, 102).
35 Ibid.
36 Qiu and Fowler (1985).
37 Childs-Johnson (1991, 93).
38 Ibid.

character and mental states, which found expression in non-verbal patterns. Also, Dragon's behavior, consistent and predictable, endowed it with social capacities that satisfied the social needs of populations who bonded with it. These prosocial conditions made regular interactions with Dragon meaningful.

The Turtle and Dragon stellar zoomorphs both derived meaning from their relationship with Sky River, their forms emanated from the holistic process of "reading" astronomical verities. I claim that observing their seasonal habits was likely an influential factor in the assessment of a ritual site's "visual affordances," which was an essential part of the selection of Hongshan ceremonial sites.[39] Zhang et al. provide a succinct and evocative description of the spatial logic reflected in Hongshan ritual centers: all reveal a preference for the "southwestern margins of the overall Hongshan cultural area… on the tops of low hills, within river valleys, and with high mountains as background which led to their having expansive views of the surrounding countryside and potentially high levels of connection between individual locations."[40] The authors claim that these shared contexts served as a conduit for "micro-cosmographical expressions," which include possible symbolic meanings of the material culture recovered at the sites.[41] Resonance between jade objects including turtles and dragons are found in the landscape, such as an altar complex at the Hongshan site of Caomaoshan.[42]

Site choice, ritually oriented ecological engineering, and jade object symbolism, all operated as visuographic devices for storing collectively important—I argue astro-calendrical—information. Looking closely at how the "visual affordances" carried representational meaning beyond the site-specific context brings to the fore a reliance on visual devices to shape a north-south line of sight that operated as a syntactic pattern relating visual participants to each other in meaningful ways.[43] These visual devices formed the basis of a space-based semiotics shared by and thereby connecting the ritual centers. Similarities in the surrounding material and visual landscape offered by each individual site demonstrate a wide scope of semiotic literacy.

From a psychological perspective, "visual affordances" that included optimal conditions for watching the "pareidolia alligator," would have animated the important celestial space, making it legible to farmers and astronomical experts alike. Consider the striking, unobstructed visibility of Tail and Heart that would reward an observer standing at the southeastern facing site at Niuheliang around 3500 B.C., and compare with a Hongshan "dragon" type jade (Figure 4.3 a–c):

39 Zhang et al. (2013).
40 Zhang et al. (2013, 19).
41 Ibid. (20).
42 Ibid. (17). See also Childs-Johnson (1991).
43 Zhang et al. (2013)

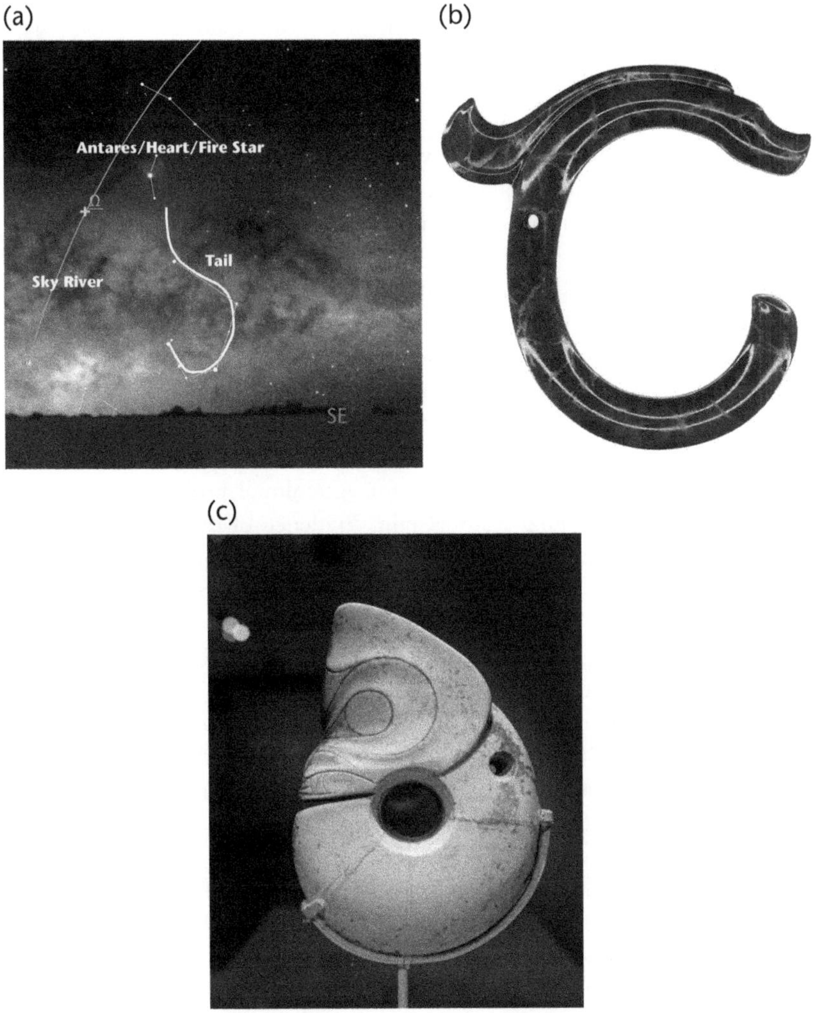

FIGURE 4.3 (a): Dragon's Hooked Tail; (b) Hongshan Jade Dragon; (c) Hongshan "Pig-dragon"

Source: (a) Redrawn from screenshot based on Stellarium, an open source software; (b) chengdu120.icu on Shutterstock; (c) Shan_shan on Shutterstock.

The integration of social rituals within the context of a space's "visual affordances" intimates the pre-existence of conceptions that the locations could express. In other words, the spaces were chosen because they were deemed appropriate for symbolic representations of astro-calendrical spatial knowledge transmitted as ecological inheritance. All of these components carried representational meaning based on pre-existing internal structures of coherence.

These semantic structures also intersected with the voluminous jade object discourse that found expression in tombs close to the ceremonial centers.

The link between the dragon and turtle shaped objects and prestige is that the former display access to ecological inheritance, which represents proximity to the suprasensible entities associated with seasonal regulation. Childs-Johnson has proposed that associations between "pig-dragon" shaped objects and female "goddess" figures were a reflection of the "needs of an early settlement for agricultural and domestic fertility."[44] The source of Turtle and Dragon's fertility associations lies in the transformation that occurs between winter, death, and spring, rejuvenated life. The discovery of three jade turtles that were placed in the crotch of the deceased in a Lingjiatan cultural site, behavior, which has been interpreted as a gesture praying for continued lineage fertility, indicates the tenacity of these astro-calendrical associations even as cultural styles and emphases evolved and diverged.[45]

Dragon was a social actor important for agricultural production and protection, including controlling seasonal rain. Evidence of the use of alligator's body, its scutes and skin, to produce highly prestigious objects, attests to the suitability of the icon for generating new forms of signaling prestige. Surfaces of pottery on which alligator figures were engraved were recovered at a Liangzhu (3300-2300 B.C.) site; polished scales and osteoderms found at Longshan (3000-1900 B.C.) cultural sites; while huge drums made of alligator skin, and which may have mimicked to the alligator's springtime bellow, were found at Longshan Taosi (2300-1900 B.C.) culture as well.[46] Ancient as well as contemporary ethnographies are consistent in their representation of the prominence of dragon-oriented behavior in agrarian life.[47]

The celestial ecosystem inhabited by Turtle and Dragon resonates with the Hongshan water network generated by the Daling River. Flowing from west to east across the mountains that served as the backbone to the ceremonial sites, the river facilitated access to Hongshan ceremonial sites spread across inter-linked river valleys. Moreover, the *northeast to southwest direction* of the many streams that flowed off the river made them convenient for both

44 Childs-Johnson (1991, 93), citing Sun (1984, 7–10).

45 Childs-Johnson (2021b, 110), provides dramatic details of the grave scene: "The corpse apparently was laid on two to six layers of jade and stone adzes, chisels, and axes—none showing use—and within a lacquer-painted coffin decorated with sets of suspended jade *huang* rings. The body was dressed with additional layers of sets of jade bracelets, jade armlets, and jade ornaments. Three turtles in fan array lay within the corpse's crotch, signifying fertility in the afterlife."

46 Liu (1996); Wu et al. (2019). For drums and the alligator's bellow see Porter (1996, 54).

47 Childs-Johnson (1991); Qiu and Fowler (1985). For debates about the origins of the dragon symbol, see Chen (2012). See also Pang (2007).

land and river transportation.[48] I highlight this orientation because it evokes a segment of Sky River that is diagonally angled in the same way. It is impossible to discern if there was a conceptual link between the Daling River and Sky River, but a proclivity toward foregrounding aqueous conditions as a spatial meaning-making cultural marker has been identified by Bin Liu, in his analysis of the capital city of Liangzhu culture (3400-2250 B.C.) in Zhejiang Province.[49]

The city, Mojiaoshan, reveals massive control over waterways that surrounded it, a conservancy system, a large-scale astronomical observatory and connected raised outdoor platform altars.[50] Liu suggests that the design of this "water city"[51] and the cultural artifacts found within, bore Hongshan cultural inflections. The existence of cultural affiliation among these cultures has been emphasized by several scholars.[52] Of specific interest is more evidence of a link between complex water control systems and the northwest direction, which in the celestial context is occupied by Sky River, where Tail resided. More precisely, Tail is situated at Sky River's renowned fork, right below Heart, a location known in ancient astral nomenclature as Sky's Ford (*tianjin*).[53]

Elsewhere I have delineated a lexical chain of associations found in first millennium B.C. texts that linked this celestial area to a (fragmented) written discourse involving a cataclysmic flood and its control.[54] I argued that the discourse communicated, in imagistic language, important astronomical information, including the astro-calendrical and astroligical significance of the fork in Sky River. This fluvial split was conceptualized as a model for hydraulic management to complement and transcend problems not redressed by damming techniques. Note that the idea of a "ford" implies the sun's need to traverse the river during its journey around the ecliptic.[55] The river's location at northwest corner of the northern, winter, quadrant, meant that the sun would cross it at the time of the winter solstice, that potent seasonal juncture when the season of death transforms into the season of life and growth.

The hydraulic system located in the northwest of the Liangzhu city settlement, between two mountain ranges, was divided into a "northern" and "southern" set of systems. These spatial arrangements strongly evoke the split tributaries formed by Sky River's fork. Archaeologists have demonstrated a preoccupation of Liangzhu culture with measurements related to the location of sunrise

48 Zhang et al. (2013, 101).
49 Liu (2021).
50 Ibid.
51 Liu (2020, 124–125).
52 Childs-Johnson (2021a; 2021b).
53 Porter (1996, 32, 36).
54 Ibid.
55 Ibid.

evidenced in a whorl-shaped altar found near aristocratic cemeteries outside the city. The altar shapes and the color schema manifested through different materials are reminiscent of Hongshan altars. The alignment of the four corners of the altar is internally consistent enough to suggest it served as a solar observatory.[56]

In contradistinction to the waterscape context suggested by Hongshan ritual organization, Drennan et al. argue that Yangshao culture emerges from social conditions that were as densely organized as Hongshan was fluid. Such density reflects the choice of a risk strategy based on prosocial cooperation. The strategy, grounded in "mutual (and mutually beneficial) obligation,"[57] "mitigate[d] subsistence risk" posed by the ecological conditions of vast flood plains that were susceptible to both drought and flood.[58] People would cooperate to construct "drainage ditches to protect crops and homes in low areas, wells or canals for irrigation in higher areas, or terracing of gentle upland slopes for better water retention. These kinds of cooperation and interdependence do not necessarily require management or leadership, but they do require much more interaction between households than do the risk-buffering strategies" used by Hongshan settlements in the Western Liao Valley.[59] The centralized and communal storage space for grain discovered at a late Yangshao village at Dadiwan may be a reflection of the positive effects of interdependent strategies of risk buffering.[60]

Cooperative subsistence strategies are credited with catalyzing an expansion of Yangshao villages into the central river plains. The expansion extended the existing "interdependence between households within villages" to "interdependence between villages in contrasting environmental zones."[61] Implicit in this expansion is the transmission of essential astronomical and calendrical information that had a bearing on agricultural success. Yangshao culture was scaffolded on the same mental architecture that undergirded Hongshan culture. However, because the expansion created hierarchical regional societies, and because these patterns led to the formation of chiefdoms, and ultimately dynastic states, the scope of Yangshao's impact on Central Plains cultural epigenesis was also far-reaching.

The spectacular remains of a large and elaborately staged mortuary scene uncovered in a Yangshao culture grave (circa 3500 B.C.), in, Puyang, Henan, have consistently been cited as evidence that Neolithic cultures possessed a sophisticated grasp of calendrical calculation.[62] The tomb-master's body was

56 Liu (2020, 122).
57 Drennan et al. (2020, 6).
58 Ibid. (5).
59 Ibid.
60 Ibid. (7).
61 Ibid. See also Peterson et al. (2010).
62 Pankenier (2013, 337).

aligned on a north-south axis, with his feet to the north and head to the south. He was accompanied by three youthful sacrificial victims. Mussel shell mosaics shaped into zoomorphs identified as a tiger and a "dragon"—a reptilian like figure—were found placed to the west and east of the deceased. This positioning led scholars to propose that they represented the stellar configurations associated with the seasons of spring and autumn, Dragon and Tiger, respectively. A third mosaic figure "comprising a triangle and two human tibias," was found to the north of the tomb-master's feet.[63] The triangular object has been construed as a representation of the circumpolar constellation, the Dipper, which was conceptualized as a celestial clock hand that signaled the passage of the seasons"[64] (Figure 4.4).

Interpretations of the scene in grave M45 have included claims that it represents a map of celestial space, "a pictorial representation of a cosmological worldview," while others see it more "simply [as] a 'shamanic' burial."[65] David Pankenier focuses on how the scenario represents

> the prime importance of the principal constellations, Sun and Moon in their timekeeping roles, and allusion to their management by uniquely empowered individuals closely connected with rulership. The Dipper, in particular, is supremely emblematic of the mysterious power at the center of the sky to which the cosmo-priest paid homage in life and with which he perhaps hoped to be united after death. Its depiction [of astronomical space] in reverse may, in fact, be specifically evocative of this relationship, as such inversions are common in certain mystical contexts. Just as in the parallel case of Han Chang'an three millennia later, the numinous power of the Dipper is being conjured by mimicry in the tomb of this Neolithic cosmo-priest.[66]

---

63 Ibid. Pankenier goes on to explain how "the cardinal directions associated with the dragon and tiger are precisely the same as in the correlative cosmology of some 3,000 years later, with the Cerulean Dragon to the east (the constellation comprising Vir–Sco) and White Tiger to the west (corresponding to And–Ori). At that time the Dragon was associated with spring and the Tiger with autumn, although their seasonal appearances are retarded by one season today." For commentary on the cosmological meanings inferred from the tomb setting see Feng (1990); Porter (1996); Loewe and Shaughnessy (1999); Chen (2013).

64 The Dipper's handle functioned as a celestial clock hand for the Chinese: "When the handle of the Dipper points to the east (at nightfall), it is spring to all the world. When the handle of the Dipper points to the south, it is summer to all the world. When the handle of the Dipper points to the west, it is autumn to all the world. When the handle of the Dipper points to the north, it is winter to all the world." Pankenier (2013, 92).

65 Ibid. (339).

66 Ibid. (327).

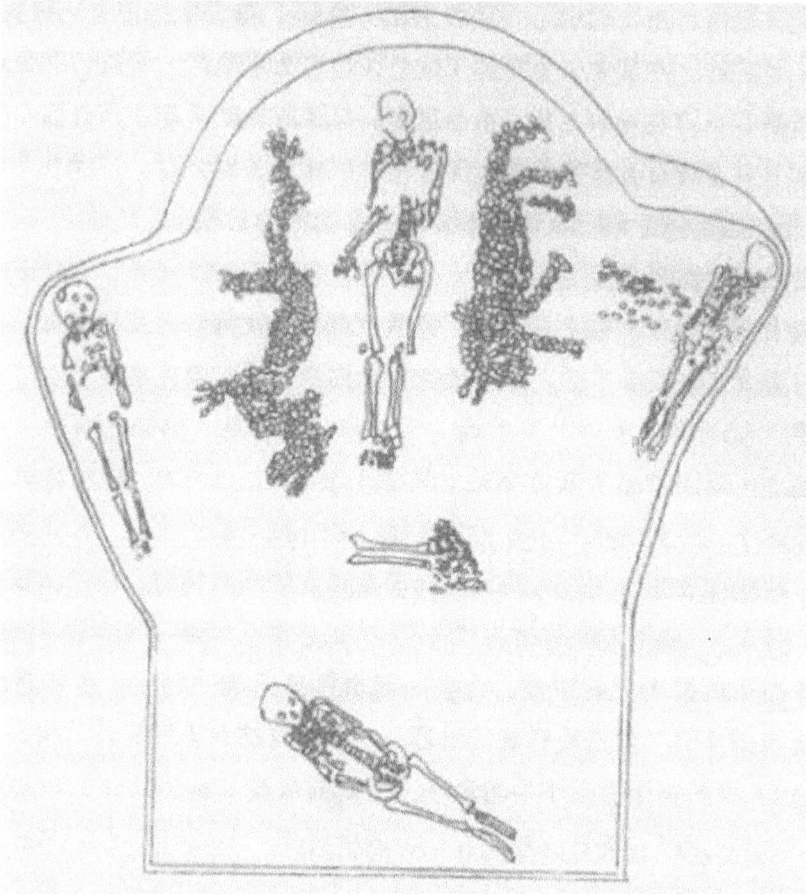

FIGURE 4.4 Drawing of Puyang burial scenario found in a Yangshao culture grave (Note, the skeleton's feet point northward).

Source: Portal to the Heritage of Astronomy.

Pankenier emphasizes the intentionality of placing a body at an oblique angle "near the north edge of the tomb," which had "been carefully arranged with the head pointing southeast to azimuth 124 degrees, the direction of winter solstice sunrise." He remarks that such accuracy "can only have been intentional and empirically established by paying close attention to the Sun's rising points along the horizon throughout the year."[67] He concludes that the preservation of azimuth information allowed for its application and replication in different contexts.

67 Ibid. (339).

The intensity of investment devoted to measuring and calculating the sun's position at the winter solstice also convokes an emotional logic, namely pleasure stimulated when the sun's apparent retreat from the earth halted, only to return to close proximity with increasing warmth. These emotional conditions may have enhanced behavior devoted to measuring and maintaining alignment with the location of the winter solstice. The resonance between the southeastern prospect and the winter solstice azimuth around 3500 B.C. raises the possibility that the southeast "visual affordances" offered by Hongshan cultural sites may have also involved rituals devoted to the arrival of the winter solstice. Feng Shi has linked the distances separating a platform made from three concentric circles at the Niuheliang ritual landscape site to winter and summer solstice measurement practices.[68] The fact that winter solstice rituals could have been attended by Hongshan farming society who were without agricultural preoccupations at that time, ties in with the logic of constructing the sites in the first place.

Still, the symbology does not speak in the same way as the aligned figure of the tomb-master of grave M45 at Puyang. The precision with which the tomb master's body was socially situated with the other bodies, and the accuracy of aligning this socially situated context along an imaginary line that extended from the deceased's body to the southern celestial location of the sun at the winter solstice, make it impossible to dismiss an astronomical level of meaning. The detail of the Tiger suggests that while Dragon symbology was centrally featured in both Hongshan and Yangshao cultural expression, its astro-calendrical basis was integrated into local astro-calendrical frameworks that had evolved due to their capacity to reduce agricultural risk. Thus, Hongshan symbolic discourse evoked a conception of Dragon contextualized by the familiar marshy ecology of Turtles, while Yangshao symbolic discourse evoked a conception of a Dragon contextualized by its relationship to the celestial Pole. This is likely the context driving the meaning of the Tiger symbol. For example, Tiger imagery has been archaeologically linked to local characteristics in Shaanxi province.[69]

The symbols of space-boundedness also evoke a psychological attitude characteristic of avoidant behavior aimed to prevent isolation.[70] They disambiguate with clear intentionality the degree of the tomb-master's—himself a proxy for the interdependent community's—commitment to maintaining proximity to the Pole Star through accurate and consistent calendrical measurements.[71] A similar intensity of "attention to the cardinal directions and the seasonal variations in the Sun's location"[72] is reflected in burial culture in

68 Feng (1993).
69 Wu (2012, 54).
70 Grecucci et. al. (2015).
71 Pankenier (2013, 88, 91).
72 Ibid. (83).

"early Yangshao dwellings at Banpo": "The entrances... were oriented toward the location of the mid-afternoon winter Sun when at its warmest a month or so after the solstice."[73] The salience of these cardinal orientations suggest that a normative standard for conferring prestige in Yangshao culture evolved around the capacity to coordinate and manage activities related to measuring, observing, predicting, and ritualizing astro-calendrical phenomena.

The Puyang scene dramatizes the joint intentionality of an interdependent group conferring prestige on a valued member, a leader, a "cosmo-priest."[74] The complex intersection of lines of bounded space reveals a level of co-ordination and communication that probably reflected on the deceased's own similar gifts. The geometric inflection of the symbolic discourse, comprised of lines and angles delineating social relationships, contrasts with the Hongshan tombs, which reflect the deceased's prestige status but did not yield more social information. This has been seen as a function of the separation between settlement business and ritual ones.[75] The Puyang burial scene, on the other hand, engendered a "we."[76] The display marked out normative expectations embodied by a competent coordinator and communicator of important social identity information.

"We-ness" is also reflected in remains of "small-sized wall towns (from ca. 2100-2000 BCE) scattered in Henan Province of the Central Plain." These towns "took a cardinal square or rectangular shape, aligned exactly north. It seems that central axes of such walled towns were integrated into the guide lines of a celestial pole."[77] However, the fact that precession also rendered difficult the identification of a Pole Star may be added to the issues confronting those charged with designing and laying out constructions including graves such as that discovered in Puyang.

At the time of Dragon's equinoctial appearances (ca. 3000 B.C.), the star closest to true north, that is, the Pole Star, was Thuban (Alpha Draconis). By 2700 B.C. precession made it appear as if it was moving closer toward true north. An archaic link between harm-avoidant strategies and Pole Star alignment would have imbued this phenomenon with positive valence, as suprasensible encouragement of behavior organized to sync with the rise and descent of stellar seasonal determinants. Nonetheless, because the cardinal standards themselves derived from the Pole Star's positionality, Thuban's increasing proximity to true north also made it necessary to make calendrical adjustments. These conditions are important for understanding the challenges faced by leaders of agrarian collectives; the situation catalyzed a space in which

73 Ibid.
74 Pankenier (2013, 337).
75 Drennan et al. (2020).
76 Tomasello and Carpenter (2007, 121).
77 He (2018a, 23).

up-to-date and applicable astro-calendrical measuring techniques became a crucial tool for accruing and sustaining power.[78]

These competitive conditions heightened a preconditioned sensitivity to precession caused deviance, which continued to disrupt calendrical systems, even Fire Star's. As a settlement's leader's reputation became more and more a matter of demonstrating command over astro-calendrical affairs, providing predictability and risk buffering effects to a community, accurate techniques for measuring and predicting time became a necessary asset for signaling control and political authority.[79] Evidence of different methods for assessing and measuring true north is seen in distinctions among cardinal orientations of square and rectangular settlement walls. For example, walls of palace and palace enclosure of urban Erlitou (1950-1500 B.C.) were found to align "rather close to magnetic north," while the axis orienting the alignment of the metropolis associated with the preceding Taosi culture (2230-1900 B.C.) differed by forty-five degrees.[80]

Putting aside the question of whether this city served as the last capital of a putative Xia dynasty, the different standards for orientation suggest the use of different measurement techniques. Du Jinpeng has attributed differences to the data yielded by the use of a compass or sundial to assess axial positionality.[81] One explanation for the axial orientation found at Taosi invokes the geographical location related to a diagonal waterway that ran (like Sky River) from the southeast to northwest. The river bordered the settlement's east and north boundary.[82] The spatial resonance between the river's orientation and the diagonal orientation of Sky River may have been important.

Another explanation, which is not mutually exclusive, suggests that the observatory's orientation was a function of Taosi elite's preoccupation with the southwest, which afforded a view of the location of the sun's movements on the day of the winter solstice.[83] The riches found in tombs of deceased presumed to have been associated with the observatory point demonstrate that it was a source of knowledge production. The inclusion of polished alligator scutes and alligator skin drums, among the prestige objects recovered from the tombs of those buried within the observatory proximity, attest to the continued salience of the Dragon for signaling power over astro-calendrical affairs.[84] A life-size form of a turquoise mosaic recovered in an Erlitou culture discovered in Yanshi, Henan evokes the

78 Pankenier (2004, 225; 2013, 98–100). Pankenier (227), discusses the migrations as a "handoff of Pole Stars."
79 Pankenier (1995, 2013).
80 Ibid. See also He (2021, 6, 17).
81 Du (2007, 141–146), cited in He (2018a, 23).
82 He (2018a, 23).
83 Ibid. (23, 24). See also He (2018b, 218ff).
84 Ibid. (22). Also recovered were a ceramic tray painted with a dragon design and a big chime stone.

Puyang composition, and has been interpreted as a signal of a ruler's endowed status as having proximity with the Dragon, be it as avatar or spirit founder.[85]

The discovery of Taoisi of what is believed to have been a "gnomon and shadow template" reaffirms the critical role played by the observatory and calendrics in prestige conferral.[86] While it is impossible to prove that the flaws of the Taosi efforts to track the winter solstice sun's movements were directly responsible for its violent demise,[87] it is clear that calendrical management played an important role in public prestige conferral, and that this was related to the settlement's cultural dominance and fall. Evidence that points to the "razing" of the observatory suggests a need to annihilate the intellectual foundations upon which Taosi had garnered prestige.[88]

Planetary Deviance and Shang Royalty

Something happened between this time and the putative beginning of the Shang (1576-1046 B.C.), when evidence of a "royal demesne" first appeared.[89] The social landscape drawn from archaeological evidence reveals a "patchwork" topography in which a schema of three spheres can be inferred, the royal sphere, the sphere of the "heads" (*ding*) of other potential competitors for dominance who were military allies, and, finally, the outer realm occupied by polities who were inconsistent allies, or constant and intrepid foes.[90] There is nothing in the record that directly accounts for the emergence of conceptions of royalty premised on ancestral lineage, even though the earliest extant written records date from a time when the family memory had already extended over twenty generations.[91] As Roderick Campbell has noted, the status of a Shang king, "though of a higher order [in Shang society], was nevertheless of the same type as that of other leaders of powerful lineages whose settlements dotted North China."[92]

The 4500-5000 individual graphs that make up the extant Shang written system do not reveal much about its evolution[93] (Figure 4.5). Although signs incised on pots have been recovered from Erlitou in north Central Henan and the early Shang site Erligang, and while earlier examples of signs may have been

85 Smith and Fan (2021, 247).

86 He (2021, 148); see also Pankenier (2013, 29).

87 See Pankenier (2013, 27–28).

88 Ibid. (21).

89 Campbell et al. (2009, 838).

90 Ibid. (835–836). For the use of the nomenclature "Ding" to refer to a lineage head, see Schwartz (2020, 58–62, especially 60).

91 Smith and Fan (2021, 229) discuss how this ancestral line was reconstructed.

92 Campbell et al. (2009, 827).

93 By "mature" I mean that the graphs "show the effects of graphic conventionalization and are not readily recognizable as realistic depictions of anything specific" Boltz (1994:56). See also Boltz (1999, 88–89). Keightley (2006, 183) claims that only half of these have been deciphered with certainty.

FIGURE 4.5 Shang dynasty Wu Ding era turtle plastron inscribed with earliest example of Chinese written system

Source: Shan_shan on Shutterstock.

precursors of oracle-bone graphs, the systems used at these sites were not unified.[94] Most scholars assume perishable materials were used as media during, if not preceding the occupation of the Anyang settlement site.[95] Chinese art historian Robert Bagley suggests that the use of writing to record divinations may have been the Shang King Wu Ding's (d. 1189 B.C.) invention, an observation that aligns with the discussion below concerning Wu Ding's psychology[96].

The plastron inscriptions recorded conversations between the Shang kings, Di, whom we have seen was a supernal lord associated with the Pole Star, and dead ancestors, who were members of the social and political community, as well as other suprasensible entities. Divination inscriptions reveal that the king and all the ancestors were subject to the authority of Di; "in short, the prosperity and continued existence of the king and his people" hinged on the discretion of Di.[97] The records also reveal a belief in Di's power to curse or find fault with the dynastic rulers.

What set of conditions would yield a discourse of royal power that took form as an "idiom of hierarchical kinship expressed through the language of

94 Keightley (2006, 180).
95 Bagley (2004); Keightley (2000); Smith (2010).
96 Ibid.
97 Campbell et al. (2009, 826).

tribute and reward, commanding and reporting, transgression, and punishment"?[98] Why would such a manner of figuring authority have elicited support from heads of separate lineages?[99] Scholarship that seeks to explain Shang political identity and prestige to conceptions of authority derived from their relationship between the Shang Dynasty founders and Di, spans from the philological to epigraphical to the astronomical.[100] Both David Pankenier and Sarah Allan argue that the relationship between the Shang and Di was as much astronomical as it was ancestral.[101] Still, as we have seen, a belief in a Pole Star entity was in and of itself not a distinguishing enough feature to warrant singularity among contenders for regional dominance. Cognizance of this reality is suggested by Shang valuation of Hongshan jades, replete with their Pole Star symbolic intentions.[102]

Considering the broader astro-calendrical traditions that I suggest explain the prevalence of cultural sites with shared features even though they were not necessarily politically united, we can imagine that the Shang's performance of "sovereignty across the landscape in counterpoint to that of rivals and rebels,"[103] was based on something else, something unexpected, deviant, which altered what had been a paradigmatic structure of power and prestige. David Pankenier proposes that a key to "what happened" is contained in a "much abused" historical annals. The annals record observation of a planetary massing, the densest such massing in hominid existence, that occurred in 1953 B.C.[104] Modern calculations validate the record, showing that the five planets visible to the naked eye amassed in a cluster spanning no more than seven degrees.

Because this date correlated with the time during which the Xia were believed to have ruled, and because we know that the repetition of this phenomenon occurred in 1059 B.C., albeit across a slightly wider span, and in a different celestial quadrant, the possibility that the 1953 B.C. conjunction

98 Ibid. (827).

99 Clark and Winslett (2011) argue that the emergence of High Deities was a function of evolutionary psychology wherein powerful people ascribe the authority to punish and reward to an external "moralizing agents." My claim is that even with the externalization of authority, the object of "moralizing" and attendant monitoring remains the capacity of the ruler to regulate agricultural and ritual schedules.

100 Pankenier (1981, 1985).

101 Pankenier (2004, 225); see Allan (2007, 20).

102 Bagley (1999, 202).

103 Campbell et al. (2009, 827).

104 Pankenier (1981). The text, the *Bamboo Annals* (*Zhushu jinian*) has a tortured bibliographic history though it is known to have been buried in the fourth century B.C., antedating many later texts viewed without suspicion. For the discovery of this text as well as another relating to the Western Zhou Dynasty King Mu, see Porter (1996). Pankenier validates the remarkable historicity of the astronomical observations preserved therein.

catalyzed the founding of the Xia dynasty has been discussed.[105] The archaeological evidence that does not yet support the notion of a pre-Shang political unit whose sphere of influence matched the scope of the Shang prevents me from considering this as an option. But rejecting a forced conception of a political unit does not preclude me from appreciating how such a phenomenon would be considered so deviant, so powerful, that it would have catalyzed cultural interpretation and material production.

The deviance of the event argues against an immediate and coherent response, time was needed to digest and process its meaning, which we can now imagine first triggered an archaic fear network. But the proximity of this deviant event to Turtle, a familiar celestial context, thanks to Dragon, filtered the novelty of the deviant experience, making it legible and meaningful. What seems to have happened is that the event was not just "duly noted," but triggered intense scrutiny for further such signs. In the meantime, Turtle's ancient meaning as a model of the cosmos underwent re-fashioning once again to imbue this unprecedented and inexplicable gathering with awesome but positive valence. Pankenier has demonstrated an incontrovertible link between ancient concepts of river animals (turtles and dragons) on whose backs were signs that demarcated cosmic verities and a collective memory of the 1953 conjunction. The memory implies an interpretive bent toward linking the event to the emergence of cosmopolitical thinking, even if there is nothing to tie it specifically to a dynasty per se.

This hypothesis helps explain why members of the Shang clan who were vying with others for regional dominance, would have responded to "odd" planetary behavior that occurred about five hundred years after the 1953 conjunction, this time occurring in another familiar and legible celestial space: Tail. According to the same "abused" *Bamboo Annals* cited above, four planets were "observed just before dawn near the eastern bank" of Sky River, (the exact location of Fire Star/Heart), toward the end of the purported Xia dynasty's last ruler.[106] Pankenier describes the "curious behavior of planetary behavior in the fall of 1576 as the planets reversed horizons and times of visibility from dusk to dawn and dawn to dusk. Four of the planets excluding Venus clustered above the southeast horizon at 5:31 local time in Xi'an on 20 December, 1576 B.C." Because the planets had been invisible, some for more than a week, "they would have been last observed after sunset, just above the northwest horizon, rather than just before dawn in the southeast" as they appeared that morning.[107]

Pankenier links this "curious behavior" to the founding of the Shang dynasty. The archaeological evidence supports a view of royal Shang authority as having

105 Pankenier (1985).
106 Pankenier (1995, 132).
107 Ibid.

exerted significant regional influence, though it is not until the last two centuries of the dynasty that social organization and political behavior merge to match the image of ancient dynasties projected back into Middle and Late Neolithic times. The record reveals a gradual process of centralization, with some gaps about the precise relationship between the huge cities that preceded the evolution of the "Great Shang Settlement" ("Da Shang yi") at Anyang, and the Shang lineage. A collective memory involving Shang dynastic founder Cheng Tang's performance of a self-sacrificial gesture in response to a devastating drought suggests that even if the Shang had access to a tradition of auspicious associations related to planetary massing phenomena, and even if they were savvy enough to invoke the phenomenon as an expression of the Polar Deity's intentions that its lineage rule supreme, the leaders needed to acknowledge fault when agrarian livelihood was unsustainable.[108]

To what degree witnessing the odd "criss-crossed" behavior of the four planets was the crux for Shang assertions of lineage distinction cannot be discerned clearly at this time. However, there is little doubt in my mind that the foregoing discussion about Turtle offers substance for situating the Shang's veneration of the turtle plastron as a mantic tool in the context of a collective memory of the 1953 conjunction. Reinforcement is found in the unique representation of the turtle in Shang writing, which includes both dorsal and profile images, unusual in zoomorphic representations.[109] The dorsal view evokes the ovoid celestial form (Figure 4.6).

Studies of the Shang's costly preference for turtle plastrons as a medium for communication with celestial suprasensible entities concur that cosmological intentions underlie the practice.[110] To this we may add the seasonally legible background of the four planets' odd movements, and the fact that it would have likely been witnessed by enough settlement leaders that a Shang claim

108 Pankenier (2020) claims that the drought might have been caused by the "mid-16th century BCE eruption of Thera (Santorini)," the smoke plumes of which affected growing cycles.

109 Larrivé-Bass (2015, 66n. 134).

110 Allan (1991); Childs-Johnson (2018, 2021c, 2021d). Allan has argued that the Shang choice to use a plastron as the medium for communication with suprasensible entities was informed by a correlation between the plastron's shape and a cosmological mentality. She claims that the plastron's shape figures a conception of spatial organization—four quadrants that encircle a central one—evocative of a cruciform shape. She identifies this cruciform-shaped model of the cosmos as the source of later five-based numerological theories. We could also cite the references to "five officials" (*chen*) in the inscriptional record, who are ascribed powers to serve as Di's proxy. Childs-Johnshon conceptualizes the zoomorphic symbols as indicative of the lineage's claim to claim to transcend boundaries that separate the living from the dead and suprasensible. Her interpretation of the significance of masks as symbols of this power, if read with knowledge of Dragon's stellar origins in mind, provides a powerful account of the interpersonal dynamics between Dragon and its human relations.

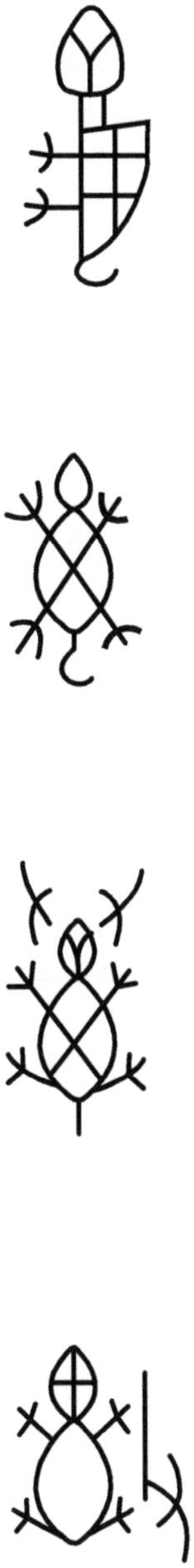

FIGURE 4.6 Early Chinese graphs depicting the word "turtle" representing both profile and dorsal views.

would have been persuasive, and made especially so with military might to back it up. While a pre-existing astrological association between the Shang and Fire Star may explain why the Shang were able to claim themselves as the intended recipient of a planetary sign ascribed to Di, evidence of sacrifices to Bird [star], Fire Star, and in one case a "new star" (*xinxing*) complicate that picture.[111]

At that time precession had narrowed Heart's seasonal signaling function to marking the sun's location at the autumnal equinox: its first appearance after a period of invisibility when the sun coincided with the star, occurred in 1554 B.C. "on or about October 26."[112] Moreover, evidence that a new zoomorph was added to Sky's lexicon is found in Shang divination texts that reference sacrifices made to a Bird Star (*niaoxing*). Pankenier has shown the persistence of a collective memory concerning the Shang's coordination of "both ritual and agricultural practices" to align with the "seasonal locations" of the Fire Star and Bird Star, the latter which was also known as "Quail Fire."[113]

Quail Fire is the legible celestial space "known as the Vermilion (or Red) Bird in which the summer solstice sun resided during Shang and early Western Zhou times"[114] (Figure 4.7). The Vermilion Bird zoomorph evokes the bird/sun imagery seen in Hongshan and other Middle to Late Neolithic cultures. Shang records show how the idea of the sunbird was situated within (translated into) the language of stellar configuration. During the Shang, "[w] hen the star Quail Fire first culminated on the meridian in spring they knew it was time to transport the hearth fires into the fields and to begin the agricultural season. In the same way, when [Fire Star] was on the western horizon at sunset in mid-autumn, they knew it was time to carry in the hearth fires and prepare for the rigors of winter."[115] Around the solstice, Fire Star "would have been on the meridian. At the same time the center of the portion of the bird asterism known as Quail Fire, marked by the star Alpha Hydrae… would have hovered on the western horizon. The name Quail Fire is thus a kind of mnemonic device for denoting this relationship between Great Fire and the Quail when the fiery" sun's power culminated.[116]

111 For mention of Fire Star and Bird stars in Shang dynasty divination records Xu et al. (2000, 21–24). Allan (1991, 69) reads mention of a tiger as a stellar reference.
112 Pankenier (1981, 21).
113 Ibid. (7).
114 Ibid. (8).
115 Ibid. (7).
116 Pankenier (1981, 9): "Zhu Kezhen confirmed the identification of Alpha Scorpii or Antares as the Fire Star (R.A. 13h 35m in 1059 B.C.) and Alpha Hydrae as the Bird Star (R.A. 6h 55m in 1059 B.C.) and confirmed also that both would have accurately performed the function described in the 11th century B.C. or early Western Zhou."

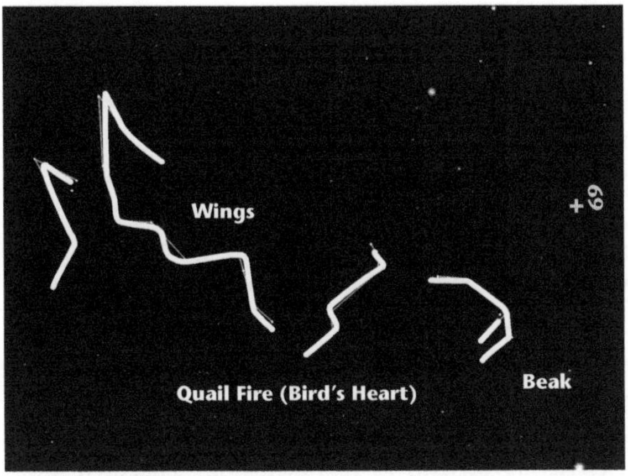

FIGURE 4.7 Stellar configurations comprising the Vermilion Bird at the time of the summer solstice 1000 B.C.

Source: Redrawn from screenshot based on Stellarium, an open source software.

The reason I emphasize Shang attention to shifting astro-calendrical realities is because I want to foreground how successful astro-calendrical management was central to Shang conceptions of behavior that would warrant Di's continued conferral of prestige on their lineage. Because Di's authority derived from power over celestial motion, it extended to the control of time and the proper course of the seasons. A shift in the "architectural orientation from a few degrees west of north at Erlitou [a cultural power that preceded the Shang] to a few degrees east of north in Erligang [e.g. Early Shang] sites, such as Yanshi and Zhengzhou" may be understood as correlate expressions of political identity.[117] These details signaled the Shang's standard of true north to demonstrate proximity to Di.[118] Childs-Johnson, following Li Ji, draws attention to the manipulation of a color palette to distinguish a square altar that "[lay] exactly to the magnetic north" at the heart of the Shang citadel. She views these visual affordances as a descendant of "Jade Age Hongshan altars."[119]

The extensive water channel system found in the northeastern sector of the Shang capital also evokes earlier displays of water-management that represented power over the cosmos.[120] We saw how these displays resonated with Tail's transcendence over its wet environment to merge, via Heart, with the power of a dry one. In light of the location of the 1578 B.C. planetary behavior, it is reasonable to imagine why Dragon imagery would figure significantly in Shang visual representations of power. At this

117 Song (2021, 262).
118 Ibid.
119 Ibid. (336).
120 Ibid.

point overlaps between liturgical and agricultural intentions had not been clearly delineated. Keightley surmises that the "start of the year" for the "numbered moons" or months that appear in the inscriptions, might have been "pegged" to begin with the first lunation after the winter solstice. At the same time, the farmers "might have tied their agricultural calendar to the observation of the stars and constellations."[121] The aforementioned references to seasonal determinative stars in the Shang divination record suggest the king was cognizant of both. The king demonstrated respect for the "time-honored seasonal customs and festivals of the general populace ('what the people respected')."[122]

This archaic norm, which linked prestige status with successful astro-calendrical management, can be extrapolated from the symbols selected to represent Shang metamorphic power. The royal language was at once legible and inaccessible, given the extravagance of the materials devoted to its representation. The divinations reveal concern with arable lands, grain tribute, and land development within the realm of the Shang ruler's own crops, understood in the terms of "dynastic agriculture." But they also reveal an acute attention to agricultural news from beyond.[123] Keightley's discussion of how Shang techniques of time management evolved in tandem with regulations for scheduling ancestral sacrifices emphasizes the role calendrics played in reinforcing sovereign claims.[124]

The urgency driving this attention suggests that increasing agricultural production was necessary to demonstrate Shang royal fitness. Effective calendrical regulation, manifested in bounteous harvests, would have been an implicit tool for moral recruitment among Shang foes in a sociopolitical context shaped by "coalitional dynamics."[125] Lapses in managing time due to the cumulative effects of precession could be claimed (and was, ultimately, by the Zhou) as a reason to contend Shang authority.[126] Agricultural success implicitly functioned as a "credibility-enhancing display" that simultaneously institutionalized cultural codes.[127]

Wu Ding's divinations provide an example of behavior resulting from the internalization of these cultural codes, including the choice of a chelonian plastron to serve as the royal divination tool. Many view the mantic properties ascribed by the Shang to the turtle's plastron as a reflection of religious and cosmological thinking. Sarah Allan has argued that Shang cosmology took form in the "shape of the turtle," which represented the turtle-based cosmovision discussed in the preceding chapter.[128] Elizabeth Childs-Johnson claims Shang cosmology derives from a belief in "metamorphism," the royal power "to

121 Keightley (2000, 44).
122 Pankenier (1995, 157).
123 Keightley (2012, 132–135, 136–173).
124 Keightley (2004, 37–53).
125 Pietraszewski (2016).
126 Pankenier (2013).
127 Chvaja and Řezníček (2019).
128 Allan (1991, 104–105).

identify with the spirit world."[129] She traces a salient "visual vocabulary of royal power symbols" that evokes the visual affordances operating in Hongshan and late Longshan sites.[130]

Although Childs-Johnson does not link these "imaginary" animals to their (potential) stellar referents, I submit that the profusion of Dragons and Birds as visual symbols for royal metamorphic power derives from the astro-calendrical realities I delineated above. The Dragon represents the location where Di's planetary massing expressed its intentions to confer the prestige of sovereignty onto the Shang lineage; together with Bird (Qual Fire), Tail, and Heart it served to regulate and manage agricultural behavior. The stellar determinants helped the king keep in sync with the seasons. Moreover, by this time, Turtle's disappearance below the western horizon soon after dusk in late autumn announced the arrival of winter.[131] Its association with the Pole Star, and, the cosmologically potent winter solstice, may explain the suitability of turtles to function as media for royal metamorphism. The zoomorphic nomenclature ascribed to the winter quadrant in a fifth century B.C. star map is "Black Tortoise," *xuanyuan* or Sky Tortoise, *tianyuan*. The *yuan* (*Pelochelys cantorii*), is a large fresh-water tortoise. The name likely derived from Turtle's association with the season, as no other stellar configurations in the quadrant are named as parts of that animal.[132]

Celestial associations are also suggested by representations of turtles in Shang art, especially the consistent whorl motifs that surround a central circle, which evoke the Box Turtle rim design.[133] A composite emblem read as denoting the animal has been found inscribed in Shang bronzes. Interpreted as a lineage insignia, which was sometimes combined with a cruciform-shape, some scholars have suggested the sign signals the lineage's high status.[134] A recent study on clan emblems inscribed on Shang and Zhou dynasty bronzes has concluded that they are inextricably linked to family lineages whose names and identity derive from their professional service to the Shang. For example, a bronze inscribed with a family emblem characterized by the figure of a turtle, has been linked to the profession of managing the import and preparation of plastrons for divination.[135] If the attribution to the graph frequently read as Sky Tortoise is valid, then it would be reasonable to assume that this family may have been responsible for astro-calendrical calculations or winter solstice rituals. The fact that the family bearing this emblem survived

---

129 Childs-Johnson (2021c, 285).
130 Ibid.
131 Porter (1996, 57).
132 Ibid.
133 Allan (1991, 107).
134 Luo (2007; 2019).
135 Gao (2019, 40).

into the Zhou dynasty, raises the possibility that the lineage may have been preserved for its ecological inheritance.[136]

The discovery of a late Shang dynasty bronze figure cast in the shape of a *xuanyuan* (Sky Tortoise) with four arrows protruding from its back, echoes the astro-calendrical valence I suggest is pressed in the semantic meaning of the turtle plastron.[137] An inscription recounts the king's ritual capture of the animal, and relays his desire that a bronze figuration of the animal commemorate the event.[138] Some scholars link the tortoise's capture to similar first millennium B.C. rituals that were carried out during the summer solstice. A symbol of the winter solstice, the capture of the turtle at the summer solstice demonstrated the capacity to balance the cosmic properties of wet and dry, those whose excesses, flood and drought, posed the most risk to agricultural production.[139]

In sum, the deviant input conditions—planetary massings that occurred within the legible space of seasonal determinants—stimulated an archaic neural strata and correlate mental architecture forged by threat precaution systems. These systems required high levels of epistemic vigilance and subordinate level discrimination. To become an expert at being open to the presence of suprasensible communication required practice and fine-level discrimination to train attention and especially sensory imagination. The visible marks of communication manifested on the plastron, which were audibly matched by the popping sound made when heat was applied to the plastron's axis, demanded careful monitoring and conscious appraisal of emotional experience within an intersubjective context. This shaped Shang kings' intuition of the presence of the listening agents.

Shang Intuitions about Di, Agricultural Abundance, and Political Status

Shang intuition that successful agricultural yields was tantamount to praise from the listening agents, especially Di, was a Neolithic legacy. It is reflected in the Shang's concern with displaying a royal commitment to calendrical regulation, testifying, as it were, to their fulfilment of prestige-worthy obligations. Divinations oriented toward ascertaining Di's support of plans to inspect fields, to "open new lands and establish farms," as well as grain diversification initiatives, show how deeply these

136 Ibid. (44). Gao's interpretation of the symbol differs from mine. He reads the symbol as a representation of a spiritual founder conceptualized as a frog instead of a water turtle. His reasoning, which is based on the reading of the representation of a frog's angled legs that make it a distinctive jumper, loses strength in the face of recent scholarship that links the angled shape of the back legs of Hongshan turtle shapes to the fresh-water turtle species to which the Box Turtle belonged. See Li and Wang (2013).

137 Yuan (2011); Zhang and Shao (2009).

138 Ibid.

139 Yuan (2011).

issues shaped the intersubjective relationship between the Shang ruler and Di.[140] The logic of Di's authority, which derived from its power over celestial motion, control over time and the proper course of the seasons, also drove Shang royal acts.[141]

"The disposal of people, land, and resources was also analogous to Di's power to approve or end settlements and thus control the distribution of people in the landscape."[142] Divinations related to reports on local production, discernment of the best time to harvest sorghum, the best time for harvesting in general, the best time to dispatch officers to supervise "land cultivation (*xiaoji chen*)" and officers to supervise the "harvest (*xiaoyi chen*)," point to the importance of opening waste-lands.[143] The "quasi-military nature of land opening excursions" was reflected in the collective tilling activity that was assigned to masses of people whose precise identity and status is still debated.[144] Sending out "royal followers or retinue" (*zhong*) to engage in agricultural rituals and activities also reflects the importance to the court of distributing the king's authority in this realm.[145]

Agricultural bounty would depend in part on the quality of ecological information, including astro-calendrical systems, that could be distributed through the work carried out by the "many field officers" (*duotian*).[146] Presumably they would be applied as a strategy for administering and supervising farming activities in newly captured lands, as well as ensuring the fulfilment of grain supply obligations. While war was a constant preoccupation for the Shang, the possibility of colonizing the land into new settlements suggests itself as a motivation. For example, Wu Ding displayed much concern with the status of a newly established "Tang settlement" (*Tang yi*) in the lands that previously belonged to a western polity called Tu Fang.[147] Because of its geographical advantages, the settlement served as a self-sufficient military colony, where farmer/soldiers helped the Shang solidify its position in Shanxi.[148] The fate of the settlement, and the basis of Wu Ding's political prestige, rested on the capacity to manage and produce agricultural sustenance for the colony.

140 Wu (2013, 103) lists several grains that appear in inscriptions, including millet, wheat, oats, barley, sorghum, buckwheat. Millet and wheat were two of the most commonly mentioned grains, and the king expressed deep concern about them at every step of production.

141 Keightley (2000, 185); Lewis (2010).

142 Campbell et al. (2009, 834).

143 Ibid. (109).

144 Keightley (2000, 280). Smith (2021) provides an account of debates over the meaning of this term, but reveals consensus that this category of people are distinct from another category of group that were sometimes involved in the king's agricultural-related activities.

145 Wu (2013, 121). I follow Kenichi Takashima's (2014, 239, 244, 242) translation of the word *zhong*, because he demonstrates how this group remains maintains proximity to the king rather than being sent off.

146 Ibid. (108).

147 Wu (2012, 42–43).

148 Ibid.

This line of thinking merges with conclusions of modern scholars who view Shang war efforts in southern Shanxi as driven by economic conditions. While most focus on the access to metals, weapons, and other luxury items, the opening up and domestication of newly acquired land should not be ignored.[149] Keightley emphasized the close connection between hunting and farming, wherein hunting served farming by clearing the land of animals destructive to agriculture.[150] Childs-Johnson's discussion of the role played by "royal-house male[s] in charge of a particular area for husbandry" yields a similar conclusion. She finds that husbandry officials "were extensively represented throughout the Shang kingdom, and often at great distance."[151] This points to the prioritization of labor mobilization toward the ultimate aim of manifesting Shang control over the transformative realms of reproduction.

Seasonality and Shang Leadership Psychology

The degree to which Shang rulership had accommodated precession-induced changes in Sky's text is indicative of their sensitivity to ensuring that agricultural practices are in sync with astro-calendrical realities. When viewed through the lens of Wu Ding's idiomatic deployment of divination, which tended toward obsessiveness, a view of the impact that these ruling paradigms exerted on his psychology and behavior emerges.[152] Because there is no evidence of when the practice of divination began, we are not in a position to ascertain if Wu Ding's anxiety is a function of his personality alone, or if it might represent a royal psychology formed when use of this technique first began. Regardless, Wu Ding's expressive behavior is fascinating because it reverberates with the psychoemotional conditions that led to the production of Turtle architecture, including deviant astronomical events, complicated grief, suspended verbalizations, and idiosyncratic behavior. Moreover, we have evidence of how Wu Ding's divination idiom affected that of his sons. I am interested in the vertical transmission of Wu Ding's psychology to that of his sons because I want to trace the evolution of ruling idioms in tandem with cultural shifts as they are transmitted down royal family lines.

For example, the concern with making King Wu Ding happy was an organizing theme of recently discovered well-preserved divination records believed to have been produced under the patronage of one of Wu Ding's sons, Prince Rong.[153] The prince's records also revealed a shared propensity to attribute

149 Ibid. (44).
150 Keightley (2012, 161–178, 227).
151 Childs-Johnson 2021c, 299).
152 Keightley (1978, 33–35, 122)) discusses the narrowing of topics from Wu Ding's "scrambled mix" to a more systematic clustering of divinations, such as those concerned with hunting and the sacrificial cycle.
153 Schwartz (2020, 19, 35, 79 et passim)

physical ailments to curses that emanated from Wu Ding's father, "Near Ancestor Yi," and his consort Lady Geng. Both Wu Ding and Prince Rong suffered from bouts of tinnitus associated with Ancestor Yi. On another plastron an inscription records a prayer entreating the grandfather not to torment the prince.[154]

Possible tension between Wu Ding and his father is faintly alluded to in a late Western Zhou text, suggesting a collective memory of a problematic context surrounding Wu Ding's ascension.[155] While this late text does not constitute evidence, it does help focus attention on a more specific rationale motivating Wu Ding's broad anxiety, which has implications for the evolutionary trajectory of ancestor worship specifically, and Chinese culture more generally. In these texts, Wu Ding references the experience of being cast away from his father's court, into the "hinterlands of the [Yellow] River" (*He huangye*). Wu Ding also bemoans losing track of a teacher along the way.[156] The text that recorded the observation of the planetary conjunction states that Wu Ding was sent away during his father's sixth year of reign, four years before the latter's death.[157]

Other references to Wu Ding having been isolated in a "mourning hut" (*zhong*), and suffering from muteness when he exited, portray the conditions of his father's death as impediments to expression.[158] These afflictions are also seen in inscriptions that record bouts of "illness of speaking" (*ji yan*) and "sick tongue" (*ji she*), which has been interpreted as stuttering.[159] In Chapter 2 we discussed how even if traumatic experiences interrupt or overwhelm a person's capacity to process it into language, these experiences remain present in a person's psyche and language as an absence that may be felt, seen, and passed on to linguistic heirs. This raises the possibility of a link between conflicting emotional conditions surrounding Wu Ding's ascension to the throne and the heightened anxiety that marks his divinatory idiom.

Wu Ding's divination records document a mental process of self-fashioning that obscured the true source of psychic suffering. His unsystematic attempts to manage the ancestral cult suggest a resistance to psychic (re)organization. Perhaps this may be because it risked making knowable a parental or ancestral saga that was transmitted to him by the fact of absence, along with an unconscious pre-existing obligation to continue the same pattern of verbal suspensions.[160] At the same time, his efforts to maintain proximity with his close ancestors through

154 Schwartz (2015).

155 See the "Yue ming" and "Wu Yi" chapters of the *Shujing* (*Book of Documents*), which purports to record Wu Ding's speech, some concerning his youthful memories. The *Shujing* was probably written during the centuries after the Zhou conquest. See Shaughnessy (1993, 378).

156 *Shujing*, "Yue ming xia," cited in Chang (1986, 8).

157 *Zhushu jinian*, "Xiao Yi".

158 *Shujing* "Wu Yi," cited in Chang (1986, 4–5).

159 Ibid.

160 Abraham and Torok (1994, 166, 168).

constant divinatory interaction made it difficult to reduce the salience of emotional investments in and entanglements with departed relational objects. The static status of salience cues impinged on the process by which Wu Ding could psychically accommodate his ancestor's (father's?) post-mortem reality.

These conditions may account for the royal idiom of the second of two sons who succeeded Wu Ding, Zu Jia (r. (1177-1158 B.C.), after his brother ruled for less than a decade. Keightley identifies Zu Jia as the author and enforcer of radical reforms that reorganized the ancestral cult schedule and practice. While Keightley acknowledges that antecedents of the reforms were evident in Wu Ding's divinations, he also notes that the rigor of Zu Jia's reforms effectively eradicated the need to divine about when to perform ancestral sacrifices, and therefore reduced "room for personal idiosyncrasy, either on the part of the living or the dead."[161] In this view, the idiosyncrasies, a feature of Wu Ding's ruling idiom, had a catalytic (aversive) effect on his son's rule.

The radical reform initiated by Zu Jia "tied ancestors rigidly to their day-names" and "regularized the five-ritual cycle of sacrifices, so that each ancestor and ancestress knew his and her place."[162] I construe the reform as a "sequel" to Wu Ding's ruling idiom. Recognizing how Wu Ding's emotional state would have been an active constitutor of social structures that wove through the memories of several generations, we can appreciate how a "tension" may have "existed between [Wu Ding's] more personal, emotional form of kinship commemoration," and Zu Jia's more systematic impersonal structure. If Wu Ding was unable to fix a cult schedule due to unresolved intersubjective relationships with recently deceased relations; if his proximity maintenance habits were not conducive to "efficient" rulership; then Zu Jia's system, which instituted the use of names to reflect the fact that the ancestors' absence had been acknowledged, mourned, and psychically buried, offered a new language that allowed the collective Shang psyche to separate the lives of the living and dead while still accommodating the ancestors' demand for sacrifices.

The fact that Wu Ding was buried across the Huan River in the Xibeigang cemetery, and not within the royal compound, as was Wu Ding's consort Fu Hao, and the obvious protracted nature of the lavish funeral, which was used by his sons to assert legitimacy, exemplify this inclination.[163] Keightley has argued that the legacy of Zu Jia's reform extended to modernity inasmuch as ancestor worship remained a central feature of Chinese cultural identity. The next chapter investigates the implications of Zu Jia's royal behavior for understanding the emergence of an equally radical reform that was institutionalized more than three hundred years later during the Western Zhou dynasty. I will argue that the conditions that converged to yield the latter

161 Keightley (2004, 30).
162 Keightley (2006, 43).
163 Keightley (2000, 185).

reform, known as the "Western Zhou Ritual Reform," recapitulated those identified as driving Zu Jia's reforms.

A constant variable linking the two dynasties generally and these two sets of ritual reforms specifically is the vulnerability of maintaining prestige status conferred by a suprasensible entity's assumed monitoring of royal affairs. I compare the conditions surrounding the ascension of the fifth Western Zhou king, King Mu (r. 956-918 B.C.), to those experienced by Wu Ding. In short, King Mu's ascension was complicated by the unexpected and ominously perceived death of his own father, King Zhao (r. 977/75-957 B.C.); King Mu's son, King Xiao (r. 882-? B.C.), profoundly affected by his internalization of his father's emotional state, initiated a ritual reform organized along rigid taxonomic rules akin to those instituted by Zu Jia.

The Zhou as the Shang's Psychopolitical Heirs

It is impossible to distinguish if the Zhou, located at the base of Mt. Qi in the west of Shaanxi Province northwest of the Shang, were aware of Zu Jia's reforms. Their first appearance on the historical stage occurs within a Wu Ding era inscription.[164] We know a Zhou polity had sporadic interaction with the Shang as part of a "network of states centered in the southern part of present-day Shanxi province, more or less along the Fen River."[165] States within this network were sometimes considered allies of the Shang, sometimes enemies. Later, according to legend, the Zhou migrated, perhaps looking for arable land, before settling at Mt. Qi. Remains that might be considered proto-Zhou culture in the Wei River Valley date to the middle of the twelfth century B.C.[166]

By the time the Zhou conquered the Shang in 1046 B.C., it was clear that they had been culturally and behaviorally assimilated within the upper echelons of Shang royal power. The Zhou rulers had intermarried with the royal family, likely as the need for western protection grew for the eastern Anyang settlement.[167] Not only is there evidence for the Zhou use of divination, but the inscriptions involved the Zhou ruler's performances of sacrifices to the Shang cult.[168] When the Zhou ruler known to the Shang as the "Western Lord" (*Xibo*) claimed to be the intended recipient of a message communicated by the planetary massing that occurred near the Beak of the Vermilion Bird in 1059 B.C., his prestige was also a function of his family status as the grandson of a previous Shang king, and the son-in-law of the reigning king.[169]

164 Shaughnessy (1999, 305); Khayutina (2021).
165 Shaughnessy (1999, 305); Khayutina (2021, 367).
166 Ibid.
167 Khayutina (2021, 347–375).
168 Ibid. (375). Shaughnessy (1985).
169 Shaughnessy (1985, 190).

There is no doubt that the capacity of the "Western Lord" to interpret the planetary cluster as the conferral of prestige and royal prerogative to the Zhou was a function of his access to knowledge about the Shang's own assumption of power.[170] Participating in cult rituals was a conduit for drawing "close to the source of dynastic power."[171] The Zhou also knew how their close attachment to the Shang lineage rendered their overthrow of Shang authority problematic for recruiting trust. Some scholars have suggested that the Zhou's emphasis on Sky (*tian*) as the entity associated with the planetary message, as opposed to Di, reveals an intention to universalize the source of their authority in contradistinction to the Shang cult.[172]

Such rhetorical diffusion may have also been useful to minimize and conceal the degree to which Zhou political claims constituted an intrafamilial breach. Indeed, studies concur that early Zhou communication of their authority relied on a "sophisticated suite of administrative, ritual and technological methods," many of which "had Shang provenance."[173] The justificatory tone that suffuses many early speeches made by kings and high officials that are recorded in bronze inscriptions, as well as the exhortations not to lose the status and prestige conferred by the planetary "mandate" (*ming*), reveal the degree to which Zhou rulers had internalized the cultural codes buttressing a conception of sovereignty premised on the fear of its possible withdrawal.[174] This context is essential for comprehending the magnitude of the obstacles to Zhou self-fashioning posed by King Zhao's unexpected and catastrophic death. According to Pankenier:

> The epoch-making Shang-Zhou dynastic transition consequently surfaced a fundamental tension at the start of ancient Chinese political thinking about the mandate and the nature of legitimate succession that was henceforth to

---

170 Pulleyblank (2000, 9) claims that the archaeological record has elicited "agnostic doubts…about the possibility of identifying a 'proto-Zhou culture in Shaanxi before the Zhou conquest." See Bagley (1999) and Rawson (1999) for similar conclusions.

171 Keightley (2000, 260).

172 Pankenier (1995, 123); Wang (2017, 10).

173 Vogt (2021, 406–407); see also Sun (2021, 452).

174 See, for example, locutions that intimate a need to be vigilant in manifesting qualities that would attract Sky's favor in this speech inscribed in the Da Yu ding cast during King Kang's reign: "At (the time) King Wu succeeded Wen and made the state, (he) ridded its evil, extending to the four quarters, and governed their people… therefore *Sky* respectfully looked down and treated (him) as a son, and greatly protected the former kings… I have heard that Yin's [Shang] losing the mandate was due to the Yin border-lords and fieldsmen and the Yin governors… often indulging in wine, and they lost the troops. Yi! I approach the pattern and follow King Wen's upright virtue… [in order to] secure virtue's continuance… Hasten to be awed by *Sky's* awesomeness… Do not neglect my command. Shaughnessy (2011, 389–381). Shaughnessy also translates two bronze inscriptions, one dating from King Cheng's reign and the other from King Kang's, in which the Kings express an anxiety over losing the mandate and exhort their courtiers to be constantly vigilant in their manifestation of cites a number of early Western Zhou bronze inscriptions.

> manifest itself repeatedly in the political life of early China… [due to the] Zhou claim to have re-established the continuity of an ancient tradition that took its cues from Heaven and the natural order.[175]

Pankenier suggests that the Zhou's invocation of the planetary massing implicitly impugns Shang privileging of an ancestral sacrificial regime "above those dedicated to the High God (Heaven) in ritual or theology." The Zhou, he claims, objected to what they saw as a "process of gradual encroachment by the royal ancestors on the former prerogatives of the High God."[176] Pankenier assumes that "there can be little doubt of the priority originally attributed to the power and influence of the supernal lord [High God] as the ultimate cosmic source both of the dynastic lineage in the mythical genealogy and its sociopolitical organization."[177]

Pankenier concludes that the Zhou's invocation of the conjunction to justify their overthrow of the Shang constitutes a "return to Neolithic pessimism" as they "reasserted the primacy of universality and inclusiveness, in marked contrast to their former overlords' indulgence in exclusive hegemony, itself a logic outgrowth of the Shang preoccupation with the cult of their royal ancestors."[178] He views the subservient relationship between the Zhou and "Heaven," which ascribes supreme authority to the latter, as a means to broaden the role of kingship at the expense of the ancestral cult in a manner consistent with the pattern followed by similar religious restorations elsewhere, which "brought back to life ancient supreme Gods of Heaven who had been turned into *dei otiosi*."[179]

Pankenier also foregrounds the Zhou's critique of late Shang rulers' negligence regarding astro-calendrical management. The Zhou's self-representation derived in part from its identification with the location of the planetary massing in the Vermilion Bird's Beak. Regardless if the Zhou were correct to impugn the last Shang kings as guilty of calendrical malfeasance, there is no doubt that with their assumption of royal status, they emphasized the "sacred task of scheduling ritual observances and promulgating the calendar… [I]n the case of the Zhou conquest in particular, this would help to account for the demonstrative piety in these matters of the successful usurpers."[180]

I argue that this pre-existing psychological mindset was a factor contributing to the implementation of a radical reform toward the late Middle

175 Pankenier (2013, 241).
176 Ibid. (231).
177 Ibid. (260). Cf. Puett (2002, 54), who denies there were any important religious differences between Late Shang and Early Western Zhou ritual practice and idem. (2010).
178 Pankenier (2013, 269). See also Lagerwey and Kalinowski (2008, 7) for a discussion of the impact on political conceptions of legitimacy exerted by "the notion of [Sky]," especially the associations that link political legitimacy to natural cycles and omens.
179 Pankenier (2013, 232), citing Mircea Eliade (1958, 75).
180 Pankenier (1995, 161).

Western Zhou, referred to as the "Western Zhou Ritual Reform". Initially observed by art historians, who noticed a dramatic almost sudden shift in the type, quality, and number of vessels used in ancestral cult rituals, the new practices reveal a shift in the way social status was enacted and expressed.[181] The fact that the reforms received no mention in either transmitted or paleographical texts, notwithstanding the overwhelming archaeological evidence that attests to their dramatically rapid and complete implementation, invites interrogation into its apparent elision. While the reform has been attributed to "the dissolution of a political and religious network based on personal ties forged during the initial years following the Shang overthrow," I approach it as a cultural unit whose spiral line of descent may be traced back to the emotional dynamics driving Zu Jia's reform.

What we know is that the Zhou experienced military resistance to their claim of sovereignty, especially from the Shang descendants and those lineages still loyal to the dynastic house, but also from other directions.[182] Royalty, in the beginning, resembled the Shang demesne form, but Mt. Qi emerged as a growing center for ritual hosting and display.[183] This dynastic unfolding is reflected in the post-mortem names ascribed to the early Zhou rulers, which enunciate a definite historical perspective. I italicize the posthumous nomenclature in the following account to emphasize this orientation. It begins with King Wen, the one who saw the (planetary) *pattern* but who died before executing its intentions; King Wu, the son whose *martial* act against the Shang actualized his father's response to the planetary pattern; King Cheng, the one who *completed* the grandfather's royal intentions by establishing a defensive settlement to monitor activity near the Shang ruins; King Kang, whose ascendance coincided with increased agricultural *bounty and satedness.*

The memory of King Zhau the fourth ruler (excluding King Wen who predeceased the Shang's collapse), proved more difficult to name. This is because of the catastrophic conditions surrounding his unexpected drowning and the concomitant decimation of the army, as they attempted to cross the Han River.[184] Although hinted at in the traditional historical record, the cataclysmic loss was rhetorically elided in two bronze inscriptions that

181 Sun (2021).

182 Shaughnessy (1992, 1999): Li (2006).

183 Shaughnessy (1992, 1999); Li (2006); Khayutina (2010).

184 Shaughnessy (1999, 321). Shaughnessy cites the *Bamboo Annals*: "Nineteenth year [i.e., of King Zhao's reign; 957 B.C.]: There was a comet in [the lunar lodge] *ziwei*. She Gong and Xinbo followed the king to attack Chu. The heavens were greatly obscured, and pheasants and hares were all shaken. They lost the six armies in the Han River; the king died." He goes on to explain that the "six armies," which are often referred to in bronze inscriptions as the "western armies" as opposed to the *yin* eight armies stationed in the eastern territories, were the backbone of Zhou military might.

mention King Zhao. Western Zhou historians have noted this was a turning point for the dynasty.[185]

Although there is robust scholarship on how its impact catalyzed the emergence of cultural institutions during the long reign of King Zhao's successor, his son, King Mu, Edward Shaughnessy's assessment that King Zhao's death had "far-reaching repercussions" may be extended beyond the intellectual and (political, social, and religious) institutional legacies normally identified as consequential to King Zhao's demise.[186] No one has focused on the affective implications of King Zhao's demise for a royal family, never mind one psychologically preconditioned to experience deviant experiences as signs of Sky's disfavor. In order to understand the emergence of the Ritual Reform as a cultural unit it is essential to recognize the psychological threat of placing awareness of this crisis within the conditions of the Western Zhou royal family's emotional existence.

Because the conditions surrounding King Zhao's demise were so extreme and deviant, the shame of the suprasensible castigation so intense, conventional words were inadequate to break down this overwhelming emotional experience lest they exacerbate the pain of the loss and further threaten maintenance of the lineage's prestige status. Without words to name and identify a post-mortem status, King Zhao could not be psychically buried; mourning was suspended. Although silenced, the pain of King Zhao's death and the shame it incurred remained present; I argue that the institutionalization of the Ritual Reform should be construed as a symptom or symbol produced in response to these conditions. If the Zhou "never recovered" from King Zhao's demise, it may be because the loss was so traumatic that it created a disturbance in the process of mourning.

Indeed, I propose that the Ritual Reforms staged, through rigid taxonomic regulations, a private anguish, a grandson's obsession with restoring honor to his *kaogong*, or deceased grandfather, so as to make his father (King Mu) happy. The central people involved in this dynamic are the inundated King Zhao, his son King Mu, and his grandson, King Mu's son, King Xiao. The length of King Mu's reign, as well as his ruling idiom, as we shall see, did much to stabilize the royal house after he ascended the throne in the wake of his father's ignominious death. But after his reign there was a change in the normal patrilineal line of descent, when King Mu's grandson, King Yih (r. 899-884 B.C.), was succeeded not by his own son but by his uncle, King Xiao.

The ascension of this senior paternal uncle was recorded in the *Bamboo Annals* in terms of capital relocation, stating that the seventh king of the Zhou Dynasty, King Yih, relocated to a northwestern region close to the geographical

185 Ibid. (320–325). Cf. Reinhart (2015) where the author critiques "ethnography of funerary ritual for its failure to consider the emotional aspects of death and bereavement." Kern (2007, 140) speaks about the transformative consequences of King Zhao's death with regard to the emergence of new rituals.

186 Ibid. (320).

"homeland" of the Zhou lineage.[187] While this may appear to document what one scholar has seen as a trend toward "bureaucratization" of Zhou administrative practices, which expanded the reach of Zhou authority beyond the ritual-religious centers established by the dynasty's founders,[188] the consistent threats posed by polities who inhabited this area documented in bronze inscriptions, not to mention the absence of archaeological data that might confirm the Zhou's relocation, invalidate this claim. The area, called Quanqiu or "Canine Hill," was inhabited by tribes, sometimes referred to as the Quanrong (Canine-warrior-like Rong tribe), who perturbed Zhou territorial stability.[189]

The phonetic and semantic correspondence between the words "mound, ruins, grave, empty," (*qiu*) and "empty" (*xu*), and "large hill, mound, site of a ruined city" (*xu/qiu*), suggest that King Yih may have been buried there, even intimating that these events portended a fate similar to the Shang dynasty. This is suggested by the locution "the ruins of Yin (Shang)," which the Zhou used to refer to their predecessor.[190] Thus, although fragmented, these historical details indicate that King Yih's successor, King Xiao, ascended the throne amidst yet another catastrophic loss that implicated the Zhou's claim to prestige status.[191]

Kai Volgesang has remarked on the important role genealogies played in Ritual Reform rhetoric.[192] Whether they related to Zhou royal lineage, or to family lines that intersected with it, genealogies permeated repertoire performed at seasonal festivals. Genealogies appear as well in paleographical accounts written by Western Zhou aristocrats. Historiographers have observed how this cultural form emerged in response to transformations wrought by sociopolitical breakdowns, such as those that required King Xiao's ascension.[193] Genealogies attempt to bridge a gap between the present and an estranged past. I posit that the estranged past inscribed in the Ritual Reform genealogies was the catastrophic drowning of King Zhao.

Lothar von Falkenhausen proposes that King Xiao's ascension to the throne in the wake of King Yih's demise was almost a necessary usurpation, though he notes that there was most likely an opposing faction.[194] As an elder family member, King Xiao would have been respected, but the proximity of his relationship with King Mu surely enhanced his credentials. Having witnessed his father's navigation of the challenges to royal ascension in the wake of King

187 Fang and Wang (1981).
188 Li (2008, 94–95, et passim).
189 Pulleyblank (2000, 26).
190 Shaughnessy (2011).
191 Shaughnessy (2011, 387) thinks that King Yih was forced into exile.
192 Volgesang (2014).
193 Ibid.
194 Von Falkenhausen (2006, 59, 60, 63). Li (2006, 99), suggests that King Xiao's ascension involved a succession dispute.

Zhao's untimely and hence shame-inducing drowning, King Xiao was a compelling descendant who likely had the skill set necessary to transcend a similar obstacle to dynastic self-fashioning.[195] King Xiao's suitability for kingship may also have been enhanced by the memory of King Mu's successful campaign against the Quanrong, who lived in the geographical area associated with King Yih's death. According to legend, King Mu's success resulted in the transportation the "the five kings of Quanrong back to the east and relocated them at Taiyuan..."[196]

There is growing scholarly consensus that King Xiao's reign is connected to the Ritual Reform. Early China scholars for the most part concur that the reform occurred sometime around the late middle Western Zhou.[197] Lothar von Falkenhausen's rigorous attempts to untangle the complex nexus of religious, political and social triggers that led to the production of the ritual reforms, emphasizes that central to the reforms was "an effort to define social relationships more stringently and to create a more differentiated kin-based hierarchy."[198] The ritual manifestation of this differentiation reform is rooted in the practice of splitting lineages, which, according to von Falkenhausen, may have been instituted to ease the growing unwieldiness of the ancestral cult and the attendant ritual schedule.

For evidence von Falkenhausen cites an extraordinarily vivid genealogy inscribed in a bronze discovered among a cache in 1975, the Shi Qiang-*pan*. He dates the production of the vessel to King Xiao.[199] Especially relevant to our inquiry is the reliance of the genealogy on a new system of post-mortem naming, which evokes Zu Jia's reforms. The temple names used in the bronze inscription are preserved in a lexicon entitled Explanations for Rules for Posthumous Naming (*Shifa jie,* hereafter, "Rules"), which was unearthed in 279 A.D. from a tomb dating back to 300 B.C. The text involved rituals aimed to choose posthumous titles for the deceased (royal ancestors). The titles were used to memorialize the deceased during sacrifices. The comments take the form of annotations for each title, which assume a link between lived actions and posthumous commemoration. In addition, they provide an interpretive grid for evaluating and linguistically containing a deceased's behavior. This is the case for the word chosen as a posthumous title for King Xiao.

---

195 Porter (1996), reads a fourth century B.C. narrative entitled *The Accounts of King Mu* (*Mu Tianzi zhuan*), as a symbolic account of King Mu's actions following the traumatic watery death of King Zhao. For the foreign invasion, see Li (2006, 97); for historical and archaeological evidence involving King Zhao's death see Li (2006, 327–328). The inscription on the Shi Qiang-*pan* vessel puts a positive spin on King Zhao's actions, stating only that he "opened the way toward the south."

196 Li (2006, 346).

197 Rawson (1990, 1999).

198 Von Falkenhausen (1997, 4–9).

199 Idem. (2006, 62).

Von Falkenhausen sees "Rules" as an articulation of "new" customs for referring to the dead, which he ties to the Ritual Reform.[200] In this text *xiao* is annotated as appropriate for someone who engaged in specific acts, such as: settling and regulating the five generations [of a lineage]; harmonizing, (*he*), the relationships between kin (*qin*), and establishing (*zhao*), new (*xin*), rituals involving seasonal regulation and coordination with the ancestral cult schedule.[201] This definition of *xiao* contrasts both with early Western Zhou usage of the term to refer to specific food offering rituals for the ancestors, as well as with later Eastern Zhou (772-221 B.C.) usage, which refers to ethical behavior grounded in children's attitudes toward their parents, filiality.[202] The next chapter argues that a key to solving this semantic enigma lies in the recognition of the shared psychological roots of King Xiao and Zu Jia's reforms, even as the contents of the cultural idioms are distinct. The implications of this historical explanation are far-reaching since they present a model for illuminating the genesis and evolution of social institutions, such as Chinese filiality.[203]

Cited Sources

Abraham, N., & Rand, N. (1979). The shell and the kernel. *Diacritics*, *9*(1), 16–28.

Abraham, N., & Torok, M. (1994). *The Shell and the Kernel: Renewals of Psychoanalysis* (Vol. 1). University of Chicago Press.

Allan, S. (1991). *The shape of the turtle: Myth, art, and cosmos in early China*. SUNY Press.

Allan, S. (2007). On the identity of Shang *di* and the origin of the concept of a celestial mandate (*tianming*). *Early China*, *31*, 1–46.

Bagley, R. (2004). Anyang writing and the origins of the Chinese writing system. In

200 See von Falkenhausen (1997, 18). Names by which we refer to the later Western Zhou Kings are temple names. Scholars have shown that the earlier names by which Zhou Kings are referred were used during their lives as well as death. It has been argued that these names were redolent of the glorified actions of the establishment and extension of Zhou dynastic rule. For a good summary of the debates surrounding the customs of royal references see Huang (2012). Reign dates, due to the obscure nature of records referring to his reign, are approximate, and for convenience follow Shaughnessy (1992, xix; 236–297). The question of whether a *shi* temple or posthumous name was used in Western Zhou times during an individual's lifetime is still debated. Von Falkenhausen (1996) makes a persuasive argument that the posthumous names listed in the *Shifa* could not have originated before the middle of the Western Zhou, for it is linked to the major restructuring of the Zhou ancestral cult which occurred during the Ritual Reform.

201 See the *Yi Zhou shu* (1911, 6.7b-8a). For a description and analysis of the *Yi Zhou shu* see Huang (1976), and Shaughnessy's (1993) discussion of the text.

202 See, for example, the poem "Yong" of the *Zhou Hymn* (Zhou song) section of the *Shijing*. See also Masari (1994, 13–25), where he discusses Western Zhou usages of the term *xiao*, and (372–441, where he provides a seemingly exhaustive list of bronze inscriptions that refer to the ritual of *xiao*. See also Wang (1992); Li (1974); Hsiao (1978).

203 Abraham and Torok (1994, 169).

S. Houston (Ed.), *The first writing: Script Invention as history and process* (pp. 190–249). Cambridge, UK: Cambridge University Press.

Bagley, R. (1999). Shang archaeology. In M. Loewe and E.L. Shaughnessy (Eds.), The Cambridge history of ancient China (pp. 124–231). Cambridge: Cambridge University Press.

Barrett, J. L. (2004). Why would anyone believe in God? In A. Smith (Ed.), *Thinking about religion. Extending the cognitive science of religion*. Palgrave MacMillan.

Barrett, J. L. (2011). *Cognitive science, religion, and theology: From human minds to divine minds*. Templeton Press.

Bo, S. R. (1996). *Zhongguo tianwenxue shi (History of Chinese astronomy)*. Wenjin chubanshe.

Boltz, W. G. (1994). *The origin and early development of the Chinese writing system* (Vol. 78). Eisenbrauns.

Boltz, W. G. (1999). Language and writing. In M. Loewe & E. Shaughnessy (Eds.), *The Cambridge history of ancient China: From the origins of civilization to 221 BC* (pp. 74–123).

Campbell, R. B., Baines, J., Flad, R., Jigen, T., Min, L., Olsen, J. W., & Campbell, R. B. (2009). Toward a networks and boundaries approach to early complex polities: the Late Shang case. *Current Anthropology, 50*(6), 821–848.

Campbell, R., Jaffe, Y., Kim, C., Sturm, C., & Jaang, L. (2021). Chinese Bronze Age political economies: A complex polity provisioning approach. *Journal of Archaeological Research*, 1–48. doi:10.1007/s10814-021-09158-0

Chang, J. Y., & Sun, Y. G. (2017). Chahai yizhi shengzhi chongbai kao. *Chifeng xueyuan xuebao, 8*(38), 5–8.

Chang, K. C. (1988). Puyang sanqiao yu Zhongguo gudai meishu shang de renshou muti. *Wenwu, 11*, 36–39.

Chang, K. C., Xu, P., Lu, L., Pingfang, X., Wangping, S., Zhongpei, Z., & Renxiang, W. (2005). *The formation of Chinese civilization: an archaeological perspective*. Yale University Press.

Chang, T. (1986). A new view of King Wu Ding. *Monumenta Serica, 37*, 1–12.

Chvaja, R., & Řezníček, D. (2019). An integrative framework of commitment displays in religious systems. *Human Ethology, 34*, 41–52.

Chen, S. (2002). Son of heaven and son of god: Interactions among ancient Asiatic cultures regarding sacral kingship and theophoric names. *Journal of the Royal Asiatic Society, 12*(3), 289–325.

Chen, J. J. (2013). Puyang Xishuipo longhu bangsu de tianwen jiazhi. *Puyang zhiye-jishuyuan xueyuan xuebao, 26*(2), 1–4.

Chen, W. T. (2012). Long qiyuan zhushuo bianzheng. *Shixue Yuekan, 10*, 124–126.

Childs-Johnson, E. (1991). Jades of the Hongshan culture: The dragon and fertility cult worship. *Arts asiatiques, 46*, 82–95.

Childs-Johnson, E. (2018). Urban daemons of early Shang: Urbanism in ancient China. *Archaeological Research in Asia*, 14, 135–150.

Childs-Johnson, E. (2021a). Introduction and background. In E. Childs-Johnson (Ed.), *The Oxford handbook of early China*. Oxford University Press.

Childs-Johnson, E. (2021b). The Jade Age revised, ca. 3500–2000 BCE. In E. Childs-Johnson (Ed.), *The Oxford handbook of early China*. Oxford University Press.

Childs-Johnson, E. (2021c). Late Shang ritual and residential architecture at Great City Shang, Yinxu in Anayang, Henan. In E. Childs-Johnson (Ed.), *The Oxford handbook of early China*. Oxford University Press.

Childs-Johnson, E. (2021d). Shang belief and art E. Childs-Johnson (Ed.), *The Oxford handbook of early China*. Oxford University Press.
Clark, K. J., & Winslett, J. T. (2011). The evolutionary psychology of Chinese religion: Pre-Qin high gods as punishers and rewarders. *Journal of the American Academy of Religion*, *79*(4), 928–960.
Donald, M. (2000). The central role of culture in cognitive evolution: A reflection on the myth of the isolated mind. In L. Nucci, G. B. Saxe, E. Turiel (Eds.), *Culture, thought, and development*(pp. 19–38). Psychology Press.
Drennan, R. D., Peterson, C. E., & Berrey, C. A. (2020). Environmental risk buffering in Chinese Neolithic villages: Impacts on community structure in the Central Plains and the Western Liao Valley. *Archaeological Research in Asia, 21*, 100165.
Eliade, M. (1958). *Patterns in comparative religion*. Sheed and Ward.
Fang S. M., & Wang X. N. (Eds.) (1981).*Guben zhushu jinian jiaheng*. Guji chubanshe.
Feng, S. (1990a). Henan Puyang Xishuipo 45 hao mu de tianwenxue yanjiu. *Wenwu*, *3*, 52–60.
Feng, S. (1990b). Zhongguo zaoqi xingxiangtu yanjiu. *Ziran kexueshi yanjiu*, *9*(2), 108–118.
Feng, S. (1993). Hongshan wenhua san huan shi tan de tianwenxue yanjiu. *Beifang Wenwu*, *1*(33), 9–17.
Flad, R. K., Allan, S., Campbell, R., Chen, X., von Falkenhausen, L., Fang, H., … & Flad, R. K. (2008). Divination and power: A multiregional view of the development of oracle bone divination in early China. *Current Anthropology*, *49*(3), 403–437.
Gao, J. N. (2019). *Shang-Zhou qingtongqi zushi mingwen lishi laiyuan fenlei yanjiu* (Ph.D. Dissertation. Shandong Daxue).
Grecucci, A., Theuninck, A., Frederickson, J., & Job, R. (2015). Mechanisms of social emotion regulation: From neuroscience to psychotherapy. *Emotion regulation: Processes, Cognitive Effects and Social Consequences*, *57*, 84.
Guo J. Y. (2010). Shiqian xinyang zhong shenlong xingxiang laiyuan chuyi. *Yindu Xuekan*, *31*, 66–75.
He, N. (2018a). Taosi: An archaeological example of urbanization as a political center in prehistoric China. *Archaeological Research in Asia*, *14*, 20–32.
He, N. (2018b). Archaeological indicators for Chinese early states: a case study of Taosi in Shanxi. *Social Evolution & History*, *17*(2), 205–234.
He, N. (2021). Longshan culture issues: Taosi and cosmology. In E. Childs-Johnson (Ed.), *The Oxford handbook of early China*. Oxford University Press.
Henan Puyang Xishuipo yizhi fajue jianbao. (1988). *Wenwu*, *3*, 1–6.
Hsiao H. I. (1978). A preliminary interpretation of the origin of the concept of hsiao in the shang period. *Chinese Culture*, *3*(193), 5–19.
Hu, Z. W., Jinyi, R., Guo, Jiuli, Hu, Xianliang, & Xu, Dengli. (1999). A Chinese observing site from remote antiquity. *Journal for the History of Astronomy*, *30*(3), 231–235.
Huang S. S. (2012). Cong *Zuo zhuan* zhong shi 'Ling' guojun lun qi ding shi zhi you. *Donghua Hanxue*, *16* (2012), 89–114.
Huang, P. R. (1976). *Zhoushu yanjiu* (Ph.D. dissertation, Taiwan University).
James, J. M. (1993). Is it really a dragon? Some remarks on the Xishuipo Burial. *Archives of Asian Art*, *46*, 100–101.
Jiang, J., Wagner, A. D., & Egner, T. (2018). Integrated externally and internally generated task predictions jointly guide cognitive control in prefrontal cortex. *Elife*, 7.
Keightley, D. N. (1978).*Sources of Shang history: The Oracle-Bone Inscriptions of Bronze Age China*. Berkeley: University of California Press.

Keightley, D. N. (2000). The ancestral landscape. In D. N. Keightley (Ed.), *Time, space, and community in Late Shang China (ca. 1200–1045 BC)*. Centre for Chinese Studies and Institute of East Asian Studies.

Keightley, D. N. (2004). The making of the ancestors: Late Shang religion and its legacy. *Religion and Chinese Society: Ancient and Medieval China, 1*, 3–63.

Keightley, D. N. (2006). Marks and labels: Early writing in Neolithic and Shang China. In M. T. Stark (Ed.), *Archaeology of Asia* (pp. 177–201). Wiley.

Keightley, D. N. (2012). *Working for His Majesty: Research notes on labor mobilization in Late Shang China (ca. 1200–1045 BC), as Seen in the Oracle-bone inscriptions, with particular attention to handicraft industries, agriculture, warfare, hunting, construction, and the Shang's legacies*. Institute of East Asian Studies, University of California.

Kern, M. (2007). The performance of writing in western zhou China. In S. la Porta (Ed.), *The poetics of grammar and the metaphysics of sound and sign* (pp. 109–175). Brill.

Kern, M. (2009). Bronze inscriptions, the Shijing and the Shangshu: The evolution of the ancestral sacrifice during the western Zhou. In J. Lagerwey and M. Kalinowski (Eds.), *Early Chinese religion, part one: Shang through Han (1250 BC–220 AD) (2 vols.*, pp. 143–200). Brill.

Khayutina, M. (2010). Royal hospitality and geopolitical constitution of the Western Zhou polity. *T'oung Pao, 96*(1), 1–73.

Khayutina, M. (2021). Western Zhou cultural and historic setting. *The Oxford handbook of early China* (pp. 335–400).

Lagerwey, J., & Kalinowski, M. (2008). Introduction. In J. Lagerwey and M. Kalinowski (Eds.), *Early Chinese religion*, part one: *Shang through Han (1250 BC–220 AD*). Brill.

Larrive-Bass, S. S. M. (2015). Embodied materials: The emergence of figural imagery in prehistoric China (Doctoral dissertation, Columbia University).

Launonen, L. T. (2017). Cognitive science of religion and the debunking debate. In H. Appelqvist (Ed.), *The origin of religion: Perspectives from philosophy, theology, and religious studies* (pp. 151–162). Luther-Agricola Society.

Lewis, M. E. (2010). Evolution of the calendar in Shang China. In I. Morley and C. Renfrew (Eds.), *The archaeology of measurement. Comprehending heaven, earth and time in ancient societies* (pp. 195–202). Cambridge University Press.

Li, X.Q. (1992-3). A neolithic jade plaque and ancient Chinese cosmology. *National Palace Museum Bulletin, XXVII*, 5–6 (November/December 1992-January/February 1993), 1–8.

Li, F. (2006). *Landscape and power in early China: the crisis and fall of the Western Zhou 1045–771 BC*. Cambridge University Press.

Li, F. (2008). Bureaucracy and the state in early China. *New York*.

Li, R., Lv, F., Yang, L., Liu, F., Liu, R., & Dong, G. (2020). Spatial–temporal variation of cropping patterns in relation to climate change in Neolithic China. *Atmosphere, 11*(7), 677.

Li, R. C., & Wang, X. J. (2013). Guanyu Niheliang Hongshang wenhua chutu "yugui" huo "hubie" de mingming wenti jiqi jiazhi de sikao. *Liaoning shi zhuan xue bao, 2*, 134–136

Li, Y. M. (1974). Yin Zhou Jinwen zhong de "xiao" he Kong Qiu "xiaodao" de fantong benzhi. *Kaogu xuebao, 2*, 21–26.

Liu, B. (2021). Liangzhu Culture and the ancient city of Liangzhu. In E. Childs-Johnson (Ed.), *The Oxford handbook on early China*. Oxford University Press.

Liu, L. (1996). Mortuary ritual and social hierarchy in the Longshan culture. *Early China, 21*, 1–46.

Liu, L. & Xu, H. (2015). Rethinking Erlitou: Legend, history and Chinese archaeology. *Wenwu, 81*, 886–901.

Loewe, M., & Shaughnessy, E. L. (Eds.). (1999). *The Cambridge history of ancient China: From the origins of civilization to 221 BC.* Cambridge University Press.

Lü, F. C. (2018). Chaihai yizhi muzang fenxi. *Chifeng xuehuan xuebao, 3*(39), 16–19.

Lü, Z. (2016). *Shang Zhou zhengzhi tizhi bijiao yanjiu—cong Shang Zhou gongqing xingshi de jiao du* (Ph.D. Dissertation. Hebei shifan daxue).

Luo, Y. C. (2007). *Shang Zhou qingtongqi zuhui wenzi zonghe yanjiu* (Ph.D. Dissertation. Shaanxi Normal University).

Luo, Y. C. (2019). Jinwen zuihui de gongneng jiqi shidai bianhua. *Zhongyuan wenhua yanjiu, 5* (7), 102–108.

Lü, Zhi. (2016). *Shang Zhou zhengzhi tizhi bijiao yanjiu—cong Shang Zhou gongqing xingshi de jiao du. (Comparison of Shang and Zhou political systems—from the perspective of lineage and clan labels)* (Ph.D. Dissertation. *Hebei shifan daxue*).

Masari, I. (1994). *The Philosophy of Filiality in Ancient China: Ideological Development of Ancestor Worship in the Zhanguo Period* (Ph.D. diss. University of British Columbia).

Pang, J. (2007). *Zhongguo longwenhua.* Chongqing chubanshe.

Pang, K. D., Yau, K. K., & Chou, H. H. (2002). Astronomical dating and statistical analysis of ancient eclipse data. In S. M. Razaullah Ansari (Ed.), *History of oriental astronomy* (pp. 95–119). Springer.

Pankenier, D. W. (1981). Astronomical dates in Shang and Western Zhou. *Early China, 7*, 2–37.

Pankenier, D. W. (1985). Mozi and the dates of Xia, Shang, and Zhou: A research note. *Early China, 9*(1), 175–183.

Pankenier, D. W. (1995). The cosmo-political background of Heaven's Mandate. *Early China, 20*, 121–176.

Pankenier, D. W. (2004). A brief history of Beiji 北极 (Northern Culmen), with an excursus on the origin of the character di. *Journal of the American Oriental Society, 124*, 211–236.

Pankenier, D. W. (2009). Locating True North in Ancient China. In *Cosmology Across Cultures. Vol. 409*, 128.

Pankenier, D. W. (2013). *Astrology and cosmology in early China: conforming earth to heaven.* Cambridge University Press.

Pechenkina, K. (2018). Of millets and wheat: diet and health on the Central Plain of China during the neolithic and bronze age. In *Routledge handbook of early Chinese history* (pp. 39–60). Routledge.

Peterson, C. E., Drennan, R. D., & Bartel, K. L. (2016). Comparative analysis of Neolithic household artifact assemblage data from northern China. *Journal of Anthropological Research, 72*(2), 200–225.

Peterson, C. E., Shelach, G., Bandry, M., & Fox, J. R. (2010). The evolution of early Yangshao Period village organization in the middle reaches of northern China's Yellow River valley. In M. S. Bandy (Ed.), *Becoming villagers: Comparing early village societies* (pp. 246–275). University of Arizona Press.

Pietraszewski, D. (2016). How the mind sees coalitional and group conflict: the evolutionary invariances of n-person conflict dynamics. *Evolution and Human Behavior, 37*(6), 470–480.

Porter, D. L. (1996). *From deluge to discourse: Myth, history, and the generation of Chinese fiction*. SUNY Press.

Puett, M. J. (2002). *To become a god: Cosmology, sacrifice, and self-divinization in early China* (No. 57). Harvard University Asia Center.

Puett, M. J. (2010). Theodicies of discontinuity: Domesticating energies and dispositions in Early China. *Journal of Chinese Philosophy*, *37*, 51–66.

Pulleyblank, E. G. (2000). Ji 姬 and Jiang 姜: The role of exogamic clans in the organization of the Zhou polity. *Early China, 25*, 1–27.

Puyangshi wenwu guanli weiyuan hui. (1988). Puyang Xishuipo yizhi shijue jianbao. *Zhongyuan Wenwu, 1*, 1–6.

Qiu, X. G., & Fowler, V. K. (1985). On the burning of human victims and the fashioning of Clay Dragons in order to seek rain as seen in the Shang Dynasty Oracle-Bone Inscriptions. *Early China*, *9*(1), 290–306.

Rand, N. (1994). Editor's note for the phantom. In N. Abraham & M. Torok (Eds.), *The shell and the kernel: Renewals of psychoanalysis. Volume 1*. Trans. Nicholas Rand. University of Chicago Press.

Rawson, J. (1990). *Western zhou ritual bronzes from the arthur M. sackler collections*. The Arthur M. Sackler Foundation.

Rawson, J. (1999). Western Zhou Archaeology. In M. Loewe & E. Shaughnessy (Eds.), *The Cambridge history of Ancient China* (pp. 352–449). Cambridge University Press.

Reinhart, K. (2015). Religion, violence, and emotion: Modes of religiosity in the Neolithic and Bronze Age of northern China. *Journal of World Prehistory*, *28*(2), 76–109.

Richler, J. J., Wong, Y. K., & Gauthier, I. (2011). Perceptual expertise as a shift from strategic interference to automatic holistic processing. *Current Directions in Psychological Science*, *20*(2), 129–134

Schwartz, A. C. (2015). China's first prayer. *Journal of American Oriental Society*, *135*(1), 93–113.

Schwartz, A. C. (2020). *The Oracle Bone Inscriptions from Huayuanzhuang East*. De Gruyter.

Shaughnessy, E. L. (1985). Extra-lineage cult in the Shang Dynasty: A surrejoinder. *Early China, 11*, 182–194.

Shaughnessy, E. L. (1992). *Sources of Western Zhou history: inscribed bronze vessels*. University of California Press.

Shaughnessy, E. L. (1993). The Yi Zhou Shu. In M. Loewe (Ed.), *Early Chinese texts: A bibliographic guide*. Society for the Study of Early China and the Institute of East Asian Studies.

Shaughnessy, E. L. (1999). Western Zhou history. In M. Loewe and E. Shaughnessy (Eds.), *The Cambridge history of ancient China: From the origins of civilization to 221 BC*. Cambridge University Press.

Shaughnessy, E. L. (2011). History and inscriptions, China. In A. Feldherr & G. Hardy (Eds.), *The Oxford history of historical writing, Vol. 1*: Beginnings to A.D. 600. (pp. 371–393). Oxford.

Shelach-Lavi, G. (2015). *The archaeology of early China*. Cambridge University Press.

Shelach-Lavi, G. (2018). Main issues in the study of the Chinese Neolithic Gideon Shelach-Lavimain issues in the Chinese Neolithic. In *Routledge handbook of early Chinese history* (pp. 15–38). Routledge.

Shangshu. Maoshi zhengyi; Shisanjing zhushu edition, (Chinese Text Project).

Slone, Jason, & McCorkle, W. William Jr. (Eds.) (2019). *The cognitive science of religion: A methodological introduction to key empirical studies*. Bloomsbury Publishing.

Shijing Maoshi zhengyi Shisanjing zhushu edition, (Chinese Text Project).

Sieratzki, J. S., & Woll, B. (2002). Neuropsychological and neuropsychiatric perspectives on maternal cradling preferences. *Epidemiologia e psichiatria sociale, 11*, 170–176.

Smith, A. D. (2010). The Evidence for Scribal Training at Anyang. In D. Branner and Li Feng (Eds.), *Writing and literacy in early China.* University of Washington Press.

Smith, J., & Fan, Y. (2021). The cultural and historical setting of the Shang. In E. Childs-Johnson (Ed.), *The Oxford handbook of early China.* Oxford University Press.

Song, Y. (2018). Divination and deviation: The problem of prediction and personal freedom in early China (Doctoral dissertation, University of Pennsylvania).

Song, G. D. (2021). Early and Middle Shang PERIODS. In E. Childs-Johnson (Ed.), *The Oxford handbook of early China.* Oxford University Press.

Sosis, R. (2009). The adaptationist-byproduct debate on the evolution of religion: Five misunderstandings of the adaptationist program. *Journal of Cognition and Culture, 9*(3-4), 315–332.

Sun, S. D. (1984). Sanxingtala Hongshan wenhua yulong kao. *Wenwu, 6*, 7–10.

Sun Y. (2020). Bronze vessels: Style, assemblages, and innovations of the Western Zhou Period. *The Oxford handbook of early China* (pp. 451–469).

Sun, Y. (2021). Bronze vessels: Style, assemblages, and innovations of the Western Zhou period. In E. Childs-Johnson (Ed.), *The Oxford handbook of early China.* Oxford University Press.

Takashima, K. I. (2014). Working for His Majesty. *T'oung Pao, 100*(1-3), 237–263.

Tian, C. W. (1998). On the legends of Yao, Shun, and Yu and the origins of Chinese civilization. *Chinese Studies in Philosophy, 19*(3), 21–68.

Tomasello, M., & Carpenter, M. (2007). Shared intentionality. *Developmental Science, 10*(1), 121–125.

Ventura, P. (2014). Let's face it: Reading acquisition, face and word processing. *Frontiers in Psychology, 5*, 787.

Ventura, P., Fernandes, T., Pereira, A., Guerreiro, J. C., Farinha-Fernandes, A., Delgado, J., … & Wong, A. C. N. (2020). Holistic word processing is correlated with efficiency in visual word recognition. *Attention, Perception, & Psychophysics, 82*, 1–12.

Vogelsang, K. (2014). The shape of history: On reading Li Wai-yee. *Early China, 37*, 579–599.

Vogt, N. (2021). Western Zhou government and society. In E. Childs-Johnson (Ed.), *The Oxford handbook of early China.* Oxford University Press.

Van de Cruys, S., & Wagemans, J. (2011). Putting reward in art: a tentative prediction error account of visual art. *i-Perception, 2*(9), 1035–1062.

Van de Cruys, S., & Wagemans, J. (2011). Gestalts as predictions: Some reflections and an application to art. *Gestalt Theory*, 33(3), 325–344.

Vogelsang, K. (2014). The shape of history: On reading Li Wai-yee. *Early China, 37*, 579–599.

Von Falkenhausen. (1993). On the historiographical orientation of Chinese archaeology. Antiquity,*67*(257), 839–849.

Falkenhausen, Lothar von. (Luó Tài) (1997).Youguan Xī-zhou wangqi lizhi gaige jí Zhuangbai qingtongqi niandai de xin jiaoshuo: Cong shixi mingwen shuoqǐ. Li Ling, trans. In Zhongguo kaoguxue yu lishixue zhi zhenghe yanjiu. Tsang Cheng-hwa (Ed.), Integrated studies of Chinese archaeology and historiography (Vol. 2, pp. 651–676). Taipei: Academia Sinica, Institute of History and Philology.

Von Falkenhausen. (1996). The concept of wen in the Ancient Chinese ancestral cult. *Chinese literature: Essays, articles, reviews, 18*, 1–22.

Von Falkenhausen. (2006). *Chinese society in the age of Confucius (1000–250 BC): the archaeological evidence* (*Vol. 2*). ISD LLC.

Wang, S. X. (1991). Lun Xi-Zhou xiaodao guan de benzhi. *Renwen zazhi, 2*, 70–76.

Wang, Z. Z. (2017). Shang Zhou zhi shang shen de yanbian: Cong Di dao Tiandi tongyi xing zhuanbian de yuanyou. Zhongguo zaoqi lishi fazhan daolu yu gedi wenminghua juncheng. *Lishi yanjiu, 5*, 4–10.

Wong, A. C. N., Bukach, C. M., Hsiao, J., Greenspon, E., Ahern, E., Duan, Y., & Lui, K. F. (2012). Holistic processing as a hallmark of perceptual expertise for nonface categories including Chinese characters. *Journal of Vision, 12*(13), 7.

Wu, S. H. (2012). Fighting for his majesty (I): Accretion of the Greater Shang (1200–1045 B.C.) *Journal of Military History, 1*, 24–60.

Wu, S. H. (2013). Fighting for his majesty (II): The Shang art of war. *Journal of Military History, 2*, 89–126.

Wu, X., Zhang, X., Jin, Z., Song, Y., Luan, F., & Xue, X. (2019). Strontium isotope analysis of Yangtze alligator remains from Late Neolithic North China. *Archaeological and Anthropological Sciences, 11*(3), 1049–1058.

Xigui, Q., & Fowler, V. K. (1985). On the burning of human victims and the fashioning of clay dragons in order to seek rain as seen in the Shang Dynasty Oracle-Bone Inscriptions. *Early China, 9*(1), 290–306.

Xu, H. (2021). Introduction to the Xia Period: Definitions, themes, and debate. In E. Childs-Johnson (Ed.), *The Oxford handbook of early China*. Oxford University Press.

Xu, Z. T., Yao, K. C. C. & Stephenson, Richard. (1989). Astronomical records on the Shang Dynasty Oracle Bones. *Archaeoastronomy, 14*(20), S61–S72.

Xu, Z., Pankenier, W., & Jiang, Y. (2000). *East-Asian archaeoastronomy: Historical records of astronomical observations of China, Japan and Korea*. CRC Press.

Yi Zhou Shu Jiaoshi, ed., Zhu Yuzheng(1911). E guan shucong rpt. edition. (Chinese Text Project)

Yin, D. F. (1978). 西汉汝阴侯墓出土的占盘和天文仪器/Xi Han Ru Yin hou mu chu tu de zhan pan he tian wen yi qi. *Kaogu, 5* (1978), 338–343.

Yuan, J. J. (2011). Zuoceban tongyuan mingwen xinshi bulun. *Zhongyuan Wenwu, 1*, 43–52.

Zhang, H., Bevan, A., & Guo, D. (2013). The Neolithic ceremonial complex at Niuheliang and wider Hongshan landscapes in northeastern China. *Journal of World Prehistory, 26*(1), 1–24.

Zhang, X. H., & Shao Q. S. (2009). Zuoceban tongyuan mingwen cihui. *Heilongjiang Jiaoyuxueyuan Xuebao, 1*, 100–101.

Zhang, Z. L. (2015). Cong zhongyuan longshenhua kan "Zhonghua diyi long" de wenhua shi jiazhi. *Puyang Zhiyejishu Xueyuan Xuebao, 2*(28), 5–9.

Zhushu jinian jizheng. Chen Fengheng (Ed.) (Chinese Text Project).

5

THE DEEP HISTORY OF THE WESTERN ZHOU RITUAL REFORM

As the title foretells, this chapter engages in a deep dive. A wide range of evidence is marshaled to argue that the Ritual Reform must be seen first and foremost as concomitant to King Xiao's implementation of a newly constructed agrarian and cult schedule. My claim is premised on the gloss for King Xiao's posthumous name in "Rules," which attributes to the ruler acts that interpolated cult sacrifice into an archaic seasonal ritual system. This description was not a mere figure of speech. Rather, this sole reference to the Ritual Reform's aims and content preserved in the transmitted record convokes the context of a full-fledged astro-calendrical reform, including the invention of new asterisms. Once the system is excavated, reconstructed, and reconciled with paleographic and transmitted textual evidence, we will be positioned to appreciate the neuropsychological implications of King Xiao's royal acts, which I argue may be construed as a symptom (symbol) of complicated mourning.

Although King Xiao is attributed as the instigator of the Ritual Reform, it did not occur *ex nihilo*. My approach construes the reform as a cultural unit whose symbolic idiom marked the failure of ordinary language to convert into words the traumatic experience of King Zhao's death. The astro-calendrical realities that undergirded King Xiao's alignment of royal cult with archaic seasonal habits will be shown to have been the product of an evolving process beginning with his father's reign. The conditions surrounding King Mu's ascension, and how they would have impressed the linguistic surround in which his son King Xiao was socialized, serve as an organizing principle for the analytical line advanced in this chapter. This chronology of the Western Zhou Dynasty will be helpful as we delve deeper into interpersonal lineage dynamics:

DOI: 10.4324/9781003215134-5

Western Zhou Ruler Chronology*

King Wen	1059-1050 B.C. (Pre-conquest)
King Wu	1046-1043 B.C.
King Cheng	1042-1006 B.C.
King Kang	1005-978 B.C.
King Zhao	977-957 B.C.
King Mu	956-918 B.C.
King Gong	916-900 B.C.
King Yih	899-883 B.C.
King Xiao	882-866 B.C.
King Yi	865-858 B.C.
King Li	853-828 B.C.
Gong He	841-828 B.C.
King Xuan	827-782 B.C.
King You	781-771 B.C.

*Following Shaughnessy (1992, xix) with modifications for King Xiao's reign length.

To facilitate the excavation of this "intrapsychic" site, I identify four Phases or strata, each of which provides data for sketching the psychoemotional history of the Ritual Reform. Recalling how Abraham and Torok understood symbols as dynamic structures of meaning making that reside at the root of all symptom/symbolic behavior, my method assumes that "[w]e read fragments of semantic or phonetic elements that, if joined to their missing parts, would signify something (a drama, a scene, or simply a lexical or phonetic element) that must for some reason be kept hidden or out of circulation."[1]

This reading strategy assumes the possibility of identifying the traumatic source that catalyzed the production of a symbol by looking for rhetorical and lexical cues that reveal "the direction or 'sense' in which a variety of symbols must be held to fit its complement." This "allow[s] us to reconstruct the lines or traces of the direction or sense of [the symbol's] 'voyage' or displacement from its other half."[2] In other words, the methodology offers a way to identify the underlying emotional conditions that propelled the formation of the symbols as a mediating response. Because the concept of the symbol "is not informed by any predetermined axiom of human psychosocial development," it holds significant interpretive potential for neurocultural research. The versatility of the concepts of symbol formation justifies its application to a broad range of cultural behavior even as it narrows our focus on its source. In the case of the Ritual Reform, to construe it as a symbol is to see it as a fragment of an emotional experience that inhibited a subject's psyche from the activity of mourning.

1 Rashkin (1992, 38–39).
2 Ibid. (39).

The link between symbols and their traumatic experiential source can "only be verified or dismissed in the process of uncovering specific structures of organization and coherence that preserve intact the specificity of what is obscured."[3] In the four-phase analysis I engage in below, I identify dominant and overlapping lexical patterns among the symbols, sounding them out with alternate verbal possibilities.[4] I look to identify how these other possibilities "inhibit the emergence of meaning by concealing the significant link within a chain of words."[5] From such linguistic operations of displacement, such as synonymy and homophony, emerges a "verbarium," whose entire lexicon is shaped by the *specific* components of the traumatic drama *that must at all costs be shut up and excluded or transformed.*[6] The verbarium contains those distorted or camouflaged lexical fragments that make up a symbol and silently evoke an excluded reality.

Phase I focuses on the immediate aftermath of the crisis, beginning with King Mu's psychological state when he succeeded his father. Traditions of collective memories related to King Mu's aversion to ruling and concomitant desire for pleasure hint at the overwhelming nature of the emotional reality.[7] Western Zhou historian Yang Kuan has demonstrated truth in legends that reflect a collective memory of King Mu's travel, though he contextualizes it in terms of the soft-power efforts King Mu would have had to ply in order to persuade proximate polities in the Yellow River region to support Zhou supremacy.[8] Even this, though, which sounds more realistic, represents the desperate conditions in which the royal scion, King Mu, found himself at the beginning of his reign. I trace evidence that documents strategies used by King Mu to transcend obstacles to mourning King Zhao and point to the way feasting functioned to catalyze psychic digestion of the aversive event.

Phase II refers to the time following King Mu's death. I raise the possibility that the retirement of King Mu's sacrificial cult repertoire by his successor and

3 Ibid. (45).

4 By "ritual repertoire" I refer to the *Book of Poetry* and Book of *Documents*. As mentioned in the preface, these texts comprise the primary cluster of transmitted sources that have authentic Western Zhou roots. Scholars have emphasized the inextricable relationship between many passages in the repertoire and the context of royal court ritual. Bronze inscriptions on vessels that were used in sacrificial rituals also form a major part of this ritual repertoire corpus. See Kern (2001; 2005; 2007). Cf. Kern's (2000) "reconstruction" of a "proposed protext" that reveals patterns of intentional repetition influenced by Western Zhou rhetorical patterns that normalize legitimacy anticipates the linguistic orientation of my present study.

5 Abraham and Torok (1994, 17).

6 Abraham and Torok (2005,16–19, and Appendix, 107–113).

7 Porter (1996) analyzes legends surrounding King Mu's travels, as well as the implications they had for his memory construction and reputation.

8 Yang (2003). See also Zhao (2008), who discusses historical accuracy of King Mu travel references in the *Yi Zhou shu*

son King Gong may have led to the establishment of political factions. I zero in on historical records that show astro-calendrical schedules were out of sync with seasonal realities to suggest that King Xiao's faction would have continued the legacy of King Mu's intense interest in astro-calendrically determined junctures of transformation, such as the winter solstice. Astronomical techniques developed by those astronomers in King Mu's retinue who supported King Xiao's faction, would have prepared King Xiao to take advantage of celestial phenomena that occurred at the time. I argue that these conditions endowed King Xiao with the authority to initiate the Ritual Reform.

Phase III analyzes the Ritual Reform symbolic systems to show they were motivated by King Mu's unfinished business. I excavate the astro-calendrical structure that serves as a tacit organizing principle for the symbolic and rhetorical strategies that characterize Ritual Reform language. The analysis links the underlying theo-political ideation of kingship, and the sumptuary rituals that anchored this framework, to a context of suspended bereavement. The material and cultural objects emerge as products borne from the need to transcend an obstacle to mourning.

Finally, Phase IV traces the spiral line of evolution that connects the cognitive dissonance and subsequent distress triggered by the King Zhao crisis to the evolution of cultural production. Zeroing in on two texts that belong to the classical canon, one poetic, one mantic, the analysis demonstrates how both texts are tacitly driven by an absent complement—King Zhao's unspeakable loss—that is nonetheless central to their signifying function.

The following section provides a brief account of the astro-calendrical conditions and practices during the reigns of King Mu and King Xiao. Their interactions with Sky make clear how the latter's Ritual Reform was radical to the extent that it sought to subsume an archaic Turtle-Sky River-Dragon complex under new axial based astro-calendrical system. The radical shift to the new system reverberates with an earlier, similar shift that directed attention away from Turtle toward the celestial Pole, a turn catalyzed by ambiguous loss. I suggest the same neuropsychological conditions drove both acts.

The Evolution of a Bird Star Semiotics

Although it was not my intention, research into the Ritual Reform uncovered evidence of its role in the evolution of the Chinese zodiac, whose final form was comprised of twenty-eight constellations. Called "lunar stations" (*xiu*) due to their spatial accommodation of the moon as it traversed the ecliptic, the constellations were divided evenly among the four cardinal directions.[9] The

9 Pankenier (2013, 8), states that "originally conceived, the lodges did not technically constitute a zodiac."

foregoing chapters have implied that the zodiac began with Turtle and perhaps Sky River; even though Turtle was not included in the extant zodiac, we have noted how it likely was the source of the winter northern quadrant's zoomorphic nomenclature.

I submit that Fire Star, Heart/Tail were next integrated into the system in the fourth millennium, to constitute a transregional core. Local ancient traditions surrounding the movements of other asterisms, including Orion's belt (ζ Ori), *known to the Chinese as Three Stars (shen),* Three Stars and Pleiades (17 Tau), Hairy Head (*mau*), along with other autumnal constellations, are also preserved in historical records.[10] What has become clear to me is that Dragon's form, up through the Ritual Reform, remained defined by Tail and Heart. While Eastern Zhou texts contain many references to the Dragon constellation envisioned as a configuration made of six asterisms spread over a span of seventy-five degrees across the Eastern Quadrant, I claim that this extended formation only emerged after the new system established by the Zhou became tarnished as a result of the Zhou's shameful fall in status (Figure 5.1).

Understanding this, we are in position to reassess semantic intentions in the nomenclature ascribed to the other parts of the Dragon, which were forced into being, as it were, by the fact of precession, which rendered the zoomorph's seasonal function completely obsolete. I argue that these names, as well as the names of other constellations not recorded in the Shang record, reflect a system that was distinct from even as it accommodated the Turtle-Sky River-Dragon framework. In sum, originally the four configurations extending northward from Heart belonged to an independent system premised on a different method for counting time.

In Chapter 4 we saw how Great Fire and Qual Fire seasonal markers were imbued with specific symbolic significance for Zhou power and royal self-construal (Figure 4.6). This astro-calendrical relationship is mentioned in the "Canon of Yao" (*Yao dian*) chapter in the *Book of Documents,* a late first millennium text that describes acts undertaken by an imagined Neolithic ruler, Yao, who commissioned officials to regulate the calendar. One of the duties was to establish seasonal determinant stars to align collective agrarian efforts: he charged officials "to calculate and order the movements and appearances of the sun, the moon the stars, and zodiacal stations."[11] Historian of science Jiang Xiaoyuan claims this was Yao's one political merit;[12] Kai Volgesang views the vocabulary and political theory surrounding the astro-calendrical narrative as part of a larger debate on appropriate forms of governance: Yao's actions

10 Pankenier (2013, 95ff). Cf. *niu*, Ox (β Cap); *nü*, Girl, and *xu*, Emptiness (β Aqr). Ox was the location of the winter solstice during the Western Zhou.

11 Modified from Legge's translation, *Shangshu zheng yi*, "Yao dian."

12 Jiang (2021).

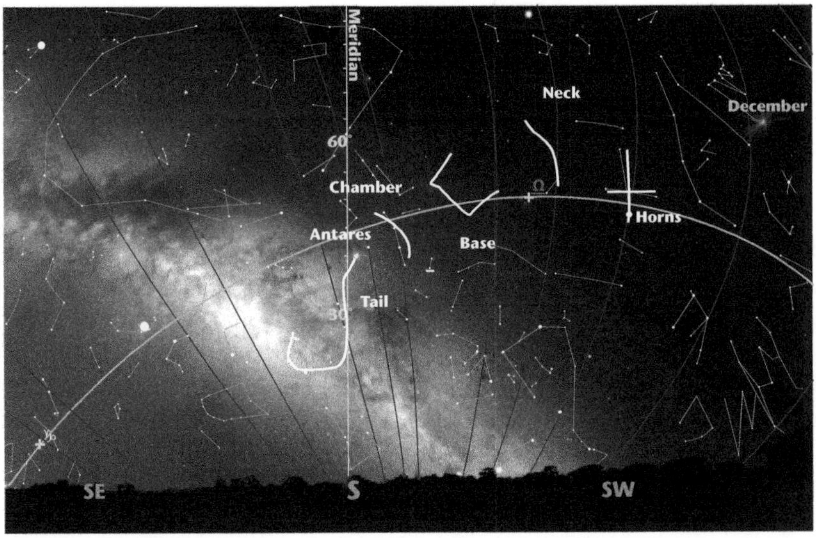

FIGURE 5.1 The six separate configurations that make up the Eastern Dragon. Note the proximity of Chamber, Base, Neck, and Horns to the ecliptic.
Source: Redrawn from screenshot based on Stellarium, an open source software.

reflected a bureaucratic understanding of rulership.[13] In Chapter 6 I will propose that this "split-personality" representation of Yao's rule tacitly points to a dissonance created by conflicting memories about King Xiao's astro-calendrical reforms; the "Canon of Yao's" dual perspective is a symbol of a problematic memory.

The configuration identified as the Vermilion Bird's Beak in Figure 4.6, was called Willow (δ Hya) in the transmitted zodiac system. Many Eastern Zhou annular accounts of summer phenomena reference Willow, the nomenclature derives from the configuration's semblance to the tree's full bough at summertime. The name Willow seems incongruous with the holistic association suggested by the zoomorphic semantic sense conveyed by the names Wings, Quail Fire/Bird/Star/Heart, and Beak. This raises questions about the chronology of astral nomenclature, a central focus of this chapter.

The type of measurements that Yao insisted be consistently conducted involved a technique of calculations based on measurements obtained by observing when legible asterisms "transited the meridian," the highest point of a constellation's arced trajectory from its ascent above the eastern horizon after sunset, to its descent on the west before sunrise. This method relied on the ancient shadow-measuring tools, or gnomons, similar to those discovered in Taosi graves proximate to the observatory. Data derived from meridian transit observations

13 Volgesang (2017, 88).

expanded the scope of astro-calendrical frameworks beyond the parameters of spring and autumn achronycal sightings alone. Pankenier recounts a tradition during the winter solstice that required one to "set up an eight *chi* [long] gnomon, tie a cord to its top" and using it as a plumb line watch the shadows so as to know the length of them at sunrise.[14]

The antiquity of the use of the plumb line is beyond doubt. Christopher Cullen claims the gnomon "was the basic instrument of ancient Chinese astronomy and surveying."[15] Shadows of the sun at sunrise and sunset were measured by use of the gnomons to lay out north-south and east-west lines. What was innovative was the application of this instrument to establish a new sightline for measuring the cardinal directions, and the consequent identification of seasonal determinants that were proximate to, sometimes straddling, the ecliptic.

Cullen's discussion of the technical term *canwang* used in an astronomical text appended to a famous compendium of Han cosmological perspectives, calls attention to the way the word references a holistic perceptual process aimed toward alignment: the locution refers to visual apperceptions of "situations where two objects defined a line of sight running in the direction of a third."[16] Recognizing that "an ideal plane of the earth measured out to the sides of [a] square defined within the celestial circle by the equinoctial and solsticial" points, the "true meaning of the early Chinese concept of a square earth," will help us understand how King Xiao's astro-calendrical topography melded with the terrestrial.[17] When the nomenclature of the new asterisms (Chamber, Base, Neck, Horns) are Read in tandem with the axial orientation on the Pole, it becomes clear that they point to a concrete origin for the iconic concept of the celestial temple, "Bright Palace" (*mingtang*).[18]

In sum, the axial-based approach of establishing seasonal determinants undergirds the astro-calendrical logic driving the Ritual Reform. With this technology in place, the Zhou were more equipped to seize upon predictable celestial occurrences as fresh proof for Di's sanction, making it imperative for the elite to valorize Zhou sovereignty and the legitimacy of their calendrically based religiopolitical rituals. We will see that similar to the way elites configured Hongshan ritual landscapes, the Zhou exploited unique topographical and astronomical configurations to enhance their self-presentation as supreme. The new system reveals that the Ritual reform emphasized not just the Zhou's capacity to synchronize agrarian cycles with celestial ones, but rather, that an innate

14 Ibid. (129).
15 Cullen (1993, 269).
16 Ibid.
17 Ibid. (273).
18 Pankenier (2013, 63 et passim).

potency provoked Di to confer prestige on their patrimony and charged them with sustaining it.

Phase I

King Mu's Public Mourning of King Zhao

Investigation of Phase I starts from the idea that archaic cognitive architecture was recruited to exempt King Mu and his son's psyches from the painful processes of psychic reorganization following the trauma of King Zhao's death. The exemption was necessary because placing awareness of the crisis within the conditions of the royal Zhou family's emotional existence threatened the preservation of a psychological integrity defined by belief that their rule was sanctioned by Sky. To "safeguard" the royal Zhou psychic "topography marked by [the crisis'] impact, linguistic networks and discursive structures were recruited to operate"[19] like a "'restricted code,' *guarded* by strict intertextuality" (emphasis mine). These discursive networks generated a selective memory or "history-conscious ritual ideology." This chapter aims to trace the underlying nueropsychological processes that worked toward preserving a royal psychic topography.[20]

In "Rules" we find a structure of lexical patterns that screen the Zhou family's complicated grief. Glosses for clusters of posthumous titles reveal an over-determined chain of linguistic deferment. Deferment is effected via synonymy and homophony, but when all the items in the chain are gathered up we can discern a pattern of coherence. The pattern emerges from the aversion of words that were spurned or deemed contaminated by salience cues related to King Zhao's ignominy. "Rules" offers a template for deciphering embedded intentions undergirding the Ritual Reform. The text sheds light on the complicity of a wide range of sources in preserving a "structured amnesia" to screen King Zhao's shame all the while symbolically commemorating him publicly among a community of empty mouths. Symbolic production acknowledged and accommodated the reality of his absence as a fact of Zhou self-fashioning.[21]

Recent research on social and cultural behaviors that emerged during King Mu's reign frequently invoke the political consequences of King Zhao's death as a shaping condition.[22] This is especially the case in conversations about the emergence of a new ideology of Zhou kingship, and the institutions to support it. Joern Peter Grundmann, like other Western Zhou historians, views King Zhao's death as a crisis but he also

19 Abraham and Torok (1994, 126).
20 Kern (2009, 192), invoking von Falkenhausen (1993, 152–156).
21 Porter (1996).
22 Shaughnessy (1999, 323 et passim); Vogt (2012, 245).

offers an insight about the psychoemotional conditions it would have generagted. He opines that among the threats experienced in the wake of the trauma, perhaps most fearful was the potential of "*falling back into a state of cultural oblivion* (emphasis mine)."[23]

Grundmann links this fear to the evolution of Zhou kingship ideals. His discussion of the etymological links between the words "to revere" (*jing*) and "fear, surprise" (*jing*), reveal a neuropsychological dimension of the evolution of kingship ideology.[24] Grundmann views the evolution of Zhou kingship rhetoric as an expressive behavior triggered by deviant (crisis) conditions. For him, the rhetoric symbolized a reification and reinforcement of a threatened bond between the king and the aristocrats. In turn, the rhetoric conditioned an aristocratic mindset and identity that was established along the lines of a "quasi patron-client relationship."[25] Grundmann's interest is not neuropsychological, but his observation that the royal Zhou response was animated by a desire to tighten a threatened relational bond recalls the proximity maintenance strategies that were generated by an archaic, primary experience of unspeakable loss.

The decimation of both King Zhao and the armies ended Zhou expansionist aspirations, so King Mu had had to recruit for defensive purposes. The ritual and political center located at Mt. Qi (located one hundred kilometers west of Xi'an, twenty-five kilometers to the south of the Qi Shan mountain range, and about the same distance to the north of the Wei River in west central Shaanxi province), began during King Mu's reign, which suggests that hosting and feasting were deployed as dominant strategies to rebuild a coalition.[26]

Archaeological evidence recovered in graves dating to the early years of King Mu's reign reveal influence of a northwest regional steppe culture.[27] King Mu's interest in horses and chariots bespeaks affection for aspects of northwestern steppe culture with which pre-conquest Zhou was familiar.[28] Focus on an interests shared with polities in predynastic conditions would have strengthened the Zhou efforts to recruit new allies. Maria Khayutina interprets the growing centrality of hospitality as "a convenient tool for claiming and representing authority and sovereignty, as well as for constructing and reconfiguring hierarchy in the social space."[29] This interactive orientation is also reflected in bronze

23 Ibid.
24 Ibid. (192, n. 166). See also Kern (2000, 75) where he discusses the Zhou fear of dissembling.
25 (2019). Cook (2020).
26 Khayutina (2010, 51).
27 Jessica Rawson (1999, 397); Grundmann (2019).
28 Cf. Vogt's analysis of the rite of "catching foals," which he suggests posed the Zhou king as the ultimate source of military resources, (2012, 217).
29 Khayutina (2010, 47). Her use of the word "sovereignty" is qualified with regard to what Li Feng refers to as the Zhou core region, which was directly administered by the Zhou royal house. See Li (2006, 98–99).

inscriptions that reveal a geopolitical preoccupation with the northwest. Inscribed records of royal hospitality during the mid-late Western Zhou differ, in both form and content, from records of early Western Zhou hospitality, which reflected a more "ambulatory" understanding of political authority.[30]

If hospitality was the literal means for reorganizing the Zhou political apparatus, we can also raise the figurative implications of feasting as an act that places food into an empty mouth when words capable of initiating collective mourning processes are absent. The regression to the language of literal ingestion and digestion intimates obstacles to psychic processing presented by world-changing experience.[31] A text in the same compilation that contains "Rules" preserves a remonstration made by Duke of Zhai to a young King Mu that paints a vivid scene of this psychic landscape. Duke of Zhai was a historical figure and an important Zhou elder during King Mu's reign.

> Do not let family [affairs] implicate the royal house (*wangshi*), concern yourself with what is external to it; above all abide by the seasons to center the many states (*zhong wanguo*). Wuhu! Three Dukes! Consider [these injunctions]. You [including King Mu] all must not be chaotic (*minmin fenfen*), thicken your [skin→]face (*yan*), endure the shame (*chi*).[32] The seasons are what must not be neglected. During the time of the first kings, I too was endangered by difficult conditions (*xian yu nan*), but never [did we] lose sight of squaring with [true north] (*bu shi zheng*). I also used this [behavior] to avoid destroying my lineage (*yimian mou wo shi*).[33]

An earlier part of the remonstrance suggests it was formulated to curtail King Mu's behavior. The injunction against "using tears to overturn the criminal affliction (*zuiji*)" evokes a chapter appended to the fourth-century text about

30 Khayutina (2010).

31 Cook (2005, 21–22), discusses the relationship between food and religious purification in the context of Bronze Age rituals

32 Following Wei (2016) amendment to text, based on a recently recovered text written on bamboo slips.The word in the transmitted text is written with an alternate graph, *chi*, "shame," which has been accepted as the accurate transcriptions.

33 *Jizhong Zhoushu*, "Zhai Gong jie." Recent archaeological discoveries of texts that point to a widespread tradition of Zhai Gong, and especially comparisons among different lexical items used in the same places, have furthered understanding. For example, included among bamboo strips donated anonymously to Qinghua University in 2008 is a similar text; the 1993 discovery of bamboo strip texts at Guodian, near Jingmen, Hubei Province, also yielded a text. See Gao (2013) for a discussion of the transmission of the speech and a comparison of the Qinghua strips' and transmitted versions' lexicon. Li (1998) compares the Guodian text with the transmitted version. Li (2012) compares Zhai's remonstrance with another text included in the Qinghua strips and in the transmitted *Book of Documents* (*Shangshu*), which he claims are politically aligned.

King Mu's travels. This chapter describes an excessive mourning ritual carried out by King Mu and his children for a favored concubine.[34] The narrative all but makes clear that King Mu's funerary rites are inappropriate given the status of his consort, Sheng Ji. While no evidence has been adduced to argue this account is based on a historical event, the intertextual relationship between a text that romanticizes King Mu's journey and one that portrays symptoms of complicated grief, yields a profoundly historical perspective of how King Mu's psychological status was preserved.[35]

King Mu's performance of a public sacrice to commemorate the memory of King Zhao demonstrated the gradual reorganization of the collective royal psyche. The capacity to name his father posthumously indicates accommodation of the psychological, emotional, relational and political landscape wrought by the crisis. King Mu performed the *di*, the Great *Yue* and the *wan* sacrifices in conjunction with rituals sacrificing to King Zhao.[36] The *di* sacrifice, mentioned frequently in Shang texts, involved animal sacrifice, and was performed for the recently deceased. The *yue* and *wan* sacrifices were grain based.[37]

Inscriptions on bronze vessels cast by non-royal aristocrats reveal that they also performed these rites.[38] According to Nicholas Vogt, the rites performed for King Zhao belonged to a shrinking toolkit of "Shang-style ancestral ritual techniques."[39] The reduction resulted from the death of King Zhao, which "sounded the death knoll for expansion of the Zhou state."[40] He suggests King Mu may have wanted to capitalize on the prestige associated with their antiquity, and thereby reinvigorate the "rhetorical capital" of mortuary ritual.

A reinvigorated rhetorical capital was cognitively distributed to promote a specific vision of King Zhao's post-mortem journey. The temple name, *zhao,* "reflective brightness," ritually chosen to memorialize King Zhao, is key to its coded value.[41] In "Rules" the glosses for the temple name distinctly focus on King Zhao's post-mortem capacities, unlike the glosses for the temple name *xiao,*

---

34 *Mu Tianzi zhuan*, chüan 6.

35 Liu (2016) rejects the historical validity of the courtesan, but argues that Zhai Gong's message implicitly warns against licentious behavior that could lead to excessive favoring, which would damage political relations.

36 The two vessels that record King Mu's sacrifice to King Zhao are the Xian-*gui* (dated to the thirty-fourth year of King Mu's reign) and the Lie *ding*. See Vogt (2012, 94–100); Feng (2020a, 9).

37 Vogt (2012, 94–95); Feng (2020a, 14). Sterckx (2018, 306), lists the five grains (*wugu*) conventionally referred to as staples: "two millets [e.g., panicled and glutinous millet], rice, wheat, barley." As for vegetables, "legumes, hemp and beans." Soybeans are attested during that time. See Liu and Chen (2012, 85–91).

38 Ibid. (100–102).

39 Vogt (2012, 312, 318).

40 Ibid. (312).

41 Von Falkenhausen (1996, 9), described the ritual for choosing temple names based on a Han dynasty idealized reconstruction.

which accurately account for deeds the king accomplished while alive. Thus King Zhao's temple name directed attention to his *post-mortem* capacity to "reflect brightness" on Zhou "lineage potency" (*de*).[42] This, according to "Rules," was the source of his renown. Moreover, the glosses take pains to emphasize that awareness of this renowned was accessible via speech; in other words, information about his capacity for reflective brightness relied on something that was *heard*.

> When effort has been expended to *reflect* (*zhao*) *lineage potency* (*de*), it is called "reflective brightness" *zhao; w*hen one's awesome comportment is *reverential* toward [the] bright [symbols], it is called *zhao*; when one's *apperceived* wisdom pierces the [communication] circuits [of the] Zhou, it is called *zhao.*[43]

King Zhao's temple name symbolically, posthumously, summons his memory through the proclamation of his "reflective" renown.[44] The summons envisions an imagined community of invocators capable of sensory-based, integrative intelligence, denoted by the words "brightness" (*ming*), and "wise" (*sheng*).[45] William Boltz has shown that both words refer to the "specific knowledge, perception, or capacity that can be associated with the aural and visual faculties,"

---

42 *De* is conventionally translated as "virtue," though the word's semantic range includes the sense of "spiritual endowment" and "a principle of genus." I follow Cook (2012–2013), who translates the word viscerally as "lineage potency," because it captures the dimension of transmission which is important in Western Zhou rhetoric. We will discuss the concept of "lineage potency" in much detail below. Cook (2020, 3–4) more recently broadens her definition of "lineage potency" in the context of Western Zhou and Eastern Zhou kingship discourse. She links potency to the development of musical performance as a clear manifestation of the presence of the power. She later links this discourse to the important position of the lineage heir, the *xiaozi*.

43 *Jizhong Zhoushu*, "Shifa jie." My translation of the word *da* as "piercing" follows Shaughnessy's (1992, 185), translation of the same word as it appears in the King Xiao era vessel, the Shi Qiang basin. The context of the latter usage relates to the eulogy for King Wu, who was revered for his abilities to "pierce the Yin [Shang] and govern its peoples."

44 Scholars who have looked at the relationship between writing and ritual have long noted the close connection between concepts of (ritually) inscribed writing, *ming*, and concepts of naming, in the sense of "having made a name for oneself," to explain the implicit ritual objective of inscribed writing on the vessels, namely to communicate the renown of a descendant's actions in order to receive reciprocal blessings in return. William Boltz has adduced graphic evidence to show that that an earlier referent of the graph "name" is the verbal sense of "to call," linking oral articulation, or representations of it, to the act of naming. Boltz (1994, 63).

45 In another Eastern Han account by Wang Chong, King Mu's grief related governing negligence is framed in terms of disastrous approaches to re-establish social organization, see his *Lunheng*, "Fei Han." Here, King Mu's reign is identified as a time of decline (*shuai*), when the king "deployed models to order governance, [it was] chaotic without merit. Lord Fu remonstrated with him, [and, because] King Mu's potency dwelled within; he was able to offer sacrifices to the Zhou for a long time. As for his reign, it was chaotic, but ended in order; it wasn't that knowledge was fuzzy in the beginning and then perspicacity evolved later. In the beginning he deployed Chi You's [blunt] methods, later, he adhered to the remonstrance of Lord Fu."

often in the sense of insights gleaned through connecting or gathering various threads of information.[46] The audient wisdom derived from long-term *hearing* implies a capability to configure contexts based on information that is made known through both spoken and silenced discourse, hence the adjectival modifier "reflective."[47]

The psycho-cognitive perception suggested by "reflective brightness" reverberates with the psychoemotional terrain evoked by Zhai Gong's remonstrance. Earlier in the speech Zhai Gong invokes King Mu's spoken intentions to rely on the Zhou's "bright lineage potency" (*mingde*), as a guide for royal acts. Zhai Gong also invokes his relationship with King Mu's father (King Zhao), the latter whom he continued to refer to as "lord" (*pi*). This reverence may also have been a tacit nod to Zhai Gong's own father, who perished along with King Zhao. Raising the imminence of his own personal death, Zhai Gong muses that he occupied a metaphysical position: his "body" (*shen*) was "here" (*zi*), but his "soul" (*hun*) was already proximate to King Zhao's [celestial] location (*suo*), where [King Zhao] assiduously made [the location of] Sky's Mandate his residence (*xu zhai tianming*).[48]

We should not let the obvious anachronism in Zhai Gong's use of the word I translate as "soul," for which there is no extant Western Zhou epigraphic evidence, deter us from recognizing the message that King Zhao's post-mortem residence was imagined in the celestial realm. A precedent for this formulation appears in an Early Western Zhou bronze inscription, the Tian Wang-*gui*.[49] There, the vessel castor describes the dynastic founder King Wen as supervising his descendants, along with Di, from *above* (*Wenwang jian zai shang*).[50]

At the same time, the Duke of Zhai's reference to a "soul," however anachronistic, does call attention to the metaphysical dimension of port-mortem existence captured in Eastern Zhou texts by the word "ghost" (*gui*). The possibility arises that Zhai Gong's reference to the celestial local where King Zhao resides may in fact point to a precise celestial location especially when considered alongside the nomenclature used to designate the square, stellar configuration called *yugui*, Ghost Conveyor (θ Cnc), which straddled the ecliptic and was the (new) location of the summer solstice during King Mu's reign. According to a fifth-century text that preserves ancient star-lore, Ghost

46 Boltz (1994, 116).

47 Cf. Ching (1997), whose analysis of the word *sheng* argues that the implicit wisdom derives from an ability to hear the spirit world.

48 *Ji Zhong Zhoushu*, "*Zhai Gong jie*."

49 Bronzes inscriptions are given titles based on information related to the caster of the vessel provided in the narratives. I follow convention and link the vessel type, such as *-gui*, or *-pan*, or *-xu*, with the vessel names.

50 Wang (2017, 10).

Conveyor had many appellations, including Sky's Temple (*tianmiao*), Sky's Grave (*tiankuang*) and Sky's Eye (*tianmu*).[51]

However odd, the plausibility of a link between the Duke's indirect reference to the soul as a metaphysical entity and the astral name Ghost Conveyor is reinforced when contextualized with paleographical references to Western Zhou mortuary rites that were performed when corpses were sent via "conveyors" from the homestead to be buried at the lineage temple. The corpse-sending rite is mentioned in conjunction with the *yue* sacrifice in an early Zhou bronze inscription.[52] The text provides information about beliefs in post-mortem journeys, and thus refines our understanding of King Mu's performance of the sacrifice to memorialize King Zhao.

Post-mortem Journeys and the Yue and Wan Rites

The precise meaning of the word used to denote the *yue* sacrifice is still contested, although the antiquity of the rite, which appears frequently in Shang dynasty oracle bone-inscriptions in mortuary contexts, is universally accepted.[53] Regarding early Zhou practice, a reference in the *Bamboo Annals*recounts that "[i]n the sixth year [of the last Shang ruler's reign], the Earl of the West first performed the *yue*-rite at Bi."[54] Vogt opines that the reference provides an "unusual example of the performance of a rite 1) associated with the Shang royal house 2) by King Wen 3) in the Zhou heartland 4) before the conquest of Shang was accomplished."[55] While more evidence is needed to affirm the viability of such proto-Zhou practice, its importance for King Mu's ruling style warrants a short diversion to engage with the scholarship on the meaning of the rite.

Epigraphically, the graph used to denote *yue* is believed to represent a musical instrument made of a bamboo tube with three holes.[56] The instrument was clearly intrinsic to the aim of the ancestral sacrifice in Shang and Western Zhou texts. Some scholars have focused on the homophonic resonance between the words that denote the rite and the word for happiness (*yue*) to explain the rite's emotional objective.[57] The cognate "skylark" (*yue*) (*Alauda gulgula*) reinforces these associations. Not only is the bird known for its full-throated

51 Schlegel (1895, 475).
52 Vogt (2012, 171–174).
53 Ibid.; see also Feng (2020b).
54 Vogt (2012, 172). Vogt opines that the reference provides an "unusual example of the performance of a rite 1) associated with the Shang royal house 2) by King Wen 3) in the Zhou heartland 4) before the conquest of Shang was accomplished."
55 Ibid. (173).
56 Ibid.
57 Cf. the Han Dynasty etymology, *Shuowen*, where the graph used to denote the yue sacrifice is glossed as "pleasurable, happy" (*yue*).

melodious singing, but its behavior of shooting up into the sky, singing, and then fluttering as it descends conjures a metaphysical scenario of earthly departure for celestial realms. One observer of the bird remarks that "the song can go on for... over ten minutes without an instant's pause." Moreover, "the call can easily reach over 150-200 m."[58]

That those for whom the *yue* sacrifice was performed were destined for the celestial realm is affirmed by another early Zhou inscription, which recounts mortuary acts performed to honor a beloved mother.[59] Cast by a non-royal elite, the inscription mentions the sacrifice in conjunction with a suite of rites devoted to the preparation of the corpse for a post-mortem journey. These associations are reflected in a semantic chain of cognate words including, "to wash, cleanse, soak" (*yue*); "to ascend, climb, rise" (*yue*); "to jump, leap" (*yue*); "key, strategic [place]" (*yue/yao*), all of which may be construed as movement toward a targeted place. The vessel commissioner explains that the vessel will be used to mediate "unending grief" (*ji buyi*) after the deceased's "essence/spirit" (*jing*) is ritually "sent off" (*qian*).[60] It is an expression of grief and anticipated mourning.[61]

Feng Shi has argued that the semantic scope of the graph used to denote the word "essence/spirit" (*jing*), also included the meaning "star(s)" (*xing*).[62] This semantic association is also suggested by the dominance of light metaphors used to describe ancestors. Moreover, Feng claims that the word "essence" pictographically depicted Quail Fire (Can-Gem), the ancient marker of the summer solstice, the Heart of the Vermilion Bird.[63]

In another study he claims that the link between ancestors and celestial essences derives from more archaic practices involving the Hearth God (*zao*) and the summer solstice. Based on a complex but solid philological line of argument, the crux is the link between the word *zao*, "hearth," and the word *ao*, which, as a modifier, means "deep, dark," but as a noun, referred to "the southwestern corner of a house." There, the sun's shadows dominated, as

---

58 Cf. a description of the song flight of the *Alauda gulgula*: "The song [is] delivered by hovering at a single location and gaining height vertically until the bird reaches 30–40m above the ground. Ali and Ripley (1986), describe '… suspended in the heavens or less stationary at this pitch, hovering on vibrating wings'" Praveen (2005, 141).

59 Ibid.

60 Ibid. (209). This quote comes from an inscription on the Pi-*you* vessel.

61 Feng's (2013, 185) analysis is based on a non-royal early Western Zhou bronze inscription the Wo Fang-*ding*. The record reflects current cultural mortuary practice among the elite.

62 Ibid. (205).

63 Ibid. (205). He cites a similar reference made by the non-royal aristocrat Qiang, whose King Xiao-era cast vessel we will discuss in detail below. See Kern (2000, 77), and Cook (1990, 218–237), for the dominance of light metaphors used to refer to ancestors.

summer drew to a close, so it was where the corpse of the deceased was placed and sacrificed to just before being sent in a conveyor (*yu*), to be buried.[64]

Feng claims that this association between hearths and the southwest is seasonal. The *wan* feasting ritual that followed the *yue* sacrifice, refers to a specific congee made from braised soybeans harvested at the summer solstice.[65] References to the *wan* sacrifice appear in Shang and Western Zhou texts, leading Feng to conclude that the archaic association between fire, Hearth God, the summer solstice and post-mortem transformation lent prestige to the celestial area most closely tied to Zhou collective identity, Quail Fire.[66] As a signifier for fire's capacity to transform food and thereby facilitate the absorption of nutrients necessary for human survival, the Hearth God was a natural guide for the transformation process a person undergoes from body to stellar essence.[67]

The Seasonal Underpinnings of Zhou Refashioning

Feng's insight prepares us to see seasonality as an implicit ideation that conferred meaning to King Mu's sacrifices to his father. This possibility is strengthened considering the unique ecological conditions of the place where the sacrifices were carried out, Pangjing or Pang. King Mu performed several Great *yue* rites and *wan* sacrifices, as well as the *di* ritual, at Pang. This section will argue that seasonal associations attendant on all these rituals were used to refashion the source of Zhou authority in cosmological and astrological terms that were familiar to non-royal aristocrats. Vogt has demonstrated how their participation in Zhou state refashioning was crucial, King Mu may have "revived outmoded ritual techniques" to expand offerings that could "create non-military opportunities for interaction with and patronage of non-royal Zhou elites.[68]

Pang was located close to the royal lineage temple at the capital Zongzhou, near present-day Xi'an, Shaanxi.[69] This proximity helps contextualize the Pang landscape: its meaning was connected to the celestial source of royal prestige and sovereignty. Based on descriptions culled from contemporary sources and transmitted texts, the environs included a broad moat called *biyong*, which

64 Ibid.
65 Ibid. (204).
66 Ibid. (209).
67 Ibid. Cf. Lévi-Strauss (1983). Beliefs in a journey to the underworld post-mortem are amply manifested in Imperial era tomb texts and art. See Lai (2005), for a lucid account. He includes travel paraphernalia used during rituals as one of the objects of analysis.
68 Vogt (2012, 317).
69 Li (2006); Khayutina (2010, 7, especially n. 15).

encircled an islet on which several buildings were constructed on top of a high platform (*jing*).[70] The space was and still is conventionally believed to be an area used for royal leisure. Paleographic sources show it to have been an important hosting location as well.[71]

Most scholars link the name of the moat, or pool, as it is usually understood, to the jade *bi* discs, because of the similarities in the shapes of the park and disk. Both are formed by concentric circles represented by the center and outer circumference of the surface area.[72] In Chapter 3 we saw that Li Xinwei, among others, construe the symbolic value of Neolithic *bi* disks in terms of embedded cosmological and astrological information shaped by celestial Pole oriented astronomical observations.[73] If, as Vogt argues, *biyong* served as the dramatic set for mimetic representations of royal Zhou potency, then we must acknowledge that the mimesis is founded on an assumed symmetry between Pang and the celestial Pole landscape.

Paleographic texts that refer to buildings on a platform locate it on an islet in the middle of *biyong*. According to Feng Shi, the platform had to be raised because of the moat's dampness (*shi*). This condition, he claims, was intimated by the name of a building, "Moist Hall" (*zigong*), which is recorded in a contemporaneous bronze inscription.[74] Feng's philological point suggests an alternate interpretation for the astronomical nomenclature of asterisms surrounding the celestial Pole. Normally read as meaning "Purple Guardian Enclosure" (*ziweiyuan*), if the graph conventially read as "purple" is read, as Feng proposes, "wet," then the name of the protective walls surrounding the celestial pole in transmitted astral lore is revealed to describe the watery boundary that, similar to protects the Pole Star.

References in the transmitted literature, including the *Book of Poetry*, attribute the construction of *biyong* to King Wen.[75] Such construction would have been a guarded privilege of royal prerogative under the Shang. Whether King Wen was associated with Pang because the geography was strategically advantageous and therefore auspicious for conducting state observations of numinous phenomena, or perhaps because he in fact witnessed the planetary conjunction there, cannot be discerned. Still, the memorable image of a Vermilion Bird's beak clasping a jade disc perching on Mt. Qi, raises the possibility that it is an accurate description of what was observed from a raised platform in Pang as an observer looked west toward the Zhou ancestral

70 Ibid.
71 Vogt (2012).
72 Feng (2019).
73 Ibid. (6), provides a comprehensive account of the transmitted philological scholarship on the name of the pool.
74 Ibid.
75 Ibid. (10). See "Numinous Terrace" ("Lingtai"), *Shijing*.

homeland near Qi Mt. The fact that the platform included a place of "study" (*xue*), moreover, reinforces the plausibility that the buildings on the platform were related to (astronomical) issues of state security.[76]

While it is unlikely that King Wen, who did not live to participate in the overthrow of the Shang, would have had the time or resources to create a park of the scope described in transmitted and paleographic texts, ecological engineering of the sort suggested by the references could have been carried out over the early part of the dynasty, and intensified as hosting activities expanded. Repeated references to "numinous" (*ling*) locations, such as "platforms" (*tai*), "paths" (*dao*), and "marshy pools" (*zhao*), in the transmitted and paleographic accounts conjure a scenario that mimicked the terrestrial landscape of the celestial Pole.

Pang's numinous associations contextualize the psychoemotional dimension of King Mu's performance of the *yue* and *wan* sacrifices for King Zhao there. A contemporary inscription describing King Mu's pageantry at Pang reveals the indelible impression made by these spectacular, spiritual events, on collective memory. The castor of the vessel memorializes the sacrifice as a year marking event ("It was the year when the King [Mu] performed a great *yue*-rite at Zongzhou and then gave a *wan* feasting at Pangjing, in the fifth month...")[77]

Another inscription dating to King Mu's reign makes clear how Pang and *biyong* became a stage for dramatizing control over cosmic spacetime. The vessel castor, Document Maker Mai, describes the king's boat journey punctuated by three stops before arriving at the fourth, which served as the retinue's launching point to join him.[78] King Mu's ritual actions at Pang included arriving at the boundaries of Pang space in each of the cardinal directions, and shooting birds there. This was less a hunting party than a ritual performance, akin to the Shang king's capture of the *yuan* tortoise at the summer solstice discussed in the previous chapter. The king's mimetic performance featured his power to delineate a cosmological boundary, demonstrating his authority to establish and align cardinal and celestial coordinates. The king's square itinerary drew attention to the cardinal reach of his royal agency.[79]

76 Vogt (2012, 255) pays close attention to the relationship between studying and learning and archery contests. References to archery events support his perspective that studying archery was seen as an important means of representing one's meritorious comportment, but I reason that other topics must also have been included in the educational academy.

77 The inscription appears on three different vessels (the Shi Shang-*you*, the Shi Shang-*zun*, and the Shi Shang-*he*) recovered near Luoyang, where King Cheng established a defensive settlement. See Vogt (2012, 172 et passim) for translation and discussion.

78 Mai Fang-*zun*, translated in Vogt (2012, 296–297). See also the *ding* vessel inscription commissioned by Bo Tang Fu who was gifted for his participation in preparing the king's boat during one such journey, Ibid. (251 *et passim*); Feng (2019, 8), discusses the latter two inscriptions in terms of the *biyong* pool at Pang.

79 Porter (1996) investigates the production of a fourth-century B.C. fictional text about King Mu's travels, that focuses on King Mu's delimiting strategy as the narrative's organizing conceit.

On the level of royal discourse, King Mu's rejuvenation of Shang mortuary rituals suggests a strategy for targeting non-royal elites to reconsolidate power. An archaic Shang cosmology of post-mortem transformation provided a lexicon for "speaking" about King Zhao, one that focused on his metamorphosis into an astral spirit, and not on the events and deeds of his lived live. The incorporation of the summer solstice-related *yue* sacrifice into the context of royal memorialization also fit in with the astrological and cosmological framework of the Zhou's royal self-construal, which was generated by the planetary massing in Quail Fire. Indeed, evidence suggests that the conception of the summer season as a time-space (distinct from the event of the summer solstice), seems to be an invention of the Zhou dynasty.[80] The Shang agricultural year (*nian*) and ritual year (*si*) comprised two seasons, one during which planting and growing transpired, "spring" (*chun*), and one marked by harvesting, "autumn" (*qiu*).[81] This binary conception is reflected in the ancient astro-calendrical function of Dragon's Heart, which related to the vernal and autumnal equinoxes.

The dominant presence of "relief dragons and birds, each with a curved S-shaped extended body and reverted head," common during King Mu's reign reveals the growing importance of solstice centered ecological information.[82] The "naturalistic representative imagery" of the Vermilion Bird and Cerulean Dragon together represented the apotheosis of heat and fire, and thus served as apt accoutrements for a royal rhetoric of cosmological agency. The discovery in Shanxi of the earliest extant preserved textile dating to King Mu's reign, and identified as belonging to the ruler of the "State of Peng," provides more vivid evidence of this association. A coffin shroud, "bright red and ornamented with phoenixes," extended to over ten meters long.[83]

The next section will trace how the staging of these mourning rites, heightened by a seasonally determined iconographic discourse of dragons and birds, effectively situated the discourse of King Zhao's post-mortem transformation within the cosmological symbolic domain of agricultural cycles. This discursive

80 Wang (2016).

81 While the graph that evolved to denote "winter" (*dong*) is found in Shang oracle bone inscriptions, Deng and Wen (2012, 107) argue that the context requires reading the graph to mean "the whole time duration" of a completed sacrificial act. This meaning evolved to denote "winter," which was conceptualized by the Zhou as the season when the solstice marked the beginning and end of a year's cycle, a new meaning of "whole time duration." See also Wang and Zhang (2016). For summer agricultural harvests, see Hsu et al. (1980, 81–88); Yang (2003); Du (2018). Cf. Maria Khayutina (2009, 136), who analyzes the royal year-counting systems during the Western Zhou, which reveals a trend away from the (Shang related) means of counting years (*si*) in terms of a ritual round of sacrifice, toward a broader deployment of the term, "harvest" (*nian*) to designate the royal year-count. This may indicate the pointed agrarian orientation of the *xiao* reforms that I posit.

82 Sun (2021, 455–456).

83 Shaughnessy (2017, 142).

strategy proves key to uncovering the astro-calendrical subtext driving King Mu's royal behavior. Most important is evidence of how literally King Mu appears to have heeded Zhai Gong's remonstrance against "forgetting [his obligations to manage the] seasons (*wu wang shi*)." His sacrifices and hosting reveal him to have not "distanced" himself from the "[path of] centering [the Zhou] state (*wu yuan zhong guo*)." In fact, notwithstanding his initial reluctance to ascend to the throne, King Mu remained devoutly proximate to this path.[84]

The Cosmological Subtext of the Western Zhou Well-Field System

References in sources to centering the state, bounteous harvests, and summer solstice offerings evoke the Western Zhou agricultural management technique known as the "well field system" (*jing tian zhi*).[85] The system was at its core a land-distribution method; its name derives from the Shang graph for "well," whose form elegantly captured the conceptual image of the division: a square area divided into nine equal square sections, eight encircling the central plot. The written word comprised four strokes, two horizontal and two vertical, which were arranged in crisscross fashion, resembles that of our contemporary "hashtag," 井.[86] The eight outer squares represented land that would be privately cultivated (*sitian*) by families under a lord's rule; collectively they would cultivate the center field(s) (*gongtian*). Harvests reaped from the communal land were offered to the lord as tribute, who then in turn, offered it to the Zhou king to use at summer cult sacrifices.[87]

Eminent Chinese historian Yang Kuan makes the case that the emergence of the well-field system was a function of enhanced agricultural production techniques. He sees the system as one that supported aristocratic control over rural communities; the obligation to the lord went beyond cultivation of the communal land to include construction labor; weaving; hunting (for furs); martial needs; and even, according to a poem in the *Book of Poetry*, providing services to repair a lord's bedchamber.[88] Yang provides a thorough analysis of the

84 *Ji Zhong Zhoushu*, "Zhai Gong jie." Cf. Goldin (2008, 165–174) whose discussion of the word *zhong*, center, which has been conventionally argued to mean "loyal." Goldin argues that sentiment marked by the heart signific in the graph used to denote ethical term should be construed more in terms of behavior that is aligned, balanced and hence capable of equanimity.

85 See Zhang and Li (2019) for discussion on ancient agrarian systems; see also Lai (2001); Cai (1997) defines the system on the basis of classical references.

86 Yang (2003, 4).

87 Sterckx (2018, 312) provides more detail: "Each household gets usufruct of one hundred mu of farmland and some extra space to rear animals, grow mulberry trees, put up a cottage."

88 Yang (2003).

archaeological and textual evidence to tease out the breadth and depth of the institutionalization of this practice, and the influence it exerted on Western Zhou social, economic and political development.[89]

My interest lies in the intersection between the emergence of this system, the King Zhao trauma, and the Zhou's astro-calendrical response. Again, King Mu seems to draw from the prestige of Shang culture, this time from the repertoire of written graphs as opposed to mortuary rites. The square form of the Shang graph "well" has been likened to the square wooden beams that framed ancient wells, although evidence suggests that wooden beams were substituted with stones used to line well structures during the Western Zhou.[90] The square frame with the round well themselves recall the geometric features associated with cosmological models, as well as the shapes of the ritual platforms discovered in Hongshan ceremonial sites.

Wells were crucial in the "spread of foxtail millet agriculture, which required more water over a longer growing period than broomcorn millet."[91] Scholarship on the evolution of irrigation techniques in the pre-Longshan Neolithic period reveals an early capacity to extend agriculture "into areas of deeper groundwater, and possibly the development of new well-digging techniques."[92] We have seen how an increase in millet production has been identified as a causal factor in Neolithic population growth.[93] Wells have been found frequently in North China Plain sites dating from the sixth to the second millennium, some reaching depths of ten meters, made possible by evolving drilling techniques.[94]

Intensification of the well-field system has been traced to King Mu's reign. Some have explain this trend as a function of the Zhou's growing reliance on hosting as an alliance building strategy, connecting it to emerging irrigation techiques.[95] This behavior increased the need for resources.[96] Historians also connect the emergence of large-scale standardization in vessel shape and ornamentation during King Mu's reign to the centralization of agricultural methods that synchronized cultivation of a variety of crops with seasons.[97] Paleographical

89 Ibid.

90 Zhou et al. (2011, 1105).

91 He et al. (2020, 7).

92 He et al. (2020). Systematic well use is dated to Peiligang culture around 5480 BCE, around the time of the spread of foxtail millet. Broader use of triangular stone ploughs around "4200-4000 BP" also indicate agricultural development between Longshan culture (5200-1850 BCE) and Erlitou and Erligang cultures (ca. 1900-1300 BCE).

93 Ibid.

94 Zhou, Zwahlen and Wang (2011, 1105).

95 Zhou et al. (2011), Zhuang (2017) present findings on hydrological management that demonstrate a networking approach using vertical and horizontal channels.

96 The Western Zhou bronze inscriptions cited by Zhang (2011) that make references to the system do not pre-date the middle of the Western Zhou, King which falls within King Mu's thirty-nine-year reign.

97 Grundmann (2019, 112).

records indicate that during King Mu's reign, the well-field system was deployed as a strategy for dividing "fertile" (*wo*) cultivatable fields (*tian*) in a way that could sustain a lord and those subjects who cultivated it.[98] According to Feng Shi the royal house did not have a monopoly over the deployment of the system, but evidence attests to the Zhou's robust reliance on gifting allotments of cultivatable land to patronize non-royal elites.[99]

During the Western Zhou the graph denoting "well" was multivalent. It was used to designate the name of the official charged with management of dividing fields; it denoted the unit of measurement by which the fields were divided and aligned; it referred to a lineage who seemed to have had a long monopoly on the aforementioned official management; as well as to their own plot of cultivated lands within the royal domain.[100] A King Mu-era inscription, the Ba Bo-*gui,* cast by the ruler of the Ba polity located to the northeast of the Zhou capitol in Shanxi, brings to life the intersectionality of these meanings in the personage of a high-ranking Zhou official, one Jing Shu, who visited Ba to inspect the quality of salt that they mined and refined for royal Zhou use.[101]

In addition, Jing Shu delivered to the Ba ruler King Mu's charge to protect the salt pool from incursions by aggressive polities eager to access it. The need for a standing army to carry out these security obligations for the Zhou required a means to sustainably feed them. Toward this goal, Jing Shu provided for the Ba ruler "one hundred *jing*" to be used for the cultivation of (coarse) grains (*liang*) for military subsistence purposes.[102] The system ensured that the Ba ruler would be able to fulfill his obligation to the Zhou king, while also benefitting from the yield produced by communal cultivation of the central plot.

This practice of land distribution along with cultivation methods strengthened ties between the states who occupied the rich and fertile lands, at the edges of Zhou territory and the Zhou court. Like Yang Kuan, Feng Shi places the institutionalization of the well-field system squarely within King Mu's reign. He claims that the Zhou relied on the spread of the well-field system as a security strategy.[103] The mutually beneficial system reflected in the Ba Bo-*gui*, especially the way the well-field system could be managed by farmer/soldiers, making it an efficient mechanism for adapting to shifting geopolitical conditions,[104] explains why it became integral to King Mu's patronage repertoire. References in the *Book of Poetry* to well-field cultivation paint a stately scene: tall stalks arranged in neat rows within each plot, swaying and bending, their tips ripe to the point of

98 Ibid. Feng (2020b, 68).
99 See for example the inscription on a vessel commissioned by a ruler of the state of Ba, which we discuss below.
100 Feng (2020b).
101 Shaughnessy (2017, 148–149).
102 Feng (2020b, 68).
103 Ibid. (69).
104 Ibid.

bending; this condition is frequently denoted by the duplication of King Mu's temple name: *mu mu*.[105]

The advantages of this patronage were manifested in the surplus produce that was offered in collective summer solstice rituals. Crop rotation practices that yielded summer harvests included a multitude of grains (*wugu*), beans, and vegetables. These were first offered up (*deng*) to King Mu, who then used it to conduct ancestral sacrifices. After the completion of the rites, leftovers, including meat provided by the ruler, were distributed among those who managed the lands.[106] The Ba Bo-*gui* documents that this ritual transaction was replicated by lineage heads at their own ancestral temples.

In sum, the intensification of land grants accompanied by agricultural techniques for cultivation and irrigation infused uncultivated lands with political and cultural capital. The Zhou used this in exchange for commitments to screen its political and ritual center, and thereby reify their lineage's premier hierarchical status. Bounteous harvests resulting from well-field cultivations would have enhanced "bond-like patron-client relations between the king and lineage elites."[107] Because widespread use of the system was tantamount to widespread acknowledgment of the Zhou as a mediator of collective agrarian purpose, it defended the royal Zhou family from dynasty ending accusations of failed agrarian management. Most importantly, it contributed to the formation of a network of aristocratic actors who converged on a shared model that linked agrarian practice and production to Zhou cult sacrifices.[108]

The next section proposes that the intensification of the well-field system found cosmic reinforcement in a pareidolia event that projected the Shang graph form of the word "well" onto the Sky. The constellation Well sits at the southwestern border, that is the boundary, that separates the southern, summer quadrant from the western, autumnal one. Recall, the southwest direction figured in the ancient Shang *yue* and *wan* rites performed to send off a corpse for its transformational ascent. Moreover, I suggest that this context is implicit in the locution "bright model" (*ming jing/xing*), which appears frequently in paleographic and transmitted texts to refer to the vaunted ruling paradigms demonstrated by Zhou dynastic founders, especially King Wen. Because the graph that denotes the word "model" (*xing*), is in fact the same used to denote the word "well" (*jing*), the cognate relationship suggests the former meaning derived from the latter.

---

105 See for example the use of the duplicative in the poems "Wen Wang," in the Greater Elegantiae; "Jia le," an "Yong," within the Sacrificial Hymns of the Zhou (*Zhou song*), *Shijing*

106 Feng (2020b); Zhou (2000).

107 Grundmann (2019, 171).

108 Walton (2013), cited in Grundmann (2019).

The Astronomical Basis of Western Zhou "Bright Model" (mingxing) Discourse

Invocations of "bright models" were integral to Ritual Reform era bronze inscription discourse. Vogt argues that the idea that "living members of a lineage should attempt to conform to the example of their most illustrious ancestors, [was] a linchpin of the [Western Zhou royal] model of ancestral ritual."[109] Dedication to efforts to shape one's behavior on the acts of a deceased ancestor's service to the royal house opened a specific venue for negotiating status. With the emerging dominance of standardized ceremonies that involved the recording of official appointments during King Mu's reign, the rhetoric of "bright models" promoted the "interest of the upper echelons of nonroyal lineages in maintaining the ongoing vision of the Zhou collective with the king at its head."[110] Similarly, Grundmann finds that rhetorical references to modeling ancestors registers an effort to counter the dynasty's fear of the dissolution of collective solidarity; he argues that the rhetoric in fact "focused on an unbroken *political commitment*, stretching from forbears" (emphasis mine).[111]

From the start the deployment of a grapheme from the royal written script to make legible the conceptual idea of the well-field system surely enhanced the value of the system and Zhou authority. Scholars agree that the written word was responsible for generating a "consistent portrayal, reaching across the boundaries between elite lineage cults, of the Zhou king as the legitimizing force behind the body of officials that conducted the day-to-day operations of the Zhou state."[112] Investiture ceremonies "placed royal utterances into the ancestral-ritual material of assemblages of Western Zhou officials," including a specifically contoured written linguistic surround.[113] Martin Kern asserts the "superior cultural, social, and political status of writing in Chinese civilization," especially for its capacity to "proclaim a normative version" of reality.[114]

I argue that just as King Mu borrowed from seasonally inflected Shang mortuary repertoire to refashion (by extending) the discursive parameters within which King Zhao's loss could be publicly acknowledged and psychically buried; and just as he used the ancient Shang graph "well" to convey a version of a normative reality for agrarian life; so too did he project the graph's

109 Vogt (2012, 68).

110 Paleographical evidence attests to the early formulation of the concept of modeling, exemplified, for example, in the King Cheng era inscription cast on the He-*zun*. The expression "bright model" became a rhetorical fixture in bronze inscriptions dating from the middle Western Zhou. See Vogt (2012, 43, 69).

111 Grundmann (2019, 225).

112 Vogt (2012, 282). See also Panenier (2011); Kern (2001, 2005, 2007, 2009); Pines (2009); Von Falkenhausen (1993).

113 Vogt (2012, 282); Pankenier (2011); Kern, especially (2001, 2009).

114 Kern (2007, 109); See also Pankenier (2011); Pines (2009).

form onto an observable astro-calendrical phenomenon. Once we contextualize the idea of "normative" in terms of King Mu's efforts to center the Zhou, we can appreciate its convergence with conceptions of alignment with true north.

I suggest that measurements of the sun's shadows combined with nightly observations of asterism transits led to the projection of the Shang graph "well" onto Sky's text, resulting in the asterism known in Eastern Zhou texts as Well (μ Gem).[115] Well was inserted into the legible space dominated by Quail Fire.[116] During King Mu's reign, Well transited the north-south meridian—that is, it reached its most central and north position—at midnight on the winter solstice, that "highly symbolic" seasonal transitional juncture since the Neolithic.[117] With the Pole Star directly north, Well was an appropriate legatee for Di. Moreover, the vertical alignment of asterism and Sky River as it "arched" across Sky like a "brilliant silvery ribbon," surely heightened the cosmic valence of observations[118] (Figure 5.2).

Constance Cook also notes the Zhou attention to light angles, in her evocative description of the "visual details" of mortuary ritual performance. "First, the many images of light suggest torch, or oil-lamp lit ceremonies, which enhanced the slanted rays from the sun across a shrine courtyard at dawn to dusk on feast days… music rose as the descendant moved in [awesome] style; it reached a crescendo when he 'grasped' the ancestral "lineage potency" [the vertical Sky River]. A successful performance reaffirmed the Zhou political order, and like an oath affirmed to the spirits of the founder kings, the continued expansion of the Zhou *ming* (mandate, charge).'"[119]

David Pankenier's epigraphic argument that the grapheme denoting Di might represent the measurement results produced by Shang rulers' "practical geomantic applications" of the technique of laying out a true north-south line," suggests a precedent for the projection I attribute to King Mu. He claims that the word Di graphically depicts the linear and angular results of measurements taken to identify the Pole Star; the process necessitated laying out "right angles" based on a pair of stars aligned on the meridian.[120] The Di graph's form, argues Pankenier, shows how lines were drawn with the use of a weighted cord. A similar motivation may have catalyzed the projection of the graph "well" onto Sky's text. That is, the objective was to

115 Cullen (2007, 194).
116 The determinant star of Well is *Mu Geminorum*.
117 Cullen (2007, 194) mentions this spatiotemporal context referencing techniques used to make astronomical measurements. We will see how an incipient form of this system was a product of King Xiao's Ritual Reform.
118 Pankenier (2013, 206). Ibid. (356).
119 Cook (2020, 53). See also McCurley (2005) for an analysis of a celestial choreography and ancient Chinese ritual performance
120 Ibid.

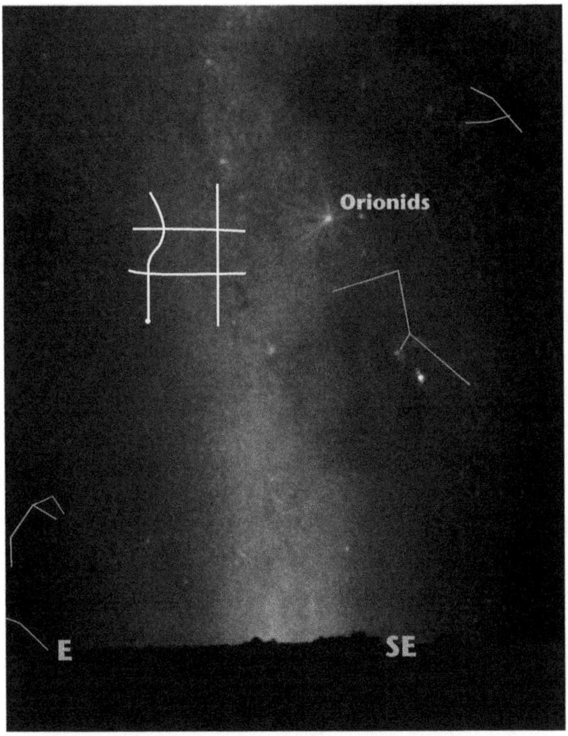

FIGURE 5.2 A vertical Sky River with Well on its bank just as it begins its transit over the meridian circa 940 B.C. Milky Way magnified by 5x for emphasis.
Source: Redrawn from screenshot based on Stellarium, an open source software.

reveal lines of measurement that could be made with stretched cord techniques.

Pankenier proposes that another constellation located in the northern, winter celestial quadrant and aptly named [carpenter's] Square (*ding*), was used for this purpose. He cites a strophe in the poem "Numinous Platform," collected in the *Book of Poetry* as evidence. There, the construction of a platform (*yingtai*), is described with the terminology of stretched cord techniques. Pankenier asserts that these methods figured significantly in efforts to achieve "cosmological alignment of high value structures."[121] The verb "to align" (*jing*) connoted specific astronomical and astrological intentions related to the terrestrial organization of space.[122] Feng Shi contends that management of the well-field system to produce summer and autumn harvests would have necessarily relied on astro-calendrical information. One

121 *Shijing*, "Yingtai."
122 (2015, 21). See Eno (2009) for evaluation of the theory.

can certainly imagine the use of the gnomon to lay out the parameters of the well-field square. He concludes that "well-field" management officials would have worked closely with or alongside royal astronomers charged with observing Sky and interpreting the (astrological) implications of its patterns.[123]

These techniques were highly valued by the Zhou. A concrete example of such high evaluation is provided by epigraphic evidence, namely, the addition of a stroke to the center square of the graph "well." Du Yong claims the added stroke relates to the growing fortunes of the Jing lineage, which were tied to their growing status as administrators and models of the well-field system. Du claims that the added stroke denoted honor conferred by the court to signal the lineage's superiority in its management of its land holdings within the royal domain (*jinei*).[124] The excellence would have been observable in the bounteous produce harvested from the central plot(s) of their well-system lands, which were offered for royal family sacrifice and consumption. From a genealogical perspective, the Jing lineage's capacity to produce resplendent harvests reflected an innate talent that was important for the Zhou's conception of their "lineage potency," a concept central to Western Zhou cosmopolitical thought to which we will return shortly.[125]

Du goes on to argue that excellence in management of ones own *jing* fields was deemed a basis on which to trust the introduction of junior officials into higher levels of royal service. Underlying excellent land management was a deep grasp of astro-calendrical information. A *jing* official would have known that the meridian transit of Square's eastern "wall" a month before the winter solstice could be used to align city walls and civil buildings along the north-south axis.[126] Well, too, functioned as a celestial too with application to ecological and social management. The cognate relationship between these two asterisms' names and the verbs "to make square," "to make upright," "to rectify," "to govern," (*zheng*),[127] conjures a shared function. As the Zhou penchant for "squaring" is reflective of the Neolithic "impulse to 'make right' of psychical alignment (e.g., to face dwellings south to capture the light and warmth of the winter sun)."[128] The names of the constellations reinforce symmetry among celestial entities designated as standards for orienting Zhou sovereign behavior.

123 Ibid. (66). "Numinous Platform" evokes the platform constructed at Pang, which may have been used for astronomical observations.

124 Du (2018, 43, 44, 48 et passim). Cf. Sterckx (2018, 301) where he discusses lineage control over agricultural logistics before evolved into a fully administrated state institution.

125 Ibid. (2018, 52–54).

126 Ibid. (320, 129): Jing/Ding:(⋆tiŋ/⋆tsjiŋ?)

127 Pankenier (2013, 132).

128 Ibid. (114).

Well's semiotic status as a marker for axial alignment, and the fact that its form was also used in Middle Western Zhou bronze inscriptions to denote the homophonic word "model" (*xing*), encouraged me to hypothesize that the concrete referent for the binominal locution "bright model" seen frequently in Middle Western Zhou bronzes was none other than Well.

In light of abundant paleographic evidence attesting to great feasts held concurrent with King Mu's sacrifice to King Zhao, it is easily imaginable that the feasts would have afforded ripe opportunity to orchestrate visual affordances of their worship spaces with an unimpeded view of the sky at the moment when Sky River appeared vertical. His power would have been magnified by positioning guests in view of the brilliant fusion when "the sub-celestial realm below [was] joined together at opposite ends of the sky by the confluence of the terrestrial [Wei] River and Sky River." Well, positioned smack in the middle of the "arched ribbon" at midnight, signaled the Zhou's centrality in the cosmos. It was proof of the Zhou's religious claim that their supremacy was a function of their relationship with the Polar Deity Di.[129]

This social choreography placed celestial phenomena in the starring role of seasonally coordinated ritual events. The image of the vertical Sky River, even without the skillset to discern Well, afforded a dramatic symbol of an axis mundi that yielded access to the celestial realm. While initially perceived as a cryptic code, awesome but indecipherable, the phenomenon became a resource for deciphering the spatiotemporal parameters of a new astro-calendrical framework. The phenomenon of Well's transit across the meridian was an essential element of the homologized layout seen in Pang.

King Mu's response to the psychological crisis posed by his father's death; bears traces of ancient nervous system forged by ecological loss and transcendence. Astro-calendrical phenomena were (unconsciously) invoked to project a veneer of perfect regularity, concealing the emotional reality of the crisis, dynastic instability and increased psychological pressure for shame aversive behavior. Johanna Broda has observed similar behavioral patterns in Mesoamerican civilization, wherein ritual performance directed attention to "concerted mystification to make social relations appear to be just ideology."[130]

A comparable condition motivated King Mu's act. Still, I think we can extrapolate an even more specific dimension of King Mu's personal grief when we recontextualize the scene of Sky River's transit in terms of the disasterous river crossing that caused it. In Chapter 2 I suggested that emotional relief may have been experienced by the cognitive turn in direction toward the celestial Pole area

129 Ibid. (329).

130 Broda (1982, 104). Broda's (81–82) discussion of ideology as "false consciousness," whose social "function is to legitimate and justify the existing order of society," bears similarities to the psychic operations I say are active in the production of the symbolic language driving King Xiao's political ideology.

due to the constancy of the circumpolar stars. A similar emotional logic is suggested by the idea of mystical, successful river transits. When read in concert with the Western Zhou belief in the astral essence of post-mortem existence, highlighted in King Zhao's temple name, a more poignant sense of the tumult that needed mystifying emerges: the unresolved distress caused by his father's terrestrial, unsuccessful river transit.

The next section offers paleographical evidence that supports the connection between the successful aplication of the well-field cultivation technology as a patronage strategy among eastern polity leaders, and Well's winter solstice transit. My source is a renowned, remarkably long and informative bronze inscription, cast by Mao Ban, a high-ranking royal, celebrated duke and contemporary of Duke of Zhai.[131] The inscription recounts distinct events related to Mao Ban's successful "quieting" (*jing*) of eastern states (*dongfang*) two years before King Mu's death: the vessel includes a reign year date of the thirty seventh year.[132] I offer a novel interpretation of the narrative, eschewing an ill-fitting chronological framework.[133] This reading strategy permits an unfamiliar perspective of Mao Ban's experience.

The Mao Ban-gui Inscription's Implicit Astro-Calendrical Subtext

Mao Ban commissioned the vessel for use in sacrifices performed for his late father. He makes repeated reference to his line of descent from King Wen, which suggests an imagined connection between Mao Ban's pacification success and King Wen's overthrow of the eastern Shang, both of which he attributes to Di's beneficence. This link between Sky's patterned legitimization of King Wen and Mao Ban's own success contextualizes the latter's reference to the "bright model" that he invokes as a determining factor driving his triumph.

Yang Kuan has argued that Mao Ban's responsibilities to construct a partition to "buffer the king's position" (*bing wang wei*) reflect Zhou family efforts to establish the Zhou capital at Mt. Qi as the center of its political reach.[134] The inscription begins with Mao Ban's recall of his geopolitical boundary making experience to establish the narrative's informational reference point—the topic. I identify five distinct narrative

131 Yang (2003, 558) identifies him as Mao Shu Zheng.

132 For a convenient and thorough account of the discovery of the Ban-*gui* as well as the dissemination of the 197-graph inscription, see Tang (2017, 45). I have also benefitted from the systematic collation of all commentaries and explications provided by Tang. The same event is mention in the King Mu vessel, Meng-*gui*,Feng (2017, 16–17). I also relied on Lan (2004), Yu (2019) for understanding.

133 Porter (1996) elaborates on the suitability for using topic-comment structures as an analytical lens for ancient Chinese expression.

134 Yang (2003).

segments, each of which may be construed as elaborations the topic.[135] Significantly, Mao Ban did not relate the result of his three year quieting excursion in terms of booty or ears captured, frequently seen in other military-related bronze inscriptions.[136] Rather, after noting the accomplishment of the task with which he was charged, provides more details about the conditions that led to this result.

First, he calls attention to "[Sky's] awesome conferral" (*pibi*) as a condition of his success.[137] Following this, Mao Ban recounts his performance of a "reporting ritual" (*gao*) directed "[to Zhou royal ancestors] above"[138] at She [a place to ford the Yellow River].[139] Because fording the Yellow River was a historically verifiable defining act in the successful overthrow of the Shang, but fording the Han River led to King Zhao and the Zhou army's demise, the location of the "reporting ritual" is pregnant with emotional context.

135 Goldin (2017) discusses how the Shang experts in writing and other governing techniques were distributed to the aristocratic families who survived the Zhou takeover.

136 Shaughnessy (1992).

137 I follow Tang Lan and others, cited in Tang (2017, 160), who read the graph modifying "conferral" as *pi* "awesome" and not the negative particle *bu*. The graph denoting conferral, *bi*, comprised a "display instrument" (*bi)* with the graph for "field" (depicted full of "grains") on top, evokes grain offerings in response to conferrals from Sky or the Zhou king. In the Zuo commentary on the Easter Zhou annals, the word is associated with land division." "Han Mao") the conferral is contextualized as a response in a reciprocal relationship.

138 Vogt views the *gao*-report as "an important link in the chain between royal and local rituals," (2012, 299n36). Following Liu Yu, Vogt claims the *gao* "ritual mechanism existed whereby such interactions that took place elsewhere could be incorporated into the ritual and social life of the local kin group" (73). The object of Mao Ban's report is unclear. I read it similarly to the way Zhou Gong, King Wen's son and King Wu's brother, performed a *gao* ritual when the latte fell ill. Not simply an update of recent events as seen in other contemporary inscriptions, Mao Ban's *gao* ritual "conveys an impression of perceived obligation, a sense that [Mao Ban] not only hopes that the ancestors will accede to his request, but expects their cooperation as an acknowledgement of his superior character and good service" (77).

139 Following Huang Shengzhang, cited in Tang (2017, 164). Huang argues that Mao Ban "gathered the garrison troops at She," a location named for its function as a place "to ford" (*she*) the Yellow River. The conventional reading of the graph Huang identifies as *she* is to view it as a variant orthographic form of the word *de* "lineage potency." If this latter reading is accepted, this changes the reading of the previous graph from *tun* "to gather the troops," to *chun*, meaning "great, big." These types of modifiers are often used to describe Sky's communicative gestures. Huang's reading makes sense discursively; the spatial location of She establishes the discursive parameters for understanding the following information about Mao Ban's performance of the reporting sacrifice. In this reading, the flow of the discourse could be rendered: "Awesome was Sky's conferral. The garrisons gathered at She (the "fording" place). The Duke performed a *gao* sacrifice to [Sky] above. Truly [Sky responded by] manifesting as a place name intersects with my understanding of the astral source of the locution "bright model," which I lay out below. Nonetheless, the conventional reading does not preclude the validity of the celestial intentions I identify.

Mao Ban then goes on to quote what he reported during his performance of the rite: "It is that [among the eastern polities' rulers] there are none who are not inept at [managing]… [astro-calendrical] constancy (*yi*), [therefore they] obscured Sky's command (*tianming*). For this reason (*gu*), [they] lost [the benefits of following Sky's command]."[140] Mao Ban segues to recount how Sky, "truly [*as expected*]" (*yun*), "brightly manifested" (*xian*) its "awesomeness" (*pi*) [in response to this report]"; and then he portrays the scene of this manifestation: "it was the revered [Zhou] lineage potency (*de*). [Once manifested] there was "nothing [no need] [for the eastern lords] to escape (*wu you wei*) [Zhou patronage]."[141]

The familiar rationale that the Shang lost their sovereignty due to astro-calendrical mismanagement is given a twist: it was an atrophied celestial literacy that accounts for their descendants' blindness to Di's (most recent) indication of Zhou superiority. Once they witnessed the vertical Sky River appear at the time Mao Ban predicted it would, however, they saw the "truth" of the Zhou's claim. One suspects that the Shang origins of the constellation's shape, which would have been familiar to literate Shang descendants, also was a compelling factor. Below I will return to discuss in more detail the interchangeability of the notion of Zhou "lineage potency" with Sky's fluvial image. For now it is helpful to note how Mao Ban concludes his account by linking the concept of "bright model" to his lineage's service to the royal house.

A *Book of Poetry* poem called "Dang," "Roiled Waters", along with other texts reverberate with details that reinforce Mao Ban's assessment of the eastern polity rulers' cognitive status. This suggests that Mao Ban's quieting event was widely circulated. For example, there was confusion over distinctions between "bright" (*ming*) and "shadows" (*hui*), mention of indicating problems with gnomon use. The ignorance led to "calculations [about the duration] of daylight that turned it into night" (*bi zhou zuo ye*). In the same vein we find references the existence of records and *models* (*xing*) that can be used to redress confusion and ignorance.[142,143]

140 Following Guo Muoruo, Tang (2017, 163).

141 This rendering of the notoriously difficult segment of the inscription draws on precedent interpretations but offers a novel explanation for the seeming lack of contiguity between the various acts recounted. See Tang (2017, 157 et passim).

142 Feng (2017) offers a persuasive philological argument to support his claim that the personal name referenced in the Mao Ban-gui is the historical figure known as the leader of a polity named Xu, located in the east. See "Chang wu." *Shijing*. Another allusion to Mao Ban's quieting excursion may perhaps also be extrapolated from "Zhengming," where a lexical cluster of references to a roiling Han River (e.g., the one where King Zhao drowned); cord measurements used to lay out the cardinal boundaries of the four quarters; reports of this success to the king, where success is defined in terms of "the seasons do not [self] contend [against each other]" (zheng). Following this, the poem exclaims over the extraordinary nature of Sky River, whose "reflective brightness" (*zhao*) encircles Sky.

143 Cf. the poem "Ji zui" ("Already sated [with alcohol]"), in which King Zhao's temple name, "reflective brightness," is associated with winter solstice imagery: "lofty and with cold clarity (*gaolang*) [it, the "bright model"] commands [winter's] end… resulting in auspicious reports [to those above] about the Impersonator." *Shijing*.

Mao Ban invoked dynastic ancestors to begin the narrative. The second time he included details about his father, King Wen's grandson. Mao Ban references the (presumably well-field divided) lands (*yili*), apportioned to his father consequent to the latter's service "manifesting [King Wen's] accomplishments."[144] The inscription's final dedication to Mao Ban's father notably addresses King Mu in familial terms, as a fellow descendant of King Wen, and not a superior. He proffers that any grandson of King Wen who wants to demarcate the blazing (*lie*) [impact of the ancestor's deeds] must "embrace" the "bright model."[145] He concludes, "I do not dare suppress this [model], and only make this [vessel] to "reflect brightness" (*zhao*) on my deceased father's memorialized [deeds] (*shi*)."[146]

Notwithstanding the reputation of Mao Ban's success, Vogt shows that we should consider his account a "swan song" of royal public ancestral offerings. These rituals ceased after King Mu died three years later.[147] He surmises that that one reason for their discontinued use might have been the "diversified strategy" driving King Mu's "overall royal ritual program," even if it did "create non-military opportunities for interaction with and patronage of non-royal Zhou elites."[148] After King Mu passed, stylistic features of vessels commissioned by the elite, as well as bronze inscription rhetoric, reflect a turn away from sharing with the non-royal elites a "common" set of practices.[149] This explains a noted "divergence of the ritual concerns of non-royal elites and those of the royal house… [the] narrative of royal offerings did not play the role in the inscriptional record that they previous had."[150] The following section seeks to explain the conditions that account for this turn and to elucidate its implications for the production of the Ritual Reform.

Phase II refers to evidence that points to the psycho-emotional conditions that impacted King Mu's son King Xiao. The evidence permits me to lay a foundation for recognizing the psychological role played by ritual behavior to transcend the agony of social pain. Vogt explains the shift away from the public cult sacrifices as

144 Tang (2017, 45).

145 The notion of demarcation is implied in the sense of locational boundary connoted by the word *jing*, often seen in the binome: *huanjing*, "environment." Tang (2017, 196).

146 There are different opinions about the categories of nomenclature used by Mao Ban's reference to his deceased father. I see Mao Ban's use of the adjective *zhao* –the same word used in King Zhao's temple name—to refer his late father as evidence that the temple name system had not yet evolved. If it had, then it would be highly unlikely that the father of an aristocrat, even a royal elder, would share the same temple name as the deceased king. This suggests that the word *zhao* here means "reflective of brightness" and not "reflective brightness," making it parallel to the other adjective, *shuang*, "dewy brightness" invoked by Mao Ban to describe his father.

147 Ibid. (317).

148 Ibid.

149 Ibid. (315).

150 Ibid. (289).

economically driven: it was necessary to conserve royal resources, which were used too liberally by King Mu as the basis of cultivating broad patronage.[151] Grundmann, too, finds that a rhetoric that emphasized transgenerational commitment to following ancestral modes of patronage obligations was a "conservative reaction" to the wide-spread adoption of ritual practices.[152]

Their enormous contribution to our understanding of the evolution of Western Zhou rhetoric related to Zhou kingship, ideology, and social networks notwithstanding, Vogt and Grundmann's conclusions still leave unresolved the question as to *what precise conditions motivated* wide-spread adherence to the "symbolic forms of an enhanced politico-religious identity" promoted by the Zhou after King Mu's reign, especially as the Zhou continued to be challenged by ongoing attacks. This issue is especially pressing because, as Vogt suggests, the theo-political ideology promoted by the Zhou upon their founding assumed the "interchangeability of elite lineages, implying that the Zhou royal house, like the Shang before them, could be replaced." Identifying what would compel polities to acknowledge Zhou supremacy when other possibilities existed is the main aim of the investigation into the second strata of the intrapsychic site, Phase II.[153]

Phase II

King Mu's Problematic Legacy and King Xiao's Ritual Resolution

My hypothesis about the correspondence between political and personal trauma, King Mu's rehabilitation of the Zhou and King Zhao's memory, Well, and the well-field system, advances a distinct way of thinking about the driving forces of culture. King Mu's psychological state influenced his ruling idiom as well as the linguistic surround in which his royal progeny were socialized. Whereas King Mu's early prioritization of feasting placed food in an oral vacancy to fill in for words that were previously unavailable due to their association with King Zhao, his own death and the disruption of the collective mourning sacrifices he instituted by King Gong, recreated a cultural and social environment once again characterized by gaps where (the feasting and sacrificial ritual) language for loss was absent.

Extending this logic implies that a generative source of the Ritual Reform is none other than the same repressed shameful event that drove his father's acts, which he unwittingly inherited, along with the unconscious obligation to preserve it as concealed. This shame aversive mindset was organized by linguistic and behavioral habits that find coherence in the way they avoid words contaminated

151 Ibid. (191).
152 Grundmann (2019, 330–332).
153 Ibid.

by association with King Zhao's shameful fate. The eradication of rites from the royal repertoire that King Mu had used to commemorate King Zhao also eliminated the established public channels for mourning him. The result was a weakening of the psychological defenses that were conditioned by King Mu's feasting style. Had there been no family trauma threatening the royal family's status, King Mu wouldn't have needed to transform himself and the memory of his father. Had public sacrifices continued so that King Mu's transformed memories would be transmitted and shape the way he himself was memorialized, then King Xiao wouldn't have needed to (re)create his father's symbolic language in the form of a full-fledged astro-calendrical reform. I want to emphasize how King Xiao's Ritual Reform flows from the traumatic emotional event it inscribes within itself as a founding silence.

Astro-calendrical problems caused by precession offer an alternative rationale for King Mu's successor's apparent disposal of his father's sacrificial program. The shift in the iconographic focus of ritual vessels produced during King Gong's reign, manifested in the disappearance of elaborate bird and dragon forms, may reflect the reality of Quail Fire's obsolescence as a viable summer solstice determinant. Dynastic astronomers surely would have observed this. However, if this awareness was enough to influence ritual vessel form, it did not seem to lead to necessary changes. An entry in the *Bamboo Annals* critiquing King Gong's successor, and King Xiao's predecessor, King Yih, specifically points to mismanagement of summer solstice recalibrations.[154]

The implied mismatch between terrestrial and celestial realities would have had grave implications regarding the Zhou's naturalized claim to authority. King Mu's charisma—a function of his personal participation in the recognition and distribution of royal wealth to his "client elites through the medium of ancestral ritual"[155]—may have been enough to thwart would-be contenders for lineage status, but his death left the difficult job of seasonal recalibration to his descendants.

Contention over how to redress these astro-calendrical issues may be implicated in a royal factional split suggested by the co-existence of two incompatible royal calendars that David Nivison discovered deployed in bronze inscriptions dating to after King Gong's reign. This reverberates with Zhai Gong's injunction that King Mu "not let family [issues] implicate [you] in a "tangled skein" (*luan*) that would damage "royal house (*wang shi*)."[156] Nivison attributes the discrepancy to ritual mourning practices, which required that sons ritually abstain from self-proclaiming their new status. He invokes the "three-year system" of mourning we discussed in relation to Confucius' paradigmatic filial son.

Less anachronistically, Lothar von Falkenhausen explains the discrepancy in terms of a family faction. Based on the evidence, he concludes that "[f]or perhaps

154 *Zhushu jinian*.
155 Grundmann (2019, 39).
156 "Zhai Gong jie."

as long as a half century, two distinct royal calendars were used, most likely reflecting a split of the dynasty into two contending rival houses."[157] This scenario of knotty royal succession is also discerned through an analysis of royal year-count discourse, conducted by Maria Khayutina. Khayutina observes a growing concern with royal chronography in bronze inscriptions dating from the mid to late Western Zhou.[158]

These findings shed light on a problematic historical context underlying the meaning of the temple name *gong*, chosen for King Mu's successor. The striking number of glosses provided for the temple name *gong in* "Rules," and the clear variance among the eight different definitions offered, suggests confusion over how to memorialize him. Some are laudatory, and some indicate a problem with King Gong's reign.[159] Besides the word's general sense of "to be reverent," the glosses hint that the reverence shown by King Gong may have been in response to errors in his royal behavior that had to be redressed through reverent behavior.[160]

Because "Rules" is a cultural product of the Ritual Reform, it would be understandable to also read the broad range of glosses for King Gong's temple name as a reflection of confusion over King Mu's succession wishes. Faint evidence of a tradition that King Gong agreed to anoint his younger brother as heir apparent to succeed him—following his father's wishes—appears in some explanations for King Xiao's temple name.[161] This reading interprets the assignation of the word *xiao* to the king to honor his restraint when his older brother King Gong betrayed his promise to King Mu, and identified his own son, King Yih, as his successor.[162]

I cannot accept this conclusion about the source of the meaning of the temple name, since I accept the gloss for King Xiao's temple name as an accurate description of deeds he accomplished during his reign. However, given the subsequent turn away from King Mu's ritual program manifested in King Gong's ruling idiom, and the *return* toward it, albeit in disguised form, manifested in King

157 Von Falkenhausen (2006, 63). See Nivison (1983, 49–50).

158 Khayutina (2009).

159 "Rules" lists eight glosses for the temple name *gong*. The graph used in the text is a variant of the graph used in the bronze inscriptions to refer to King Gong.Paleographical evidence has shown that the former is used in contexts that make sense only if the semantic connotations of the latter graph are considered. See, Quan (1989, 233–245).

160 The Qing dynasty commentator Zhu Youzeng, explains the meaning of the word *gong*: "The host and the guests prioritize reverently upholding rituals in order to "supplicate" (*ya*) the gaps amongst kin and thereby elongate their "spiritual endowment" (*de*) as a way to contain them" "Shifa jie." We will see that the invocation of "spiritual endowment" links these glosses to an entire discourse of genealogical divinity based on King Xiao, and not King Gong's authority.

161 Gassmann (2009, 104).

162 Ibid.

Xiao's Ritual Reform, we can see in that attitude, a commitment to finishing King Mu's unfinished business. In this case, the temple name *xiao*, in addition to accounting for the deeds carried out by King Xiao to complete his father's intentions, also represented an interpersonal psychological commitment. Ultimately, that commitment would evolve to become a central feature of Confucius' conception of a paradigmatic filial son.

King Xiao's sanctioned authority

King Mu reigned for thirty-nine years. It is easy to imagine a relationship between him and a young, favored, charismatic son emerging toward the middle of his reign. This would explain why a faction supported and followed the prince after his father's death, when his half-brother ascended the throne. Knowledge of King Mu's aspirations for his son, named Pi, "field opener, ruler," would have attracted to the future king some of his father's loyal astro-calendrical experts, whose techniques and knowledge were crucial to justify King Xiao's claims for authority. These techniques, passed down hereditary lines, would continue to be refined.[163] Bronze inscriptions that reveal the Jing clan's contiguous access to power from King Mu to King Xiao's suggest similar relationships were forged with lineages whose members were endowed with celestial literacy and mastery over calendrical measurements.[164]

Further support for the idea that King Mu may have intended King Xiao to succeed King Gong may be found in eminent Chinese historian Wang Guowei's contention that after "the Zhou conquest of Shang, the Zhou maintained—at least initially—many of the Shang royal institutions."[165] We saw this to be the case with King Mu who availed himself of Shang precedents to reinvigorate Zhou social capital. Wang includes "the Shang royal succession policy of younger brother succeeding elder brother" as one of the institutions carried over by the Zhou. Thus, according to Wang, "when King Wu died just two years after the conquest, he was naturally succeeded, as king, by his younger brother Dan, the Duke of Zhou. When the Duke of Zhou then stepped down seven years later in favor of King Wu's eldest son, Song (i.e., King Cheng), this represented not an isolated act but a conscious reform of royal succession policy."[166]

Edward Shaughnessy rejects this as historically invalid but in his analysis of the *silence* surrounding the Duke of Zhou in Western Zhou paleographical sources he reconstructs an interaction between the Duke of Zhou and his brother the Grand Protector Duke of Shao, in which royal succession issues are contested. Shaughnessy's reconstruction of a royal family discussion, and his historical

163 Ibid.
164 Li (2006, 128–129) discusses the Jing lineage. Du (2018).
165 Shaughnessy (1993, 45).
166 Ibid.

conclusions, both resonate with my understanding of a structured silence that defines royal Zhou expression.[167]

King Xiao would have been keen to redress the astro-calendrical chaos that impacted his father's memorialization and legacy. A new standard of measurement was needed to recalibrate the effects of precession. Competition over astro-calendrical methods may have figured in King Xiao's succession to his nephew, whose lapses were of "cosmic proportions."[168] Portents, magnified by security issues stemming from incursions by northwestern polities, galvanized Zhou astronomers to "reduce to rule as many astronomical phenomena as possible, with the ultimate aim of predicting" omens so as to be prepared.[169] Thus, a solar eclipse that was observed in 899 B.C., was likely foremost in the minds of King Xiao and the faction that supported his ascension; it may have even been predicted by calculations. This suggested by the *Bamboo Annals* record of the eclipse, which occurred during the first year of King Yih's reign.[170]

Edward Shaughnessy, among others, has convincingly demonstrated that the locution "heaven twice dawned at Zheng," refers to a solar eclipse that occurred on April 21, 899 B.C. Moreover, Shaughnessy suggests that certain fully dated vessels, which date to the reign of King Xiao, "are consistent with a royal calendar beginning in the year… 882… what makes this dating particularly interesting is that the year preceding the first year of such a calendar, 883, would have been, if the chronology proposed here for King Yih is correct, the fifteenth year of his reign [when King Yih was said to have relocated his capital]… King Xiao's interregnum might officially have begun in the following year 882."[171]

While Shaughnessy ultimately rejects his "proposal entailing such a radical departure from traditional interpretations of Western Zhou history," astronomical evidence, along with considerations of the influential role played by "field-allocation" astrology in early Zhou military decision-making, has convinced me that Shaughnessy's proposal needs to be seriously investigated for the light it sheds

167 Ibid. (72).

168 See the "ancient" version of the *Bamboo Annals*, *Guben zhushu jinian,* where commentator Fang Shiming, states that an official in charge of establishing the summer solstice was unable to do his job. The inability to measure the location of the summer solstice may reflect a disjunction between a "ritual bureaucratic calendar, with all its political symbolism, and a more popular calendar of seasonal festivals, market days, and the like." Pankenier (2013, 257).

169 Cullen (2007, 5–6). The astro-calendrical recalibration it catalyzed recapitulates the conditions that gave rise to the enculturation of alignment behavior among Neolithic communities.

170 *Zhushu jinian*; Shaughnessy (1992).

171 Shaughnessy (1992, 256); Nivison (1983, 549–551) also identifies 882 B.C. as King Xiao's first reign year based on different criteria.

on the religiopolitical context motivating the Ritual Reform's practical implementation.[172]

Studies that demonstrate how the Zhou undertook specific military acts, including the definitive battle with the Shang at Muye in 1046 B.C., in response to Jupiter's movements, support the idea that similar influences may have informed significant decisions regarding civil affairs as well.[173] Most relevant to the issue at hand is the tradition that Jupiter's presence in an asterism "energized" the asterism, and, by extension, the terrestrial location or state associated with that celestial portion of the sky. Descriptions in ancient texts state that the heliacal rising of Jupiter (i.e., when the planet first becomes visible above the eastern horizon at dawn, not having been seen for some thirty odd days because of Jupiter's annual conjunction with the sun) was a particularly important criterion for defining which celestial (and terrestrial) space would be energized by the planet for the year (Jupiter rotation). Thus, Jupiter's presence in Quail Fire after its *conjunction* with the sun played a central role in the Zhou's perception of having a strategic advantage during the early years of the Western Zhou.

This context explains why the appearance of Jupiter in the Vermilion Bird in 882 B.C. would have been closely watched (and probably anticipated) by royal astronomers. Jupiter appeared after its conjunction with the sun in Gemini just north of Quail Fire in Leo. At this time, Jupiter began what would turn out to be an elongated sojourn in the Vermilion Bird. This culminated in a stunning, vertically aligned four-planet conjunction of Saturn, Jupiter, Venus and Mars for two weeks leading up to the summer solstice, July 2, 880 B.C. this location was proximate to the location where King Wen's "mandate" appeared in 1059 B.C. Mercury was not far off, and might have even been considered a part of the conjunction. As we shall see below, however, in the context of King Xiao's self-proscribed status as founder of the first branch lineage off the main Zhou line, the four-planet conjunction may have been deemed ritually appropriate (Figure 5.3).

Current evidence does not tell us whether, or how often, Jupiter's yearly celestial dance was established by observation or simply by counting through the cycle during the Western Zhou. It is entirely possible that either 882-881 or 881-880 B.C. could have been considered a "Quail Fire" year. Or, Jupiter's long sojourn near Alpha Hya could have rendered the whole period auspicious. Nonetheless, the rationale underlying the inauguration (*zhao*) of new rules in response to Jupiter's energizing presence would have been deemed an act suitable for redressing an "out of joint" astro-calendrical system.

172 Ibid.
173 See Pankenier (1999, 261–279, 268 et passim).

Indeed, note how the planets align on the ecliptic. This is important because the new astro-calendrical system clearly aimed to introduce asterisms whose configurations fell on or were very close to the ecliptic. We saw above, for example, how closely the four configurations that eventually comprised Dragon's upper body parts lay to the ecliptic. The almost vertical alignment of the planets on the ecliptic within the Vermilion Bird may have been read as a signal of Sky's sanction of King Xiao's political maneuvers. It's possible to imagine that events may have been orchestrated to coincide with Jupiter's movements in Vermilion Bird.

Not only was the period rendered auspicious by Jupiter's presence near Quail Fire, but the trajectory of the other planets toward a conjunction must have been apparent within six months of the initiation of the lunar year if not earlier.[174] It is beyond doubt that "recurrence of such portentous planetary phenomena in precisely the same location as that witnessed by the Zhou founder would have profoundly impressed" members of the ruling elite who had access to this information.[175] Given these implications, and the probability that the massing was anticipated by the court astronomers, one might infer a deep-seated rationale informing the exigency of King Yih's "relocation" and the initiation of the Ritual Reform.

The occurrence of the conjunction yields an explanation for the affective bond of trust and commitment that Grundmann sees reflected in bronze inscription rhetoric. It also offers a response to Grundmann's query about why a rhetoric expressing solidarity to protect and serve the supremacy of the Zhou lineage coincided with the implementation of the Western Zhou Ritual Reform. He viewed the aims of the latter as proscriptive, "assign[ing] to each individual a fixed non-negotiable position in elite society," not personal and spiritual, animated by a "conception of the heart."[176] But if we recognize that a rare astronomical event was witnessed and believed to have sanctioned King Xiao's policies, then it does not seem so incongruent that the social reorganization effected by the Ritual Reform would simultaneously manifest as an increase in the valence of a "conception of the heart."

These cultural and ecological interactions imbued the apperception of this conjunction with agentive power insomuch as it triggered, by appearing to sanction, King Xiao's symbolic project. These conditions contextualize our investigation into Phase III, of the sedimented Ritual Reform; here we zero in on evidence that demonstrates the astro-calendrical roots of the reform. Keeping in mind that King Xiao inherited his father's mindset, structured to

174 Jupiter's location on returning to visibility after conjunction with the Sun determines how the twelve-month Jupiter year (*sui*), that follows is designated astrologically.

175 Pankenier (2013, 293) is referring to a different coincidence of planetary repetitions, but his point holds for the phenomenon under discussion.

176 (2019, 330).

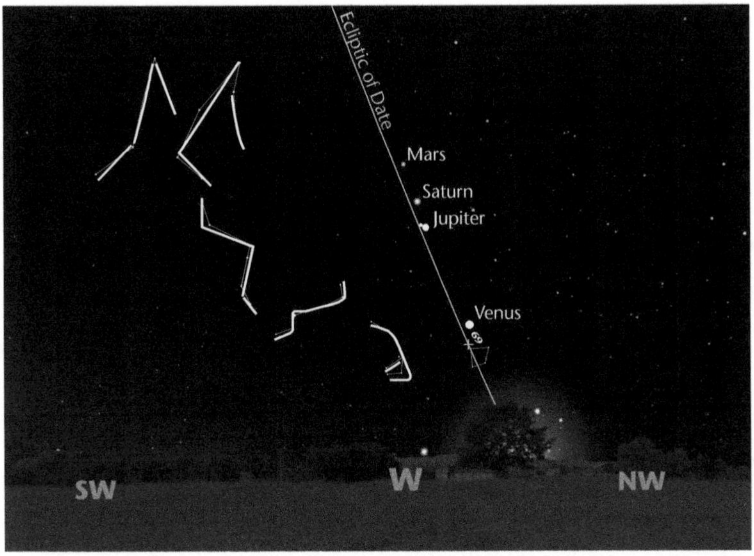

FIGURE 5.3 880 B.C. Conjunction of the four planets Mars, Saturn, Jupiter and Venus in vicinity of Quail Fire, after dusk, circa summer solstice.
Source: Redrawn from screenshot based on Stellarium, an open source software.

avoid and decontaminate words associated with King Zhao's ignominy, will heighten appreciation of his intention to systematize and taxonomize ritual expression.

Just as Zu Jia's ritual reform was a response to his father, Wu Ding's, charismatic rule, so too was King Xiao's radical Ritual Reform a response to his father, King Mu's, charismatic ruling idiom. Put another way, the birth of the Ritual Reform suggests an epigenetic line of cultural descent. Whereas Zu Jia's reforms sought to systematize sacrifical schedules for ancestors within a (calendrical) system based on a sixty-day cycle, King Xiao's system integrated ancestor rituals into a calendrical system based on the ascents, meridian transits, and descents of astral seasonal harbingers. The new framework encompassed the warp and weft of the Ritual Reform. With King Mu's view of Zhou supremacy serving as the longitudinal warp yarns, King Xiao's Ritual Reform was the transverse weft, drawing through and inserting over and under the warp.

Phase III evidence demonstrates how King Xiao embraced his father's deployment of the well-field system as an important patronage technique. This is reinforced by the continued salience of the expression "bright model" in bronze inscriptions. King Xiao's novelty lies in his extension of Well's signifying role to involve the determination of seasonal coordinates. The following section will argue that Well's evolving role paralleled the refinement of measurements for identifying asterisms close to the ecliptic. Well's location on the winter solstice and its proximity to the ecliptic allowed astronomers to identify new seasonal determinants that could rectify an out of sync Zhou lunisolar calendar.

Phase III

Well and the Systematization of New Seasonal Determinants

About this new system. Well's spatiotemporal position made it a useful tool for measuring and determining the celestial seasonal markers. How the cardinal and ordinal positions might have been ascertained is suggested by a technique for determining the distance between stars mentioned in the *Zhou bi suanjing*, a first century A.D. collation of astronomical measurement methods. The method required erecting a gnomon at the center of a circle on level ground, while a "moveable gnomon," positioned on the circumference of that circle, would be used to conduct "a series of sightings" of standard stars "with the object of determining" the width between them.[177]

Christopher Cullen, an expert on Chinese astronomical mathematics, points to a couple of "statements relating to the seasonal position of the sun relative to a stellar reference system," that directly concerns Well's function in a new astro-calendrical system.

> #G7 [60b] When [the lodge] Well is centered at midnight [on the winter solstice], the beginning of Ox falls over the middle of *zi* [due north]. When Well is 30 du and 7/16 *du* to the west of the central standard gnomon, and falls over the middle of *wei* [30 degrees west of south], then the beginning of Ox falls over the middle of *chou* [30 degrees east of north]. With this, heaven and earth are matched together.
> #G11 [62h] The distance of [the asterism Chamber] and Horn from the pole is 9\ *du* 610 // 264 *bu* and 1296/1461 *bu*.
> #G13 [63b] The distance of Well from the pole is 66 *du* 1481 *li* 155 *bu* and 1245/1461 *bu*.[178]

Cullen claims the method could obtain only a "crude approximation of differences in right ascension,"[179] because "ancient astronomers had no direct means of observing the sun's position amongst the stars. It could only be inferred indirectly from other observations."[180] Nevertheless, he concludes that the methods were likely formulated in response to mismatches between seasonal

177 Cullen (2007, 48).
178 Ibid.
179 Ibid.
180 Ibid. (97).

determinants and terrestrial realities. While he found "no internal evidence connecting this section with any particular epoch,"[181] the following will argue that an incipient form of this system underlies King Xiao's astro-calendrical reforms. Here I follow Cullen's nuanced point that although measurement techniques most certainly were systematized to redress disjointedness between astral and terrestrial realities, which arose in an "objective natural world 'out there,'" perceptions were also "dictated" by mindsets that were culturally constructed.[182]

Well lies just below the circumpolar stars, where the asterism Celestial Ford (*Tianjin*, Cygnus), straddles Sky River. This area was designated as the "Center Field," marking true north, in the earliest strata of an astrological system preserved in a transmitted text called the "Nine Fields Allocation" system. The system carved up and correlated celestial with terrestrial space.[183] Pankenier argues that the Zhou possessed a technique for precisely locating true north at the autumnal equinox, which likely "supplanted an increasingly inaccurate method of alignment using the circumpolar stars."[184] Rectification of the cardinal directions of north and south was needed to key in new seasonal markers to redress this inaccuracy.

Such a conclusion may be drawn from a telling distinction between the "Nine Field" correlative system and the fourth-century B.C. version of an astrological system that divides the sky and its terrestrial correlates into twelve fields. Whereas the southern cardinal point—the location of the summer solstice—is listed as located within the asterism Ghost Conveyor in the "Nine Fields" version, the later system inaccurately reassigns the task to Quail Fire, whose ancient role as the place where the summer solstice sun resides had been rendered obsolete by precession.[185] We will have the opportunity to offer an explanation for this

181 Ibid. (140).

182 Ibid. (xiii). Indirect evidence that relates to the emergence of measurements techniques at this early date may be gleaned from the *Accounts of King Mu*, which evinces an overdetermined emphasis on counting the distance traveled by King Mu on his journey (Porter, 1996). Although King Mu's reign cannot be credited with the measurement advances, the account reflects effort to align his memory with these innovations. King Mu generated a similar sense when he spoke to royal elder Zhai Gong, who was on his deathbed invoking Kings Wen and Wu's "measuring of the sub-celestial states" (*du xia guo*). These measuring acts were analogized with Di's meausrement of the founding Kings' intentions (*duo qi xin*). Consequential to the scrutiny, Di planted within the Zhou lineage the bright potency. This is what was was spread (*pu*) to the extreme cardinal points (*sifang*). See *Yi Zhou shu*, "Zhai Gong jie."

183 Ibid. (145 *et passim*).

184 Pankenier (2013, 147) argues that the eastern and western walls of the asterism align perfectly with the meridians converging on the pole over seventy degrees to the north at mid-autumn, an astronomical phenomenon whose legacy is reflected in transmitted literature on star-lore.

185 Pankenier (2005, 265).

conservative act in Chapter 6 below. For now, it is important to reiterate the fact that during King Mu's reign, Quail Fire's lag would have been noticeable, and would have been perceived as implicit commentary on the longevity of Zhou sovereignty.

The use of Well as a yardstick for measuring true north undergirded a new concept of centeredness, the "heart" of the Zhou's dominion. In the "Nine Fields" system, the space occupied by Well is not allocated to any specific direction, nor was it included among those asterisms designated as belonging to the "Center Region." I interpret this as negative evidence that Well functioned as the lynchpin for and not within the entire system (Table 5.1).

As the table indicates, an ancient relationship between the three asterisms Horns, Neck (*kang*), and Base (*di*), is suggested by their allocation to the "Center Region" in the earlier "Nine Fields System." By the time the "Twelve Fields" system emerged, these same constellations had been allotted to the "Eastern Region" to form the upper portion of the Cerulean Dragon. The "Nine Fields System" reinforces the idea that at the time of its formation, Dragon's form had not yet extended beyond the two asterisms recognized in the Neolithic: Tail and Heart. The invention of a new asterism called Chamber, invented to rectify Dragon's obsolescence, anticipates the salience of construction acts that links Base, Neck and Horns.

The introduction of imagery whose pareidolia source was the *built environment* into the space that had been legible as a marshy environment for Turtle, Sky River, and Dragon, alerts us to momentous changes in the cadence and semantic intentions imbuing the new astro-calendrical language. The shift from the natural to the built environment might also be a function of the role played by the Dipper, a domestic utensil, to key seasonal coordinates. According to a transmitted text called the "Monthly Ordinances" "*Yue ling,*". The astral indications derived from interpreting Dipper's handle's orientation could be mapped onto the seasonal sky to produce a seasonal schedule.[186]

Use of the dipper's handle as a clock-hand is conventionally understood to have relied on the assumption of an imaginary line that connected the asterism's first, fifth and seventh stars in a straight vertical line when the handle pointed downwards.[187] The counting of stars begins with Dipper's "ladle" and extends clockwise up through the handle. The destination of the assumed imaginary line is usually assumed to correspond to a twelve-month luni-solar calendar, although some ancient calendrical systems that used the Dipper as a time-keeper were

186 I refer to the "Yueling" chapter of the canonical *Book of Rites*(*Liji*), a Han Dynasty text. Pankenier (2011, 2013).

187 Ibid. (18n. 28).

based on a ten-month year.[188] Chen Jiujin shows evidence references that pertain to two different systems of accounting for yearly lunations, appear in the *Book of Poetry*.[189]

Most relevant for our discussion is differences in the destinations of an imaginary line that extended from Dipper's handle. In the twelve-month system, the line arrived at Antares. But in the other system, the imagined vertical line made by the same three stars *did not* continue straight down from the fifth start (Alioth, ε Ursae Majoris) to Heart. Rather, "the two stars at the very end of the [Dipper's] handle [were] aligned on Arcturus [Horns], *da jiao* and *pointed to lunar lodge Kang*(κ Virginis)" (my emphasis).[190] This is the same spatiotemporal organization suggested by the "Nine Fields" system, which includes Horns, Neck(=*kang*), and Base as circumpolar stars.

The determinant star of Chamber and all three asterisms, Neck, Base, and Horns, like Ghost Conveyor and Well, lie on the ecliptic. This alignment reveals that the nomenclature of the asterisms later identified as belonging to the Dragon's upper body were not intended to be understood zoomorphically. The later link between the trio of configurations and Dragon has obscured a semantic level of meaning involving *building contexts*: a core etymon of the word "horns" is a sound whose original meaning was (sharp) "point." This earlier meaning was used in contexts of building construction to refer to the highest point of a room's ceiling.[191]

This association explains why Horns is allocated to the "Center Region" of the "Nine Fields" system: it conveys the star's alignment with Dipper at the northernmost point of the cosmos. In this context, the words "base" and "neck" also reveal themselves as technical terms for building large constructions using the carpenter's tool, the I-square. Base refers to a chamber's foundation, Neck to the cross beam(s), all of which work in concert to support a building's pointy (ceiling), Horns.[192] The names reveal that the establishment of the new system was analogized in terms of the construction of a new royal residence, a new celestial Chamber.[193]

In sum, Well's role evolved beyond being a blazing emblem of a royal land distribution program aimed to dramatize Zhou supremacy. Paralleling the advances of astronomical observation and measuring techniques used to divide celestial space, the centrality of Well's spatiotemporal position allowed

188 Chen (1982, 305 et passim). See also Pankenier (2020, 20).
189 Ibid. (314).
190 Pankenier (2020, 20).
191 *Kangxi zidian*.
192 Cf. semantic and phonetic clustering around the terms *kang*, translated as "neck"; *hang*, "to stretch the neck, " and *heng*, meaning "cross-beam." Schuessler (1987, 348) cites two examples of the word "neck" in the *Book of Poetry* that designate "high outer gates" and "structures," evocative of cross-beams.
193 Ibid. (45).

TABLE 5.1 Comparison of "Nine" and "Twelve Field Allocation System" distribution of seasonal determinant asterisms for spring and summer.

The Nine Fields System	
Direction	*Correlated Asterisms*
Center	Horns, Neck, Base
East	Chamber, Heart, Tail
South	Ghost Conveyor, Willow [Beak], Quail Fire
The Twelve Fields System	
East	Base, Chamber, [Dragon] Heart
South	Willow, Quail Fire, Spread

Source: Adapted from Pankenier (2005, 504–505).

astronomers to identify new seasonal determinants that could rectify the Zhou calendar. Because cult sacrifices were performed at seasonal junctures and at carefully chosen locations deemed ritually appropriate; and since extensive feasting and entertainment—with pedagogical objectives—was part of the new schedule, the new astro-calendrical infrastructure and attendant rhetoric would be something with which the aristocratic class would become familiar.

The next section investigates examples from the paleographic and transmitted record that represent how the new system was filtered through royal and non-royal elite expressions. We home in on the connection between the valorized concept of "lineage potency" (*de*) deployed by the Zhou to justify their lineage's supreme status and the way it intersects with attitudes and beliefs about Sky River's cosmological significance. The discussion concretizes how the new system generated a new rhetorical, public, space to commemorate and psychically bury Kings Zhao and King Mu.

Genealogies, Sky River and "Lineage Potency" in Ritual Reform Texts

This section examines the notion that "lineage potency" was transmitted and "grasped" (*bing*) through successful cultivation. Constance Cook has shown an association between cultivation practices and a process of "opening" (*pi*) or "broadening" (*guang*) hearts.[194] This resonates with Grundmann's findings on the emotional core of Western Zhou king-elite ritual intercourse. He asserts that the formulation of a "specific idiom of obligation and commitment" was required, in the wake of the King Zhao crisis, to transform the sociopolitical bonds between

194 Cook (2020, 196–197).

the elite and the royal house into a new apparatus to promote a community of purpose.[195]

Grundmann, like others, focuses on investiture ceremonies that make the aristocrats "the bearers of a theo-political command."[196] The seasonally timed performance of Zhou cult rituals required an intense investment in the cultural construction of "structures of feeling,"[197] which had a conditioning effect. "Lineage potency" was central to the meaning and operation of the new symbolic economy and the structures of feeling it generated.[198] Starting with its astrological association with Sky River, I will trace how the concept was (unconsciously) deployed to decontaminate words that would naturally occur in a discourse about waterways, such as acts of river crossings.

Two glosses for the temple name *de* in "Rules" provide a useful guide. Both articulate the rulership qualities denoted by the word. In one, the behavior of rulers who choose to respond to threats in a yielding manner is deemed appropriate for conferral of the posthumous name: "When [a ruler] is advised to contend [with a hostile force], but [chooses not to engage in] fierce attacks, [choosing instead to] erect boundaries, it is called *de*. When stability is installed tenderly and consistently to [Zhou] officials and their collective subjects (*min*), it is called *de*."[199]

Recalling that Mao Ban identified "lineage potency" in terms of "bright models" prepares us to appreciate the vivid portrait of "lineage potency" provided by the exemplary Ritual Reform vessel and inscription known as the Shi Qiang-*pan* (Figure 5.4).[200] This vessel was introduced briefly in the previous chapter because the inscription has been advanced as evidence that King Xiao is the king referred to as "the present king" in the inscription. This conclusion led to the hypothessis that King Xiao was the implementor of the Ritual Reform.

195 Grundmann (2019, 328).
196 Ibid. (184).
197 Von Falkenhausen (2006, 294–295) calls attention to the self-referential celebration of musical qualities reflected in bell inscriptions on bronzes dating from the mid to late Western Zhou and beyond, a "language of devotion," which evokes a "structure of feeling" in the context to which I refer. See also Brindley (2012).
198 The concept of *de*, "lineage potency" has been a subject of deep scrutiny for scholars of early Chinese philosophy because of its prominence within Warring States discussions of private and public behavior. See for example, Kryukov (1995, 315); Hansen (1996); Zhao (2009). For the concept of *de* and agrarian lifestyles, see Allan (1997), who sees the natural world rather than a religious tradition as the source of root metaphors of early Chinese thought. She argues that the concept of *de* derives from the symbolic significance of plants, which provided a model for the continuous sequences of generation, growth, reproduction, and death.
199 *Yi Zhou shu*, "Shifa jie."
200 For the discovery of the Shi Qiang-*pan*, its material features and the archaeological context, see Shaughnessy (1992, 103–113); von Falkenhausen (1993).

Scribe Qiang, a high-ranking non-royal aristocrat and officer, commissioned the vessel. He was a descendant of a lineage that had a deep history of allegiance to the Zhou. Qiang's exalted rank made him privy to valuable information; he was likely a witness to the four-planet conjunction of 880 B.C. Scribe Qiang's rhetoric reverberates with the chain of words referring to bright celestial entities exemplified in the gloss for King Zhao's name and Mao Ban's celestial references to make a strong case for the identification of "lineage potency" as a metonym of the celestial river's transformational power. His inscription represents "lineage potency" as an aqueous substance whose transmission flows from Sky to the sub-celestial population.[201] This line of transmission is especially evocative given the vision of connecting celestial and terrestrial rivers at the winter solstice, which naturalized the Zhou's cosmic endowment.[202]

Scribe Qiang traces the line of transmission through a royal Zhou genealogy, rightfully famous for its elegant presentation and artful rhetoric. The first line of the genealogy points to a boundary between Sky and terrestrial activity. Here the eulogy—understood as a linguistic structure that converts King Wen's absence into words shared among a community of empty mouths—specifically points to a transaction between King Wen and celestial power involving "lineage potency":

> King Wen the Examiner of Antiquity! The one who first *aligned grain cultivation (lihe) with squaring (zheng*=governance); the one to whom *Di* sent down refined[203] lineage potency (*de*) and great screening protection (*bing*); the one who spread it [the "lineage potency"] all above and below; the one who convened and received the many states.[204]

---

201 The inscription suggests that the transmission of *de* has a social effect akin to that effected by Yu's partitioning of celestial regions.

202 Von Falkenhausen (1993, 169), suggests that this vessel's "greatest historical interest" is "in the rhetorical thrust, and the specific form of its propaganda." Li (1991, 96), discusses the connection between *de*, matching rituals and notions of divine legitimacy. Zhao (2009) also discusses the relationship between ritual performance and political legitimacy.

203 The term "refined" here and in line 6 of the Bin Gong inscription to be discussed immediately below, emphasize that *de* is a quality received from Sky by the ancients and then continuously sustained and accrued over the generations. The modification of *de* with various adjectives (refined, respectful, unified, practiced) is common in Western Zhou inscriptions, though the use of the adjective Yih, which happens to be the temple name for King Xiao's nephew, is rare. Cf. the gloss for Yih in "Rules": "Pure and tender with audient goodness is called yih." "Shifa jie."

204 Translation modified from Valmisa (2013, 11), who persuasively argues that we should read the collection of epithets as a "titular" or "nickname" that identifies the person with his most distinctive quality." See also translations by Shaughnessy (1992, 185) and Eno (2009, 44).

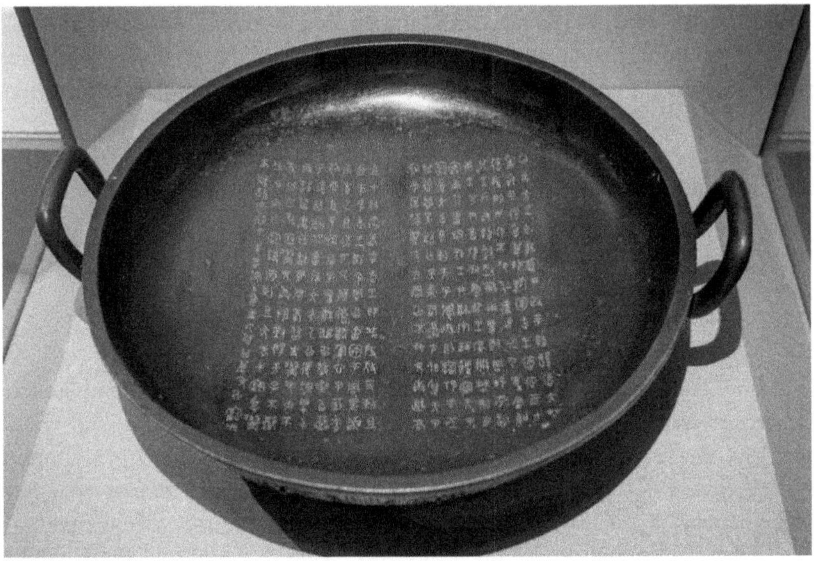

FIGURE 5.4 The Shi Qiang-*pan* genealogical inscription.
Source: Shan_shan on Shutterstock.

According to the epithets, Zhou "lineage potency" transmission was ignited by King Wen's (anachronistically conceptualized) management of the well-field system, denoted by the expression *lihe* "to bring in line the grains [e.g., management of grain cultivation.]"[205] The verb *li* "to bring in line" resonates with the stretched cord measurement terminology used in astro-calendrical discourse, as well as the vertical linearity of Sky River at the winter solstice. But the method was also used to measure and distribute the cultivatable land. The verb thus evokes the linear tic-tac-toe alignment represented in the word "well." The references to high and low reinforce the celestial origin of the Zhou's "lineage potency," which King Wen is credited with "spreading" (*fu*) among other polities.[206]

The hereditary nature of "lineage potency" transmission is highlighted in the genealogy. This is achieved through a chain of words that converge on the meaning of "descendant" and "lineage." The chain connects the eulogies for King Wen's descendants straight down to the reference to the living, "present king" (*jinwang*), King Xiao.[207] The ideation of "grandsons" (*sunzi*) serves as an

205 Shaughnessy (1992, 185).
206 See Quan (1988, 113), for examples of how these two graphs were used interchangeably in Western Zhou bronze inscriptions.
207 Cf. Shaughnessy (1992, 183), who points out the "conscious artistry of its phrasing," suggests an intention to synthesize discourse, rhyme and meter.

organizing principle for the transmission of potency in the Shi Qiang-*pan* inscription, beginning with the eulogy for King Cheng, King Wen's grandson. Lexical overlaps among words used to eulogize King Cheng and those that appear frequently in the glosses explaining the temple names *zhao* and *xiao* are discernible, suggesting familial affiliations. Italicized words represent those that occur in all three texts:

> King Cheng, the *widely renowned* (*xian*) audient (*sheng*) *Sage*! The one who [in an orderly way] left and right, cast and gathered a net; the one who *initiated* (*zhao*) the thorough integration (*che*) of the Zhou.[208]

The unambiguity of the trope of casting and gathering fishing nets to refer to lineages is reinforced by Wen Yiduo's analysis of fish as symbols of fecundity and sexual potency in ancient Chinese texts, including the *Book of Poetry*.[209] When coupled with references to integrating the Zhou state, we see an implicit intention to ascribe to King Cheng the additional quality of reproducing the vouchsafed "lineage potency" that was transmitted by his grandfather, King Wen. King Cheng, whose temple name we've seen is conventionally understood in terms of his realization or "completion" (*cheng*) of his father and grandfather's political objectives, is also represented as a caster of fishing nets that broadly extend and manage lineages.

This symbolism creates a discursive space wherein King Cheng's grandson, (the problematic) King Zhao, may be memorialized publicly. Eulogized as "vast and high-yielding" (*honglu*), replete with connotations of reproductive fertility, the words portray King Zhao as the heir and recipient of King Cheng's transmission of "lineage potency." As for King Zhao's watery demise, the inscription euphemizes it in terms of the gentle and pacific methods he used to "tame" (*neng*) those populations he (ostensibly) sought to subdue. It is this act that bears witness to his "lineage potency."[210] As if to seal this interpretive position, the inscription includes, unusually, a comment that drives home the significance of King Zhao's taming actions: [King Zhao was] the one who broadly struck the lands of Chu and Jing; [he was] the one who campaigned through to the south (*wei guan nan xing*).[211]

---

208 I follow Valmisa's (2013, 11) titular reading approach, but follow much of Shaughnessy's translation. My interpretation of the first epithet for King Zhao differs from that of Shaughnessy (1992, 106); I translate the words he translates as "model" (*xian*) and "wise" (*sheng*), according to the glosses provided in "Rules." *Shifa jie*.

209 Wen (1956). Cf. the reference to ropes and ancestors in the *Book of Poetry* poem "Si zhai."

210 Cf. Pines (2009, 317) also notes the revisionist inclination.

211 Shaughnessy (1992, 186). Cf Dorofeeva-Lichtmann (2010, 27), where she discusses the word "to make communicate" (*tong*), which is a synonym of the word *guan* "connect," used in the epithet for King Zhao, and identifies *tong* as a central technique used to control flood waters in the flood myths. Much of her work in this are

The emphasis on King Zhao's pacific as opposed to aggressive intentions is important because it is this quality that rendered his deeds illuminative of the Zhou's refined "lineage potency." References to great power immanent in a yielding nature evoke Great Yu the flood controller's "gentle" draining methods of channel construction. In "Rules," cognate words related to peaceful water control methods intersect consistently in glosses that invoke the ideation of "lineage potency." This linguistic nexus conveys the idea that the transmission of "lineage potency" is a cosmogonic and regenerative act.[212]

The ascription of a motive for King Zhao's southern campaign emphasizes the south, a cardinal direction fundamental to Zhou lineage status. It attributes to the campaign a project of expansion, reverberating with the "Rules" gloss for his temple name, which mentioned "piercing [the communications circuits] of the Zhou." The logic that links King Zhao's connecting act with the transmission of "lineage potency" becomes clear if we recall how King Zhao's temple name refers to his status as a reflective light that shines on the "bright model" located in Sky River. This status is also suggested as the particular context for the grand "counsels" (*mou*) and "models" (*jing/xing*), for which King Mu was eulogized. King - present king - was praised for "reverently glorifying [his father's] great plan (s)" (*huanmou*) and "diligently sacrificing to (the spirits) above and below" (*jian she shang xia*).[213]

The rare mention in this inscription of Di and a legendary Zhou "spirit founder" and progenitor, Hou Ji[214] is noteworthy, as is the fact that references to them are contextualized within prayers for abundant harvests. Together, these elements all point to the reigning king as an agent of seasonal productivity, making him worthy of attention from all borderland peoples. Exalted as one who "extends tranquility" (*shenning*) King Xiao was also lauded for his appropriate reflection of his grandfather's (King Zhao's) potency. Like King Zhao, King Xiao opened communication circuits to expand Zhou sovereignty.[215]

Rhyme and meter patterns within the inscription has found a prevalence of *yang* and *geng* rhymes in the first stanzas devoted to King Wen. These rhymes patterns, which reveal greater concentration among the verses

---

212 According to William Boltz, the cognate relationship between the word "tender"> "infants' flesh" (*rou*), shares common etymological origins with the word "flow" (*you*), as well as other cognate words related to a word family devolving on the concept of parturition: "childbirth/child-rearing; incubate/protect; parent-child bond; flow." Boltz (1994, 112). Cf. his suggestion that the three strokes that occur in the form of the graph for King Xiao's father's temple name, *mu*, may indicate a relation with the word family for "flowing."

213 Shaughnessy (1992, 10).

214 Hou Ji is invoked by Zhai Gong in the "Zhai Gong zhi guming" text discovered in 2003 and included in Li Xueqin's edited publication, Li (2010). We will return to this figure in the following section.

215 Vogt (2012, 230.)

devoted to Kings Cheng, Zhao and Xiao. parallel those that link the words Square and Well.[216] Rhymes identified by Martin Kern as belonging to [-ang] scheme, such as "bright" (*ming*), "golden bright" (*huang*), an ancestor's "return [upon being summoned to receive cult]" (*huang*), not to mention the celebratory "feast" (*xiang*), resonate with the Shi Qiang-*pan* phonic motif. Together they form a soundscape to replace an untenable sociolinguistic surround.[217]

Scribe Qiang's scripted genealogy of his own Wei clan follows suit in its emphasis on a pronounced affinity between grandfathers and grandsons. The non-Zhou genealogy includes epithets devoted to Grandfather Xin whose "[reflective] brightness" (*zhao*) was manifested with the "transfer" (*qian*) of his lineage," which many believe to be a reference to the establishment of a branch lineage.[218] Scribe Qiang linked the timeliness of this lineage transfer to good fortune associated with the well-field system agricultural success. This led him to boast proudly about the fact that his father, Duke Yi, was never remiss in providing the (summer) harvests yielded by the collective cultivation of the central fields of his lands.[219] The pride expressed in this detail is expressed with the locution *bugu*, literally "not [enough] grain." Feng Shi claims the term conveyed self-deprecation during the Western Zhou. It was used self-referentially, by regional lords who were unable to fulfill their obligation to contribute to the royal cult.[220]

The parallel between Qiang's and the royal Zhou genealogies highlight "important facets of aristocratic self-image in late Middle Western Zhou times."[221] Visually, the parallel genealogical narratives evoke the image of two pillars, two families who are represented as assistants to Di; visually, both are *equally* important to holding up Zhou sovereignty. The shared self-construal as assistants in carrying out Sky's mandates is most pertinent. The concurrence of topics related to the well-field system; "lineage potency"; Di; Sky; Hou Ji; abundant descendants; and special familial affinities between alternating generations of a lineage, all affirm the Shi Qiang-*pan*'s status as an exemplary Ritual Reform court product.

The inscription's inclusion of parallel royal and non-royal genealogies recalls King Mu's "diverse" ritual program.[222] In other inscriptions the king

216 Tharsen (2003, 9).
217 Ibid. (83).
218 Shaughnessy (1992, 190).
219 Ibid. (191).
220 Feng (2020a, 89). He likens the self-deprecatory gesture to that used by kings when they refer to themselves as "alone" (*du yi ge ren*) or as "orphans" *gu*.
221 Von Falkenhausen, (1993, 169–170).
222 Vogt (2012, 245) also talks about King Mu's emphasis on rituals associated with feasting that served to reframe Zhou authority as aligned with natural order. See also Cook (2005).

makes clear that an ancestor's past assistance to supporting a Zhou king's hold on power became a form of valuable social capital that could yield material benefits and status.[223] The shared memory of a "wise ancestor and deceased-father" who "accompanied and assisted the past [founding] kings to have merit and care with the great mandate,"[224] was the primary currency exchanged. The more illustrious an ancestor's contribution to "stabilizing the Zhou state" was, the more indelible was the royal memory: "I have not forgotten the wise-men's grandson."[225] These networks impacted collective psychology by including members of Zhou and other lineage descendants as potential recipients of the kings' "spread" of their "lineage potency." They supported the evolution of a sense of "we-ness" (*yi*); a gloss for the temple name *mu* in "Rules" defines the word in terms of the "allegiance to the we group"[226] that a ruler generates.[227]

Peter Boodberg has noted how "the intrusion of" concepts such as "we-ness" on the consciousness of philosophers, throbbed "with the live problems that faced the Zhou."[228] The broad dissemination of the "lineage potency" trope facilitated the formation of Zhou 'we'-group identity in a new social context, wherein "the amalgamation of small social units into larger lineage groups" was necessary for dynastic perpetuation. Rituals and genealogies that emphasized "fellowship" and "otherliness," not only served to distinguish and hence preserve the smaller 'we'-group; but they also served as "material intermediaries" to cultivate "a fixed image of a social order" as dominated and mediated by the king, lest the newly created sociopolitical groupings disintegrate.[229]

The following two sections offer an analysis of two texts, one transmitted, one paleographical which have a lot to say about the sacrificial rituals carried out by King Xiao, and which Scribe Qiang singled out for praise. These included sacrifices devoted to Hou Ji and Di worship. Both texts devolve on a homology between a ritual and the hoped for result of prayers. Most significantly, both texts reveal the homology to hinge on reconceptions of family.

223 Kern (2000); Grundmann (2019).
224 Shaughnessy (2011, 389).
225 Shaughnessy (1992, 173). He dates the vessel to King Yih's reign, though it could have just as easily date to that of King Xiao's.
226 Boodberg (1937, 361).
227 This is drawn from the gloss for King Mu's temple name, *mu*: "To spread 'lineage potency' in order to uphold allegiance to the we group (zhiyi) is called mu." See "Shifa jie."
228 Boodberg (1937, 362).
229 Ibid.

"Birth of a People," Creation of New Family Parameters

Differences in target audiences suggested by the text's form and content reinforce the broadening conceptions of family permitted by the new astro-calendrically based parameters. We begin first with a poem whose elegance rhetorical structure and rhyme pattern reflect an aristocratic court sensibility. The poem, called "Birth of a people" (*shengmin*), is a sophisticated court product.[230] The astro-calendrical intentions underlying the imagery have been ignored by commentators who focus on the homology of agrarian production and human reproduction. While this of course is an essential component of the poem's meaning, it is also important to emphasize the context of obligation to proffer what was reaped from the well-field central plots to the king or regional lords who followed the royal ritual lead.

This extended, rhythmic ballad celebrates the expansive generosity shown by dynastic "spiritual founder" Hou Ji, credited with teaching humanity the technique of field cultivation. Scribe Qiang specifically linked Zhou prosperity under King Xiao to his worship of Hou Ji along with Di. Although Hou Ji was an icon of Zhou agrarian supremacy, Stephen Owen argues that the sacrificial rites devoted to his commemoration bespeak an anxiety about preserving rituals that will not result in fault and cause for regret." [231] The aversive cadence in the strophe "For Lord Millet [Hou Ji] began the rite/and hopefully free from failing or fault,/ it has lasted until now," suggests that Hou Ji worship rituals were an institution that emerged to resolve a problem and prevent its recurrence.[232]

The astro-calendrical intentions organizing the Ritual Reform convince me that Hou Ji worship was the product of King Xiao's merging of two venerable traditions, one organized around harvest worship of natural deities, and one related to royal cult sacrifices. One problem that Hou Ji worship resolved was the need to establish a distinct line of lineage from Di that would validate the Zhou's claim of a divine "lineage potency" and therefore could buttress their claims to supremacy (ironically, this was the very Shang behavior that was implicated in the Zhou's conquest). Hou Ji worship situated the Zhou's claim to supremacy within the parameters of their relationship with Di.

Worship of Hou Ji as a lineage "spirit founder" focused on his technical contribution to agricultural methods, which benefitted all humanity. Hou Ji modeled for the public how well-field system agrarian methods were a function of his relationship with Di.[233] The rhetoric of assistance and matching is central to the effect of the homology presented in "Birth of a people." It combines cultic "ritual lore" about the Zhou ancestress Jiang's divine conception, with

230 "Shengming." Shaughnessy (2015) provides a nuanced argument for the dynamic between orality and written texts that must be considered when analyzing the communicative intent if poetry collected in the classic.

231 Shaughnessy (1992, 173).

232 Owen (2000, 27).

233 Ibid. (28).

agrarian lore related to the "cycle that [wa]s supposed to be accurately reproduced at the end of the poem."[234] Jiang's production was anthropomorphized as a son, Hou Ji, a term that could be literally rendered as "the parturition," (*hou*), of "millet" (*ji*), the dominant product of summer harvest.

Vogt has shown that Hou Ji was also the title of Zhou officials charged with managing cultivation-related rituals.[235] This official would have had to time his ritual performances to align with seasonal verities, and thus, like the well-field officials titled Jing, would have had to rely on astro-calendrical predictions and calculations to be effective. The sequential presentation of spatial images to demonstrate temporal progression in "Birth of a people," such as moving from Hou Ji's issuance from the womb, to the pens of hoofed animals, to forestland that is being cleared for agricultural production, mimics agrarian reliance on astral movements across space to coordinate collective agricultural activity. While Stephen Owen has hypothesized that the first two spatial images may refer to the migratory path taken by leaders of the pre-dynastic Zhou until they embraced an agrarian lifestyle, he admits to being at a loss for how to relate this trajectory to the last spatial image, ice, from which Hou Ji is protected with bird feathers.[236]

Resolution for this conundrum may be found if the spatial images are construed as seasonal scenes. This schemata views the scene of Hou Ji's conception as having occurred on the winter solstice; his birth depicted with verbs associated with reproductive vegetation cultivation, represent spring; the "narrow alley" or pen, with growing yearlings who split the stream of their comings and goings in order to avoid trampling him, the summer scene;[237] the forestland, an autumn one that transpires after harvests have been completed; while the ice represents a return to the spatiotemporal location of conception. Following this logic, the bird feathers that protect Hou Ji from the extreme cold are those of the Vermillion

234 Ibid.

235 Vogt (2012, 207, n. 67).

236 Owen (2000, 26). According to Sima Qian's "The Annals of Zhou," one Zhou ancestor, Gong Liu, was credited with facilitating the full transformation from steppe to agricultural lifestyle; he is recorded as having settle at a location known as Bin, an area within close proximity to Mt. Qi. Cf. Michael Puett (2002b, 72) who understands Hou Ji's prelinguistic survival as ensured only "because figures on earth protected him from Di's wrath" (over Jiang Yuan's appropriation of his potency to impregnate herself).

237 The novel locution that describes the hoofed animals' mode of protecting Hou Ji's summer sojourn implores comment: the animals splitting act is conveyed with reference to the form of a Chinese graph, *pai*, which means to "split." The image of a line of hoofed animals diverging as they approach Hou Ji resonates with the location of the Sky River's split, and its regenerative cosmological associations. We shall see how a special relationship between solstitial moments is intimated in the poem. Cf. Sterckx (2018, 306), where he discusses the deforesting and other clearing that was carried out after harvests.

Bird, whose promise of warmth is imagined at its own initial stage before reaching its apotheosis at the summer solstice.[238]

Hou Ji's resounding cry after overcoming the cold symbolically marks his transcendence of the winter solstice; the vocal emanation dramatizes language acquisition exemplified in his penchant for naming the object and project of agricultural reproduction. Several commentators have reflected on this lavish attention devoted to taxonomy, concluding that the repetition served a pedagogical and mnemonic purpose directed toward spectators of the ritual.[239] "Birth of a people" exemplifies how the Ritual Reform expanded the domain in which ancestral sacrifices were performed.[240] Hou Ji worship aimed to shore up a broad coalition of aristocrats who were linked by their shared commitment to supporting and protecting the Zhou's status as Di's sanctioned purveyor of agricultural bounty and social stability.

Feng Shi has argued that Hou Ji was also the title of an official who managed rituals organized around grain production. The equivalent to the rank and title given to the Grand Protector (*Dabao*), or Grand Scribe, (*Dashi*), the official called Grand Grain Cultivator, *Da He*, was an overseer.[241] Bronze inscriptions also record the existence of an official called *Tianji*, Sky's Millet [Manager]. Feng claims the word *tian* here delineated a specific lineage within the Zhou clan, which oversaw astronomical affairs.[242]

Peter Boodberg's analysis of the mutual interaction between Chinese mythic memes, and Chinese language development yields an important lexical clue linking Hou Ji's worship to axial perspectives. Boodberg asserts that a key to understanding the connection between Chinese mythic memes, such as axial pillars and floods, and language development, is to understand how the linguistic fragments that comprise the memes work together to reconstruct an original phoneme. Boodberg explains the dissipation of the original phoneme as a function of a gradual dimidiation of the complex cluster of consonants, a feature of archaic Chinese phonetics.

238 Schlegel (1875).

239 Scholarship on the *Book of Poetry* that accompanied ritual performances has shown how these rituals mark a distinct break with a tradition of royal rituals that had previously been private, intimate occasions See Shaughnessy (1997, 187); Kern (2000).

240 Li (1991, 84–86), offers graphic evidence to support his argument that late Western Zhou kingship ideology was based on the allineation of seasonal and ancestral sacrifices. Li sees a common origin of the graphs for the word "altar" (*qi*) used as a semantic signifier in words having to do with sacrifices in temples, and the graph for the word *zong*, which denotes clan or lineage affiliation.

241 (2020a, 88) The southwestern part of Shanxi was linked to the agricultural spirit's place of origin (74–75).

242 Ibid. (90). Feng emphasizes that to administer his business the official would be bureaucratically linked to those related to astro-calendrical observations and regulations.

In this view Hou Ji's name may be a product of linguistic evolution: it emerged from the need to reconstruct lost phonetic forms, but along the way the new sounds accrued new semantic meanings. In Boodberg's account, Hou Ji's name reconstructs the phoneme *chu*, "pillar," which itself derives from the etymon "horn." "Horn" is also identified as the etymonic source of the words "'altar,' 'ancestor,' 'torch.'"[243] It is also, recall, the word used to designate the roof of the celestial palace, as indicated by its association with Neck and Base in the "Nine Fields" allocation system. These intentions reveal the degree to which the Zhou's image of clan supremacy depended on the superiority of an axial based astro-calendrical system to ensure consistent prosperity.

"Birth of a people" is a polished ritual thanksgiving ritual that was performed in a royal hosting setting. The diction, the rhythm, the poem's cadence, all reflect literary workmanship aimed to cultivate devotion among the aristocratic celebratory audience. The recent discovery of another verified Ritual Reform era text inscribed on bronze vessel and inscription, provides an extraordinary counterexample. Called the Bin Gong-*xu*, the text invokes the Great Yu is as a "spirit founder." There is scholarly consensus around the idea that the inscription recounts a thanksgiving ritual organized by a regional lord for those farmers whose labor was the backbone of the well-field system. A comparison of this text with the Shi Qiang-*pan* inscription and "Birth of a people" deepens our understanding of how Ritual Reform ideals were disseminated.[244]

The Bin Gong-xu Inscription: A "Wild" Thanksgiving Ritual

The Bin Gong-*xu* inscription reflects how the cultural complex surrounding the Great Yu was recruited to expand the symbolic economy of Western Zhou political representation. I propose that the Zhou persuaded Yu worshipping populations of the value of the new Zhou axial oriented astro-calendrical schedule by coopting Sky River as an icon symbolizing their "lineage potency." Several texts point to Zhou efforts to represent Hou Ji as "picking up where Yu left off," and the vessel inscription validates them.[245]

Constance Cook's incisive analysis of the Bin Gong-*xu* inscription uncovers a lexical network connecting narratives related to "celestial assistants."[246] These assistants included Yu; Hou Ji; and Gong Liu, the putative first Zhou ancestor to

243 Boodberg (1937, 345–346).

244 For an account of the discovery of the vessel as well as incisive analyses of the inscription Cook (2012–13); Chen (2012).

245 Cook (2012, 81). Other poems that celebrate either one or the other as spirit founders reflect the *Book of Poetry's* inclusivity of a variety of local perspectives. *Shijing*, "Si wen" for Hou Ji's matching; and "Xin Nan Shan" and "Hanyi" for Yu's. In the latter poem, Yu's acts resemble those described in the Bin Gong-*xu*.

246 Cook (2012–2013).

settle and establish a sedentary agrarian lifestyle. Cook concludes that the narratives concerning the latter two figures share structural features with Yu narratives. Although, following Mark Edward Lewis, she acknowledges an implicit astronomical dimension underlying the "occult of Yu," which might explain these representational similarities, she stops short of identifying its source.

If we accept, as I've argued elsewhere, that the "occult of Yu" relates to Dragon worship, then the first two lines of the Bin Gong-*xu* inscription may be seen to invoke a celestial position: Yu was endowed with the capacity to measure and establish new coordinates because Dragon's identity itself derives from its archaic calendrical regulating function. Situated at that transformational, cosmological space between the northern and eastern quadrants, between winter and summer, Yu/Dragon emanated the power to rectify the seasonal coordinates. This power source is alluded to in the inscription:

> Sky charged Yu to spread [e.g., cultivate] the earth (*putu*); leveling mountains and channeling [Sky] river, [Yu] thereupon [balanced the] differences (*cha*) to select the [four cardinal] regions (*fang*)[247] in order to square [rectify] (*zheng*) [the seasonal determinants];[248] thereupon [Yu] descended among the people and examined the [extent of their] lineage potency. Thereupon, [Yu] made himself a match to [Sky] to feast the collective (*min*), giving birth to Our King and creating officers, their merits were *de*. The people cared for the bright (*ming*) *de*, assuming the obligation to rely on it in the sub-celestial realm (*tianxia*). Using its reflection (*zhao*) for good situations (*hao*), increasing… the refined (*yi*) *de* [to the extent of] prosperity (*kang*), there will be none who are not diligent (*bu yu*) as offering friends (*xiaoyou*). The constant brightness (*yiming*), [aids in keeping fields] measured and tidy (*jingji*) [to provide] good sacrifices without flaw. Marriage relations that care for *de* also assist Sky.[249]

The word used to designate the act Sky commands, *pu*, "spread" is ancient. Shang records show its original form denoted a process of clearing the fields of weeds to increase grain production.[250] The field clearing was likened to spreading out a new (earth) plane upon which new cardinal parameters were established.[251] But,

247 For *cha* as "difference," see Liang (2003, 51–56).
248 Liang Shaomin interprets this locution *yi zheng*, as a version *li zhong*, "to establish the (axial) center. See Chen (2012–2013, 141).
249 Slightly modified after Cook (2012–2103, 81–83).
250 Ibid. Cf. Sterckx (2018, 303), describes ancient agronomic knowledge as something that "tends to be formulated as a menu of instructions or a catalogue of rules that need to be enforced, reinforced or sanctioned. We learn about beginnings and outcomes, that is, what the farmer should or should not do on the one hand, and, on the other hand, how the farmer should ge rewarded or punished for the outcome of his labor."
251 Sometimes this would be accomplished through contained fire.

because the inscription makes clear that following his clearing and rectifying of coordinates (*zheng*), Yu descends (*jiang*) to the "collective," we are forced to conclude that the earlier acts were completed above, that is, in Sky. Metaphorically, Yu's establishment of seasonal determinants with distance measuring techniques, shapes a new geobody.[252]

Cook notes that "the 'mandate' to Yu was not a conquest over a former regime, but a fundamental reconfiguring of the earth for civilized life."[253] Yu's suitability to serve as Sky's assistant is demonstrated in his first act, "his making the world fit for human habitation and agriculture."[254] Moreover, Yu's celestial acts established a standard for behavior that would be available for inspection after his descent to the terrestrial realm. The inscription emphasizes the order of actions to imply a causal relationship between Yu's reconfiguration of astro-calendrical coordinates and his scrutiny of peoples' *de*. Yu's recalibration became a benchmark for measuring the degree to which "lineage potency" imbued a ruler and his subjects' behavior. Put another way, "conversion to the way of *de*" meant accepting the new seasonal coordinates established by Yu. The Zhou were able to sublimate Yu worship to their overarching cosmo-ritual program by ascribing to Yu the establishment of the Zhou's new astro-calendrical framework![255]

The extensive accounting of kin groups who benefit from Yu's rectification of seasonal boundaries names groups of people who are open to receiving "lineage potency" and cultivating it. Presumably, these people were those conscribed to work the well-fields. Significantly, the line of transmission reflects a permeability of boundaries that separate family lineage and collective identity.[256] "Parents" (*fumu*), "people" (*min*), "*our king*" (*wowang*), "marriage alliances" (*hungou*), are all in line to cultivate "lineage potency" so long as they assist with promoting and cultivating fields in accordance with Yu's newly rectified framework.[257]

---

252 Dorofeeva-Lichtmann (1993, 2005, 2009, 2010) has contributed a body of work related to imagainary geographical schemata in transmitted and recently excavated texts.

253 Cook (2012–13, 85).

254 Ibid.

255 One factor that may have contributed to this reformulation is the importance of the number nine for cosmological and religious conceptualization. Porter (1996, 46, 121) argues that valorization of the number derived from its association with Tail, a configuration comprised of nine stars. This is the origin of the myth about Yu's division of land into nine parts. The nonary basis of the well-field's division of cultivatable land may have been easily likened to Yu's own land dividing acts.

256 Shaughnessy (1999, 327) sees this discursive shift reflected in sections of the *Book of Poetry*.

257 Cf. Pines (2005, 91), discussion on "universalistic" approaches to "establishing the imaginary, not only the physical boundary" of inclusion as pre-imperial governing tendencies; and Rawson (1989) on distinctions between "barbarians" and the Zhou as reflected in bronze inscriptions.

The Bin Gong-*xu* inscription implies that cultivating "lineage potency" is discernible in the commitment to the performance of timely sacrifices (*si*) year in and year out. The religious logic proscribes that external alignment manifested in behavior that showed "care of the annual sacrificial performance," had an internalized counterpart, a "care of *de*" (*hao de*). In the Bin Gong-*xu*, these qualities were shared by a group who identified as "offering friends" (*xiaoyou*), a term that Scribe Qiang also used self-referentially.

The next section continues this line of inquiry to explore identity formation dynamics in the face of such spatiotemporal conditioning. I focus on the term "offering comrade" *xiaoyou*, especially, but not exclusively, in this binomial form. I argue that the locution communicates concisely the interpersonal structure of the reimagined family.[258] Summer and winter solstitial rituals were attended and then mimicked by lords of the regional states who buffered the Zhou center. Ritual was a mechanism for extending the spatial realm of cognitive distribution. It externalized important information based on a politico-religious lexicon and concomitant mental structure redolent of familial tones. Grundmann aptly identifies this sense of inclusivity as an "esprit du corps."[259]

King Xiao, Zhou Sovereignty, Inclusivity, and Xiaoyou Identity

The previous sections demonstrated how the Ritual Reform symbolic economy, generated by the astro-calendrical reform and distributed through multiple media, was characterized by its aim to reorganize royal family relationships so that King Xiao could psychically bury and mourn both father and grandfather.[260] This section my focus centers on the *xiaoyou*, whose sociopolitical status was unique to the Ritual Reform. The fact that both Scribe Qiang and the people supervised by Yu have access to this status, thanks to their transmission of Zhou "lineage potency," is evidence of a shift toward appealing to a broad public audience.[261] Shaughnessy has singled out an evolved preference for vessel quantity over quality, reflected in the repetitive blandness of décor in exemplary Ritual Reform vessel shapes, as evidence of spectacularizing intentions. Aesthetic valorization of vessels that could be displayed as sets reduced the valence of ornate quality that required proximity for maximum aesthetic effect.[262]

The fractious family dynamics driving the broadening of public appeal is reflected in the editorial license taken by Qiang. His excision of Kings Gong and

258 Anderson (2006).

259 Vandermeersch (1980, 111–151) discusses the Zhou rites and the "esprit" they generated.

260 Ibid. 23. Cf. Von Falkenhausen (2006, 53–56), where he suggests that the function of ritual vessels expanded to include the role of preserving a lineage archive.

261 Ibid.

262 Shaughnessy (1995).

Yih from the genealogical record, substituting King Xiao as the direct successor of King Mu, figuratively severs an older brother and nephew from the royal genealogy. A similar violence is also reflected in the sudden ousting of vessel shapes and motifs of ritual vessels in favor of new ones. While Rawson and Kern's view that a propensity toward "visible ordering" in the archaeological and textual record represents a deliberate archaism is persuasive, I see the archaism as paradoxically suffused with a pronounced iconoclastic cadence: although the past is invoked, it is only to reshape it to accommodate, through the language of mortuary ritual, the psychic need of a grandson to mourn the loss of his father and grandfather.[263]

The Shi Qiang-*pan* inscription's pruned genealogy exemplifies what I mean. It publicly endorsed a standard of differentiation among lineages based on segmentation through the valorization of Qiang's ancestor, who transferred his lineage. His description of a lineage structure based on segmentation evokes a definition provided by one of the glosses for the temple name *xiao* in "Rules."[264] The gloss implicitly attributes to King Xiao a system that involved acts of splitting and "settling lineages every five generations" (*wuzong anzhi*). The rule would have justified King Xiao's self-representation as the direct issue of the fifth generation of Zhou rulers (excluding King Wen who did not actually rule). As such, he would be the appropriate heir to establish the first branch off the Zhou lineage trunk.[265]

Eastern Zhou texts' use of the term *zhaomu* to refer to a cycle of generational distinctions in mortuary rites becomes perhaps more intelligible if understood in the context of King Xiao's own patrimony: Zhao and Mu, of course, refer to his grandfather and father.[266] Regardless if the expression "settlement of the five generations can be definitively linked to the Eastern Zhou *zhaomu* system itself, the clustering of King Zhao along with four other rulers as a collective object of

263 Rawson (1999, 449).

264 Von Falkenhausen (2014, 66, 67). The complementary genealogy of the ancestors of the caster of the Shi Qiang-pan presented in the inscription reveals how members of an elite lineage positioned themselves as parallel to the house of the Zhou kings. The specific reference to a Gaozu—the first ancestor in a lineage segment spanning five generations—silently reflects on King Xiao's own lineage position as the first descendant of the trunk to establish a branch lineage.

265 Cf. A chapter in the *Book of Rites* (*Li ji*), a Han dynasty idealistic reconstruction of Western Zhou ritual, "Rules for Sacrificing" ("Jifa") states that "The Zhou offered supernal sacrifices to Gu, and suburban sacrifices to [Hou] Ji; they made King Wen into a founding [dynastic] ancestor, and made King Wu into the founder of a lineage." *Liji*.

266 Kern (2009, 161). Kern's assertion that attendant upon the change to the temple system was "the fusion of religious and administrative practices" is relevant. As he recounts, "nearly all references to the temple in middle and late "Western Zhou bronze inscription point not to the offering of ancestral sacrifices but to the performance of appointment ceremonies during which the king bestowed a new position, complete with a wealth of ritual insignia, on an appointee."

worship recalls Jessica Rawson's observation that remains from Middle Western Zhou burials incline toward family grouping "suggest[ing] a wish to cluster close relatives together."[267] Rhetorically clustering King Zhao along with a set of previous kings effectively camouflages his singularity to conceal ignominy surrounding his death. Erecting a boundary between the first five rulers and subsequent branches tidied up his memory by immersing it within a more general and over-arching commemoration of dynastic-founding events.

In sum, the institutionalization of systematized branching turned on the radical severance of ritual form from an original politically and religiously significant context. What sanctioned this symbolic violence was the astro-calendrical framework that refashioned the Zhou's cosmo-ritual dominion. Multiple genres of Eastern Zhou transmitted texts corroborate the existence of a deep collective memory pressed within their accounts of Western Zhou governance. Summer and winter solstitial gatherings left an indelible impact on collective agrarian habits. The psychotropic effects of intense and repeated attention and resources devoted to seasonal cult sacrifices and feasting also exerted a strong conditioning factor on the esprit du corps. Galvanized by the Zhou house with consistent presentations of them as the "obligatory passage point" for power enhanced a sense of solidarity among attendees replete with an auspicious sense of success among a range of guests regardless of rank level.

An example of how seasonal associations contoured the *esprit du corps* is reflected in the value of royal gifts that emblematized the Zhou's astrologically based authority. For example, red garments such as knee-pads, usually denoted by the word "vermillion" (*chi*), were frequently bequeathed to Zhou officers in investiture ceremonies.[268] These sartorial objects were identifying markers, as the Zhou are referred to as "the ones with the red knee covers" in transmitted texts. Knowledge of the astronomical context that I hypothesize sanctioned King Xiao's implementation of the Ritual Reform is suggested by gifts of banners with "four stars," which were included among Zhou royal gift repertoire. Banners with "five stars" have also been recovered, leading some to suggest it refers to the five planets whose conjunction signaled the ascension of the Zhou house.[269]

The occurrence of the locution *xiaoyou* in the Shi Qiang-*pan* and Bin Gong-*xu* inscriptions despite the distinct differences in the contexts of their practical use, suggests the term had instrumental value as well as a symbolic function. The

267 Rawson (1999, 422).

268 Wang (2019).

269 Pankenier (2013, 312), cites the discovery of an "Eastern Han Silk brocade bowman's armguard bearing the legend "when the Five Planets appear in the east it is beneficial for China," that could be used as indirect evidence to support the possibility that the five stars represented planets.

binome denoted a new paradigm of relationships with the royal lineage. This index points to an expansion of the signifying currency of the verb *xiao*, from a more narrow, liturgical domain in which the term denoted the royal practice of "offering" [food to ancestors]," to the broader realm of social distinctions.[270] I propose that *xiaoyou* relations created new membership criteria for participating in royal lineage sacrifices.

The term *xiaoyou* marks a radical shift in religious orientation. Distinct from what David Keightley and others have observed in ancestor sacrifice during the Shang and early Zhou, which was implicitly oriented toward "making a good ancestor," bronze inscriptions from the late Western Zhou evince a "shift in early conceptions of eternity from backward memory to forward expectation."[271] The currency of the phrase *xiaoyou* reveals that it is not the ancestor who has to be "made," it is the subjects of the Zhou state who were made into Sky's assistants.

The seasonal schedules that regulated when *xiaoyou* would enjoy the privilege of participating in royal sacrifices cemented a shared acknowledgment of the Zhou's "lineage potency." Coordinated to feature brightly manifested astronomical phenomena, believed to be communiques from Sky, the gatherings heightened the king's "ethic of presence," and "created powerful new motivations for enrollment in the Zhou state identity."[272] These seasonal associations also nuance the new preference for vessels specific to grain and other vegetarian offerings insomuch as the aesthetic is appropriate for the summer foodstuffs harvested from the central plots of lands. This produce was offered to the lords who feasted in response.[273] Rituals that relied on materials to demarcate lineage ranking displayed who had the privilege to offer foodstuffs to the royal house and thereby fulfill the well-field system obligation.

As an identity label, *xiaoyou* promised integration of various devotions of people into the Zhou fold through parallel bonds of mutual obligation.[274] The king assumed a double position as the object around which *xiaoyou* relations were structured. He was the scion of the Zhou lineage, whose celestial sanction was iteratively demonstrated through ritual performance. As the founder of a branch lineage, he also represented a reorganized and expanded view of the Zhou family.

270 Knapp (1995, 200). Knapp observes that although a "majority of recipients of *xiao* offerings in the bronze inscriptions are the vessel maker's father, grandfather, or both," at the same time, *xiao* offerings were also dedicated to higher ranked personages other than one's parents or grandparents, such as "one's uncles, the lineage, lineage elders, the sub-lineage, the lineage temple, friends, in-laws and spirits. This suggests the broader social currency of the practice. See also Knapp (2005).

271 Keightley (2004); Puett (2005).

272 Vogt (2012, 230). It also "opened up the possibility of a Zhou elite identity separate from the royal house," Pines (2000, 2).

273 Hosting strategies may have also driven the dramatic reduction of smaller drinking vessel shapes; scholars have explained it as a reflection of the Zhou's desire to control when libations can be consumed.

274 Kutcher (2006).

In sum, the impulse "to make right," which we have traced through history, is amply displayed in Ritual Reforms' implicit and explicit fixation on alignments: astro-calendrical cardinal coordinates rectified; the lines of royal genealogy reorganized; cult liturgical rites merged into an archaic system of ancient seasonal sacrificial schedules; sumptuary vessel sets spectacularly displayed in lines during ancestral sacrifices; these were all symbolic behaviors aimed to "square" and therefore decontaminate memories of an excluded father, and shamed grandfather.[275] If the term *xiaoyou* captures the transformation of subjects into assistants mandated to protect Zhou sovereignty, it also created a community of empty mouths into which lexical structures built to avert bringing shame to Kings Zhao and Mu could be inserted.

The implications for Chinese cultural evolution of these conditions orient the analysis of the last and latest strata of the intrapsychic site, Phase IV. My focus turns to two texts whose composition, consumption, transmission, and preservation have been universally seen as having exerted a strong shaping force on the formation of a collective memory about the Western Zhou. The first, again a court poem from the *Book of Poetry*, "Thorny Caltrop" (*Tribulus terrestris*), has been construed as a "hypotext for much if not all the 'systematizing' description of ancestral ritual" found in late first millennia texts." The other, the renowned mantic text, *Book of Changes (Yijing)*, represents a collective *xiaoyou* mentality.

It is not my intention to rehearse all that these texts embody as a reflection of the spirit of Chinese culture.[278] Instead, my discussion focuses on the texts, embodiment of as cultural traits shaped by vicarious dissonance. In other words, the texts are approached as artifacts of a mental structure forged by the collective cognitive dissonance caused by King Zhao's demise. They were produced in response to obstacles preventing its accommodation within social emotional awareness. The symbolic language articulated in "Thorny Caltrop" and the *Book of Changes* operates along expressive channels via "mutual implication," reflecting a mindset, in which "qualities of experience are perceived to be most essentially present at the time of their nominal absence." Tracing patterns of silence or emptiness that were nonetheless replete with power reveals the texts' source is the saga that they were produced to disguise.[277] I apply the concept of "vicarious dissonance" to propose that both texts are imbued with a neuropsychoanalytical historicity.[278]

---

275 Pankenier (2013, 472, 473).

278 Jung and Wilhelm (1975, 141).

277 Ibid. (60). Cf. the name of the asterism that marked the winter solstice, *Xu* "Emptiness." (β Aquarii).

278 Cooper and Hogg (2007); and Cooper (2019). My thinking about dissonance in China was significantly influenced by Michael Puett's groundbreaking work that questioned assumption of holistic understandings of Chinese cultural perspectives. We noted his research regarding the "ambivalence of culture" and its implications for understanding Confucianism. Here I call attention to his work as a rejoinder to the idea that the ambivalence is a function of the dissonance described below, see Puett (1997, 2002a).

Phase IV

"Thorny Caltrop" as Fantasy Structure

"Thorny Caltrop" vividly and viscerally stages the resurrection of a grandfather through his possession of his grandson.[279] The grandson, is ritually identified as an Impersonator, literally "corpse" (*shi*). He along with the offering son, the bereaved who hosts the sacrifice in honor of his father, as well as a kind of ritual emcee, or officiator, known as the Invocator, are the central actors of the ritual. The Invocator was the only one empowered to speak during the ritual. The graph denoting *shi* is formally very similar to other graphs, including those that denote the meanings, "person" (*ren*); "grandmother" (*bi*); "eastern polities considered foes" (*yi*). These epigraphic resemblances have caused much confusion about the word's original meaning. While there is a logic connecting "person" to "corpse" insofar as they each signify an existential status, recent scholarship has found that the word's use in Shang divination records in fact points to a metaphorical level of signification, referring to the ritual deployment of Impersonators who served the royal court's needs for mediated communication.[280]

While Zhao Fulin has demonstrated significant differences in Shang and Western Zhou Impersonator ritual roles and acts—based on "Thorny Caltrop's" account—the gesture toward revivifying an ancient Shang ritual recalls King Mu's ritual program.[281] As in the case of the performance of the *yue* and *wan* rites to commemorate King Zhao, the incorporation of an Impersonator into ancestral cult performances afforded the Zhou an opportunity to dramatize the sources of their lineage supremacy.

At the same time, the ritual enacted in "Thorny Caltrop" evokes "wordless affects and unconsciously guarded secrets."[282] Michael Puett theories that Chinese ritual practice is a form of domesticating behavior that stimulate. Puett triggered by "dangerous interactions" with a "fundamentally discontinuous world."[283] I suggest that "disjunction between the ritual space and what is outside it" may be construed from the perspective of a psychic topography. Whereas Puett focuses on ritual's capaicity to domesticate malcontent triggered by a discontinuity from which ritual afforded a respite, the ritual scenario depicted in

279 Von Falkenhausen (1995) discusses how questions about the mechanisms for this possession have riven interpretations of this scene. Although trances are hinted at, the substances or conditions for their inducement were not deemed appropriate or important enough for discussion.
280 Zhao (2016).
281 Ibid.
282 Ibid.
283 Puett (2019, 443, also 447–448).

"Thorny Caltrop" points more concretely to the mechanisms triggered to keep it concealed from the psyche's awareness."[284]

Puett explores the "productive tension" that operated in the royal processes of domesticating disjunctions.[285] He shows how the ancestor's descent from Sky to inhabit the grandson's body, and the father-sacrificer's behavior, *modeled* for his son (my emphasis), the Impersonator, "how to play the role of son. Through this role reversal, a normative father–son relationship is built up across the three generations. Within the ritual space, the [spirit] becomes a supportive ancestor and the living becomes filial descendants, with perfect father–son dyads extended across the three generations."[286]

Moreover, although he does not mention astro-calendrical observations, Puett notes how beyond the interpersonal and on the "royal level, the dyad is extended. The sacrifices are also given to Heaven, and the leftovers are spread to the various families of the realm… sacrificial space, the cosmos would become, ritually speaking, a single lineage. And the ruler would be at the center of this web of relationships."[287] Within this ritual space, "disparate lineages are connected by their ritual kinship relations with the ruler, who in turn is connected in ritual kin relations with Heaven. The ruler thus becomes, ritually speaking, a Son of Heaven, and also, going in the other direction, the father and mother of the myriad people."

Puett's account of the epistemological and ontological underpinnings of the ritual world represented in "Thorny Caltrop" is used to make a theoretical argument, so the malcontent that he identifies as the source of the poem is treated abstractly. Our neuropsychological understanding that King Xiao's domestication process recapitulated an archaic behavioral pattern to create a new cosmovision, is reinforced when we approach the poem as a mise-en-scène. This perspective yields information that is "doubly telling" as regards both the ritual content and the specific emotional danger that its construction parried.[288]

The negative valence of conditions associated with an "outside world" implores rehistoricization within the traumatic conditions of King Zhao's death. Puett's attention to the rigid regulation of the ritual world evokes a hermetically sealed space, where entrances and exits are tightly controlled: it is neither the host nor the Impersonator who greets the spirit who descends from Sky, only the Invocator engages in that interface. The Invocator ventriloquizes the sacrificer, the Impersonator, and the spirit's vocal

284 Ibid.
285 Ibid. (447, 442).
286 Ibid. (442–443).
287 Ibid. (443).
288 Abraham and Torok (1994, 126).

intentions. He is *the only one* to speak during the spiritual exchange: the grandson *remains silent.*

Martin Kern also points to the aesthetic and religious dimensions of the ritual performance depicted in "Thorny Caltrop." Most relevant to the discussion is his conclusion that "the ubiquity of formulae related to longevity and permanence, together with their narrow terminological scope, accounts for the numerous instances of identical phrases or lines. In these prayers and conferments of blessings, we recognize the interplay of ritual language and cultural memory."[289] He foregrounds how ritual literacy required cognitive reconstruction necessary to access the intentions of each item in the ritual lexicon: "one must (a) determine its extra-textual referent in the situational context of the ritual act and (b) integrate it into the complete sequence of deictic words within the text."[290] We saw a similar rhetorical pattern driving patterns of lexical items in the glosses in "Rules"; the notion that reconstruction is a function of integration of separate yet related components recalls the holistic neural processes condition by Sky literacy.

Kern's analysis of the "distribution of shared lines" between "Thorny Caltrop" and other poems provides evidence for the existence of a "common and clearly demarcated pool of ritual language."[291] He notes that the only parallel usage of a line found in "Thorny Caltrop" among poems categorized as "States' Airs" ("Guofeng"), occurs in the poem "Seventh Month," whose astro-calendrical intentions reflects a "very different situation of ritual speech."[292] Another poem from "Airs" includes the word "caltrop" in its title: "[On] the wall there is Thorny Caltrop," ("Qiang you ci") but was not considered by Kern. Categorized as representative of a lyrical tradition ascribed to the Yong region, which was associated with the Zhou ancestral capital in the "Twelve Field" field-allocation system discussed above,[293] the poem's reference to "thorny caltrop" performs the aesthetic function of stimulating or arousing (*xing*) the emotional expression that follows. This was a common rhetorical feature seen in the *Book of Poetry*. The cultural preference for a form of expression that revolves around a stimulation-response interaction between the natural environment and its impact on cultural forms exemplifies a central tenet of this this book's claim.

As in the case of "Thorny Caltrop," the plant also evokes royal psychic pain in "[On] the wall." The intertwining properties of this brambly plant, unlike in the former poem where it is stripped of its thorns, are represented as too entangled to "sweep" away (*sao*) in the latter poem. The second line of the poem gets to the heart of the matter: "Speech of the [royal] inner chamber, cannot be spoken

289 Kern (2000, 105).
290 Ibid.
291 Ibid. (53).
292 Ibid. (92).
293 Pankenier (2005, 505).

(*bu ke dao ye*). That which could be told, the speech [about it would reveal] their vileness."[294] The trope of pain caused by blocked speech is repeated in the following two stanzas, elaborating on how long and shameful (*ru*) any recitation of what is discussed in the inner chamber would be if spoken.

One ancient commentary notes that it is not just that the caltrop is so dense that it cannot be swept away, but that sweeping it away would collapse the entire entity represented by the wall.[295] Another emphasizes the disinfectant role ritual plays to distract from the thorny mess; yet another pits the desire to speak against the need to preserve the royal house. The poem's imagery and content evoke the trope of a (haunted) house to represent a psychic condition. Although "[On] the wall there are thorny caltrops" is conventionally interpreted as a scathing rebuke of the regional lord of Wei, and hence is not discussed with "Thorny Caltrop," which clearly portrays a royal sacrifice, two shared features among poems encourage reconsideration of this historical interpretation. First is the function of the bramble image as a stimulant for the following expressions in both poems. Second, and concomitant to the first, is the images' status as topics about which the following (poetic, imagistic) discourse offers new information. These evocative topics trigger or stimulate (*xing*) the expression.[296]

With this broader intertextual context in the background, we return to "Thorny Caltrop." I construe the text as a fantasy produced by a subject, in this case the protagonist grandson/Impersonator, (King Xiao). Unlike the commonplace meaning of fantasy as a simple antonym for not real, my understanding is narrowly conceived: fantasy refers to a specific psychic structure produced to exempt the psyche from reorganizing in the wake of a traumatic experience. Fantasies are stories the psyche tells itself in order to preserve a shameful secret. "Thorny Caltrop" is a fantasy because it carries out, "with the help of [its] manifest content, the repression of [its] latent content." The poem comprises a culturally coded symbolic return of the repressed.[297]

Just as "[On] the wall there is thorny caltrop]" uses the trope of a sealed up domestic realm to figure a haunted (royal) house and, by extension, psyche, so too does "Thorny Caltrop" reveal its ancestral crypt-like setting to be a psychical counterpart. Conventional interpretation of the poem tends to marvel at the apparent harmonious synchronicity instantiated by the rich and varied ritual performance presented in the lyrical tableau, even as they acknowledge its constructed nature. Martin Kern has demonstrated the complexity of rhyming devices at play within the poem's structure. The

294 "Qiang you ci," *Shijing*.
295 *Shijing, "Chu ci."*.
296 Dai (1991).
297 Abraham and Torok (1994, 94).

interaction between semantic and aural levels of communication represent an interactive milieu.[298]

I identify another structural pattern contained in the text, which reflects "[d] istinctions between two separate mimetic contexts, one that represents the reality of psychic agitation" and one that represents a fantasy structure produced to relieve the psyche. This structural feature becomes clearer if we approach the poem from the perspective of information communication, more precisely, topic-comment discursive structures. As seen in the case of Mao Ban's inscription, topics are discourse generators, they establish "given" or "old news," while comments refer to utterances that respond to the topic, offering elaboration and nuance. Chronology in topic-comment structures operates on the level of "old news"/"new news." As for comments, they do not need to be linked chronologically. This frees us to focus on other components within the comments that account for their relationship to each other.

There is an inherent psychoanalytical temporality in "Thorny Caltrop's" structure: the first stanza, contained by the [-ək] rhyme, points to an agitating affective context, while the following stanzas dramatize the psychic consequences—the production of a fantasy structure—of preserving a trauma as unknowable.[299] For example, the first stanza's imagery combine to recapitulate the affective conditions of King Mu's reign. Whereas the first image, thorny caltrop, invokes a royal psychic pain, the formulaic imagery evocative of bounteous millet production ("our panicled millet is abundant, abundant, our glutinous millet is orderly, orderly") recall King Mu's growing reliance on the well-field system and feasting as a symbolic means to transcend the conditions evoked by the caltrop image.[300] Bracketing this information as "old" intimates its alterior status within the offering grandson's psyche: it communicates that the affective center of his psyche was transmitted to him as a lineage inheritance.

Recognizing the salience of psychic agitation communicated through the [-ək] rhyme in the first stanza, and linking that to King Mu's experience, opens a new vantage point for interpreting the return to this rhyme in the fourth and fifth stanzas. Because the first and fourth stanzas are separated by stanzas that are organized by the prominence of [-ang] rhymed words, which we have seen carried positive valence in astro-calendrical contexts, and because the cadence of the poem is ostensibly one of jubilation and celebration, the question arises as to why, when the focus is on the interaction between the Impersonator and ghost, the rhyme scheme returns to the that of the first stanza with its reverberations of agitation.

This alignment implicitly links the ghost's return and speech to the affective conditions generated by the grandfather's unutterable absence. The ghost's presence, in my reading, is not a happy reunion but a haunting one; he returns to

298 Kern (2000, 55 et passim).
299 Ibid. (80–81). There is a compelling phonetic link between this set of rhymes and the word for "ghost" (*gui*, *-ədx*).
300 Ibid. (81).

protect his secret, and to ensure his descendant grasps the linguistic and consumptive regimen necessary to do the same. The danger and sadness evoked by the first stanza's imagery and rhyme scheme was metapsychological, this is what constituted the grandson's "reality."

This interpretation finds strength in the fact that music, exalted by all commentators for its mediating capacities, is not performed until the ghost is escorted away, as opposed to when he ghost arrived, or during his consumption of the feast. The absence of music from these other contexts strikes me as emotionally incongruent in light of music's capacity and function to intensify "reunion urges so as to restore social 'warmth.'"[301]

One explanation for the conscribed use of music in "Thorny Caltrop" is that it is reserved for the singular pleasure of "knowing" that the ghost's successful ingestion had led to satiety. In this view, it is the Invocator's public pronouncement of the ghost's satisfaction that triggered musical jubilation. When read in in tandem with the convergence of all expressive power on the persona of the Invocator,[302] his control over decisions about what words to use; his power to ventriloquize those whose mute intentions he professes to understand; and his control over the timing and substance of physical ingestion, it becomes clear that the Invocator's characterization is a metaphor for the psychic mechanisms that operate to preserve an inherited shameful secret. The invocator exerts control over the seat of psychic and physical digestive processes: the mouth.[303]

The fact that it is the Invocator alone who interfaces with the Ghostly Protector (*shenbao*), (distinct from Shang ritual practice), suggest to me that the Invocator and the returning ghost are one and the same character. Let me explain. Ghosts return to ensure that the unwitting descendant—e.g., King Xiao, the grandson/Impersonator—stays on task regarding preservative repression. What this task entails is the grandson's resistance to psychic reorganization, a rejection of his own assimilative inclinations. If left unsupervised, it threatened the preservation of the shameful sceret.[304] Thus, ghosts don't just show up and they don't symbolize inaccessibility of meaning. On the contrary, they return when a secret (here too an "order of knowledge" or "truth") is threatened with exposure, that is, accessibility to conscious awareness. These are ghosts who

301 Pankenier (2009).

302 Kern (2000, 88) cites a commentator who explains the Invocator's complex multivocal responsibilities in terms of a capacity to read and translate the intentions of the host and grandson: "The invocator first [i.e., in Stanza 4] invokes the intention of the impersonator(s) to announce it to the host. Then in turn [i.e., in Stanza 5] he invokes the intention of the host to make an announcement to the impersonator(s)."

303 Ibid. (89, n. 139). Kern cites ritual compendia that show the "removal of the dishes [to be] another fixed element in the process of an ancestral sacrifice. According to the Zhou li and Yi li, the invocator gives the order to remove the dishes once the sacrifice is finished."

304 Abraham and Torok (1994, 25).

return to ensure that the subject remains blind to the obliterated traumatic act. They return, in other words, to lie. The "apparent 'revelations' articulated in speech and demeanor are by nature deceitful," and this deceit is the "the entire purpose motivating" their presence. *Their returns enforce the unconscious obligation to perpetuate concealment of a specific family saga* (emphasis added).[305]

"Thorny Caltrop" recounts the ghost's disguised return and also the means by which the ghost teaches its descendant a ruse for resisting the topographical shift to accommodate a shameful loss. The fantasy's latent topic is the unconscious linguistic processes that convert experience into words and promote self-fashioning. The fantasy's illusion of a ghost's consumption of a feast tricks the psyche into thinking it had already "swallowed" and "buried" and digested the experience of a traumatic and shameful loss, thereby exempting the psyche from acknowledging it ever occurred. Abraham and Torok refer to this type of fantasy as "incorporation." It is triggered when a "subject shares a shameful and therefore unspeakable secret with [a] lost object."

> In order for the subject to safeguard the secret as unspoken and preserve the innocence of the object, the subject pretends to have had nothing to lose in the first place. This pretense is sustained by the fantasy of incorporation, which functions by effecting a false introjection or simulated "swallowing" of what has been lost. Instead of the grief being introjected and the ego's topography rearranged to accommodate its loss, the shamed lost object [e.g., King Zhao] itself is magically taken into the psyche and preserved alive in an "intrapsychic crypt"... or vault lodged within the ego, but resistant to the ego's mechanisms of assimilation. The structure of the crypt simultaneously prevents the psyche from integrating the loss, protects the secret from exposure, and maintains the (fictitious) integrity of the debased object, thereby allowing the subject to deny that a loss ever occurred.[306]

Fantasy structures "implement the metaphor" of psychic assimilation literally when the "usually spontaneous process [of linguistic conversion and psychic processing]... undergoes reflexive treatment due to an encounter with a prohibitive obstacle."[307] The fantasy imagines the "taking into the mouth the unsayable the object itself." Abraham and Torok identified this speech figure as

305 Porter (2018, 18).
306 Rashkin (1995, 370).
307 Abraham and Torok (1994, 130). Cf. the regressive implications of such fecalizing behavior. Research demonstrates that "children of about 2 years of age or less will but put virtually anything in their mouths, including what is described as and appears to be feces" Rozin (2007, 395).

"demetaphorization," the mechanism "annuls humiliation" by accommodating the literal meaning of the words causing the humiliation.[308]

In this light, the word used to designate the grandson, the Impersonator or "corpse," may be construed as evidence of these operations. The word, evocative of the macabre scene of washed up bodies on the banks of the Han River, also recalls the term "ghost conveyor." Both terms carried negative valence, they were cues whose salience disturbed Western Zhou self-fashioning. We saw how negative valence was drained from the word "ghost conveyor" by situating it within an astro-calendrical lexicon. A similar decontamination process may have devolved on the word "corpse" when situated within the ritual lexicon of ancestral sacrifice.

In "Thorny Caltrop," labeling the grandson as a "corpse" pretends that this awful word that had become "excremental to others" is appetizing by linking it to the grandson's vaunted social and religious status. It is crucial to note that this is *not* simply a reversion to a literal level of signification, "but of using [the word] in such a way—whether in speech or deed—that [its] very capacity for figurative representation is destroyed."[309] The word instantiated the grandson's (unconscious) self-construal. It staged how he was "fine to be a corpse,"[310] that being a corpse was appetitive. This context nuances the hidden motivations driving the Invocator's control over the meal and music: the fantasy reveals that the successful means to preserve the secret (and send the huanting ghost away) is to *ritually celebrate* an *illusory transformation* achieved through literal ingestion.

The incorporation fantasy suggests that the poem's foregrounding of delectable foodstuffs to be consumed by the ghost is part of the deceitful conceit to buttress the idea that it is fine to be a corpse. The fantasy's apotheosis transpires upon the Invocator's announcement of the ghost's "having been sated" (*ji zui*). This public statement about the ghost's affective status initiates the music performance, which itself is coincident with the withdrawal of ghost. The scenario reveals how a royal discourse about concrete oral fulfillment, displayed within a context of public bereavement, was a technique for protecting the secret and psychic integrity. Herein lies the source of the poem's its aesthetic effect, which derived from the effect produced by the nullification of figuration. The fantasy mediates the haunting effects of the ghost's return by making him the author of the illusive trickery, which he demands his descendants "grasp." Convinced that

308 Ibid.

309 Abraham and Torok (1994, 132).

310 Ibid. Fantasy is distinct from Broda's (1982, 82–83) account of the "false consciousness" in Mesoamerican Astronomical calendrical rituals, the purposeful crafting and projecting of which she attributes to elites, although it produces the same effect. That said, what Broda describes is quite accurate for Imperial astro-calendrical rituals.

the descendants have the fiction firmly in hand, the ghost returns to its crypt buried in the descendant's psyche.

"Thorny Caltrop" brings to life a psychic disturbance endured by King Xiao in his struggle to self-fashion. Its preservation as a vaunted text suggests the ghostly exorcism exerted a curative effect that was inextricable from its aesthetic power. The poem represents an unconscious attempt at self-cure, to transcend an obstacle to self-fashioning through a symbolic language that fantasizes not a re-union with the deceased relational object, but its expulsion, albeit in the guise of physically sating the ghost.

From a neuropsychological perspective, recent findings related to the neurobiology of schizophrenia, may sharpen our understanding of fantasy production. I rush to add that I do not mean to imply a diagnosis for the grandson–putatively identified as King Xiao, but neither do I feel the need to deny the possibility. My interest is in discovering possible intersections between the formation of a fantasy structure and brain functioning. A compelling starting point lies in George Northoff's finding that spatiotemporal mechanisms associated with "auditory cortical activity" operate differently in schizophrenic brains than in the general population. The distinction has the potential to account for the neuropsychological factors that might account for the illusion (delusion) dramatized in "Thorny Caltrop."

In Chapter 3 we saw that spatiotemporal binding and alignment to Turtle was disrupted due to the effect of the precession of the equinoxes on Turtle's spatiotemporal position. I suggested that in this phase of social evolution, there were opportunities to create new symbolic means to "speak" about the loss of Turtle and thereby transcend the state of suspended mourning and return to unobstructed self-fashioning. The rupture to the spatiotemporal mold, though catastrophic, was transcended through the reformation of Turtle into turtle; this reveals that discontinuity in spatiotemporal alignment does not predict pathology.

However, in the case of the grandson/Impersonator portrayed in "Thorny Caltrop," I submit that we see symptoms that can be explained by Northoff's hypothesis. According to my reading, the intrapsychic drama situates us in the crypt concealed in the grandson's psyche ego where King Zhao and the words associated with his humiliating saga were stored. The scenario exhibits properties of a neuropsychological phenomenon observed in brains of schizophrenic subjects. For example, findings relating to the way schizophrenic brains suppress spatiotemporal binding and alignment to external, i.e., exteroceptive, stimuli,"[311] helps account for the occasion of the grandson's torment. "Thorny Caltrop" depicts the neuropsychological condition when internal brain activity is able to suppress external activity to align and bind with an "ongoing resting state."

311 Northoff (2018, 87).

Fantasy production is dissociative, its aim is to cause the psyche/brain to reaffirm alignment with the preservative regimen, to shift away from external alignment toward "internal thoughts," albeit unconscious ones, is the mechanism that exempts the psyche from having to acknowledge the reality of psychic devastation wrought by an unutterable loss. The fact that internal stimuli are defined as features of the "ongoing resting state," moreover, also intimates the possibility that the resting state is one internally organized by the unknown presence of a secret in its midst.

Neuropsychological findings also refine our understanding of the kind of response that witnessing the performance of this fantasy of a parried psycho-pathogenic trauma would have produced. Exposure to this performance, as indicated by its canonization, would have generated a "chill or thrill" effect for aristocratic participants. This would have resonated aesthetically with their own experience of traumatic loss.[312] Panksepp argues that the archaic roots of the "chills and thrills" lie in "our capacity for separation-distress (substrate for primary-process sadness)."[313] Panksepp argues that it remains possible that our emotional nature diverted (co-opted) affective vocalizations into musical branches long before language emerged in cultural evolution and this more likely occurred in sub-neocortical rather than neocortical regions.

The relationship between separation distress, music and language evolution suggests a possibility for building on Northoff's observation of "reverse en-training" in schizophrenic neural circuitry and its implications for fantasy structure production. Because the psychic aim of the fantasy of incorporation hinges on the rhetorical figure of demetaphorization, it implicates the pre-linguistic state as an essential component of fantasy production. The linguistic subterfuge performed by the fantasy, allows the psyche to represent the unutterable secret all the while disguising it in the symbolic language of pleasurable gustatory experience. "Thorny Caltrop" paints a picture of neurobiological processes recruited to exorcise a source of psychic torment.

Finally, I want to call attention to the spirality of the fantasy's temporal structure. If its occurrences within a lifespan were figured to represent three-dimensional space, the shape would be a space curve with *one* tangent line at a constant angle. This suggests that at the time of a fantasy, when brain processes suppress spatiotemporal binding and alignment, they are aligning with the temporality of the ancestor and his secret who's haunting led to a dissociative state.[314]

The correlation between internal resting-states and the suppression of external stimuli, moreover, suggests the presence of an a priori claim over cognitive decisions. Already present and operative as a regulator of self-fashioning in a

312 Panksepp (2009).
313 Ibid. (242).
314 Northoff (2018, 87).

subject's psyche—e.g., as a function of the resting state, the a priori structure only demands full attention when the brain's efforts to resist topographical shifts are seriously threatened by the brain/psyche's spontaneous inclination toward self-fashioning. When the tension is so great that it threatens psychic disintegration, the brain prevents psychological dissolution by dissociating and aligning with the internal space time of the crypt, in which a grandfather and his shameful saga live dead by alive. This explanation has the advantage of appealing to evolutionary theory, according with neurobiological findings, and explaining the production of a cultural object whose aesthetic value lies as much in the uncanny recognition of the condition portrayed as it is the rich and complex textural fabric in which it was woven.

While it remains to be seen if the Chinese evidence compels reconsiderations of neurobiological and neuro-cultural phenomena, it is fair to say that if "Thorny Caltrop" was the "hypotext" for later attempts to reconstruct Western Zhou rituals, then the fantasy that portrayed King Xiao as the "dead but alive" corpse must be construed as a shadow "hypotext" that contoured Confucius' imagination of a paradigmatic filial son. We will explore these implications in Chapter 6 below. Before that, we will compare the structure of the *Book of Changes* to "Thorny Caltrop" to trace the relationship between the Zhou royal family's distress, and that of the *xiaoyou* who witnessed, participated, and consumed feasts offered at performances similar to what is recounted in "Thorny Caltrop."[315]

Rejoining these two texts within the context of social and psychological equilibrium brought by the Ritual Reform offers an opportunity to investigate how the same events so central to the royal family's self-construal, also exerted influence on the *xiaoyou*. The fantasy created the illusion that *xiaoyou* were indispensable to the proper execution of the rites—the exorcism of King Zhao's ghost—on which depended the recurrence of natural phenomena, the growing of the grains and other food-plants and the successful accomplishment of the well-field system. This population, who fell in line to both physically and psychically ingest and digest King Xiao's program for managing his own complicated grief, emerge as ghost authors of the famous mantic text.

The Book of Changes and the Existential Memory of Dissonance

This chapter has advanced the claim that the Ritual Reform expanded the parameters of family so that King Zhao and King Mu could be memorialized without shameful aversive consequences. Along with their acknowledgment

315 Cf. "Ji zui" which points to the winter solstice as the seasonal context for the ancestral sacrifice.

and implementation of agrarian schedules that aligned with the new astro-calendrical concept of center, *xiaoyou* were welcomed into the Zhou family. This form of alliance network formation had, from the beginning, been central to Zhou political authority. This section explores the implication for individual members of a group when the consequences of a group leader's actions generate cognitive dissonance. I aim to trace how the royal Zhou family's response to their psychic experience of dissonance evolved into a cultural behavioral modality that is represented in the form and content of the mantic *Book of Changes*.

Taking a cue from neuroscientific formulations related to testing conditions, I argue that norms valuing familial cohesion, which sustained relationships between the Zhou and their alliances, effectively "primed" the latter to identify as part of an interdependent group. Because self-worth and self-fulfillment derived from both group and members' success, the cognitive distribution of negative emotions, including "cognitive dissonance," shaped individual as well as collective responses in similar ways. Neurocultural research conducted by Lee and Jayarej shows that "having an independent or interdependent self-construal accounted for differences in dissonance experienced."[316] Interdependently primed participants experienced dissonance "when they made choices [ranking music CDs] for close others but not for themselves."[317] The sense of discomfort elicited by the dissonance recalls our discussion in Chapter 3 of the individual and vicarious nature of shame.

Studies on subjects who had been primed with the salient presence of "social eyes" meant to represent a "social other" demonstrate how perceived social monitoring influenced the interdependent self.[318] Chapter 3 raised the possibility of tracing the source of the "social eyes" influence back to the placement of a symbol on a Jiahu Box Turtle plastron, which evoked the presence of a monitoring entity. Because group membership consistently figured in interdependent self-definition,[319] and due to the salience of shame avoidance as a constitutive feature of interdependence, self-affirming values alone are ineffective tools for reducing anxiety induced by "social eyes."[320] These conditions naturally influenced the capacity to assess threats;

316 Lee and Jeyaraj (2014, 1).
317 Ibid.
318 Ibid. (2).
319 Ibid. (6).
320 Here I suggest that shame aversive behavior may nuance the assertion made by Cooper (2007, 107–108), who argues that self-esteem is not involved in comparisons between behavioral outcomes and normative standards.

"a suboptimal decision that involved social others was threatening to those with interdependent self-construals."[321]

The conditional nature of the bond between the Western Zhou and Sky, as well as with their alliances, made King Zhao's death a consensually negative phenomenon. Because it was seemingly unprovoked, and because the conditions of the bond with Sky made it impractical for the Zhou to absolve themselves of responsibility for the aversive consequence of his expansionist mission, its inconsistency with preconceived cognitive beliefs created a dissonance that was heightened by an emotional need for an "unambivalent stance toward the world."[322] The *Book of Changes* is a symptom of these conditions, as well as the symbolic means by which the elite, and then the *xiaoyou*, transcended the emotional threat posed by the crisis. The conditions influenced "attitude, perceptual [and] behavioral" changes, which were stimulated among the broad network of Zhou affinal relations to regulate their arousal.[323]

In the absence of responsibility which could reduce dissonance, the Zhou and those alliances that remained supportive, adapted to the discrepant realities by reformulating the "measuring stick" or normative standards by which members could affirm themselves. We have seen this reflected in both King Mu and King Xiao's ruling idioms, and its impact on the mentalities of aristocrats who inscribed devotional expressions to the king and lineage ancestors on bronzes. The *Book of Changes* offers a different vantage point from which to appreciate the cultural consequences of a social transformation catalyzed by an emotionally impractical social awareness.

Mantic Strategies and Collective Memory Formation

The *Book of Changes* contains results obtained by yarrow or "'milfoil' (*Achillea millifolium*) stalk casting."[324] The mantic technique used to obtain them was "a complex sortition of forty-nine stalks" that had an "evenly round and smooth texture" and were "uniform length and diameter." Because the "joints or nodes between the branches [we]re long enough to permit the cutting of stalks of adequate length (some eight to twelve inches in length), the lengths of the stalks could be manipulated.[325]

The text "is organized around sixty-four graphs or 'pictures' (known in Chinese as *gua hua*,), each of which is composed of six lines, either solid (—) or broken (- -)." These "pictures" or "hexagrams" (*gua*) representative of the

321 Lee and Jeyaraj (2014, 2).
322 Ibid. (4).
323 Cooper (2007, 107).
324 Raphals (2019).
325 Ibid. See also Song (2018).

sixty-four possible permutations of stalk selection results, are "supplied with a name and seven brief texts: a 'hexagram statement' (*gua ci*) understood to represent the entire hexagram, and 'line statements' (*yao ci*) for each of the six lines."[326]

The mantic text also included cryptic, imagistic texts that correlated with specific lines in the hexagram sequence from top to bottom. The astro-calendrical underpinnings of the system are undoubted. Most clearly, the line statements belonging to the first two hexagrams in the transmitted version of the *Book of Changes,* contain references to the movement of Dragon throughout the year. Pankenier has demonstrated the "correspondence between the line texts of the first hexagram and the changing posture of the evening dragon constellation from beginning of spring to beginning of autumn," as well as its winter peregrinations.[327]

Lisa Raphals claims that a preoccupation with stars and other celestial phenomena is a feature of the way the oracle was systematized. For example: she notes how the system operated to store data, "(1) systematic empirical observation and record-keeping; (2) early theoretical accounts of [Sky]; and (3) hermeneutic correlation with terrestrial geography and events.[328] This data correlates with this book's consideration of mental features shaped by the "world-brain" interactions of Neolithic farmers.[329] The prior architecture remains. It evolved by virtue of the integrative mechanisms that gave rise to it, even as it was contoured by ongoing elaboration and modulation of sensory information across the processing hierarchy of the brain. Upon these systems of symbols, sensory, and material information, rested the idea that transformation is the organizing principle for cosmic operations.

We have seen that neuroscientific findings demonstrate the highly edited subjective nature of perception. Chapter 2 laid out how traumatic conditions surrounding Turtle's withdrawal triggered cognitive processes that affected the "editing" of information before its presentation to the brain. I suggest similar processes governed the systematization represented in the *Book of Changes*, which bears traces of collective symptoms of disturbed memory and self-fashioning.

Latent cognitive diissonance, which required "reperception" of realities, permeates the mantic text. Recognizing how shame/self-esteem played a role in the arousal of dissonance, we can appreciate the collective need for self-affirming feedback concerning how to cooperate and fit in a social environment organized around an "unsayaable known." The strategies deployed to categorize and organize alternative future scenarios reflected in the *Book of Changes*' structure

326 Shaughnessy (2014, xv).

327 Pankenier (2013, ix, 51–55).

328 Raphals (2019, 269). She lists similar types of prognostication texts recovered from three different sites to demonstrate the salience of the practice.

329 Northoff (2018). See Chapter 3 above where I discuss this in more detail.

evoke the neural processes identified by Peek and van Beek that are triggered by oracle interpretation.[330] Mechanisms that increase cognitive attention allows for the rehearsal of future scenarios; these same mechanisms are also recruited for the interpretation of imagistic and metaphor-reliant oracular language.[331]

The text's promise of a transformational experience via its contained oracles suggests that what imbued *Book of Changes* with its inspired aesthetic sensibility was its capacity to trigger an uncanny moment of re-experienced dissonance. The "strange but familiar" nature of the moment derived from its connection to a primary (historical) collective experience of dissonance caused by obstacles to psychically bury King Zhao. The astro-calendrical imagery and lexicon found in the text reveals its connection to the royal strategy for overcoming the obstacles posed by King Zhao's failed river fording. At the same time, the text's format and content reveal it to embed an existential memory of the processes by which the collective reordered reality.

Access to the oracles in the *Book of Changes* probably involved several steps. Raphals emphasizes the importance in Chinese mantic practices of formulating "one's own intentions before initiating mantic procedures. On this view, divination was not undertaken to resolve doubt or conflict, but rather to seek divine sanction for goals and desires already formulated."[332] Based on internal textual evidence, Edward Shaughnessy shows that frequent appearances of a word he translates as "receipt" (*heng*) indicates the receipt of a favorable response to an earlier divination.

Song Yunwoo argues that the growing significance of yarrow divination during the Western Zhou reveals a trend away from belief in anthropomorphic spirits associated with turtle divination. The yarrow tool represented a universe that operates in "cosmic patterns" and not the dire consequences of individual suprasensible entities.[333] Whereas the "prerequisite" determined intentions driving Shang king mantic practice were manifested in an imagined dialogue with a suprasensible entity, the *Book of Changes* operates without a similar "explicit interpersonal interaction."[334] Eastern Zhou texts represent Zhou kings' mantic consultations, but the degree to which the oracle can be considered a product of royal divination acts in the same way we view oracle bone records is questionable. Nonetheless, there is evidence that the text instantiates an "ecology of mind" that "helps us to understand the mentalities that organize other essential aspects" of Western Zhou experience.[335]

330 van Beek and Peek (2013).
331 Ramachandran and Hirstein (1999); Johnston and Struck (2005, 11).
332 Raphals (2017, 256).
333 Song (2018).
334 Raphals (2017, 269).
335 Driediger-Murphy and Eidinow (2019).

The (ritual) process of arriving at intentions to present to the oracle may have evolved from processes to arrive at consensus on how to interpret silences about unspoken events.[336] Consideration of the application of the information conveyed by the oracle reinforces this idea. For example, it contained "data that was important for planning and preparing new settlements; people who gathered [where mantic practices were performed] would talk about 'their enterprises, their range, and probably their products' while at the same time they updated their databases regarding prospective lands," and kingly conduct.[337]

The names of certain hexagrams tacitly sketch an existential memory produced from the dynamic coalition between the brain's functional circuits. The nomenclature and clustering of hexagrams suggests cognitive representation that extends beyond "low level peripheral" processes" because they "draw information from many sources."[338] This mode of representation operates as a network, an "interconnected web in which beliefs 'cohere' with one another to avoid cognitive dissonance." [339] Because it scaffolds on other "higher-order cognitive functions, such as planning and decision-making, which require beliefs to conceptualise and evaluate the current situation, actions, and consequences… [the organization] provides a basis of action."[340]

The hexagram names denote states of being in circumstantial contexts, while the line statements provide experiential tidbits that nuance the contexts. Their interplay is "intuitively coherent."[341] This mode of communication, along with the three-hundred and eighty-four scenarios offered by the line statements for rehearsal, emerged as a response to ambiguous information. Like beliefs, "whatever their neural or cognitive structure," the linguistic interplay among hexagram nomenclature and line statements reflects a multi-distributed memory system.

Coherence provided by tropes in the oracle's symbolic language facilitates the "encoding and retrieval of memories that are consistent with the cognitive and emotional" content of the dissonant experience.[342] While the mantic process involved the recapitulation of a primary dissonance, its internal lexical networks effectively drain it of its salience by situating the aversive memory among a myriad of *future potentialities*. The rehearsals have an adaptive function to help interpret and integrate dissonant information and respond accordingly, that is, in an appropriate shame aversive manner. Consequently, hexagrams are not simply the reportable results of a cognitive and mantic process; they also catalyzed

---

336 Raphals (2017).
337 Papalexandrou (2005, 62) cited in Eidinow (2018).
338 Connors and Halligan (2015, 2).
339 Ibid. (3).
340 Ibid.
341 Ibid.
342 Ibid. (10).

expectations that reached beyond the available sensory information to accommodate a transforming social environment.

This dialectic between past and future resonates with the rhetorical shift from a past toward a future oriented gaze that we saw manifested in Ritual Reform rhetoric. The temporal polarity may be construed as an axis that implicitly organizes the text; it is a strategy that aligns with those endemic to Ritual Reform regulations in its projection of a new cosmos to accommodate an event that shattered a previous one. The new cosmos is one that can be fixed, rehearsed, planned for, projected, the antithesis of the old one where deviance proved fatal. When the *Book of Changes* is rehistoricized alongside the King Zhao catastrophe, we can see how its phenomenology was a product of it. Even as the plurality of potentialities it offers camouflaged the event that caused the dissonance, we can sense the latter's informing silent presence.

This presence is intimated in the results of sortilege divination found inscribed on two Western Zhou "pestle-shaped pottery tools used in the making of pottery vessels."[343] Given the cardinal oriented spatial semiotics that permeates Ritual Reform discourse, it is significant that the spatial representation of the results met by a Western Zhou mantic user is manipulated. Whereas on one paddle stem the numbers (before having been translated into broken or solid lines) are "lined up vertically next to each other, and in the other case four [sets of] symbols [are] arranged in a sort of ring, with two oriented vertically and two horizontally."[344] When converted into hexagram form, the two parallel vertical number sequence emerges as Jiji "Already Across" (#63) and Weiji "Not Yet Across" (#64). As for the set of four number sequences, the two vertical lines convert to hexagrams Bi "Alliance" (#8) and Lü "Stepping" (#10); the two horizontal sets convert to hexagrams Shi "Army" (#7) and Xiao chu "Lesser Livestock" (#9).

These archaeological discoveries have been cited as evidence that the sequence of hexagrams preserved in the transmitted text was extant "no later than the late Western Zhou."[345] I am skeptical, like Shaughnessy, as to whether the entire text as we know it was in existence during the Western Zhou.[346] The evidence does support the idea that sortilege mantic practice was used by the royal court; it is more likely that stories about those results and the contexts surrounding them, became the core for a system of assessing action. Eastern Zhou texts reflect the currency of stories related to the interpretation of results met by Western Zhou kings' mantic efforts.[347]

343 Ibid. (15).
344 Ibid.
345 Ibid. (18).
346 Shaughnessy (2014, 18).
347 Song (2018) provides a review of the scholarship on Eastern Zhou records that cite accounts of the results of Western Zhou ruler milfoil divination.

Neuroscientific findings reveal that the same neural mechanisms stimulated in a mantic consulter's brain when attempting to resolve an oracular message, are also stimulated in cases when stories about oracular statements *ex post facto* are circulated and heard.[348] This insight helps contextualize the performance conditions that may have led to the composition of the *Book of Changes*. This chapter's discussion of *xiaoyou* membership in an expanded conceptualization of Zhou family suggests they may have been part of a broader constituency of auditors in whose minds these neural processes would have been triggered.

Reconfiguring oracles triggered by royal determinations yielded information about what the Zhou family imagined as correctly aligned behavior. A formulaic prayer attributed to the "first kings of the Zhou dynasty" that appears on a turtle plastron divination made clear they had in mind a "measuring stick" or collective standard by which behavior was assessed: "would that it [the suggested sacrificial rites and victims] be correct[ly aligned, e.g., with true north] (*youzheng*)."[349]

If we cede validity to this hypothesis, it yields a new perspective from which to interpret the combination of hexagrams found inscribed on the pestle-shaped paddles, as well as their unique, if enigmatic spatial arrangement. First, the clustering reveals how classing phenomena and placing them in some sort of spatial relation with one another was already a means to respond to the fears that weighted Zhou rulers and motivated them to engage in mantic interventions. Moreover, early Chinese celestial/spatial literacy suggests a link between the paddle shapes and the sets of numbers as well as their spatial arrangement.

There is no evidence to suggest these numerical symbols were linked to the nomenclature found in the transmitted versions. Nonetheless, reading the hexagram names, hexagram statements and line statements in tandem does support the idea that there was a conventional interpretation of the contexts encompassed by the numerical sequences. In this light, the resonance between the names "Already Across" and "Not Yet Across" inscribed vertically on the paddle, and the salience of a trope involving fording rivers in the *Book of Changes,* adumbrate a cluster of associations that we have seen central to the symbolic language of the Ritual Reform.

These associations include 1) King Zhao's failed crossing of the Han River; and 2) transit of Sky River as a symbol for post-mortem and regenerative seasonal transformation. The vertical stem of the pestle-shaped object evokes the Zhou preoccupation with an axial-based astro-calendrical system, suggesting that the pair of numerical lines inscribed on it may be related as well. The paddle stem also recalls the name "Revolving" used in the "Nine Fields" system to refer to the "Central" location delimited by the asterism Horns. Indeed, two asterisms called Mortar (*jiu*) and Pestle (*chu*), located in the northern quadrant proximate to

348 Eidinow (2018, 449 et passim).

349 Ibid. This divination record was recovered near a Zhou temple at Fengchu, Qishan, Shaanxi, in 1977.

Square, the constellation that served as a standard for aligning new constructions with true north, gives concrete context for these associations.

I have found no other evidence to attribute Zhou agency to the invention of those asterisms, but more to the point, Pestle (π Peg), situated in Pegasus' left hoof, aligns with Mortar (μ Peg), located southeast in the winged horse's chest. Its proximity to Square, and its visibility just after the winter solstice was believed, according to first millennia texts, to signal the time to prepare tools necessary for spring's imminent arrival.[350] How or whether these asterisms may have figured more significantly in Western axial measurement practices will need to await resolution.

The literal and metaphorical centrality of Sky River in the astro-calendrical Ritual Reform, along with its association with the winter solstice, are both evoked in the language of the second hexagram in the transmitted sequence called Kun, translated by Shughnessy as "Compliant."[351] Shaughnessy's translation reflects the sensibility that the hexagram's name and meaning are bipolar complements to the name and form of the first and preceding hexagram, Qian "Vigor."[352] Because the last two line statements mention a dragon battle, and since the image of a dragon figures significantly in "Vigor," where it refers to Dragon soaring in the spring and long summer night skies, other astro-calendrical information included in the lines have not been pursued.

David Pankenier has uncovered how references to Dragon in the Kun hexagram in fact reveal sophisticated astro-calendrical knowledge about Tail, Heart, and Chamber's unique movements during the winter months, especially around the "regulated" or "first" (*zheng*) month of the year. These movements are less celebrated than the ancient knowledge of Dragon's vernal career. Pankenier shows that six weeks after the winter solstice, when Well's midnight transit of the meridian with Sky River marked a "successful fording," Dragon would appear vertically within Sky River as it rapidly transited the winter sky. The resonance between the verticality of the celestial objects and their aqueous surroundings is enhanced when read with line statements that gloss the meaning of Kun.

For example, the hexagram statement makes clear that a positive response to an initial mantic endeavor had been received. It also sums up the context of a scenario deemed relevant to the assessment of the currently divined issue: "… The nobleman has some place to go, is first lost and then gains his ruler. Beneficial to the west-south to gain a friend, to the east-north to lose a friend. Determining about being settled. Auspicious." Putting aside how to interpret the subordinate directions, we can extract an overall sense of interest in establishing a newly found settlement or means to settle that involve cardinal directions. Following this, the first line statement places the consulter within

350 Schlegel (1895, 271–273).
351 Shaughnessy (2014, xviii, 5, 160).
352 Ibid. (47, 160, 209).

the seasonal confines of autumn, even as it looks ahead in anticipation of the arrival of "hard ice," a symbol of the solstice. This context also matches conventional agrarian habits which used the autumn and winter months to engage in construction of the build environment, represented by the zodiacal imagery related to building.

The third line statement moves us to the solstice, and what could be seen as a description of Well as it appeared vertically alongside Sky River before their meridian transit at midnight: "[s]traight, square and great. [Even] without repetitions, the [measurement technique is such that] "[t]here is nothing not beneficial." The next line refers to something "[c]ontaining a pattern. One can determine [i.e., divine]. And now following the king's service. There is no completion, but the end" (*zhong*)." The word translated as "end" is one of several homophonic words related to "year's end" (*zhong*), including "winter" (*dong*), and "bell" (*zhong*). Bell music was used in regenerative rituals; their resounding euphony were acoustic counterparts of winter solstice sacrifices.[353] In this context, reference to Dragon is one of several vital pieces of information about the winter solstice that are offered for the mantic consulter's rehearsal.

The implications of this interpretation are historical. It suggests that the earliest strata could not antedate King Mu's reign. This then raises the possibility that the cluster of four hexagrams found on the other pestle-shaped pottery paddle also relate to topical events of significant import to the Zhou at that time. The hexagram nomenclature associated with the sequenced numerical lines on the second piece relate to contexts of crucial concern to the Zhou's post-King Zhao survival. *Martial* decisions; determinations about making new *alliances* in the wake of the loss of the majority of the troops; sacrificial resources for rain prayers (lesser livestock); and the progressive *steps* or stages necessary to regain status.

References to trust (*fu*) occur in hexagram lines belonging to three of the four hexagrams arived at after conversion of the number sets. In addition, two references to a "corpse conveyor" (*yushi*), mentioned in the discussion of the Impersonator above, appears in "Armies." A possible source for that scenario is hinted at in the hexagram Da Guo "Greater Surpassing" (#56), where the river fording trope appears. The last line statement of this hexagram invokes an image: "Crossing the ford and cutting off the crown [*ding*] of the head. Ominous. There is no trouble."[354]

Traditions about King Mu divining and meeting with hexagrams "Army" and "Stepping" point to a collective memory about Western Zhou oracular use.[355] Internal textual evidence is more nebulous, but two line statements refer to the timeliness of performing the grand *yue* funerary rite that King Mu performed for his father. Again, if we read the hexagram statements as a rhetorical structure whose

353 Porter (1996, 103, 84, 120); Brindley (2012).
354 Ibid. (250).
355 Ibid.

semantic and grammatical relationship with the rest of the hexagram lines resembles that seen between the opening strophes and the rest of "Thorny Caltrop," then we can see how it too establishes an epistemological boundary for the related line statements that follow. This context imbues the nomenclature of the two hexagrams with a historically evocative sensibility: one, Cui, "Gathering," recalls the geopolitical conditions preceding King Xiao's ascension and the planetary massing ("gathering") that cemented his authority; the other, Sheng "Ascending" (#46), evokes the regular offerings of foodstuffs to royal Zhou thanksgiving sacrifices.

In "Gathering," the hexagram statement functions like a cinematographic establishing shot: "Receipt. The king enters the temple. Beneficial to see the great man. Receipt. Beneficial to determine. Using the great ox sacrifice: auspicious. Beneficial to have someplace to go." Then the first and second lines continue: "There is trust, unending, then disordered, and then gathered. A scream once grasped becomes laughter. Do not worry. Going: there is no trouble… Prolonged auspiciousness. There is no trouble. Trusting then it is beneficial to therewith make a [*yue*] sacrifice." [356]

The penultimate hexagram in the transmitted system, "Already Crossed," which was inscribed on the other pestle-paddle pottery, also invokes the *yue* summer sacrifice. In this context it is used to distinguish the Zhou, identified as the "[polity located in the] Western regions, for their efficacious implementation of rites that yield bounteous fortune (*fu*). These lexical cross-currents reveal an internal structure of coherence whose historicity travels across the silence of the Ritual Reform. The sense of meaning conferred by the structure tells us something about the socioemotional conditions catalyzed by the King Zhao crisis. The preliminary reading offered here is not intended as a panacea for interpretive obstacles posed by this living ancient text. Instead, it offers a lens to refract the neuropsychological underpinnings of a mental structure whose transmission was determining factor in the evolution of the Confucian conception of filial piety.

To conclude, this section has shown how a collective existential memory of a profound social transformation was preserved in the *Book of Changes*. The mantic text contains fragments of a collective transformation catalyzed by the royal family's response to an emotional crisis of cognitive dissonance. Fragments that point to the Zhou's astro-calendrical system preserve, like amber, traces of complicated grief that propelled the oracle's emergence as a cultural strategy to accommodate and manage it. While reminiscent of Neolithic preoccupations with Polar alignment, the particular and idiosyncratic inflections of the Zhou personality, those men of the "scarlet kneepads," is also viscerally on display.[357] Serendipitously perhaps, the hexagram and line statements that comprise the

356 Shaughnessy (2014, 166).
357 Hexagram #47, Kun "Bound."

forty-eighth hexagram of the *Book of Changes*, Jing "Well," provide an eloquent summation of the persona that emerges.

Hexagram #48 "Well"

Through the prism of the Zhou royal saga, the organization of the hexagram and line statements project a range of negative to positive scenarios related to the topic of wells. This is achieved by the polysemy of the grapheme pronounced *jing*. We saw in Chapter 1 how emotions interacted with lexical, semantic, and syntactic processing.[358] The affective system, understood in terms of positive or negative valence, as well as the fact of arousal, are involved in cognitive comprehension. Whereas valence is a function of judging the "polarity of the emotional activation, going from unpleasant… to pleasant," arousal relates to the "degree of excitement or activation which an individual feels towards a given stimulus," such as hearing or reading a word.[359]

The hexagram and line statements organized around the word "well" reveal it to have been affectively arousing. The arousal hinges on the negative valence of the danger implicit in its meaning as a "trap," or its positive valence as source of community sustenance.[360] Ancient dictionaries reveal that hunting traps were conceptualized as (concealed) pits, sometimes filled with dark water.[361] The two valences are modulated by the degree of concreteness in the hexagram statement that makes unambiguous how to "read" the grapheme. The dissonance generated by the polarity of its meaning devolves on the evaluation of the affective and semantic properties of the word.

Insights from the fields of cognitive linguistics and neurosciences are helpful for conceptualizing how the evaluation of affect for polysemic words "is achieved through weighted connections that are established/abstracted through these prior experiences…"[362] Neuroscience findings demonstrate how "recent context and working memory context" are not significant factors in unconscious semantic processing associated with polysemy.[363] The discovery that high-level unconscious processes are not automatic but are flexible and sensitive to "several top-down factors" recalls Abraham and Torok's understanding of the influence exerted by shame-aversive propensities on high-level unconscious response codes in semantic processing. Polysemy is implicated in the transmission of unsayable knowns.[364]

358 Vergallito et al. (2019).
359 Ibid.
360 Shaughnessy (2014, 60–66).
361 *Shuowen jiezi*.
362 Li and Joanisse (2021).
363 Rohaut et al. (2016, 10881107). Zhang et al. (2018) present findings based on ERP evidence that links meaning complexity to heightened emotional affect.
364 Ibid.

In Hexagram #48, the word "well" functions as a type of "language-based knowledge cluster" that operates to "modulate expectation patterns."[365] A cognitive linguists perspective defines a polysemic cluster as "a whole conceptual network of matrices and their cognitive domains, where the individual senses are inalienable from their schematic structures."[366] Put another way, polysemy operates as a mechanism that linguistically links qualitatively different senses of a word on the basis of background affective knowledge.[367] The affective senses imbued in the image schemas that motivated different uses of the polysemous word "well" derived from tacitly understood judgments formed in response to the same affective conditions.[368]

Cognitive dissonance generated by King Zhao's death may have been a driving factor generating knowledge clustering. The qualitative differences among the meanings denoted by the word *jing* arose from affective expectation patterns determined by the shifting of perspectives. The hexagram statement identifies the affective experience of loss and gain (*shi de*) as the stimulant conditions of expectations and knowledge:

> Hexagram statement: Changing the city, not changing the well. There is no loss, there is no gain. Going and coming in succession, *jingjing*-like ["well-well"] in manner. Upon arrival, also not yet dipping the well, breaking its pitcher. Ominous.
> First [line statement]: The well is muddy and is not drinkable. The old trap is without a catch.
> Second [line statement]: The well[/trap?] is deep, shooting the silverfish. The pitcher is battered and leaking.
> Third [line statement]: The well leaks and is not drinkable. It makes my heart pained. It can be used to draw from. The king is bright, together receiving this blessing.
> Fourth [line statement]: The well is bricked. There is no trouble.
> Fifth [line statement]: The well is frigid; the cold spring is drinkable.
> Sixth [line statement]: The well is received; do not cover it. There is trust. Prime auspiciousness.[369]

A narrative line that illuminates the emotional conditions motivating the polysemy of the word "well" may be discerned from the semantic structure of the

365 Gibbs and Matlock (2001, 69).
366 Lewandowska-Tomaszczyk (2007).
367 Vergallito et al. (2019) find "evidence for bodily responses during word comprehension." The observed that the concreteness of the word modulated its valence, and thus the way the valence influenced arousal activation: the "lower the word concreteness, the larger affective -variable impact." See also Hinojosa et al. (2020).
368 Gibbs and Matlock (2001, 225).
369 *Zhouyi*.

hexagram texts. First, the dominant semantic meaning of the word is established with the concrete image of a well, which is contextualized in terms of its spatiotemporal properties: constancy of location in relation to sociopolitical boundaries (city), and temporal in terms of its stability amidst change. The statement emphasizes the endurance of a well, and the way its properties yield "neat and tidy" behavior year in and year out.

Then, there is a shift in cadence. A cluster of images and line statements portray dysfunction that bespeaks blockage: be it because of turgid, undrinkable water, leaks, or traps that yielded no catches (gains), all point to the loss of essential sources for sustenance. On one level, this critique resonates with similar complaints expressed about dysfunction of stellar objects named for their function seen in the *Book of Poetry*. This would suggest an astro-calendrical subtext to the hexagram line statements, which would have us read the dysfunctions as signs of astro-calendrical mismanagement.

Although this entire chapter has been about the centrality of Well for King Mu and son's transcendence over King Zhao's ignominious loss, this astro-calendrical level of meaning is only hinted at in the culminating line statement's determination records. While difficult to interpret, the embodied knowledge associated with this sense of "well" is extended to a different sense or role value.[370] The concluding image of the hexagram schema seems aimed to transform negative emotional valence driving expectations concerning the word "well" into positive ones.

As for the scenes of dysfunctional wells, I suggest that the sense of "damage" represented in the negative valence of the images of loss and absence, represents the collective embodied experience of King Zhao's death. Consider the emotional position represented in the third line statement, which expresses the pain (*ce*) resulting from the "indigestible" nature of the well's water. I contend that what couldn't be digested was the dissonance between "objective empathy" and "concealed internal distress" (*pangguan tongqing, anzi beishang*) experienced by the aristocratic elite in the face of the Zhou's shame.

The next image, which refers to the "bright" king, shifts the valence from negative to positive. Because we now are aware of the astro-calendrical intentions driving the Western Zhou locution "bright model (well)," we are in a position to appreciate why this word would have triggered a mental shift from a state marked by grief and dissonance-induced anxiety to one marked by conceptual and emotional clarity. This perceived "brightness" is represented as a catalyst for the blessings bestowed upon the king and is intimated in the concluding image of the schemata driving the sense of the word "well": The well is received; do not cover it. There is trust. Prime auspiciousness.

370 Cf. Kleinman and Kleinman (1994), vanguards in scholarship on embodied pain theorize and analyze the scars caused by Communist policies.

Once (a new) order was (re-)established, the dissonance cleared, the water (that King Zhao-shame-contaminated word-idea-concept) could be ingested, that is, psychically accomodated. No need to cover it, repress it, BLOCK it. The conduit for shared communion with empty mouths had been established so that it engendered trust among all who partook (in the discourse). Prime Auspiciousness indeed.

This analysis treats the hexagram "Well" as a neuropsychological artifact. Its internal dynamics reflect on the emotional events and responsive behaviors that shaped the evolution of a Western Zhou mental structure. Polysemy, a cluster of knowledge generated by dissonance-inducing conditions, functioned in the divination text as an interface, mediating between symbolic processes and intrapsychic trauma. The line statements attached to "Well" bear traces of an existential pain while offering up the mantic experience as the means to mediate it.

The positive valence communicated by the reduplicative expression *jingjing* to refer to the organization of the "comings and goings" (e.g., seasonal determinants) in a "neat and tidy" manner convoke a behavioral propensity that aligns with interdependent mind structures. Pareidolia Well emerged in response to necessity to neaten and tidy the emotional messiness of watery operations; the hexagram "Well" evolved in response to the cognitive dissonance generated by the shameful demise of a beloved relational object.

The archaeological record makes clear that widespread adoption of the Ritual Reforms altered the warp of Western Zhou social and cultural life. From royal ancestral temple to rural agrarian regions, populations adopted practices undergirded by ideologies such as "lineage potency" and "modeled behavior." Because the rituals regulated social life to perpetuate the internal cohesiveness of Zhou supremacy, their frequent iteration conditioned participants to experience political legitimacy as a function of natural order. It also layed the foundation for later conceptualizations of ritual as central to the proper function of state and society.

Yuri Pines' historicization of the evolution of the word *li*, which eventually came to denote "a set of rites, ceremonies and sumptuary rules inherited from the early Zhou" reveals an evolutionary trajectory that resembles the path taken by the word *xiao*.[371] Both semantic trajectories began with limited scopes related to specific rite practice, and ended as ethical concepts related to an expanded conception of these practices. The following chapter traces the evolved, Confucian, ethical concept of filiality, *xiao,* as a function of the consequences for collective *xiaoyou* self-construal resulting from the Zhou royal family's demise.

371 Pines (2000, 3).

The existential memory preserved in the *Book of Changes* prepares us to understand the *xiaoyou* response to the royal Zhou court's forced migration eastward. As we shall see, the event, contaminated by the Zhou's shame, threatened valorized group-identity but also posed severe challenges for a lineage's social survival. This conflict created conditions that complicated mourning the loss of what had been an idealized *xiaoyou* collective identity. The conditions help explain the emergence of Confucian ideations of filiality, and especially his implicit valorization of behavior manifesting complicated grief. Similar to the turtle-based cosmology and the Ritual Reform, Confucius' paradigmatic filial son will be shown to be a symbolic, ideational projection deriving from a devastating collective loss about which emotional awareness could not exist within social discursive norms.

Cited Sources

Abraham, N., & Torok, M. (1994). *The shell and the kernel: Renewals of psychoanalysis* (Vol. 1). University of Chicago Press.

Abraham, N. . & Torok, M. (2005). *The Wolf Man's magic word: A cryptonymy* (Vol. 37). U of Minnesota Press.

Allan, S. (1997). *The way of water and sprouts of virtue*. Suny Press.

Anderson, B. (2006). *Imagined communities: Reflections on the origin and spread of nationalism*. Verso Books.

Boltz, W. G. (1994). *The origin and early development of the Chinese writing system* (Vol. 78). American Oriental Society.

Boodberg, P. A. (1937). Some proleptical remarks on the evolution of archaic Chinese. *Harvard Journal of Asiatic Studies*, *2*(3/4), 329–372.

Brindley, E. (2010). *Individualism in early China: Human agency and the self in thought and politics*. University of Hawaii Press.

Brindley, E. (2012). *Music, cosmology, and the politics of harmony in early China*. SUNY press.

Broda, J. (1982). Astronomy, cosmovisión, and ideology in pre-Hispanic Mesoamerica. *Annals of the New York Academy of Sciences*, *385*(1), 81–110.

Bu, L. Y. (2004). Du "Shijing" suojian Xi-Zhou tudi zhidu. *Shijing yanjiu congkan*.

Cai, R. S. (1997). Jingtianzhi. In M. Kui, & Z. Yanjin (Eds.), *Zhonghua guocui da cidian* (p. 93). Guoji wenhua.

Chen, J. J. (1982). Lun "Xia xiao zheng" shi shiyue taiyangli. *Zirankexue yanjiu*, *4*, 305–319.

Chen, Y. F. (2012). Qinghuajian zhaigong yu Xi-Zhou Zhai shi. *Jiang Han kaogu*, *1*, 122.

Chen, S. (2012–13). Collected interpretations of the X Gong Xu. *Early China*, *35*, 135–155.

Childs-Johnson, E. (1995). The ghost head mask and metamorphic Shang imagery. *Early China*, 79–92. doi: 10.1017/S0362502800004442

Ching, J. (1997). *Mysticism and kingship in China the heart of Chinese wisdom*. Cambridge University Press.

Connors, M. H., & Halligan, P. W. (2015). A cognitive account of belief: A tentative road map. *Frontiers in Psychology*, *5*, 1588.

Cook, C. A. (1990). *Auspicious metals and Southern spirits: an analysis of the Chu bronze inscriptions* (Ph.D Dissertation, University of California, Berkeley).

Cook, C. A. (2005). Moonshine and millet: Feasting and purification rituals in ancient China. In R. Sterckx (Ed.), *Of tripod and palate: Food, politics, and religion in traditional China* (pp. 9–33). New York: Palgrave Macmillan,

Cook, C. A. (2012–13). Sage King Yu and the Bin Gong Xu. *Early China, 35*, 69–103.

Cook, C. A. (2020). *Ancestors, kings, and the Dao*. Brill.

Cooper, J. (2019). Cognitive dissonance: Where we've been and where we're going. *International Review of Social Psychology, 32*(1).

Cooper, J. , & Hogg, M. A. (2007). Feeling the anguish of others: A theory of vicarious dissonance. *Advances in Experimental Social Psychology, 39*, 359–403.

Cullen, C. (1993). Motivations for scientific change in ancient China: Emperor Wu and the Grand Inception astronomical reforms of 104 BC. *Journal for the History of Astronomy, 24*(3), 185–203.

Cullen, C. (2007). *Astronomy and Mathematics in Ancient China: The "Zhou Bi Suan Jing"* (Vol. 1). Cambridge University Press.

Chunqiu gongyangzhuan. Shisanjing edition. Chinese Text Project.

Dai, W. Q. (1991). Xing again: A formal re-investigation. *Chinese Literature: Essays, Articles, Reviews (CLEAR), 13*, 1–14.

Di Cosmo, N., & Wyatt, D. J. (Eds.). (2005). *Political frontiers, ethnic boundaries and human geographies in Chinese history*. Routledge.

Donald, M. (1991). *Origins of the modern mind: Three stages in the evolution of culture and cognition*. Harvard University Press.

Dorofeeva-Lichtmann, V. V. (1995). Conception of terrestrial organization in the Shan hai jing. *Bulletin de l'École française d'Extrême-Orient, 82*, 57–110.

Dorofeeva-Lichtmann, V. V. (2005). Mapping a "spiritual landscape." In N. Di Cosmo and D. J. Wyatt (Eds.), *Political frontiers, ethnic boundaries and human geographies in Chinese history*. Routledge.

Dorofeeva-Lichtmann, V. V. (2009). Ritual practices for constructing terrestrial. In J. Lagerwey and M. Kalinowski (Eds.),*Early Chinese religion, Part one: Shang through Han (1250 BC–220 AD)* (2 vols., pp. 595–644). Brill.

Dorofeeva-Lichtmann, V. V. (2010). The Rong Cheng shi (容成氏) Version of the "Nine Provinces": Some parallels with transmitted texts. *East Asian Science, Technology, and Medicine, 32*, 13–58.

Driediger-Murphy L. G., & Eidinow, E. (2019). Introduction. In L. G. Driediger-Murphy & E. Eidinow (Eds.), *Ancient divination and experience*. Oxford University Press.

Du, Y. (2018). Cong Jingshi caiyi can XiZhou shiqing zhidu de zunxian gongneng. *Gudai wenming, 4*(43), 43–55.

Eidinow, E. (2018). A feeling for the future: Ancient Greek divination and embodied cognition. In A. K. Petersen , G.I. Sælid, , L. H. Martin , J. S. Jensen , and J. Sørensen (Eds.), *Evolution, cognition, and the history of religion: A new synthesis* (pp. 447–460). Brill.

Eno, R. (2009). Shang state religion and the pantheon of the oracle texts. In J. Lagerwey and M. Kalinowski (Eds.), *Early Chinese religion, Part one: Shang through Han (1250 BC–220 AD)* (2 vols., pp. 39–102). Brill.

Feng, L. (2006). *Landscape and power in early China: The crisis and fall of the Western Zhou 1045–771 BC*. Cambridge University Press.

Feng, S. (2013). Wo Fang-*ding* mingwen yu Xi-Zhou sangdian li. *Kaogu xuebao, 2*, 185–212.

Feng, S. (2017). Wu Xu kao. *Zhongyuan wenhua yanjiu, 3*, 15–19.

Feng, S. (2019). Xi-Zhou Pang Jing yu Yin Zhou (xiang wan) ji—Yin Zhou yuanyu yu ji Zao chuan tong. *Zhongyuan wenhua*, 7(6), 5–15.

Feng, S. (2020a). Da He yu Hou Ji. *Jiang Han kaogu. 2*(167), 87–90.

Feng, S. (2020b). Ba Bo zhiyan yu Xi-Zhou jingtian. *Zhongyuan wen wu, 1*, 63–70.

Gao, F. (2013). *Qinghua jian "Zhao gong" pian yanjiu* (Masters thesis, *Tianjin shifan daxue*).

Gassmann, R. H. (2009). Two types of ancestors: A note on Xiao^ in *Eastern Zhou Times. Asiatische Forschungen, 153*, 93.

Gibbs, R. W., & Matlock, T. (2001). Psycholinguistic perspectives on polysemy. *Amsterdam Studies in the Theory and History of Linguistic Science Series, 4*, 213–240.

Goldin, P. R. (2008). When Zhong 忠 does not mean "Loyalty." *Dao*, 7(2), 165–174.

Goldin, P. R. (2017). Some Shang antecedents of later Chinese ideology and culture. *Journal of American Oriental Society, 1*(137), 121–127.

Grundmann, J. P. (2019). Command and commitment: terms of kingship in Western Zhou bronze inscriptions and in the Book of Documents. (Doctoral dissertation, University of Edinburgh).

Guoyu. Sibucongkan chubian edition. Vols. 251-254. Chinese Text Project.

Han, J. (2020). Ba Bo zhiyan yu Xi-Zhou jingtian—yi Huang Xianfan 'Jingtian zhi' yanjiu wei li. *Xin Jingji, 9*, 40–44.

Hansen, C. (1996). Duty and virtue. In Patrick Suppes (Ed.), *Chinese language, thought, and culture: Nivison and his critics* (pp. 173–192). Open Court Publishing.

He, H., Lawson, J., Bell, M., & Hui, F. (2020). Millet, wheat, and society in North China over the very long term. *Environment and History*. doi: 10.3197/096734019X15463432086937

Hinojosa, J. A., Moreno, E. M., & Ferré, P. (2020). Affective neurolinguistics: Towards a framework for reconciling language and emotion. *Language, Cognition and Neuroscience, 35*(7), 813–839.

Hsu, C. Y., Xu, Z., & Hsu, C. Y. (1980). *Han agriculture: The formation of Early Chinese Agrarian economy, 206 BC–AD 220* (Vol. 2). University of Washington Press.

Jin, F. T. (2019). "Mou zhi sun, mou zhi zi": Tan Zhoudai qingtonqi mingwen zhon yizhong teshu de chengwei fangshi. *Guoxue xuekan, 3*, 31–39.

Jiang, X. (2021). The astronomy in ancient China: An overview. *The Origins of Sciences in China: History of Science and Technology in China, 1*, 1–37.

Johnston, S. I., & Struck, P. T. (Eds.). (2005). *Mantikê: studies in ancient divination*. Brill.

Ji Zhong Zhoushu, Sibucongkan chubian edition. Vol. 250. Chinese Text Project.

Jizhong Zhoushu. Sibu congkan edition. Chinese Text Project.

Keightley, D. N. (2004). The making of the ancestors: Late Shang religion and its legacy. *Religion and Chinese Society: Ancient and Medieval China, 1*, 3–63.

Kern, M. (2000). "Shi Jing" songs as performance texts: A case study of "Chu Ci" (Thorny Caltrop). *Early China*, 49–111.

Kern, M. (2001). Ritual, text, and the formation of the Canon: Historical transitions of wen in Early China. *T'oung Pao, 87*(1), 43–91.

Kern, M. (2005). The Odes in excavated manuscripts. In M. Kern (Ed.), *Text and ritual in Early China* (pp. 149–193). University of Washington Press.

Kern, M. (Ed.) (2005). *Text and ritual in early China*. University of Washington Press.

Kern, M. (2009). Bronze inscriptions, the Shijing and the Shangshu: the evolution of the ancestral sacrifice during the western Zhou. In J. Lagerwey & M. Kalinowski (Eds.), *Early Chinese religion, Part one: Shang through Han (1250 BC–220 AD)* (2 vols., pp. 143–200). Brill.

Khayutina, M. (2009). The royal year-count of the Western Zhou Dynasty (1045–771 BC) and its use (r) s: A sociological perspective. In Wang-Riese Xiaobing and Thomas O. Höllmann (Eds.), *Time and ritual in early China* (Vol. 153, pp. 125–151). Harrassowitz

Khayutina, M. (2010). Royal hospitality and geopolitical constitution of the Western Zhou polity. *T'oung Pao, 96*(1), 1–73.

Kleinman, A., & Kleinman, J. (1994). How bodies remember: Social memory and bodily experience of criticism, resistance, and delegitimation following China's cultural revolution. *New Literary History, 25*(3), 707–723.

Knapp, K. N. (1995). The ru reinterpretation of xiao. *Early China*, 195–222. doi: 10.1017/S036250280000448X

Knapp, K. N. (2005). *Selfless offspring*. University of Hawaii Press.

Kryukov, V. (1995). Symbols of power and communication in pre-Confucian China (On the Anthropology of "de"): Preliminary assumptions. *Bulletin of the School of Oriental and African Studies, 58*, 314–333.

Kutcher, N. (2006). *Mourning in late imperial China: Filial piety and the state*. Cambridge University Press.

Lagerwey, J., & Kalinowski, M. (Eds.). (2008). *Early Chinese religion, Part one: Shang through Han (1250 BC–220 AD)* (2 vols). Brill.

Lai, G. (2005). Death and the otherworldly journey in early China as seen through tomb texts, travel paraphernalia, and road rituals. *Asia Major, 18*, 1–44.

Lai, Whalen (2001). "Well-Field System." In O. Leaman (Ed.), *Encyclopedia of Asian Philosophy* (p. 564). Routledge.

Lan, H. Q. (2004). "Ban-gui" mingwen xinshi. *Zhengzhou daxue xuebao: zhexue shehui kexueban, 37*(6), 105–108.

Lee, J. J. Y., & Jeyaraj, S. (2014). Effects of self-construal differences on cognitive dissonance examined by priming the independent and interdependent self. *SAGE Open, 4*(1), doi:10.177.2158244014521434.

Lévi-Strauss, C. (1983). *The raw and the cooked: Mythologiques* (Vol. 1). University of Chicago Press.

Lewandowska-Tomaszczyk, B. (2007). *Polysemy, prototypes, and radial categories. The Oxford handbook of cognitive linguistics* (pp. 139–169).

Li, C. R. (2017). Sishi bafeng: feng yu Zhongshuo gudai minzhong de shijian sheng huo. *Zhongyuan wenhua yanjiu, 5*(2), 57–61.

Li, F. (2001). "Offices" in Bronze Inscriptions and Western Zhou government administration. *Early China,* 26, 1–72.

Li, F. (2004). Succession and promotion: Elite mobility during the western Zhou. *Monumenta serica, 52*(1), 1–35.

Li, F. (2006). *Landscape and power in early China: The crisis and fall of the Western Zhou 1045–771 BC*. Cambridge University Press.

Li, F. (2008). *Bureaucracy and the state in early China: governing the western Zhou*. Cambridge University Press.

Li, G. Z. (2010). "*Shijing*" qinshu chengweici yanjiu. *Cross-Cultural Communication, 4*(2), 1–21.

Li, J., & Joanisse, M. F. (2021). Word senses as clusters of meaning modulations: A computational model of polysemy. *Cognitive Science, 45*(4), e12955.

Li, L. H. (2012). *Qinghua jian "Jin teng,"* (Masters thesis, Hebei daxue).

Li, X. P. (1991). *Wangquan yu shenquan*. Liaoning jiaoyu.

Li, X. Q. (1998). Shi Guodianjian Zhai Gong zhi gumu. *Wen wu*, 7, 44–45.

Li, X. Y. (2020). Xi-Zhou qingtongqi niaoxing zhuangshi de "Li yue" shenmei fengge suzao. *Yishu yu sheji (lilun), 9*, 2–34.

Liang, S. M. (2003). "Bian Gong-*guan*" mingwen kaoshu. *Zhongguo lishi wenwu, 4*, 51–56.

Liu, J. M. (2019). Ernan caiji qingjie zhong de jisi fengsu. *Advances in Social Sciences Education and Humanities Research, 342*, 219–226.

Liu, L., & Chen, X. (2012). *The archaeology of China: from the late Paleolithic to the early Bronze Age*. Cambridge University Press.

Liu, M. Y. (2016). "*Zhai gong*"*yanjiu* (Masters thesis, Hebei shifan daxue).

Loewe, M., & Shaughnessy, E. L. (Eds.). (1999). *The Cambridge history of ancient China: From the origins of civilization to 221 BC*. Cambridge University Press.

McCurley, D. (2005). Performing patterns: Numinous relations in Shang and Zhou China. *TDR/The Drama Review, 49*(3), 135–156.

Mu Tianzi zhuan. Sibu congkan edition. Chinese Text Project.

Nivison, D. S. (1983). The dates of Western Chou. *Harvard Journal of Asiatic Studies, 43*(2), 481–580.

Northoff, G. (2018). *The spontaneous brain: From the mind-body to the world-brain problem*. MIT Press.

Owen, S. (2000). Interpreting Shengmin. In P. Yu , P. Bol, S. Owen, and W. Peterson (Eds.), *Ways with words: Writing about reading texts from early China* (Vol. 24, pp. 25–30). Univ of California Press.

Pankenier, D. W. (1981–82). Astronomical Dates in Shang and Western Zhou. *Early China*, 7, 2–37.

Pankenier, D. W. (1995). The cosmo-political background of heaven's mandate. *Early China, 20*, 121–176.

Pankenier, D. W. (1999). Applied field-allocation astrology in Zhou China: Duke Wen of Jin and the battle of Chengpu (632 BC). *Journal of the American Oriental Society, 119*, 261–279.

Pankenier, D. W. (2001). Getting "Right" with heaven and the origins of writing in China. In Li Feng and David Prager Branner (Eds.), *Writing and literacy in Early China: Studies from the Columbia Early China seminar* (pp. 19–50). University of Washington Press.

Pankenier, D. W. (2005). Characteristics of field allocation (fenye) astrology in Early China. *Current Studies in Archaeoastronomy: Conversations Across Space and Time* (pp. 499–513). Carolina Academic Press.

Pankenier, D. W. (2011). Getting "Right" with heaven and the origins of writing in China. In *Writing and literacy in early China: Studies from the Columbia early China seminar* (pp. 19–50). University of Washington Press.

Pankenier, D. W. (2013). *Astrology and cosmology in early China: conforming earth to heaven*. Cambridge University Press.

Pankenier, D. W. (2015). Weaving metaphors and cosmo-political thought in early China. *T'oung Pao, 101*(1-4), 1–34.

Pankenier, D. W. (2020). A mythology of sibling rivalry and culture contrast

Pines, Y. (2000). Disputers of the "Li": Breakthroughs in the concept of ritual in pre-imperial China. *Asia Major, 3*, 1–41.

Pines, Y. (2005). Beasts or humans: Pre-imperial origins of the 'Sino-barbarian' dichotomy. In Reuven Amitai and Michal Biran (Eds.), *Mongols, Turks, and others: Eurasian nomads and the sedentary world* (pp. 59–102). Brill.

Pines, Y. (2009). Chinese history writing between the sacred and the secular. In *Early Chinese religion, part one: Shang through Han (1250 BC-220 AD)* (2 vols) (pp. 315–340). Brill.

Pankenier, D. W. (2005). Beasts or humans: Pre-imperial origins of the 'Sino-Barbarian'dichotomy. *Mongols, Turks, and others: Eurasian nomads and the sedentary world, 11*, 70.

Pankenier, D. W. (2009). Chinese History writing between the sacred and the secular. In J. Lagerwey and M. Kalinowski (Eds.),*Early Chinese religion, Part one: Shang through Han (1250 BC–220 AD)* (2 vols., pp. 315–340). Brill.

Pines, Y., Shelach, G., von Falkenhausen, L., & Yates, R. D. (Eds.). (2013). *Birth of an Empire*. University of California Press.

Pines, Y., Shelach, G., von Falkenhausen, L., & Yates, R. D. (Eds.). (2014). *Birth of an Empire: The state of Qin revisited*. University of California Press.

Poo, M. C. (2004). The concept of ghost in ancient Chinese religion. *Religion and Chinese Society, 1*, 173–191.

Porter, D. L. (1996). *From deluge to discourse: myth, history, and the generation of Chinese fiction*. SUNY Press.

Porter, D. L. (2018). *Collective trauma and the psychology of secrets in transnational film*. Routledge.

Praveen, J. (2005). Does the crested lark Galerida deva occur in Kerala? *Indian Birds, 1*(6), 141–142.

Puett, M. (1997). Nature and artifice: Debates in late warring states China concerning the creation of culture. *Harvard Journal of Asiatic Studies, 57*(2), 471–518.

Puett, M. (2002a). *The ambivalence of creation: Debates concerning innovation and artifice in early China*. Stanford University Press.

Puett, M. (2002b). *To become a god: Cosmology, sacrifice, and self-divinization in early China* (No. 57). Harvard Univ Asia Center.

Puett, M. (2005). The offering of food and the creation of order: The practice of sacrifice in early China. In R. Sterckx (Ed.), *Of tripod and palate: Food, politics, and religion in traditional China* (pp. 75–95). Palgrave Macmillan.

Puett, M. (2019). Life, domesticated and undomesticated: Ghosts, sacrifice, and the efficacy of ritual practice in early China. *HAU: Journal of Ethnographic Theory, 9*(2), 439–460.

Quan, G. Z. (1989). Liang-Zhou jinwen tongjiazi yanjiu. Xuesheng shuju.

Ramachandran, V. S. , & Hirstein, W. (1999). The science of art: A neurological theory of aesthetic experience. *Journal of consciousness Studies, 6*(6–7), 15–51.

Raphals, L. (2017). *Old society, new belief: Religious transformation of China and Rome, ca. 1st-6th centuries*. Oxford University Press.

Raphals, L. (2019). Which gods if any: Gods, cosmologies, and their implications for Chinese and Greek divination. In *Ancient Divination and Experience* (pp. 253–276). Oxford University Press..

Rashkin, E. (1992). For a new psychoanalytic criticism: The works of Abraham and Torok.*Family Secrets and the Psychoanalysis of Narrative*, 13–48.

Rashkin, E. (1995). A recipe for mourning: Isak Dinesen's "Babette's Feast". *Style*, 356–374.

Rawson, J. (1989). Statesmen or barbarians? The Western Zhou as seen through their Bronzes. In *Proceedings of the British Academy, 75*, 71–95.

Rawson, J. (1999). Western Zhou archaeology. In E. L. Shaughnessy and M. Loewe (Eds.), *The Cambridge history of ancient China*, 352–449. Cambridge University Press.

Rohaut, B., Alario, F., Meadow, J., Cohen, L., & Naccache, L. (2016). Unconscious semantic processing of polysemous words is not automatic. *Neuroscience of Consciousness*, 2016(1). doi: 10.1093/nc/niw010

Rozin, P. (2007). Food and eating. In S. Kitayama & D. Cohen (Eds.), *Handbook of cultural psychology* (pp. 391–416). The Guilford Press.

Salim, A. , & Ripley, S.D. (1986).*Handbook of birds of India and Pakistan together with those of Bangladesh, Nepal, Bhutan and Ceylon* (Vol. 5). Delhi: Oxford University Press.

Schlegel, G. (1875). *Uranographie chinoise*. Librairie de M. Nijhoff.

Schlegel, G. (1895). *Uranographie chinoise* (2 vols.). Reprint 1875. Ch'eng.

Schuesslelr, A. (1987). *A dictionary of Early Zhou Chinese*. University of Hawaii Press.

Schuessler, A. (2006). *ABC etymological dictionary of Old Chinese*. University of Hawaii Press.

Shangshu. Sibu congkan edition. Chinese Text Project.

Shaughnessy, E. L. (1992). *Sources of Western Zhou history: inscribed bronze vessels*. Univ of California Press.

Shaughnessy, E. L. (1993). The duke of Zhou's retirement in the east and the beginnings of the Ministerial-Monarch debate in Chinese political philosophy. *Early China*, 18, 41–72.

Shaughnessy, E. L. (1995). From liturgy to literature: The ritual contexts of the earliest poems in the *Book of Poetry*. *Hanxue yanjiu*, 1(13), 133–164.

Shaughnessy, E. L. (1997). From liturgy to literature: The ritual contexts of the earliest poems in the Book of Poetry. *In idem. Before Confucius: Studies in the creation of the Chinese classics* (pp. 166–197). SUNY Press.

Shaughnessy, E. L. (1999). The Western Zhou. In M. Loewe and E.L. Shaughnessy (Eds.), *The Cambridge history of ancient China: From the origins of civilization to 221 BC*. Cambridge University Press.

Shaughnessy, E. L. (2011). History and inscriptions, China. In A. Feldherr and G. Hardy (Eds.), *The Oxford history of historical writing: Volume 1: Beginnings to AD 600*. Oxford University Press.

Shaughnessy, E. L. (2014). *Unearthing the changes: Recently discovered manuscripts of the Yi Jing (I Ching) and related texts*. Columbia University Press.

Shaughnessy, E. L. (2015). Unearthed documents and the question of the oral versus written nature of the "Classic of Poetry." *Harvard Journal of Asiatic Studies*, 331–375.

Shaughnessy, E. L. (2017). *Imprint of kinship: Studies of recently discovered bronze inscriptions from ancient China*. The Chinese University of Hong Kong Press.

Shiji jijie. Ed. Pei Yin. Chinese Text Project.

Shijing. Sibu congkan chubian edition (Vols. 5–8). Chinese Text Project.

Shuowen jiezi. Sibu congkan chubian edition (Vols. 66–69). Chinese Text Project.

Song, Y. W. (2018). *Divination and deviation: The problem of prediction and personal freedom in early China* (Ph.D. Dissertation, University of Pennsylvania).

Sterckx, R. (Ed.). (2005). *Of tripod and palate: food, politics, and religion in traditional China*. Springer.

Sterckx, R. (2018). Food and agriculture. In *Routledge handbook of early Chinese history* (pp. 300–318). Routledge.
Sun, Y. (2021. Bronze vessels: Style, assemblages, innovations of the Western Zhou Period. *The Oxford Handbook of Early China, 451.*
Tang, M. T. (2017). *Ban-gui mingwen jishi* (M.A. thesis, Huadong shifan daxue).
Tharsen, J. (2003). *Rhyme, meter and cadence in early Western Zhou Bronze Inscriptions.*
Valmisa, M. (2013). Formulaicity in Western Zhou bronze inscriptions. https://www.academia.edu/11486919/Formulaicity_in_Western_Zhou_Bronze_Inscriptions?auto=download&email_work_card=download-paper
Vandermeersch (1980). *Wangdao ou La voie royale: Recherches sur l''esprit des Institutions de la Chine archaïque. Tome II: Structures politiques, les rites* (2 Vols). École Française d'Extrême-Orient.
van Beek, W. E. , & Peek, P. M. (Eds.). (2013). *Reviewing reality: dynamics of African divination* (Vol. 50). LIT Verlag Münster.
Vergallito, A., Petilli, M. A., Cattaneo, L., & Marelli, M. (2019). Somatic and visceral effects of word valence, arousal and concreteness in a continuum lexical space. *Scientific Reports, 9*(1), 1–10.
Vogelsang, K. (2017). 2 Competing Voices in the Shangshu. In *Origins of Chinese Political Philosophy* (pp. 62–105). Brill.
Vogt, P. N. (2012). *Between kin and king: Social aspects of Western Zhou ritual* (Doctoral dissertation, Columbia University).
Vogt, P. N. (2020). Western Zhou government and society. In E. Childs-Johnson (Ed.), *The Oxford handbook of early China.* Oxford University Press.
Von Falkenhausen, L. (1993). Issues in Western Zhou studies: A review article. *Early China, 18*, 139–226.
Von Falkenhausen, L. (1995). Reflections on the political rôle of spirit mediums in early China: The wu officials in the Zhou li. *Early China, 20*, 279–300.
Von Falkenhausen, L. (1996). The concept of Wen in the Ancient Chinese ancestral cult. *Chinese Literature: Essays, Articles, Reviews (CLEAR), 18*, 1–22.
Von Falkenhausen, L. (2006). *Chinese society in the age of Confucius (1000–250 BC): the archaeological evidence* (Vol. 2). ISD LLC.
Von Falkenhausen, L. (2014). Review. Bureaucracy and the State in Early China: Governing the Western Zhou, by Li Feng. (Cambridge: Cambridge University Press, 2008).. *Zhejiang University Journal of Art and Archaeology, 1*, 252–277
Walton, J. (2013). The obligatory passage point: Abstracting the meaning in tacit knowledge. *In Proceedings of the 14th European Conference on Knowledge Management. Vol. 2.* Academic Conferences and Publishing, 769–775.
Wang, C. *Lunheng*. Sibucongkan chubian edition. Chinese Text Project.
Wang, C.H. (1974). The Countenance of the Chou: Shih Ching. *Zhongguo Wenhua Yanjiusuo Xuebao*, 7(2), 425–449.
Wang, H. (2015). A genealogical study of de: Poetical correspondence of sky, earth, and humankind in the early Chinese virtuous rule of benefaction. *Philosophy East & West, 1*(65), 81–124.
Wang, H. (2019). Cong jinwen ceming ciqi li kan Xi-Zhou juewei zhi. *Zhongguoshi yanjiu, 3*, 35–53.
Wang, P. (2016). Xi-Zhou bangguo de fazhixu goujian: yi xintu jinwen wei zhonxin. *Faxue yanjiu, 38*(6), 191–206.
Wang, S. X. (1992). Lun Xi-Zhou xiaodao guan de benzhi. *Renwen zazhi, 2*, 70–76.

Wang, X. G., & Zhang J. T. (2016). Jiaguwen yu Yin Shang nongshi tanxi. *Zhongguo nongshi, 35*(2), 15–28.
Wang, Z. Z. (2017). Shang Zhou zhi bian yu cong Di xiang Tiandi tongyi xing zuanbian de youyu. *Lishi yanjiu, 5*, 4–10.
Wei, Z. D. (2016). Cong chutu de "Qinghuajian," "Zhai Gong zhi gumu" lai kanqing ren dui *Yizhoushu*, "Zhai Gong" pian de jiaozhu. *Xia da zhongwen xue bao, 1*, 3.
Wen, X., & Shu, C. (2012–13). The Suigong Xu Calligraphy and Inscription: A Contextual Reconstruction and Translation. *Early China, 35*, 105–134.
Wen, Y. D. (1956). *Wen Yiduo xuanji.* Wenxue chubanshe.
Wu, J. (2019). Xi-Zhou shiqi zhijian wenci de xingqi yu faxzhan. *Chongqing Gongshang daxue xuebao, 37* (3), 112–119.
Yang, K. (2003). *Xi-Zhou shi.* Shanghai: Renmin.
Yu, L. F. (2019). Zailun shoudu bowuguan cang Xi-Zhou Ban-*gui*. *Bowuyuan, 4*, 10.
Yu, P., Bol, P., Owen, S., & Peterson, W. (Eds.). (2000). *Ways with words: Writing about reading texts from early China* (Vol. 24). University of California Press.
Yü, Y. S. (1987). "O soul, come back!" A study in the changing conceptions of the soul and afterlife in pre-Buddhist China. *Harvard Journal of Asiatic Studies, 47*(2), 363–395.
Yushu, Zhang, Y.S., & Chen T.D. (1973). *Kangxi zidian.* Beijing: Zhonghua shuju.
Zhao, D. (2009). The mandate of heaven and performance legitimation in historical and contemporary China. *American Behavioral Scientist, 53*(3), 416–433.
Zhao, F. R. (2008). Qianqian zaiwei, zhuiyi wenwu: "Yi Zhou shu" zhong de Zhou Muwang xingxiang. *Lilun jie, 8*, 129–131.
Zhang, J. (2011). YeXi-Zhou jinwen zhong yu jingtian youguan de shiliao.*Nongye kaogu, 4*, 48–51, 57.
Zhang, H., & Li, R.H. (2019) Zhongguo gudai nongye jisi wenhua xingshuai de yi ge kaocha. *Nongye kaogu, 4*, 247–253.
Zhang, M., Ge, Y., Kang, C., Guo, T., & Peng, D. (2018). ERP evidence for the contribution of meaning complexity underlying emotional word processing. *Journal of Neurolinguistics, 45*, 110–118.
Zhao, D.X. (2009). Mandate of heaven and performance legitimation in historical and contemporary China. *American Behavioral Scientist November,53*(3), 416–433.
Zhao, F.L. (2016). Buci suojian Shangdai ji shili qiantan. *Kaogu xuebao, 3*, 343–364.
Zhou, Y., Zwahlen, F. & Wang, Y. (2011). The ancient Chinese notes on hydrogeology. *Hydrogeology Journal, 19*(5), 1103–1114.
Zhouyi. Sibucongkan chubian edition. Vols. 1–2. Chinese Text Project.
Zhuang, Y. (2017). State and irrigation: Archeological and textual evidence of water management in late Bronze Age China. *Wiley Interdisciplinary Reviews: Water, 4*(4), e1217.
Zhushu jinian. Sibu congkan chubianedition. Vol. 86. Chinese Text Project.

6

NEUROHISTORY, FILIALITY, AND HISTORICAL CHANGE IN CHINA

The decisive historical importance of the neuropsychological underpinning of the Western Zhou Ritual Reform lies in its potential to expand our understanding of factors driving historical change. The preceding chapter reveals King Xiao's reforms to be a product of a complex stimulant-response interaction catalyzed by the deviant conditions of King Zhao's death. We saw how the Ritual Reform mediated King Zhao's loss not only for the royal family, but for the Zhou aristocrats, whose status and wealth were inextricably connected to the vicissitudes of Zhou political stability. "Thorny Caltrop" and the *Book of Changes* are artifacts borne from this process. This foundation puts us in a favorable position to understand why the "intentional enculturation" structured by regulations that condition bereavement expression would impact the way they were memorialized after the Western Zhou fall.[1]

The psychotropic conditions in which bereavement rituals and prestige distribution were linked via a schedule of collective ancestral cult practices—including feasting and multisensory performances—had a definitive impact on the brains of attending *xiaoyou* members. These experiences coalesced to form the spiritual foundation of Zhou corporate solidarity and shaped an aristocratic mindset. The Zhou's reversion to Shang discourse of bloodlines and lineage to claim supreme status emerged to transcend an obstacle to self-fashioning. King Xiao's socialization within a linguistic surround structured by prohibition of public speech about his grandfather's death is shown to be the "parent" of the Ritual Reform. This idiom of social organization motivated participating aristocrats to describe their

1 Vogt (2012, 68).

DOI: 10.4324/9781003215134-6

relationships with the Zhou lineage with the same relational terminology deployed by the Zhou to refer to their ancestors and kin groups. We explained the profusion of words for kin forms, family and social status, temple names and corollary disambiguation applied to seasonal behavior, as evidence that attests to the efficacy of the Ritual Reform in converting the Zhou family's distress and shame into language that signals its public accommodation.[2]

This chapter proposes a neuropsychological link between the mindset of elite lineages who were immersed in the ritualized culture shared by *xiaoyou*, and cultural behaviors that emerged in the wake of the Zhou family's loss of supreme status in 772 B.C. At that time, King You (729-722 B.C.) was killed by the joined forces of Western Rong tribes, identified in some contemporary bronze inscriptions as the Xianyun. The royal family and aristocrats who lived within the Zhou royal domain were forced to flee eastward from their religious and cultural centers.[3]

Recent discoveries of late Western Zhou bronze inscriptions and Eastern Zhou bamboo strip texts have sharpened our understanding of how the Western Zhou decline was reckoned with. Li Xueqin observes that at the onset of the migration the Zhou were without a ruler, the state had "lost its head" for nine years.[4] Fu Ruixun notes there were no words to describe the end of the Western Zhou. Wordlessness, a latency in expression, is, of course, a feature of all traumatic experiences. Following this book's premise, however, I postulate that the sociopolitical decapitation resulting from the Zhou lineage's fall in political rank and social status activated the same separation distress related mechanisms that King Xiao's reforms intended to transcend. My historical argument is that the *xiaoyou* mindset had been so deeply conditioned by King Xiao's charismatic Ritual Reforms that the lineage's shameful fall was experienced as a repudiation of him and them.

In the context of this study, to claim that identification with King Xiao left a psychic legacy that helps explain contiguities and differences among Western and Eastern Zhou cultural behavior is to construe the identification as an invisible but active kernel that confers neuropsychological meaning upon the mental landscape of Eastern Zhou culture.[5] It is also to suggest that submerged

2 This is the gist of the analysis of "Thorny Caltrop" in the previous chapter.

3 Li Feng's (2006) study of the rise and fall of the Western Zhou provides an expert and elegant account of the trends in traditional and modern scholarship regarding the conditions of the Zhou's demise, and advances new theories for the sociopolitical mechanisms that he sees as responsible. See also Fu (2018) who discusses how there were "no words" for quite some time that the Western Zhou.

4 Li (2003, 66).

5 Cf. Lagerwey and Kalinowski (2009, 4), where they use the word "cataclysm" to refer to issues of continuity between before and after the fall of the Western Zhou. "Not that there was no continuity between before and after, but that the late Eastern Zhou provides the indispensable key for understanding the history of early Chinese religion and culture."

under this topography are traumatic tombs erected via a linguistic structure whose intent is to hide from the collective memory what had been torn from it. Just as the states enfeoffed to allies and kin by the Zhou founders physically functioned to screen (*bing*) the Zhou lineage to protect and secure its sovereign position, so too did the post-Western Zhou mindsets of *xiaoyou* lineages evolve to psychically screen King Xiao's (and by extension, the Zhou's) (and their) shameful plight.

The Ritual Reform shifted Zhou the political consolidation strategy from enrolling regional lords into a Zhou state project to intensifying control over the core operations of the state. These conditions shaped dynastic core operations to the degree that they established a "pendulum track between kin and king,"[6] and found coherence in the *xiaoyou* memory of these "moments of contact." This memory perpetuated a "charismatic demand" for Zhou rulership.[7] A neuropsychological lens facilitates a critical investigation of cultural reproduction mechanisms. With it I foreground "the ethic of presence in bronze inscriptions and the distributed personhood of the Zhou king" that ensues. Nicholas Vogt, like Joern Peter Grundmann, implicitly follows an emotional vector in his focus on the way Zhou rituals generated a "sense of presence and immediacy of personal interaction between both living and dead members of social groups."[8] The previous chapter's findings explain the sense of presence in terms of King Zhao's saga whose occurrence was screened by yet also pressed between the lines of the social grammar instituted by the Ritual Reform. This chapter zeroes in on social behavior that transmits the content and effects of this silenced trauma as "lexical parcels of unutterable tales."[9]

King Xiao's Memorialization

Like the ritual bronze vessels whose existence bore witness to the *xiaoyou's* protective project, which were buried in fear and haste by fleeing aristocrats, memories of a (retroactively) shamed religious idyll were secretly, psychically, entombed. The inalienable relationship between mourning and *xiao* practices, and the concomitant withdrawal and retreat from libidinal investments that this relationship requires of Confucius' filial son, is understandable in light of how it reflects an identifying empathy with the "life" of King Xiao('s reforms) *beyond the grave*. This of course is the same intrapsychic condition I argue contoured the portrait of King Xiao's self-construal preserved in "Thorny Caltrop." As I will show, just as the Impersonator stages that "it is fine to be a corpse" to appease an

6 Vogt (2012, 336); Grundmann (2019).
7 Wakeman (1977, 207).
8 Vogt (2012, 30).
9 Rashkin (1992, 46).

incorporated ancestor encrypted in a concealed part of his psychic topography, so too did *xiaoyou* descendants stage that "it is fine to be *xiao*."

Although the details surrounding King Xiao's death and succession are, like those pertaining to his ascendance, murky at best, we can extrapolate a scenario from some details provided in historical sources. The *Bamboo Annals* records a short reign, stating that King Xiao died in his ninth year, while Sima Qian focuses on what happened later: "after King Xiao's demise, the feudal lords *reinstated* King Yih's son, Xie. This was King Yi." The adverb *fu* "to repeat," which modifies the verb "to instate" (*li*), implies that the factional tension underlying King Xiao's ascendance had not been resolved. King Yi's reign did not last a decade and his son, King Li (857-828 B.C.), named posthumously for the cruelty (*li*) that marked his governance, was driven into exile in the twelfth year of his reign, 842 B.C.[10]

We have no way of discerning when King Xiao's temple name was ritually bestowed. Robert Gassmann discusses the subtle processes by which political knowledge about a reign is transformed and subsequently diffused via a ritually regulated posthumous name selection. The preservation of an inventory of implicit knowledge, "abstracted and combined... act[s] as a base to affect dispositions and expectations."[11] Gassmann argues the temple name *xiao* represented a "category" within a system of succession that allowed for "the well known (but usually disregarded) implication that the immediately preceding ancestor of a king was not necessarily the biological or genealogical ancestor."[12] He identifies "two articulations" of the concept of filiality, one for living or dead parents, and the other, "*ancestral* piety," for lineage preservation.

Gassmann surmises that King Xiao's acquisition of his temple name is a function of his reticence to assert a claim for legitimacy upon King Gong's death. He concludes that "this epithet fits more to the pattern of epithets like Zhao and Mu," which are dictated by the organization of temple names that he claims are "unquestionably already known at the beginning of their respective reigns."[13] Gassman is persuasive in linking the broadening conceptual connotations of the word *xiao* to activities related to the reorganization of lineage hereditary divisions, but his conclusion is problematic because it anachronistically assumes that King Xiao's temple name derives *a priori* from a well-wrought ancestral sacrificial system that this book's previous chapter argues was in fact initiated by King Xiao himself.[14] Also, the explanation cannot account for the later trend toward using the temple name to memorialize rulers who used excessive means to institute

10 *Shiji "Zhou benji."* See also Shaughnessy (1999, 344).
11 Walton (2013, 769).
12 Gassmann (2009, 94).
13 Ibid., 111.
14 Von Falkenhausen (2006b, 85) contends that the *zhaomu* practice has yet to receive archaeological validation.

reforms, similar to the way the term "harsh" was used to refer to a ruler's particularly fierce governing tactics.[15]

The fact that "Rules" quite straightforwardly glosses King Xiao's temple names in terms of deeds he accomplished during his reign leads me to believe that the distress caused by King Xiao's death was at first not complicated. Put another way, the temple name signals the successful conversion of his loss into a word, a sign that the reality of King Xiao's absence has been collectively commemorated and (psychically) accommodated. In an inscription on the famous Hu-*gui* that King Li himself cast, expresses a desire for "model assistance," "comprehensive counsels" and as well as an aspiration that his behavior align with that of the ancestral Zhou house. His words reverberate strongly with the epithets that figure so prominently in the Shi Qiang-*pan*'s genealogical account of the dynasty's first five rulers.[16]

King Li's self-description as someone who "take[s] the eminent warriors and presented people and elevate[s] them in line with the former kings and ancestral lineage (*zong*),"[17] moreover, reveals that he relied on a system of patronage for supplying personnel to serve the bureaucratic needs of the Zhou "royal domain" (*jinei*).[18] Du Yong's delineation of the fortunes of a branch of the Jing lineage reinforces other scholarship that claims two systems for filling positions in the Zhou bureaucracy coexisted. One was a hereditary system based on the succession of sons descending from the trunk lineage (*zong*); the sons of this lineage inherited the seat of government in the regional state enfeoffed to their lineage founder. The other one was a merit-based system, relying on "presentations" offered by patrons, for the duties involving the maintenance of the king's royal

15 For example, the temple name *xiao* is given to a Qin Lord (Qin Xiaogong, r. 381–338 B.C.), whose adoption of radical reforms helped transform Qin into a dominant state. Similarly, the name is attached to Emperor Han Wudi's posthumous title: the reign of Han Xiao Wudi (r. 141–87), who was also known for a number of radical reforms, including the great calendrical Taichu reform, which bears uncanny traces of the *xiao* reforms. Lastly, the Empress Wu Zetian, whose usurpation of the throne and subsequent establishment of the Zhou dynasty (690–705 AD) was marked by efforts to institutionalize radical reforms, was also given the posthumous name *xiao*.

16 Translated in Shaughnessy (1999, 343); Grundmann (2019). I understand that these expressions are formulaic. Nonetheless, since it is a royal voice who invokes the epithets used in the royal genealogy included in the exemplary Ritual Reform product, and because at the time the vessel was cast incursions into the areas of Canine Precipice, the place were his grandfather (King Yih) ostensibly relocated his court, King Li's prayers suggest more than simple platitudes.

17 Ibid.

18 Du (2018, 53–54) offers an explanation for the fact that lineage members who served within the royal family could, in spite of "high position and great wealth" be "a rather low-ranking member in the genealogical hierarchy of his lineage" Von Falkenhausen (2006a, 273). He notes how service to the Zhou shifted from including primary sons of lineage founder, referred to as Jing Bo, to the dominance of members of the lineage stemming from the founder's second son, referred to as Jing Shu. This shift suggests a rift in the family along the lines of the factions supporting King Gong and King Xiao.

functions.[19] Li Feng has argued that this was effectively the only bureaucracy operating during the Western Zhou, that is, one staffed by sons belonging to lineages descending from second or third sons of the lineage founder.[20]

Du emphasizes that a position in the "royal domain" system was not automatically open to a lineage member's descendants, and in fact the land proximate to the capitals that was bestowed to those who serviced the bureaucracy could be retracted and redistributed.[21] King Li's inscription reveals that he continued to staff his royal bureaucracy in the same manner used by Kings Mu and Xiao. Tradition holds that King Li's temple name derives from his excessive reliance on a duke from the state of Rong for personnel choices. Rong Yi Gong was said to have profited from slandering the progeny of lineages who had served previous kings.[22]

The waning presence of members of the Jing lineage during King Li and King Xuan's (827-782 B.C.) reign, after having held elevated positions as conduits for royal patronage during the reigns of King Mu and up through King Xiao, may be attributed to King Li's distrust of the lineage's protective attachment to King Xiao. That is, the factional history surrounding King Xiao's ascension may have been transmitted to his grand-nephew; or perhaps King Li's repressive policies elicited an effort to protect King Xiao's memory, which then exacerbated the situation.[23] Another ritual vessel cast by King Li in his reign's twelfth year, before he was forced into exile, bears an inscription that records the transfer of land ownership from the Jing to another lineage.[24] When read in tandem with the decrease of references to the Jing in patronage contexts recorded in late Western Zhou bronze vessels, both summon a scenario of a branch lineage that lost its status.[25]

Extrapolating from the Jing lineage experience, we can imagine how King Li's style may have impinged on the charismatic coherence conditioned by Ritual Reform enculturation. What once "motivated subordinate Zhou elites to conceive of their personal identities and degrees of status, prestige, and wealth in terms of the [Zhou] kinship model"[26] *(the unconscious shared obligation to protect King Zhao's/Mu's/Xiao's shame)* became a source of danger for the

19 Ibid.
20 Li (2001, 2008).
21 Du (2018, 54–55).
22 Shaughnessy (1999, 341–343).
23 Du (2018, 54).
24 For example, in the Da Ke-*ding*, the property belonging to a descendant of the trunk lineage, Jing Bo. It was it this time that the second son of the lineage founder, Jing Shu, found favor with King Xiao and King Yi's court. See Shaughnessy (1992, 327-328) for inscription.
25 Li (2006,129) suggests that the Jing lineage began to decline during the late Western Zhou when its estates were annexed by other lineages.
26 Vogt (2012, 48).

xiaoyou, who embodied King Xiao's distributed personality. Because King Li's own behavior was erratic, predicting which lineage's "Zhou-affiliated ancestor" would be deemed a worthy model for exemplary behavior was difficult. I suspect that this context explains the decline of the Jing lineage.

King Li's flight into exile occurred almost forty years after the remarkable planetary conjunction appeared proximate to the Vermillion Bird's Heart at the summer solstice in 880. Before his fourteen-year-old son, King Xuan, ascended the throne in 827, the reins of power had been held by one Earl He, whose lineage hailed from the state of Gong.[27] The *Bamboo Annals* claims it was a usurpation (*she*), but the earl retreated when presented with King Xuan, who had survived his father's exile thanks to the intervention of two powerful dukes from the states of Shao and Jin.[28] By this time the original lineage members who had experienced King Xiao's charisma were passing. The *Bamboo Annals* records a high density of deaths among lineage heads during Earl He's interregnum, including from the Central Plain states in eastern Henan: Cai and Cao, Chen, Song and Qi; it was suggesting the end of a generation.[29]

Edward Shaughnessy views King Xuan's lengthy reign "as something of a restoration" for the Zhou royal house, due to the king's quick efforts to "reassert royal authority."[30] One gloss in "Rules" tells us the temple name *xuan* is apt for a ruler whose behavior "excels in listening and is broadly expressive in [social] circulation" (*shanwen zhouda*).[31] After the shock of Li's cruelty, King Xuan's temple name suggests his rule, which endured for an astonishing forty-six years, ushered in conditions that served as an antidote. Sima Qian emphasizes that he "made adjustments to the rectified norm, and imitated the legacies and style of Kings Wn, Wu, Cheng and Kang.

Although King Xuan's reign was bedeviled with the same military threats that confronted King Li, bronze inscriptions buried by members of the Shan lineage when they migrated after the collapse of the Zhou's, suggest his ruling idiom created conditions that regained the trust of the *xiaoyou*.[32] The inscriptions reflect how the *xiaoyou* were motivated once again to "conceive of their personal identities and degrees of status, prestige, and wealth in terms of the [Zhou]

27 Shaughnessy (1992, 345).

28 *Zhushu jinian*. The text indicates that the last five years of the duke's reign were marked by drought. It also records a high density of deaths among lineage heads, including from the Central Plain states in eastern Henan: Cai and Cao, Chen, Song and Qi, suggesting the passing of a generation.

29 *Zhushu jinian*. Many of these lineages were known to have helped the Zhou secure territory that once belonged to the Shang Li (2006, 75).

30 (1999, 345).

31 *Jizhong Zhoushu*, "Shifa jie."

32 The cache of twenty-seven bronze vessels was discovered in 2003 at Yangjiacun in Shaanxi. Shaanxi sheng kaogu yanjiu suo (2003); Kaogu yu wenwu bianjibu (2003).

kinship model."[33] One inscription in particular, cast on a *pan* vessel by Qiu, who was newly mandated by the king to assume the position of Woodsman, is particularly relevant. The text includes a genealogy of his model-worthy ancestors interwoven with a rare genealogy of the Western Zhou rulers down to his own ruling king.

The remarkable inscription has been studied by eminent scholars who agree that it is a rich source of information that deepens our understanding of late Western Zhou social structure and the emergence of a historical consciousness.[34] All note the formulaic quality of Qiu's rhetoric, and how the inscription's structure conforms to generic practice. They also link the rhetoric to an ideology aimed toward representing the Zhou lineage line of succession as seamless, because Qiu includes King Xiao in his royal genealogy, notwithstanding the deviant circumstances surrounding his ascendance. The temple names designated to Qiu's model-worthy ancestors, provide historical commentary on the Western Zhou rulers served by Qiu's ancestors.

Both the genealogical form, and its inclusion of "ancestral titles," "indicators of seniority," and even "posthumous epithets" in line with the "Rules," are hallmarks of the Ritual Reform's differentiating lexicon. Especially noteworthy is the appearance of the term "subordinate ancestor" (*yazu*) in Qiu's genealogy, which we also saw in the Shi Qiang-*pan*. Indeed Qiu claims that his "subordinate ancestor," Yi Zhong, "made order by remonstrating [*jian*] and was able to support and preserve his lords Kings Xiao and Yi in their having achievements on behalf of the Zhou kingdom."[35] Just who was the subject of remonstration is not clear, but it may be that Qiu is suggesting that the Shan clan were supporters of the royal faction that legitimized King Xiao's succession.

Qiu's repeated emphasis on "protecting the Former Kings" stresses the primary aim of his service to the Zhou. He links his efforts to the practice of lineage sacrifices, which "strive to make joyful and happy the Accomplished Men of the Former Ages."[36] *Xiaoyou* lineages may have their own accomplished men, but King Xuan made clear that Qiu's ancestors', or even his own success, were no guarantee for social or political stability: "Exert yourself night and day in graciously harmonising the small and large projects of our state. In your taking control of the affairs of your official duties, dare not be wayward or nonconforming. In your interrogating apprehended criminals, dare

33 Vogt (2012, 67).

34 Li (2003); von Falkenhausen (2006a; 2011); Shaughnessy (2009; 2011); Sena (2012); Grundmann (2019).

35 Von Falkenhausen (2006a, 278).

36 Ibid. (279). He argues that the "narrative of lineage history" is couched in formulas that are ideologically suited to the needs of the occasion" to advance the glory of a lineage (276).

not be disloyal and nonconforming! Do not engage in bribery… for this you will make me, the One Man, punish you, and you will die *divested of your rank*" (emphasis added).[37]

Qiu's inscription bolsters the idea that King Xuan's strategy to reassert royal authority revitalized *xiaoyou* culture, but not to the extent that royal prerogative eased significantly the precariousness of political and social status. This historical fact may underlie the meaning of the second gloss provided by "Rules" for King Xuan's temple name, which tells us that the posthumous title is apt for royal behavior that "attempts to implement [a policy] but does not actualize it (*shi er bu cheng*)."[38]

The founder of the Jing lineage branch that served in King Mu and King Xiao's "royal domain" and the founder of the Shan lineage, Qiu's ancestors, were both second sons. Du Yong concludes that Jing's branch lineage was established prior to the systematization of King Xiao's practice of splitting lineages every five generations, which makes chronological sense given his association with King Mu in historical records.[39] He also suggests that the bureaucratization of the "royal domain," whose regulating obligations increased on manifold levels due to the implementation of the Ritual Reforms, created a demand for talent that opened up new career opportunities for second (or non-primary) sons.[40] Although the "large and messy conglomerate of branch lineages" resulting from these conditions led to a "permeable hierarchy," the solidity of the idea that lineages form "the basic units of social organisation, and of descent in legitimising claims to social prominence" was a defining feature of the late Western Zhou *xiaoyou* mindset.[41]

The growing importance of lineage as the "basis of reference" for identity development is crucial for understanding the link between the distress caused by the Western Zhou fall and the emergence of the Confucian filial complex. Returning for a moment to Qiu the Woodsman, von Falkenhausen points out how

> Qiu appropriates for himself the accumulated prestige of his lineage as a whole, taking credit for the achievements even of distant forebears; by the same token, however, he potentially speaks for all living descendants of the remote figures named, and he gives his more distant relatives a stake in his own wealth and glory. He encourages them, for their own benefit, to rally

37 Ibid. (281).
38 *Jizhong Zhoushu*, "Shifa jie.". Cf. Valmisa (2019, 51), where Early Chinese concepts of fate (*ming*) are described as "theory of inexplicability and inevitability." This book argues that the roots of this theory lie in the observed effects of precession on celestial entities.
39 Du (2018, 53).
40 Ibid. (54).
41 Von Falkenhausen (2006a, 273).

> around him in spite of his relatively lowly standing within the lineage. Vis-à-vis the king, this implies that any royal rewards obtained by him will reflect upon the lineage in its entirety and will ensure not only his own personal loyalty, but that of an extensive, prominent, and anciently established body of people. This rhetorical strategy, apparently without precedent in earlier bronze inscriptions (such as that of the Shi Qiang-*pan*), intimates a new conception of the lineage as an encompassing entity within which the members share a feeling of solidarity transcending all internal subdivisions.[42]

If the rhetorical strategy is unprecedented, I would argue, however, that Qiu's gestures recapitulate those of King Xiao, the king whose "lowly" place among King Mu's sons did not impede his ascension to the throne nor thwart his lineage from reaping royal rewards. Recalling how the gaps in the Shi Qiang-*pan* genealogy were necessary to rhetorically shore up King Xiao's claim to be the successor of the Zhou lineage's fifth king, thus legitimizing his royal branch lineage, it is noteworthy that Qiu's genealogy mirrors that structure. He identifies five ancestors with the ancestral title "High Ancestor" (*gaozu*) before narrowing his focus to the ancestor, Yi Zhong, whose sociopolitical position in his genealogy is clearly marked in terms of his founding of a branch lineage.[43]

The posthumous epithets designated to Qiu's last four ancestors are all glossed in "Rules." These glosses tacitly tell a story about the sociopolitical conditions that account for their designation. For example, the first ancestor memorialized with an epithet from "Rules" is Hui Zhong Lifu, whose name also includes his lineage rank designation, "second son" (*zhong*). *Hui* is glossed as behavior manifesting "a helpful essence [that] nurtures the people"; and behavior that exhibits "care and love for the people, favoring interaction."[44] Qiu integrates Hui Zhong Li Fu's deeds into those of the royal Zhou rulers, Kings Zhao and Mu. The temple name *hui,* meant to reflect why Hui Zhong Li Fu was selected to join "Kings Zhao and Mu in appeasing and rectifying the Four Directions and in clipping and attacking Chu Jing." The posthumous title emphasizes a temperament that would have been prized for its suitability to engage in King Mu's "soft power" offensives to bolster Zhou sovereignty.

In Chapter 5 we noted how the positive effects of soft power strategy help explain the evolution of the Ritual Reform as a cultural unit. If Hui Zhong Li Fu was in the Zhou court's inner circle, as Qiu's reference suggests, then his ancestors were intimately involved with the royal Zhou efforts to "forbid" discussion of King Zhao's shameful death. This might account for the religious

42 Von Falkenhausen (2006a).

43 Von Falkenhausen provides a helpful chart that delineates the genealogy of the Shan lineage, Ibid. (288).

44 *Jizhong Zhoushu*, "Shifa jie."

overtones that suffuse the temple name given to the next ancestor referred to by Qiu, Earl Ling, who "attentively brightened his mind and never relaxed [in his] service, thereby protecting Kings Gong and Yi[h]."[45] The "Rules" gloss emphasizes the capacity of a ruler's sensitivity to the conditions of "ghost spirits" (*guishen*): someone who "favors sacrificing to ghosts spirits is called *ling*"; someone who has "extreme knowledge about ghost spirits is called *ling*"; someone who has the "capacity to see spirits after death" is called *ling*; all bespeak a concern with post-mortem status. Of course, these glosses also evoke the word's association with the astro-calendrical lexicon generated as part of the Ritual Reform.

The temple name designated to Qiu's ancestor "Subordinate Ancestor," is the same given to King Yih, who preceded King Xiao to the throne. Qiu's use of the verb *remonstrated* to refer to the "Subordinate Ancestor's" support to "preserve his lords King Xiao and Yi,"[46] invites reflection. First, the verb evokes the act of Zhai Gong, whose remonstrance toward King Mu we analyzed as central to the memorialization of King Mu's reign. It positions "Subordinate Ancestor" on the same level of intimacy as those allies whose identities were forged by their commitment to preserving the Zhou's supremacy in the wake of the King Zhao crisis. "Rules" glosses *yih* as behavior that is "warm and gentle, wise and good" (*wenrou shengshan*)[47] If, as suggested in the previous chapter, King Yih's temple name does not refer to ruling behavior per se, but his role as a pure, sacrificial victim of Zhou familial strife, then its assignation to Qiu's ancestor may implicitly absolve him of nefarious intentions surrounding King Xiao's ascension. This suggests that by King Xuan's times, although King Xiao's succession had been historically accommodated, the deeds associated with his reign had already begun to be contaminated by negative associations.

The temple name designated to Qiu's father reinforces this logic. The *gong* that appears in the appellation "My August Deceased Father Gong Shu," who "venerated and protected his lord King Li," is the same as that given to King Xiao's older brother. We observed in the previous chapter how the range of glosses provided for this temple implies a problematic historical perspective regarding King Gong's legacy. Given the negativity of King Li's temple name, it would not be farfetched to read into Qiu ancestor's name an implicit acknowledgment that his ancestor may have been someone "who has transgressed [but] is capable of correcting [it]" or one who "covers flaws committed by family relations (*qin*)."[48]

---

45 Von Falkenhausen (2006a, 278).

46 Ibid.

47 *Jizhong Zhoushu*, "Shifa jie." The locution "wise and good" appears in the *Book of Poetry* in reference to a mother. The word "wise" also appears several times to refer to a leader's "wisdom and reverence." See Schuessler (2007, 539).

48 *Jizhong Zhoushu*, "Shifa jie."

The pattern woven by the integration of Qiu's ancestors' temple names into the royalgenealogy uncovers the degree to which *xiaoyou* lineages identified with the royal ideology that King Xiao's succession was a seamless affair. There was much more ideational reciprocity to those who committed and adhered to King Xiao's Ritual Reform than is usually acknowledged in "explanations that only emphasize the gift of a charismatic leader."[49] This is important because it sheds light on the conditioning force exerted by Zhou cultural leadership on *xiaoyou* mindsets.[50] The spiritual and affective weight of the Zhou family's supreme posture derived from its psychological decontaminating function. The Ritual Reform's rules and regulations drained King Zhao's shame from the language that memorialized him; the regimen of when and what to eat enforced by the ritual Interlocutor in "Thorny Caltrop" allegorized the presence of an encrypted ancestral ghost who vigilantly protects the words of his shame buried alongside him.

The catastrophically deviant condition of the Zhou family's fallen political status reactivated the same neural network of grief and shame that King Xiao's Ritual Reform was implemented to transcend. This time, however, it was not just the royal family's pain, it was collectively felt, thanks to the Zhou's establishment of bureaucratic institutions to mediate it. The Zhou's fallen lineage status rendered identification with King Xiao's Ritual Reform shameful and dangerous. Elite families found it hazardous to invoke their relationship to the Zhou ruling family. The likelihood that most aristocratic families consciously removed linguistic reference to their *xiaoyou* identity to avoid being implicated in their shame may account for the silence regarding the Ritual Reform in the textual record.[51]

To understand the experience of the aristocratic elite, and its link to post-Western Zhou cultural evolution, we must understand that of the many challenges facing the elite *xiaoyou* lineages and their descendants, the psychic problem of how to assimilate the loss of an idyll whose status had become illegitimate was paramount. The vertical transmission of the linguistic "trick" that accomplished the decontamination of the crisis, the (unconscious) pretense of having swallowed and psychically accommodated via ritual eating. The "sumptuary elevation of the royal house above regional lords and above other groups of nobility"[52] is the mechanism that effected the distribution of figurative "swallowing" and "digesting" of the Zhou's relational loss.

49 Wakeman (1997, 207). Grundmann (2019) and Vogt (2012) have provided the most extensive analyses of this dimension of Zhou political ideology.
50 Khayutina et al. (2010, 274).
51 See Grundmann (2019) for an alternative interpretation.
52 Ibid. (275.)

Origins of King Xiao's Negative Memorialization

Before examining the impact of this event on elite lineage self-fashioning, it is important to delineate evidence that supports the idea that the Zhou family's loss of prestige influenced the way the memory of the Ritual Reform was preserved. When the Western Zhou's ritually grounded sociopolitical structure collapsed, it implicitly tainted the rites associated with pronounced commitment to Zhou religious supremacy. In this section, I will lay out a trajectory that traces how King Xiao's memory began to accrue negative, transgressive associations. This likely began during the reign of King Li, whose repressive ruling style sullied King Xiao's policies by association. Although King Xuan's reign seems to have succeeded at least in preserving King Xiao's bureaucratic institutions and the concomitant awe that they instilled, the negative turn in the semantic evolution of words related to King Xiao's calendrical reforms invites us to consider it as an important clue about why his ruling legacy was erased from the transmitted record.

King Li's royal behavior surely shocked the collective aristocratic nervous system conditioned by King Xiao's rule, and this must have been exacerbated by repeated incursions on the capital area by the polities whose attack catapulted King Xiao to the throne.[53] Sima Qian's famous account of the neuropsychological conditions of that time captures the scene: among [the lords] from the [feudal] states, none dared speak, using their eyes on the road [instead]."[54] We can imagine that the policies and institutions used by King Li to terrorize the aristocratic lineages elevated by King Xiao's reforms were implicated by association. The slogan-like cadence of the word *xiaoyou,* and the fact of its occurrence in every genre of the ritual repertoire, hint at rigorous efforts to imprint this social and cultural label on the consciousness of a broad swath of subjects. Jessica Rawson infers heavy-handed measures when she notes the rapidity with which the new ritual practices effectively transformed the cultural landscape; widespread conformity in ritual vessel production and use were signs of consistent and strong dissimenation.[55]

Archaeological evidence shows that the social transformation catalyzed by the Ritual Reform was completed within fifty years to the extent that widespread cultural conformity supplanted long-standing east-west cultural distinctions.[56] Because King Li's exile occurred almost forty years after the remarkable summer solstice alignment of four planets that I claim sanctioned King Xiao's rule, his reign must have played an important role in promoting the adoption of the

53 Shaughnessy (1999, 343).

54 *Shiji*, "Zhou benji."

55 Jessica Rawson (1990, 110). Li (2006, 332 et passim) claims that this era is when a fundamental centralized culture that linked longstanding distinct traditions among the regional states occupying the east and west of China.

56 Li (2006).

symbolic language that marked elite social and political circulation. I postulate that the affective currency of King Li's execution of King Xiao's reforms been triggered by precession-induced phenomena. By the time of King Li's rule, precession would have rendered adherence to King Xiao's astro-calendrical framework inconsistent with ecological reality.[57]

Recall how the concept of modeling, foremost in King Li's mind when he cast the Hu-*gui*, was concretized during the Ritual Reform by virtue of its astro-calendrical associations with the constellation Well. Recall, too, how the graph that denotes Well, *jing*, was frequently used to mean "model" *xing* in Western Zhou bronze inscriptions. There are lexical clues in Eastern Zhou texts that suggest the Ritual Reform's method of keying certain circumpolar stars in alignment with Well to seasonal determinants was the culprit for the negative turn in the graph's semantic evolution. From the word "model," the graph evolved to denote the antithetical meaning of transgression, "crime, punishment" (*xing*). From its positive associations with a concrete astronomical symbol of aligned cosmic transformation, to its meaning as a standard/tool for ancestral modeling, to a narrower meaning of (punishment) requiring the application of models *to repair misaligned behavior this evolutionary trajectory*—implicates Well as the source of the late Western Zhou sociopolitical tensions.

The discontinuity wrought by precession, is viscerally voiced in poems that castigate astral objects as dysfunctional tools in the *Book of Poetry*. In the face of these realities, Yu worship practices may have offered recourse when the core of King Xiao's system became obsolete. I see the translation of the Zhou's axial-based celestial hall into the upper body of Dragon as a response to these conditions. Concealing the original building context by incorporating the relevant asterisms into the Dragon's astral body recapitulates the symbolic process that transformed Turtle into turtle. It permitted the use of Zhou zodiacal contributions, while disguising King Xiao's role in its production.

Peter Boodberg's analysis of the mutual interaction between Chinese mythic memes and Chinese language development yields an important lexical clue for recognizing how King Xiao's calendrical determinations may have been retroactively condemned as transgressive, due to King Li's attempt to implement them. Boodberg asserts that a key to understanding the connection between Chinese mythic memes, such as axial pillars and floods, and language development, is to understand how the linguistic fragments that comprise the memes work together to reconstruct an original phoneme. We saw in our discussion of

57 Notwithstanding the endurability of Western Zhou astro-calendrical knowledge, by the time of the Western Zhou collapse the alignments were no longer viable due to precession. Calendrical inaccuracy is whispered in the "Da dong" poem in the *Book of Poetry*, which "invokes stellar imagery to exemplify the mismatch between name and reality," with special irony directed toward the Dipper and Vega, the Weaving Maid. See Pankenier (2013, 376).

Hou Ji that the dissipation of an original phoneme catalyzed a gradual dimidiation of the complex cluster of consonants.

Recall that in Boodberg's account, Hou Ji's name reconstructs the phoneme *chu*, "pillar," which itself derives from the etymon "horn." Moreover, he also identified "Horn" as the etymonic source of the words "'altar,' 'ancestor,' 'torch.'"[58] When precession rendered the seasonal coordinates based on Horns' axial positionality obsolete, this apex of the Zhou lineage's celestial temple, was implicated in criminality. This explains the turn in the word's semantic valence from signifying divine omnipotence to the narrower negative meaning that emphasized a zoomorphic sense of the word "horn" in the verb "to butt."

The interpolation of the Zhou's building themed zodiac nomenclature into the upper body of Dragon followed a recursive logic. Unlike the cultural logic of transporting traditional signs out of their familiar habitat and situating them within broader semantic contexts that we have seen drove cultural evolution, the displacement of the conceptual kernel of the Zhou's system all the while holding on to its signifiers raises questions about the mode of perceiving necessary to bring the new zoomorphic pattern into view. I see the problem of reconciling recognizable cultural identity shaped by ecological conditions that no longer pertained as an obstacle for *xiaoyou* self-fashioning. The cultural signs that functioned as demarcations of their identity had become, for all intents and purposes, illegible.

The disintegration of cultural boundaries represented by Dragon's acquisition of a torso and horned head, generated questions about the nature and stability of cultural identity. These conditions contextualize the evolutionary path of other words associated with the Zhou's astro-calendrical system that accrued a negative valence. For example, the semantic evolution of the word *gui* "spirit ghost" parallels that of "horn." Whereas the nomenclature Ghost Conveyor implies an orderly process—and vehicular transport—for post-mortem ascendance to the celestial temple, Eastern Zhou texts refer to ghosts as dangerous presences on earth that required serious attention and domestication.[59]

Michael Puett theorizes that anxiety over ghosts' direction of anger toward humans and the fear of their potential withdrawal of interest or care in human events drove "the ritual work of dealing with the dead."[60] The anxiety required ritual mediation to keep the worlds of the living and dead separate. We have traced the neuroemotional roots of the latter fear back to Turtle's withdrawal. The resolution to the problem of dealing with ghosts in the Eastern Zhou cannot be separated from the shameful nature of the "set of problems" that catalyzed the anxiety in the first place.

58 Boodberg (1937, 345–346).
59 Puett (2019, 442).
60 Ibid.

While Puett sees ritual domestication in terms of transforming the ghost into an ancestor, the analysis of "Thorny Caltrop" suggests that ritual expressed a fantasy of having swallowed and digested, that is psychically accommodated, an unutterable loss. The fantasy was produced in response to a "haunting" by an ancestral ghost; the threat of linguistic slippage triggered the ghost's appearance. The defensive motivation driving the production of the psychic structure was the transcendence of an intrapsychic crisis that blocked self-fashioning and self-expanding processes. "Thorny Caltrop" revealed that containing the ghost required preserving a pscyhic status quo. Preservation entailed the grandson's speech and actions adhere to an unstated yet vigilantly enforced decontaminating grammar: "it is fine to be a corpse, look how happy I am to ingest the sacrificial feast."

The implications of this interpretation for understanding the evolution of the word "ghost" converge on the transformation from corpse to ancestor as an analogue for human post-mortem transformations, from the status of mourner to one of sacrificer, an offering descendant.[61] I perceive the transformation of ghosts into an "entity supportive of humans" that Puett assumes is central ritual's operational aims instead as part of the ruse that unwitting descendants are obligated to perpetuate.[62] In other words, the supposed transformation in fact is illusory, the mourner, caught in the deceit built into the sacrifice, is fated to perpetuate it through behavior focused on the literal ingestion of sacrificial food.

The collapse of the Western Zhou created conditions that were ripe for the ghosts' return. Whereas the inclusion of the word "ghost" in the nomenclature associated with King Xiao's astro-calendrical reforms intimate a positive valence, Eastern Zhou texts use the word to designate a malevolent spiritual force in funereal or post-mortem contexts. Han historian Sima Qian's "Treatise of Celestial Offices" (*tianwen zhi*) provides additional evidence to support the idea that the accrual of negative valence may have been a function of slippage between the astro-calendrical system and earthly seasonal signs. To wit, alongside the clear change in Well's nomenclature to Eastern Well, asterisms near Ghost Conveyor were given ominous labels, such as Broadaxe [referring to the white cloudy form in the middle of Ghost Conveyor]. Sima Qian explains: "Broadaxe accomplishes injury. Eastern Well accomplishes disaster and Headman's Block [another nearby asterism] accomplishes punishment."[63]

These semantic processes occurred over an extended amount of time, so I must make it clear that while I situate the negativity associated with King Xiao's temple name within the historical context of King Li's harsh ruling idiom, the problematic aspects of ensuring conformity to King Xiao's astro-calendrically based cult schedule transcended King Li's short reign. Nonetheless, King Li's

61 Ibid.
62 Ibid.
63 Pankenier (2013, 465).

cruel policy methods may have been triggered by regional lineage rulers who failed to enforce uniform adherence to the official calendrical and ritual schedule.[64]

That the royal house was deeply concerned by the instability caused by the incapacity of its bureaucrats to behave in ways that reflect alignment with the Western Zhou founders' models is reflected in a complex and difficult inscription discovered during the Song dynasty. Because its provenance was not recorded, the inscription has elicited suspicion, but it is generally regarded as an authentic representation of a late Western Zhou inscription cast by a figure named Mu to commemorate

his having been mandated to take up a new post by the reigning king. The inscription narrates an account of the king's *cri de coeur* over reports of the abuse of rank in the (royal) dispensation of justice. The king declaims the officers who work where "impartiality" (*zhong*) and "modeled behavior" (*xing*,) graph are egregiously lacking.[65] While the full context of the inscription still awaits comprehensive elucidation, it is fair to say that the inscription offers insight into how the concept of the Zhou's "bright model" may have been implicated in the breakdown of Western Zhou social order.

This context of challenges posed by precession to the astro-calendrically premised socio-religious structure nuances the implications of the record of solar and lunar eclipses that occurred during the first year of King You's official succession in 781 B.C, barely a decade prior to the Western Zhou's forced migration[66] The *Book of Poetry* contains a memory of this event, seen as malevolent and woeful.[67] Not only did it prefigure the ominous failure of the seasonally based rituals that reinforced Zhou religious potency, but it also presaged a more general darkening of the Ritual Reform as an event that was central to lineage identity formation. The following looks at the semantic evolution of words associated with temple as opposed to astronomical practice. Although in toto the evolutionary paths suggest a shift in the process of memorializing King Xiao's legacy, the process by which words' *ritual referents* were implicated in the Zhou's decline evolved in a distinct manner.

The Semantic Evolution of Eastern Zhou Ritual Terminology

Extant Shang records show that the graph conventionally translated as "ritual" (*li*), originally denoted a sacrificial vessel, which came to connote, through

64 Cf. Li (2006, 105) who mentions how King Li's cruel reputation may have attracted to him blamed for problematic land grabs made by the Zhou to enrich their royal house.
65 Goldin (2008, 171–172); see also Li (2004).
66 *Zhushu jinian*; Shaughnessy (1992).
67 Shaughnessy (1999, 349).

metonymic derivation, practices associated with ritual vessels and then, by extension, the ideology of ritual practice itself.[68] Yuri Pines argues that the last leg of this semantic evolution reflects an effort to make sense of the Western Zhou collapse.[69] Its association with government administration, including judicial responsibilities, bears traces of the role ritual bronze vessels played in bureaucratic functioning during the Western Zhou. Pines links the growing importance of the word *li* in Eastern Zhou discourse to as an indication of its centrality in efforts to provide an "intellectually coherent" response to sociopolitical disintegration.[70]

I propose a complementary but distinct account of the word's evolution starting from the word's close connection with the word *fa*, which denotes "rules and laws" and especially the dispensation of punishments, understood as corrective models for rectifying speech and behavior socially deemed "out of line." This association convokes the silent impact of the criminalization of the Ritual Reform on the Eastern Zhou *xiaoyou* mindset.[71] Significantly, unlike the evolutionary paths undertaken by words associated with the astro-calendrical details of the system, which evince a tendency to narrow the semantic range in order to emphasize a (new) negative valence, the trajectory of *li*'s semantic range reveals a broadening of meaning.

The reason for the divergence in evolutionary paths taken by astro-calendrical and ritual terms, notwithstanding the fact that both were shaped by the same aversive event, can be explained in terms of the specific collective topology emblematized in "Thorny Caltrop." The semantic evolution of *li* implicitly dissociate's the word off from its connection to *xiaoyou* sacrificial and feasting rituals. In other words, the word *li's* evolution points to the problematic memory of the Ritual Reform, and especially those objects that symbolized the sumptuary premise of the entire structure: the ritual vessels. The broadening of the semantic appears to compensate the need for a lexical substitution for those associations. These conditions may also underlie an ideological shift that coincided with growing "interest in the concept of *li* and in its social value." This shift was responsible for the proliferation of signifiers generated over the course of its evolution.[72]

The same conditions are also intimated in the semantic evolution of the word *xiao* outside of its temple name function. From the Western Zhou verbal meaning "to offer," as in "to provide food and drink to ancestors through sacrificial rituals," to its denotation of an emotional child-parent bond, the shift in the word's semantic focus resonates with Confucius avoidant attitude toward

68 See Pines (2000; 2002; 2008) for significant contributions to our understanding of the word's meaning and significance as it evolved during the Eastern Zhou.

69 Pines (2002, 99–103).

70 Pines (2000, 6).

71 Li and Yi (2005, 513).

72 Pines (2017); Nowosad (2017); Qiang and Lambert (2020).

spirits. That is to say, the broadening of the word's semantic range cuts off from view its relationship with Western Zhou communal acts of ancestral sacrifices and feasting. Yet this broadening led to unresolved ambiguities. We noted how Confucius demeaned the view that merely feeding a living parent merited consideration as "filial" behavior, waving such behavior off as merely superficial; the implication was that physical ingestion is repellant to the sincere filial son in grief.

Because *xiaoyou* relationships were cemented via a sequence of rituals including sacrifice to the royal cult, sacrificial meat splitting, and communal consumption of that meat, the screening of the word's historical associations reinforces the idea that it was triggered in response to a disturbance in self-fashioning involving the memory of King Xiao and *xiaoyou* identity.[73] The link between not eating and paradigmatic filial behavior invites us to consider it a symptom of the repression of an important experience or memory about the *xiao* reform era cannot be collectively, psychically, "swallowed" and "digested." It recapitulates, albeit in refracted form, the same intrapsychic experience endured by King Xiao, itself encrypted within "Thorny Caltrop's" fantasy structure. Keeping in mind that shameful knowledge that cannot be psychically digested *because it has been subjected to a form of "repression" before its transmission down family lines* sets the stage to understand the word's salience in Confucian thought.

This book's conceptual premise that shameful secrets led to the production of linguistic structures intended to conceal them is strengthened by a profound observation made by Peter Boodberg about the unique characteristic of glottological evolution in Chinese. The fact that glottological evolution was, as it were, "contained" by linguistic retention of the original word sheds light on psychic processes involved with preservative repression. The linguistic mechanisms are capable of preserving intact the, while making unintelligible, an unspeakable shameful drama. Boodberg's incisive observation that nowhere except in China "did the 'plus' and 'minus' of [glottological change] drift so little away from the etymonic core where they were originally merged one in the other" brings into clearer view how the neuropsychological conditions of the Western Zhou fall may have exerted influence over the evolution of Eastern Zhou linguistic pathways.[74]

73 Puett (2005). Von Falkenhausen (2011, 259) discusses the "twofold exchange of messages and goods based on the *do ut des* principle: the visitor, in presenting tribute, expects to be given royal rewards, and the king bestows the latter in the expectation of future tribute."

74 Boodberg (1937, 371).

Post-Western Zhou *Xiaoyou* Mindsets

One can easily suppose the fragility of lineages whose status and reputation were inextricably linked to the *xiaoyou* identity in the face of the Zhou's fall. Unable to openly grieve the loss of collective belonging conditioned by the ritualization of sociopolitical life, not to mention the prestige generated by these practices, mourning was suspended. These conditions led to a concern to instill loyalty to one's patrimony as a form of protection, perhaps survival, a concern that likely "manifested itself in more intrusive parenting modes, so that mothers and fathers, as well as older siblings, would have to impose greater discipline on the actions and statements of the younger children."[75]

Loss of a sense of security in public life and commerce for the parents would also mean that home life was influenced by "feelings of anxiety and discomfort, with obvious and hidden consequences for the children growing up in these distressed families."[76] Though mothers, fathers, and siblings might wish to shield the infant from these dangers, the distress and tensions would enter the domestic realm and affect care-giving. The disruptions to normal ritual practices and relations with the extended family surely had an impact on the household as well. One can imagine that in the once powerful lineages it was seen as important to keep small children ignorant of the family's historical identity, and to exclude them from the very *xiaoyou* ceremonies and customs which previously had been the primary means of social bonding. Indeed, the fear that the young child might betray the family (however inadvertently) through speech suggests itself as a pathogenic source of behavior. These conditions may have contributed to the way familial roles came to have normative force, substituting for the absent external markers "guidelines for how [one] ought to proceed and what… to do next."[77]

Jin Fangting's recent study on self-identification patterns seen in Springs and Autumns (Chunqiu 770-453 B.C.) bronze vessels provides an example of how children may have be socialized to refer to themselves in the conditions outlined above. The grammatical structure "so and so's distant grandson (*zengsun*), so and so's son," found in bronze inscriptions with a wide distribution pattern, offers two descent vectors, the intersection of which "displayed" (*jieshi*) the aristocratic child's aristocratic status. Jin concludes that the distance implied by the word *zeng* indicates the reference to be a "false reference (*xuzhi*)." The rhetorical aim of this trope was to affirm while keeping vague aristocratic origins. The pretense of specificity by combining both descent vectors served to obscure them.

75 Simms (2006, 91).

76 Ibid.

77 Rosemont and Ames (2016, 76). Cf. *Lunyu,* 2.21, where Confucius deliberately distinguishes *xiao* behavior from government, emphasizing the secular "friend" (*you*) dimension of the binome *xiaoyou*.

Significantly, Jin found that ancestors to whom these vague references pointed invariably were aristocrats who established a branch lineage off of the trunk; I have argued that "Rules'" attribution to of this segmentation system to King Xiao is historically sound. Jin's findings reinforce the idea that aristocratic self-identification required a new means to sustain aristocratic status while concealing explicit link to the Zhou. Adherence to the founder of a branch lineage as the valorized origin of descent became a tacit linguistic means to protect status while continuing to secretly valorize King Xiao, the author of the segmentation system. The self-identification formula articulates the experience of children as they absorbed the emotional insecurity caused by the disappearance of collective boundaries by which to pinpoint one's place in society.

These sociohistorical conditions form the neurohistorical context for the evolution of the Chinese filial complex. The complex encapsulates a neural signature of post-Western Zhou families. Over time, the strategy of linguistic avoidance and the imperative to adhere to these rules were internalized to the degree that they became features of the archaic interdependent mindset. For example, according to *Analect* 9.4, "The Master banished four locutions from his vocabulary: "I suppose" (*yi*); "necessity" (*bi*); "intransigence" (*gu*), and "I" (*wo*).[78]

The idea that collective secrets may emerge in behaviors that "stage" them publicly, so as to exorcise the effects of their presence in the social realm, helps me conceptualize the conditions that led to the emergence of a filial complex.[79] I understand the complex as behavior adapted to relieve the collective psychological burden of unspeakable lineage grief and shame. The mechanism operated in the same way that the ancestral sacrifices provided relief to King Xiao—and the extended *xiaoyou* family who inherited and lived in adherence to this linguistic structures and behavioral norms. Borne from the linguistic environment of *xiaoyou* lineages, pruned of words that might betray the devastating distress over the loss of sociopolitical prestige and rank, the filial complex emerges as a symptom of complicated grief, which "conceals [the *xiaoyou* shameful saga] within its own purposive force."[80]

The prominence of a Chinese historiographical tradition renowned for its intent to "to hide [the flaws of] the exalted; to hide [the flaws of] kinsmen; to hide [the flaws of] the virtuous"[81] invites a rethinking in light of the possibility

78 I follow Jean Levi's French translation (Levi 2018), cited in Harbsmeier (2019, 180). Cf. *Lunyu,* 9.1, where Confucius is described as rarely speaking about profit and destiny.

79 Abraham and Torok (1994, 176).

80 Simms (2006, 44). Li (2006, 202), discusses the story of the femme fatale Bao Si, who is castigated for the Western Zhou decline, as a narrative that expresses the contradiction between the prestige of the Western Zhou dynasty and its humiliating end

81 *Chunqiu gongyangzhuan* "Min Gong yuannian.". For critical assessments of this form of historiography, see Liu (1990); Pulleyblank (1962); Yu (1988); Li (1999); Wang (2000).

that shameful knowledge about a lineage's *xiaoyou* identity was subjected to a form of repression before its transmission down family lines. This is how the Chinese historiographical canon called the Springs and Autumn [Annals]. The annals record events that occurred at or were reported to the court of the Lu state (1042-249 B.C.). Confucius, who served at the Lu court, is often attributed as the author.[82] Yuri Pines argues that a more accurate grasp of the text's historicity requires an understanding of its ritualistic form and rhetorical intent, which he claims descended from Western Zhou forms of communication with the ancestors.[83]

Pines resituates the text in a ritual as opposed to a historiographical context, suggesting the content of the events were "reported" (*gao*) to the lineage ancestors, an ancient practice seen in the Mao Ban-*gui* inscription. The *Springs and Autumns* annals were a record of the reports made in the Lu court, they recapitulated the affective conditions during seasonal festival feasts when *xiaoyou* members would make an "announcement of merit." At the same time, the shame avoidant strategies that early commentators identified as a coherent strategy aim to conceal the ritual origins of the behavior, to deny that anything had been lost.[84] This is reflected in "some of the [peculiar] recording patterns in the Annals," structured around taboos.[85] Pines observes that the text's "emphasis on ritual precision" devolves "to the point of denying sociopolitical changes such as 'the ritual 'upgrading'" of the rank nomenclature used to designate "powerful rulers of such states as Chu, Wu, Yue and Qin."[86] Note that this last feature of the *Springs and Autumns* describes an affliction of naming, precisely the neuropsychological context advanced by this line of

82 Confucians associate the discursive strategy of the *Springs and Autumns* with the maintenance of order. Yang (1981); Pines (2009) argue that there is a dearth of evidence that supports the idea that Confucius or his disciples edited the historiography, but suggest that Confucius may have had a hand in its publication or transmission.

83 Pines (2009, 318). Von Falkenhausen (1999, 544) describes Early Eastern Zhou ancestral worship in terms of a lingering cultural homogenization, a legacy of the Western Zhou Ritual Reform: "such archaeologically observable phenomena as the use of more or less uniform sets of ritual paraphernalia, and the adoption of largely comparable burial customs throughout a wide area, may reflect an underlying shared system of politicoreligious values." For other important studies on post-Western Zhou ancestral worship that resonate with this interpretive position, see Cho-yun Hsu (1999, especially 545–562); Cook (2008); Brashier, (2011).

84 Pines (2009, 318, 323). Cf. Kao (1985), who discusses the notion of "criticism by indirection," and Kroll (1985) where rhetorical devices deployed to achieve this objective are concretely analyzed.

85 Kirkpatrick (1995) discusses an implicit "concern with audience and the relative status and power of the writer vis a vis the receiver(s) [which] has a long tradition in China." He suggests that rhetorical practices of inhibited expression were connected to ethical norms of filial piety, which were harnessed for the purpose of promoting a well-ordered and harmonious society.

86 Pines (2009, 320).

inquiry. The verbal suspensions adumbrate fracture lines in a collective psyche that point to the devastating, unspeakable collective experience of the Western Zhou collapse.

The valuation of a discourse characterized by evasive expression during the early Eastern Zhou intersects with the increasing salience in Eastern Zhou texts of discourses on family obligations. If the *Springs and Autumns* functioned as a "quasi-legal means of judging" behavior,[87] it also implicitly served as a family injunction that models a specific grammar, for *how to speak*. It exemplifies the way *xiaoyou* lineages pruned their linguistic surround, to establish new parameters for social discourse.[88] With this in mind, we are in a position to appreciate how Confucian notions of filiality refract the expectations implicit in a lineage grammar established to occlude sight of a traumatic, unmourned loss.

The Evolution of the Confucian Filial Complex

The idea that filiality is the foundation of Confucian social ethics is a widely accepted scholarly view, though there is disagreement over the historical validity of attributing to early Confucian thought a sophisticated conception of it.[89] We saw in the Chapter 2 that tenets of Confucian thought were formed in praxis around a hundred years or so before Confucius articulated them.[90] Rosemont and Ames view Confucian filiality as a "narrative site of conveyance of the cultural corpus of knowledge—linguistic facility and proficiency," that preceded Confucian discourse on it.[91] If the practice predated Confucius, then his attention toward it makes sense; but it does not explain its eventual emergence as a central tenet of Confucian thought.

Given our understanding of the *Springs and Autumns* as a record of ritual reporting rituals that covers up an experiential reality, it is significant that Confucius' views on filial behavior intersect with his concern over his perception of a misalignment between the semantic meaning of words and the real world phenomena that they are deployed to represent. His plea to "(re)align [the relationship between] words" [and reality] (*zhengming*), bespeaks an awareness of disturbances to the social expressive function of language, a consequence of social breakdown. Lisa Raphals argues that the word *zheng* in the *Analects* should "be understood to encompass alignment in multiple senses, including the

87 Ibid.

88 See Chan (2004), which brings together incisive studies of Chinese filial piety by a range of expert sinologists. See also Kutcher (2006), where he delineates how filial piety functioned as the touchstone of a well-ordered society through the propagation and staging of elaborate mourning rituals.

89 Ibid. (130).

90 Von Falkenhausen (2006, 398).

91 Rosemont and Ames (2016, 92).

epistemological, physical, and even cosmological."[92] We have seen how the concept of alignment lies at the core of interdependent mindsets. Its neuropsychological function relates to processes of recalibration necessary to stabilize one's relationship with the environment.

Confucius' own fastidious care with speech is seen by some as a reflection of a concern "that speech not outpace or *conceal* the reality of the speaker's character" (emphasis mine).[93] Although it is true that this sensitivity, also reflected in Confucius' demand that filial grief be sincere, suggests an attitude that favors transparency, I raise the possibility that his outward concern for authenticity is behavior conditioned by the need to screen a lineage secret. The emphasis on sincerity in mortuary contexts screens out the cultic associations of Ritual Reform mourning practice all the while preserving the intrapsychic obligation pressed within its praxis. Confucius' insistence on authentic grief evokes the presence of an unconscious aversive knowledge, like the "Thorny Caltrop's" Interlocutor, who symbolized a gate keeping mechanism for aligning speech and behavior to protect the ancestor's secret.

Confucius models how to behave with this type of transmitted knowledge; it is this aspect of his teaching (*jiao*) that is so visceral. The cognate relationship "between the written forms of the words *xiao* and *jiao*" encourages us to approach Confucius' behavior itself as an implicit model for *xiao* behavior, one shaped by the sociolinguistic conditions of his own upbringing.[94] A closer look at Kong Qiu the man, in comparison with Confucius, the one who teaches about filiality and other social norms, reveals that encoded in Confucius' famous sensitivity to people and situations, is a shameful drama involving the need to keep concealed a lineage secret.

Robert Eno's brilliant investigation into textual traces of Confucius' patrilineal genealogy uncovers disciples' efforts to whitewash biographical information at odds with efforts to preserve an idyllic image of the renowned teacher.[95] His account paints a picture of factions among Confucius' followers, who struggled to subsume Ruist identity under that of Kong Qiu, the name of the man referred to as Master Kong. An obstacle to fashioning a Ruist identity based on Kong Qiu's, teachings, according to Eno, emerged from what appears to have been lexical traces of a tradition that identified Kong Qui as a descendant of a lineage from Zhu Lu or Zou. This territory was considered outside the cultural sphere of the Zhou people, the very object of Confucius's expertise.

Of particular interest is how textual fragments point to Kong Qiu's detachment from his paternal lineage, represented in the oft repeated detail of his *not*

92 Olberding (2014, 12); Raphals (2014).
93 Loy (2014); Olberding (2009).
94 Rosemont and Ames (2016, 93).
95 Eno (2003). See also Goldin (2018, 11).

knowing where his father is buried.[96] Might we not read the psychological strain that Masari Ikezawa has observed in Kong Qiu's views of filial behavior as linked to his own experience of losing a father, the mourning of whom implicitly positioned his attachment to a paternal lineage in conflict with his attachment to a cultural identity that denigrates his patrimonial culture?[97] Could the repeated story of Kong Qiu's unawareness of the place where the literal, physical remains of his father were interred reflect on some level an obstruction to the process of psychically burying and thus mourning (his father)? If so, then the pointed concern with a filial son's sincerity may converge with Kong Qiu's own (unconscious) attempt to retroactively bury and mourn his father.

If the validity of these links can be substantiated, it would unveil a fascinating dimension to the overall cultural processes that the foregoing analysis has proposed. That is, Kong Qiu's personal attempt to bury and mourn his patrilineal inheritance in the face of obstacles posed by an identity deemed clandestine by political realities, intersects with broader collective lineage efforts to bury the traumatic loss of their *xiaoyou* status. In light of Ruist claims to be experts on Zhou ritual precedents, Eno's discovery of efforts to excise or revise records related to Kong Qiu's patrilineal origins reveals Kong Qiu's or early Ruists' failed capacity to accommodate or integrate an outsider cultural status in processes of self-fashioning.[98] This phenomenon mirrors the *Springs and Autumns'* preservative resistance to changing the nomenclature for rulers of polities to reflect real sociopolitical conditions.

Eno's findings suggest that the attribution of a strong association between Confucianism and conceptions of filiality is justified not merely because Confucius and his students established it as a central theme of ethical interest *per se*. Rather, gaps left by efforts to silence what was perceived as clandestine components of his family history call attention to a method of post-mortem identity reconstruction that mimics, albeit on a micro-level, the conditions that led to suspended collective mourning in the wake of Western Zhou collapse. Indeed, upon deeper comparison, one may detect a genealogical relationship between the two: the process of refashioning Confucius' teachings as an "entry point for developing moral competence,"[99] evokes the psychosocial context that

96 Eno (2003, 25). Pulleyblank (2000, 10–11) claims that according to commentary in the *Zuozhuan*, the ruler of Zhulu "received the [Zhou] king's mandate at the request of Duke Huan of Qi…[who] we may infer… had done this as a deliberate attempt to weaken his neighbor Lu. Relations between Zhu Lu and the state of Lu, where Confucius was born remained bad throughout the time Confucius lived, "probably out of resentment on the part of Lu at the changed status of its former dependency." See Pines (2005) for a discussion of the barbarian-civilization dialectic during the Eastern Zhou.

97 Ikezawa (1994).

98 For an argument that the Western Zhou "outsider" status referred to the status of political alliances, not cultural differences see Di Cosmo (2002).

99 Rosemont and Ames, (2008, 124).

lead to King Xiao's Ritual Reform. It is perhaps this resonance between structures of feeling that accounts for the eventual emergence of Confucianism as the dominant creed in imperial China; the evolution of Confucian ideology was informed by this neuropsychological dimension of Chinese cultural reality.

The need for the deliberate elisions and revisions in the construction of Kong Qiu's post-mortem identity arose during the time when Confucius' loosely connected commentary on observed patterns of social behavior started to undergo textual systematization. I submit that this historical juncture is also the time when Kong Qiu takes on the role of cipher. As the word for his patronym, Kong, denotes, he became an "empty space with a huge holding capacity,"[100] in which the fragments of an unutterable collective loss were stored. Kong Qiu's own saga of obstructed mourning made him a perfect emissary of unspoken sagas, yet an emissary whose words and actions can be heard to tell the secret history generating their existence.[101]

This interpretive position offers an optic to understand the ambiguous treatment of the concept of Sky in the *Analects*.[102] For example, Confucius refers to the Pole Star in a simile about good governance: an effective leader's power should emanate in the same way that the celestial north pole exerts its force on the constellations that circle it.[103] This astronomical knowledge of course undergirds all alignment behavior. Confucius suggests the Pole Star's force is one way that "wordless" Sky conveys its principles, about which he claims to have become prescient (*zhi*) at the age of fifty.[104] Nonetheless, in other places, the *Analects* reflects Confucius' ambivalence about the role played by Sky in human affairs. Tensions between optimism that proper performance of rituals effects modulation on the self in ways advantageous to maintaining personal and social integrity even in contexts of social conflict, on the one hand, and a fatalistic notion that life's trajectory is predetermined by the celestial agent Sky, begs the question of why ritual cultivation is necessary in the first place.[105]

The few times that the term Sky is invoked in the *Analects*, other than in combination with the locative word "under" (*xia*), which combined to form a locution that refers to earth below, it is linked to specific affective contexts. These include: the excruciating pain that Confucius experiences at the loss of his favorite student, Yan Hui, whom he loved as a son; or the experience of

100 Kangxi zidian (1985).

101 Cf. Goldin (2018, 108) for a sensitive discussion of the way cultural objects such as the *Analects* "betray their engagement with the intellectual world into which they were released."

102 Song (2018),

103 *Lunyu,* 2.1 Cf. 19.2, where Confucius likens a bad ruler to "an eclipse of the sun and moon in that when he errs the whole world sees him doing so."

104 *Lunyu,* 2.4. Cf. 17.19, where Confucius speaks about Heaven's silent but clear communication through the seasons. Cf. Valmisa (2019, 51).

105 Puett (2019) also addresses these issues from a theoretical perspective.

submitting to Sky's evaluation of the propriety of his actions, in the knowledge that if Sky did not find them aligned it would lead to Sky's disgust (*yan*) (and implicitly Confucius' social rejection); contrastively, Confucius invokes Sky to express self-assurance that the virtue it instilled in him protects him from other's harm; finally, Confucius invokes Sky when he speaks of the pleasure of self-satisfaction upon cognizance that his disposition had developed to the extent that every desire and deed automatically aligned with Sky's principles.[106]

Confucius' reference to his own behavior as something that could be measured with a "carpenter's I-square [*ju*], an instrument that measures celestial alignments,"[107] resonates with the Ritual Reform notion of "modeled behavior" (*xing*), and its concrete source of inspiration, the spatiotemporal position of Well. It also evokes the alignment of the planets which the Zhou invoked as proof of Sky's bestowal of a mandate to rule. Although Csikszentmihalyi views Confucius' concept of a celestial mandate as an "abstract classical political theory," (and hence devoid of astronomical intentions), he persuasively calls attention to Confucius' mediating role in adapting the concept of a Sky mandate,

> a doctrine that originally supported the ruling clan, to argue that [Sky's] influence was expressed through particular concrete expressions of individual virtue. As a result of this adaptation in writings associated with Confucius, the ruler's conduct of imperial rituals, performance of filial piety, or other demonstrations of personal virtue provided proof of moral fitness that legitimated his political authority. As with the rituals and the virtues, filial piety and the mandate of [Sky] were transformed as they were integrated with the classics through the voices of Confucius and the rulers and disciples of his era.[108]

What is missing from this edifying account is an explanation for why, if concepts of a celestial mandate relate to a ruler's political claim to legitimacy, it would find relevance in the context of a filial son's grief over a parent's death or filial behavior more generally. Why, especially since Confucius' focus is consistently more directed toward rituals' regulating functions in terms of tempering bad

---

106 *Lunyu,* 11.9 for Sky and grief; 3.13 and 6.28 reference Sky's agency to reject, 7.23; for Sky's protection see 7.23; for self-satisfaction see 2.4

107 *Lunyu,* 2.4. Pankenier (2013, 117–121), attributes the concept of a celestial pivot around which stars wheel to Thuban's function; likewise, he similarly attributes the late Zhou metaphysical focus on a mysterious void to obsolescence of Thuban as a signifier for true north.

108 Csikszentmihalyi (2020).

behavior, does the concept of an external source of political legitimacy, and agency, even have salience?[109]

I submit that the integration of the Western Zhou belief in Sky's agency into a framework of family rooted values and injunctions about how to enact them is a function of the fact that the *xiaoyou* lineage identity origins were inextricably linked to the royal Zhou family's state project. As investiture-related bronze inscriptions have shown, *xiaoyou* saw themselves as having received the mandate by virtue of the king's distributed personhood. This process is reflected in the inscriptional record by the word "mandate" (*ming*) to refer to the king's orders.[110] What the king distributes is the potency of his lineage (*de*). As receivers and consumers of the potency, symbolized by dried meat which had been sacrificed, sliced, distributed, and collectively ingested by *xiaoyou* members, they were linked to Sky's and the celestial ancestors' intentions in their efforts to support and protect the Zhou's supremacy.[111]

Confronted with the question of how to make sense of their part in discharging the royal Zhou family's charge to carry out Sky's intentions, the *xiaoyou* lineages had to navigate the shame and dissonance caused by Sky's behavior, reifying Zhou supremacy with a planetary conjunction one day, and the next, within three generations, withdrawing support to the degree that the Zhou were knocked off their high status axis.[112] The social effects of this psycholinguistic process are intimated in a couple of odd statements uttered by Confucius related to Sky. I point to these because they seem grandiose or inappropriate for Confucius' social position; his behavior implies a prerogative premised on an intimate relationship with Sky. We've noted a positive cadence to Confucius' self-biographical account of his progress toward intuiting Sky's mandate by the time he turned fifty. When compared to another fifty-year old whose fine accomplishments—great renown earned through achieved status and rank—Confucius praised, the former seems unusually lofty.[113]

There are also statements in which Confucius' represents himself as one whose acts would be observed and responded to by Sky, as a Zhou ruler, in other words. For example, he appears to ventriloquize the distress of a royal leader confronted with a deviant sign that implies Sky's disfavor when he wonders if his end is near since the "Phoenix and River Chart" have failed to appear. Whose royal perspective does he express when he claims to have not observed astronomical phenomena that portended dynastic founding? Whose concern does he express

109 Cf. Pines (2002, 64), where he suggests that "actively seeking [Sky's] support was replaced by the implicit recommendation to avoid direct conflict with its laws."

110 Von Falkenhausen et al. (2011, 258).

111 Ibid.

112 Scholars have pointed to poems in the *Book of Poetry* that evoke grief and hardship. See Riegel (1997); Raphals (2021).. Cf. the poem "Jie Nanshan "in *Shijijng*: "Grief is burning in their hearts, not daring to jest or speak… the state lies in ruins."

113 *Lunyu*, 9.23.

over the meaning of their absence? In the same vein, why does he express rage at Sky, who he impugns as the source of his misfortune when confronted with his favorite student's *premature death*?[114]

Edward Slingerland interprets Confucius' inconsistent use of the word *ming* as a signal for a bifurcated conception of "reality"; "*ming* refers to forces that lie in the outer realm," while cultivation is to be carried out in the internal realm, which should be the primary focus of all "gentleman."[115] Slingerland suggests that Confucius' conception of self-cultivation was inherently rewarding for those who commit to self-cultivation within the concealed, internal arena, before turning outward to deal with the vicissitudes of *ming*. Slingerland concludes that this bifurcated conception reflects a "realistic and mature redirection of human energy toward the sole area of life in which one does have control, the cultivation and moral improvement of one's own self, coupled with a faith in the ability of self-cultivation to produce in one an attitude of joyful acceptance of all that life may bring."[116]

The theory that Confucius' "slippage" into a discourse of "blind fate" might be construed as a "device to distinguish between the realm that is solely under one's own control and the one that is not" makes psychological sense.[117] While Slingerland does not go so far as to claim that this conception may itself be a compensatory strategy to assuage the Master's career disappointments, his sensitivity to the possibility that that defensive mechanisms may be a factor invites us to read between the lines a bit more. Confucius' preference for carrying out the work of cultivation on the inner realm resonates with his proscription to a filial son to observe carefully his father's demeanor so that his speech and actions may be imitated by the filial son for the three years post-mortem. Internal cultivation aims to facilitate the "grasping" of an ancestor's aversive grammar and semantics. Internal self-cultivation, in other words, may be understood as an adapted iteration of the fantasy structure where alignment of "internal stimuli" and suppression of external stimuli were required for the preservation of psychic integrity.

---

114 For the "Phoenix and River Chart" comment see *Lunyu,* 9.9. For Confucius' inconsolability and Sky see: 11.9.

115 Slingerland (1996, 568). See also Goldin (2014, 55).

116 Slingerland (1996, 568–569). Cf. (567), where he cites David Hume for an epitaph: "We hang in perpetual suspense between life and death, health and sickness, plenty and want; which are distributed amongst the human species by secret and unknowable causes whose operation is oft unexpected and always unaccountable." See also Song (2018, 119), where she contextualizes Slingerland's interpretation in the evolutionary history of divination techniques. Song links Confucius' unfixed concept of *ming* to the evolution of divination assumptions and practices. She sees Confucius' concept of fate as representative of yarrow divination presuppositions, that view a cosmos that operates according to inherent patterns, as opposed to Shang bone divinations, which presumed "a universe in which willful spirts exercise their power on human beings" (12).

117 Slinglerland (1996, 576–577).

While Slingerland claims Confucius' use of *ming* is descriptive, when read with the what he describes in fact emerges as much more "normative" than he allows. Reading between the lines, the inconsistency with which Confucius deploys this term points to a disturbance in the memorialization of King Xiao among *xiaoyou* members who engaged in the king's distributed personhood through ritual participation and feasting.[118] Put in other terms, I interpret Confucius' seemingly personal interactions with Sky as "ventriloquized" expressions representative of a mental topography in which King Xiao and his (retroactive) ignominy were secreted internally, separate from the "external world." From this perspective, if internal self-cultivation leads to joyful acceptance, we must also understand the acceptance to be a tacit statement of the same relief experienced by King Xiao when the illusory feast effectively ushered the ghost away.

Returning once again to Confucius' famous self-description that he "transmits [knowledge] but not to establish [an independent position]" we can now appreciate how it exquisitely and poignantly articulates the neuropsychological mindset of a filial son; his processes of self-fashioning is constrained by the unrecognized pact of concealment between him and an ancestor who transformed an event into a secret and transmitted it transgenerationally down *xiaoyou* family lines as a lexical structure, a mindset.[119]

We are now in a position to suggest that Confucius' implicit requirement that a bereaved filial son deny fulfillment of an appetitive affective is an ideational byproduct of the evolution of the structure of feeling I have traced in the preceding chapters. More specifically, I see in its logic a mutation of the psychic topography represented in "Thorny Caltrop." Whereas the ghost's exorcism was accomplished through the fantasy of incorporation, which conveyed "it is fine to be a corpse" through the dramatization of successful ingestion of the food, the crimes imputed to King Xiao upon the Western Zhou collapse implicated this exorcistic strategy of illusory fulfillment. The filial son's rejection of libidinal satisfaction reimagines King Xiao's "corpse" status in order to screen its associations with gustatory pleasure (albeit illusory).

Unlike the ghost in "Thorny Caltrop" who returns to teach his ancestor the ruse of illusory satiety as a technique to resist topographical transformation, the ghost in Confucius' paradigm returns to "test" the commitment of the living son to preserve the secret as he continues to exist in life. Confucian filiality proclaims that it is desirable to deny all libidinal satisfaction in order to demonstrate one's sincere commitment to being *xiao*. The consistent link between filiality and withdrawal from gustatory pleasure recapitulates the fantasy structure even as its

118 Cf. Li (2006, 198–203) where he suggests that the famous femme fatale story that explains the Western Zhou fall may have arisen from the need to blame someone for the shame.

119 Rashkin (1992, 44).

content represents a mutation. Both evoke the way a concealed secret takes over a subject's mind, and both offer a strategy to subdue, if not completely eradicate its tormenting power. In place of the "it is fine to be a corpse" Confucian filiality silently transmits "it is fine to be *xiao*."

The psychic source of the filial child's prolonged grief is the same one that drives Confucius' apparent fastidiousness, and "seriousness with regard to words."[120] "If the mat was not "straight" (the same word used to describe the filial son who conceals father's shame), he did not sit." Both behaviors speak to the subject's need to "verify congruence," so that speech and act align with unconscious lexical rules for concealing shame.[121] Thus does the filial complex stage the identity of the son and ancestor as secret sharers, complicit in guarding an undivulged secret association with a retroactively shamed King Xiao, whose posthumous name came to signify a practice devoted to its concealment.[122] Confucius' historical channeling capacity may account for his status as "ghost" author of texts, such as the *Springs and Autumns,* a lineage record organized by a grammar renders its context illegible to all but the psycholinguistically initiated. Confucianism served to safeguard the collective *xiaoyou* secret as it also served to cryptically transmit it.

Representations of Avenging Ghosts and Ghoulish Filial Behavior: A Kinship

The filial complex was generated in response to a drama that had to be cut off from view. This section turns attention to representational behavior, manifested in texts where narrative structures and tropes (written and imagistic) depict and comment on filial behavior. The focus is narrow but lends itself to broader application in the analysis of many other forms of Chinese cultural production. Because we are interested in the drama that required occlusion, Stephen Feuchtwang's analysis of "the avenging ghost as a paradigm of a shameful past" in narrative texts serves as a helpful jumping off point. Feuchtwang argues that Chinese avenging ghost stories "enact a drama of unbidden retrieval... ghost stories seem to be telling us about a line of repression such that what might have been the past is silenced and then returns."[123]

---

120 *Lunyut* 1.14.

121 Pankenier (2013,142–143), uses this term to refer to the psychological motivation driving Chinese divinatory behavior, which sought to verify the Shang dynasty kings' acts as seeking to "verify congruence" with celestial conditions.

122 Cf. Rosemont and Ames (2008, 125): "Xiao is certainly the support that succeeding older generations enjoy form the progeny that follow, but it is also the vital process whereby the younger generation is transformed into and becomes a novel yet persistent variant of those to whom they have deferred...The older generation literally lives on in the bodies and lived experience of the generations that follow."

123 Feuchtwang (2003, 11).

Feuchtwang's insight can be deepened when contextualized with our understanding of preservative repression. "Stories of avenging ghosts set up two alternatives: forgotten pasts and pasts that return to haunt and possess. Moreover, the second of these is a demand for a third past, which is that of due recognition or bidden recall."[124] This chain of repressions and returns evokes the haunting effects on descendants of forbidden knowledge about an ancestor's shame. Feuchtwant is alert to the way that the narratives point to the inability to assign the ghost "to a past" as the cause for its return.

We are now in a position to recognize the blindness to the avenging ghost's past as a function of a mindset organized by preservative repression. Stimulated by emotional conditions that threaten activation of unconsciously prohibited (taboo) words, "Thorny Caltrop" revealed the existential experience of haunting was a function of a psyche's sense of the presence of something alterior to itself yet exerting control. Ghost stories offer a reprieve from haunting in the same way a fantasy does, they give expression to a family secret through patterns of lexical deferment that effectively hide it. The writing and consumption of ghost stories "sanction what is repressed and fantastic."[125]

Avenging ghost stories dramatize the influence on the living of catastrophes experienced by their ancestor. The same can be said for representations of extreme filial behavior, which also articulate a pain without awareness of why it is there or that it is shared with an ancestor. The blurring of existential boundaries between life and death—a mainstay in ghost stories—is implicit in representations of extreme filial behavior. This may explain a persistent focus on "obsessive," "exaggerated," or "bizarre" actions in representations of Eastern Zhou, Han, and medieval filial behavior, especially some that are particularly extreme in the degree of "self-sacrifice" and "self-abnegation" involved to actualize filial obligations. Donals Holzman's observation that this type of behavior was a quasi-religious expression of "fanaticism" recalls the charismatic relationship between King Xiao and *xiaoyou*, as well as the messianic dimensions of Qin self-representation, to which we will return shortly.[126] Although Keith Knapp observes that such extreme representations reflect efforts by patriarchs to use *xiao* behavior to preserve a "politically fragmented world,"[127] he does not directly explain why representing bizarre behavior is the best means to achieve this.

Still, the insight that representations of extreme filial behavior respond to the challenges of a "politically fragmented world" emphasizes the emotional conditions that gave rise to their mediating function. This study suggests that filial complex functions to sustain the integrity of a collective psyche fragmented by suspended mourning. From this position, representations of

124 Ibid.
125 Ibid.
126 Holzman (1998, 198).
127 Knapp (2005, 188).

obsessive and bizarre filial behavior conjure a subject who is haunted by an avenging ghost, even though the ghost's presence is not overt as in the stories. This interpretation reads the fanaticism as a symptom of the noxious effects of a transmitted family secret that distorts the personalities of filial sons. At the root of avenging ghost stories and representations of extreme forms of filial behavior lies a noncoherence loaded with pains, humiliations, and constant threats to self-fashioning. The knot of ambiguities and anxieties that made ghosts into avengers and filial sons into self-abnegators can be unraveled to reveal co-evolutionary contiguities.

Gegu liaoqin as Cryptic Dramatization

Perhaps the filial behavioral form that most viscerally evokes the context of haunting is a behavior called *gegu liaoqin*. The nomenclature for this behavior describes it: "slicing one's thigh to repair an ailing parent." The earliest representations of this extreme behavior have been traced to the 8th century, and they were viewed by contemporaries as problematic.[128] The unease and inconsistency with regard to how representations of extreme filial behavior should be assessed among intellectuals and officials, derives in part from the conventionalization of Confucian filial norms into precepts for shame-avoidant behavior.[129] The main issue was the incongruity of self-mutilating acts and normative ideas about filiality and protection, such as the prohibition against harming one's body, which was popularized by the *Canon of Filiality* (*Xiaojing*) compiled during the third century B.C.[130]

This prohibition was linked to the Western Zhou *xiaoyo*u identity as protectors; whereas during the Western Zhou the object of protection was the king and his sovereign status, in Eastern Zhou the object of protection had become the descendant's body. The shift can be explained in terms of the transgenerational transmission of an encrypted secret: in order to perpetuate the crypt that concealed King Zhao and his shame in King Xiao's psyche, an inherited obligation, King Xiao too had to be "swallowed" and incorporated. The hyperbolic commitment to protecting the physical body is understandable if we construe the body as an analogue for psychic integrity. For collective self-fashioning to continue, the body that the filial sons must at all cost protect is not in fact their own, but rather *his*, that is, King Xiao's.

This framework helps contextualize *gegu liaoqin* acts and explain why they were socially perceived in terms of filial devotion. It is deeply entrenched in the

128 Qiu (1995).

129 Ibid.

130 Qiu (1995, 49–51) For an in depth discussion of the compilation, composition and philosophy of the *Xiaojing*, see Ikezawa (1994). Rosemont and Ames (2008, 105) claim vigilance in protecting the body is where filiality began.

popular imagination, the topos continues to appear in contemporary culture such as film and literature.[131] The following analysis first interprets the behavior outside of its representational context, and then reconciles this interpretation with the historical conditions in which the first representations of the behavior emerged.

Gegu liaoqin is maladaptive behavior which stages a filial child's haunting by a shameful family secret. The salience of shame as a motivating source of extreme filial behavior we saw ubiquitous in Eastern Zhou, Warring States and Han dynasty texts, and this is the case in accounts of *gegu liaoqin* behavior. Although a filial child's sense of shame is sometimes (vaguely) linked to his inability to materially or spiritually offer devotion to his living or deceased elders,[132] extreme behavior more often than not is represented as just as concerned with the *avoidance* of bringing shame to their family.[133]

The first step toward reconstructing the secret that the filial child stages with *gegu liaoqin* behavior is to show how the words that refer to the acts—in the epithet—in fact are words that articulate the secret by disguising it. We have seen how secrets may be uncovered by identifying lexical patterns of deferment that work in concert to conceal a shameful event. A logical starting point is to consider how the words describing the act of "splitting the thigh" (*gegu*) may in fact disguise the true source of the represented extreme behavior.

The verb *ge*, "to slice," the first word of epithet, has a deep history in Chinese written texts, where it originally connoted the act of "ritually splitting meat used for ancestral sacrifices."[134] The splitting rituals were most certainly carried out with the expectation of incurring the blessings of the objects of sacrifice, the dynasty's founding ancestors.[135] By ingesting the meat sacrificed to the ancestors, the feudal lords were in line to receive the benefits received by the ruling clan. Most certainly associated with *xiao* offering rituals, the practice of *ge* "splitting and separating

131 See Bachner (2018), for example for an analysis of the trope in contemporary contexts.

132 Qiu (1995, 51–50) cites many examples of narrative from the Tang histories, *Jiu Tang shu* and the *Gujin tushu jicheng*, in which shame figures in the motivation of the filial child's slicing of flesh.

133 See for example the chapter entitled "Stimulated Responses" (Ganying) in the *Xiaojing*, (1980, 2559). Cf. the description of the filial child as one who does not disgrace one's relatives, which is listed as the second most important way to manifest filial behavior, in the *Liji*. See also Ikezawa (1994, 222), where he discusses textual issues of filiation between the *Liji* and the *Xiaojing*. Liu Qingping (2003; 2006) engages in a lengthy discussion of this paradoxical position, as does Zhang (2006). For an in-depth analysis of a Ming Dynasty gegu tale, see Sibau (2018).

134 This is how it is defined in China's oldest dictionary. See Zhou (1984, 26).

135 Yang (2017) he resonance between this ritual and slicing/dividing within Jewish culture/history is a topic that may yield further insights. Acts of splitting/slicing to enact or seal a covenant have been discussed as "key fossils" to understanding the psychoanalytical dimension of the emergence of certain practices (Lewis, 2006).

meat" and *zuo* "distribution of the meat to feudal lords" was thus crucial for maintaining the balance between kingly and feudal power. The expectation of reciprocity is also indicated by the frequent use in bronze inscriptions of the word "to split" as a variant for the word "to beg for ancestors' blessing" (*gai*). During the Western Zhou these two words were exact homophones.[136]

I have emphasized how a bond of reciprocity between subjects who sacrifice to the dynastic founding ancestors animated the relationship between the Zhou king and his subjects. After the sacrifice, the divided meat was distributed to and a share was *eaten* by *xiaoyou*, to commemorate publicly the reciprocity. The *xiaoyou* "would in turn present a share of the meats to their respective regional subjects and receive meats from their followers in turn."[137] We have seen how these ritualized acts of division, presentation, and consumption symbolically functioned as a form of bereavement language that simulated mourning, that is, "swallowing" and "digesting" King Zhao's shameful death. These ritualized acts of communal food consumption established the foundation on which social contracts were built and bound *xiaoyou* members together.[138]

Figurative swallowing and digestion are also the motivating aim of *gegu liaoqin* behavior. This overlap between the aims of the extreme behavior and the King Xiao's reforms is sensical given the evolutionary link between the filial complex in general and suspended mourning triggered by the Western Zhou's collapse. The apotheosis of all *gegu liaoqin* stories is the transcendence over health obstacles catalyzed by a parent's consumption and digestion of a son's self-carved thigh flesh. To understand the internal logic that explains these curative results, we must comprehend that the specific object to be consumed, thigh flesh, functions as a word that hides another, shameful, word. It is a cryptonym. This is to say that the true source of the curative effect attributed to the consumption of thigh flesh lies in the way the word cuts something off from view and thus allows a pretense of having swallowed and digested something that in fact is psychically prohibited, in other words, it reflects yet another cultural behavior whose neuropsychological origins can be traced to the same emotional source.

I argue that the visual vivacity of the image of a sliced "thigh" diverts attention from other like-sounding words, homophones, such as the word "shameful crime" (*gu*).[139] I consider the latter to be a spurned word concealed by the word

136 Quan (1989, 454).

137 Li (1991, 39); Li (2013, 146).

138 Li (1991, 96–97). In addition to facilitating mourning processes, the acts performed a double sociopolitical function: they sanctioned the establishment of branch lineages as a way to legitimate control over a geographical domain, while they also reined in this authority by subsuming it under the larger lineage pattern of the Zhou ruling clan

139 Bernard Karlgren (1957, 33, 34) and Axel Schuessler (2007, 259) provide phonetic reconstructions that reflect a homophonous connection between the word "thigh" and the word *gu*, "ancient, which functions as a phonetic determinant in the graph that means "shameful crime." Both of the latter two words were used interchangeably in Western Zhou bronze inscriptions, Quan (1989, 84).

"thigh." Not only is the spurned word rendered edible but its ingestion is assumed to be a catalyst for healing. The "kin" (*qin*) who are cured are the kin referred to in the "Rules" gloss on King Xiao's temple name: those *xiaoyou* lineages whose relations King Xiao's reforms aimed to harmonize. Once again the behavior bears witness to the existence of mechanisms that adopt the literal meaning of one word to elide others that were used as metaphors to shame the kin annuls humiliation. Metaphors of dejection and self-abnegation seen in representations of obsessive forms of filial behavior, are neutralized in *gegu liaoqin*, which pretends, rather, that disgraceful metaphors refer to valued objects, such as thigh flesh. *Gegu liaoqin* implements literally something that had "figurative meaning, ('swallowing a loss'), by "openly adopting the literal meaning of the words associated with the humiliation."[140]

From this perspective, we discern the internal logic driving the production of *gegu liaoqin* story as a fantasy of swallowing produced to reassure an avenging ghost that his secret is in fact secure. Although the fantasy's reassurance rests on its denial of the magnitude of the *xiaoyou* ancestors' shameful loss, its very existence as a cultural object reveals that the shameful memories cannot accept exclusion, and the related words continue to engage in subversive action,[141] waiting, as it were, for the right cocktail of neuropsychohistorical conditions to summon their emergence in the form of radical practices. Deeper investigation into the historical conditions in which the first representations of *gegu liaoqin* practice emerged, may yield evidence that explains what summoned the return of the avenging ghost.

For example, the fact that the practice emerged during the Tang dynasty (618-907), soon after a time of unprecedented female rule raises the possibility that this sociopolitical deviance triggered the ghost's return. Consider the fact that Empress Wu Zetian (r. 690-705), after *usurping* the throne, named her dynasty after the (Western) *Zhou*; and the fact that she attempted to justify her rule by instituting *radical new policies* that redefined concepts of *sovereignty*; and the fact that these conditions coalesced in a reign of *censorship*. As the italicized words highlight, these repressive sociopolitical and linguistic conditions created an environment in which social circulation of metaphors of censorship and repression threatened the preservation of the "kin's" secret, borne from similar circumstances. While the historical validity of this hypothesis cannot be resolved now, it highlights one type of research that this book hopes to generate. Recent studies on the politics of mourning and the evolution of specific mortuary practices during the Han Dynasty reinforce the potential of this approach.[142]

140 Abraham and Torok (1994, 126).
141 Ibid.
142 Brown (2012) and Brashier (2011).

The Shaping Legacy of the Ritual Reform on Qin Imperial Identity

Embedded within a chapter about the Qin Dynasty (221-206 B.C.) founder's royal genealogy, the Han dynasty historian, Sima Qian, narrates a scenario that attributes the establishment of the Qin state to King Xiao. The passage records a conversation held between King Xiao and Shen, a ruler of a northwestern polity and old ally of the Zhou.[143] This polity was located within the crucial geographical area surrounding Canine Precipice, where King Yih—King Xiao's nephew—purportedly died. Sima recounts Shen's objections to King Xiao's desire to settle on Feizi, his extraordinary horse breeder, leadership over the Daluo clan. Shen resists, arguing that King Xiao's intentions betray marriage alliances between his and the Daluo tribes, and he reminds King Xiao of the latter's dependence upon their support for his royal succession.[144] Upon hearing Shen's remonstrance, King Xiao subsequently changed his mind and instead "partitioned" (*fen*) a parcel of Zhou land and installed Feizi as the founder of a Qin state:

> King Xiao said: "In the past, Bo Yi took charge of domestic animals for Emperor Shun and the animals were proliferous; therefore he received land and was awarded the surname Ying. Now, his descendant also breeds horses for me. I will partition my land and make [his descendant, Feizi] a dependent [of Zhou]." [King Xiao] settled [Feizi] at Qin, where he carried on the ancestral sacrifices of the Ying clan; [Feizi] was called Ying of Qin. [King Xiao] also did not abandon the heir of the Daluo lineage, who was a son of the Ruler of Shen's daughter, in order to harmonize the relationship with the Western Rong.[145]

This extended dialogue, noted by historian Li Feng as unique to Sima's history, intersects with this investigation's line of inquiry in several significant ways.[146] First we might point out the thematic resonance between King Xiao's infatuation with Feizi and his father, King Mu's, relationship with his renowned charioteer, Zao Fu.[147] King Mu's reputation as the first to ride extensively beyond China's northwestern borders was widespread in Warring States (448-

143 Li (2006, 202 et passim) discusses how Shen's displeasure with King You (781–772 B.C.) catalyzed the concerted attack with other northwestern polities that caused the Western Zhou fall.

144 Li (2006, 270) suggests that a relationship between Shen, Daluo, and the Zhou formed a "triangle [which] may have served as the foundation of the security of the Zhou's western frontier."

145 Ibid.

146 Ibid.

147 Ibid. For King Mu and Zao Fu see *Shiji* "Zhao shijia."

221 B.C.) texts.[148] Scholars have shown how "the horse was a critical element in the establishment of [Western Zhou] military, and hence political, authority," especially with regard to his rebuilding of the Zhou army with the support of their western nomadic neighbors.[149] King Xiao's interest in installing Feizi thus implies a desire to provide an equine source for strong defense as modeled by his father.[150]

Second, the narrative implicitly raises concerns about the rise of the state of Qin, whose post-Western Zhou ascendancy though ignored in the Springs and Autumns period, nonetheless constituted "one of the most significant developments in the aftermath of the fall of the Western Zhou." Paying heed to the "symbolical importance of the Qin occupation of the Zhou heartland," which acknowledges how the Qin had successfully posited itself as both the proximate ally and the rightful heir of the Zhou house, this section examines trends in Qin political self-representation as an example of behavior that was conditioned by the Qin's early relationship with the Western Zhou.[151]

Archaeological evidence discovered at what scholars believe to be remains of three Qin cities dating from the late Western Zhou strongly demonstrates a comprehensive adherence to rituals put into place by the Ritual Reform.[152] Paleographic sources attest to the loyalty of the Qin, perhaps in part because of marriage alliances: in an early Eastern Zhou bronze inscription, Zhou princesses are depicted as performing ancestral rites to the Qin.[153] These two sets of data suggest the Zhou and the Qin shared a high degree of intimacy, something that is reflected in the fact that Qin is the only state visited by a Zhou king after the Western Zhou fall, when the practice of royal excursions was abolished. Yuri Pines goes as far to suggest that the Qin royal house enjoyed a "special relations" status with the Zhou, citing Falkenhausen's claim that the "Qin stretched its ostensible loyalty toward the Zhou to the point of identification with the Zhou—an identification that could, and eventually did lead to the latter's replacement by a new Qin dynasty."[154] These insights into the affective nature of the Qin relationship with the Zhou prepare us to trace the development of Qin identity in terms of the neuropsychological response

148 Cf. Khayutina (2010, 55), whose study of the "geopolitical polyphony" of Zhou administrative practices reveals that King Mu "entered into privileged partnership with some non-Zhou rulers, entrusting to them the communication with other aliens." She concludes that King Mu performed investitures of non-Zhou regional rulers in order to include them in the Zhou political hierarchy.

149 Silbergeld (1985,160). For Zaofu's reputation, see Knoblock (1994, 43, 107, 162).

150 Cf. use of epithet for King Mu, "model" or "correct template," (*xing*), on the Shi Qiang-pan, Shaughnessy (1992).

151 Khayutina et al. (2010, 275).

152 Zhao (2013, 6); Teng (2013, 80).

153 Pines et al. (2013, 16).

154 Ibid., 16, 44.

to the sociopolitical humiliation experienced by the Zhou royal family when they were forced to migrate, a time that coincided with the birth of the Qin state.

Although Sima's record of King Xiao's role as catalyst for a Qin state contains anachronisms that raises doubt about its veracity,[155] and even if Sima's history betrays an effort to cast aspersion on the legitimacy of the Qin's imperial claim,[156] the account is remarkable for its portrait of a vision of King Xiao whose vision of royal prerogative reveals it to be starkly at odds with the dependence of the Zhou on marriage alliances to bolster their hold on lineage supremacy. In other words, the account of the origins of the Qin state encodes negative perceptions of King Xiao's reforms. Edwin Pulleyblank has shown that the Shen shared the same surname as the female progenitor of the Zhou clan, Jiang, and was an old marriage partner of the Zhou, extending back to pre-dynastic times.[157] These relationships are the source of tension that runs through the account of King Xiao's desire to install Feizi as the Daluo lineage head.

King Xiao's recorded intention evokes the role lineage segmentation played in establishing his own political legitimacy. Sima contextualizes this favoritism as a source of strain amongst those polities who were already considered *family* through maternal marriage alliances. King Xiao's means for resolving the conflict was to absorb Feizi into the broad ritual fold of agnatic affiliations—the *xiaoyou* system—by installing Feizi as the heir to the lineage of his father's charioteer. King Xiao's insistence that this settlement involves the performance of ancestral sacrifices to the Ying as well as to the royal Zhou lineage, articulates the reciprocal contract guaranteed by Zhou sovereignty to its *xiaoyou*. The contract was likely sanctioned by the ritualistic distribution (*fen*) of sliced meat.[158]

155 The narrative includes a reference to "Emperor Shun," a figure who many scholars believe to have been a culturally "constructed" Warring States meme signifying an ideal of sage kingship. Cf. Peter Boodberg (1937, 187) who suggests that the origins of the Yao and Shun mythic narratives lie in the "semanticization of bisyllabified (or dimidiated) forms of words that emerged to register the increasing obsolescence of consonantal clustered initials."

156 Hans van Ess (2013) advances the provocative argument that Sima's historical depiction of the First Emperor reflects a pointed historiographical intention to critique the reigning emperor, Wudi more than an interest in "objective" historiography. This position is premised on what he sees as the deliberate deployment of narrative strategies that emphasize the megalomania of the First Emperor as excessively hubristic.

157 Pulleyblank (2000).

158 Li (1991).

Sima's juxtaposition of this contract with Shen's cautionary warning, tacitly impugns King Xiao's actions as hubristic. It may be this perception of excess as the source of the Qin dependency that elicits from Sima's pen an implication of illicitness,[159] a position suggested by the literal meaning of Feizi's name, "not" (*fei*) [the] "son" (*zi*).[160] While this cadence might be explained in terms of Sima rigorous interrogation of the legitimacy of the Qin state's eventual claim to imperial power (and by extension the claim made by the reigning emperor of Sima's time),[161] the accurate depiction of geopolitical and social conditions that existed during King Xiao's reign offers compelling reasons to consider the historian's account as transmitting something of historical value.

Although the singularity of Sima Qian's account requires caution when using it for historical reconstruction, the record reflects, on the intuitive level, that something about the preservation of King Xiao's memory was for some reason relevant to the historian's understanding of the factors that explain the Qin's political ascendance. The scenario painted by Sima reflects his renowned psychological apperception, but I am inclined to suspect that the source of Sima Qian's punctiliousness toward the First Emperor's display of hubris, and the way it was reproduced as per imperial operation, may lie beyond the historian's own awareness.[162]

This is to say that Sima's narrative tacitly transmits an ancient, buried historiographical position that King Xiao was a usurper, a ruler who arrogated power transgressively. Although we saw traces of a criminalization of King Xiao's calendrical reforms in the negative turn taken in the semantic evolution of astro-calendrical terminology, Sima's account brings to the fore the genealogical implications of viewing Qin as the result or issue of a bond between them and King Xiao: Qin is framed as inheriting King Xiao's hubris. He paints a portrait of the Qin state's patrimonial origins, and in doing so reveals the Qin state as an illegitimate issue of King Xiao's reforms.

In addition to the overwhelming archaeological evidence that testifies to a single-minded devotion to King Xiao's ritual system, it is pertinent to consider the historical fact that the Qin lineage was elevated from the position of dependency to the position of regional lord as a result of the "crucial support" provided "to the Zhou dynasty during the crisis of 771," as the Zhou was forced

159 Pines et al. (2013, 43). Pines (2013, 272) discusses the hubris of the First Emperor's "peculiar self-representation" as the initiator of something novel, different, non-contiguous to conclude that it is reflective of "serious political considerations." Van Ess (2013, 257) interprets Sima Qian's focus on the First Emperor's hubris as indirect criticism of his reigning Emperor, Han Wudi.

160 The historical delegitimization of King Xiao's reign bears traces of the processes used by King Xiao to delegitimize Kings Gong and Yih who preceded him, which severed them from the group of royal ancestors who always received sacrifice.

161 Pines, (2013, 227–238).

162 Van Ess (2013).

into migration.[163] This rank elevation, which would have been publicly displayed in accordance with the sumptuary rules of the Ritual Reform, and would surely have been a huge source of pride as it would have made the Qin central players in the *xiaoyou* coalition.

That the birth of statehood coincided with devastating political and social crises, however, nullified the prestige that had previously accompanied such ranking, given that the Zhou lineage had lost all but a modicum of real power. Isolated geographically in the wastes of the Western Zhou territory, devoid of the affective relations created by the then defunct Zhou coalition, the Qin state existed as a social orphan. Moreover, the fact that, notwithstanding the symbolic value of the Zhou's acknowledgment of Qin service, it is likely that they were viewed with as much if not deeper suspicion than the aristocratic lineages regarded each other, given that Qin assistance presumably included negotiations with the attacking enemies.[164] The disappointing reality of the emptiness of the Zhou king's recognition of Qin statehood, combined with the fact that public bereavement of Western Zhou decline became impractical, convokes a set of specific psychosocial conditions, that shaped the emergence of a royal Qin identity.

The coalescence of these conditions presented obstacles to Qin self-fashioning in the early years of its development. The central role in Qin identity formation played by King Xiao's sumptuary rules is borne out in the archaeological record, which clearly reveals the extent to which the Qin drew affective sustenance from mourning rituals and norms organized according to rank. Sima's account of this birth emphasizes how it was marked by the public excoriation of King Xiao's hubristic abrogation of power. While the emergence of social behavior such as the filial complex tacitly enunciates the collective consequences of blocked mourning, the singularity of the Qin lineage's rhetorical audacity with regard to their self-identification with King Xiao, suggests a vantage point from which to view the shaping effect of this psychological condition on the development of a single family line's identity. Whether it is because, as Sima's account suggests, King Xiao was the one who personally included the Qin into the agnatic system of *xiaoyou* relations, or because the rituals they adhered to so reverently were products of the *xiao* reforms, the Qin's projected self-image bears traces of an

163 Pines et al. (2013, 13).

164 Lord Mu of Qin, "represent[ed] the [Zhou] central states" in negotiations with the polities who continued to plague the northwestern territories of the former Zhou. These qualities are the very qualities attributed to King Mu, King Xiao's father, a connection that we also saw implied in Sima's narrative of King Xiao and Feizi. It is quite possible that Duke Mu's temple name is meant to draw attention to this very association as well. See Pines et al. (2013, 14). The fact that Lord Mu is credited with "restoring the ousted King Xiang (r. 651–619)," recalls the context of Zhou political factionalism that also resonates with the conditions under which King Xiao assumed power.

identification with King Xiao that extends the parameters of our comprehension of the factors contributing to its emergence as a formidable state.

The picture painted by scholars who research the social, religious, economic, political, and cultural factors that informed the birth of the Qin empire all point to an intrinsic contiguity in Qin self-representation, especially the degree to which Western Zhou ritual antecedents were preserved. Even when the Qin instituted a break with this tradition, the series of reforms that sought to restructure society in a way that emphasized the centrality of a sovereign as a force for action aligned with Di,[165] still mirrored in aim those instituted by King Xiao.[166]

Thus, to the testimony provided by the archaeological and paleographic records from which can be discerned a historical Qin state "agenda" dating from the seventh century B.C.,[167] we may add the idea that these inclinations may also be explained in terms of a neural substrate conditioned by the social distress borne from the shame and humiliation suffered by their benefactor King Xiao. This perspective permits a view of Qin actions that explains them in terms of conditioned responses to the isolating conditions of the state's birth, when it was distrusted.

In this vein we may perhaps reevaluate the hubris of Qin expressions of royal prerogative as a function of the work of self-fashioning in response to these conditions. For example, the self-important projection revealed in Qin texts that appropriate a Western Zhou royal voice neutralizes the Qin's distress over being spurned when orphaned. The claim to singularity, unparalleled in the discourse of other states and family lines, promotes initiative and precedent breaking acts. If the Qin are hubristic, it is because the imago of a king who was castigated as a usurper lies at the source of their political identity.

The same conditions may account for the "split personality" quality of the way the memory of the First Emperor was preserved, "alternatively as a hero or a villain, the proud creator of an empire that lasted for two millennia or the savage destroyer of China's traditional civilization, a model universal villain" reinforce this supposition.[168] Split personalities reveal a rupture in representational possibilities. Pines' delineation of the "Messianic" dimensions of the First Emperor's "peculiar mindset" invites a reading that explains the emperor's mindset in terms of human development, a mental structure forged by emotional conditions impacting the relational bond between King Xiao and his Qin forbears.[169]

---

165 For Qin "usurpation" of rituals related to sacrifices directed toward God on High, see Pines et al. (2013, 16). There is evidence that suggests a connection between the veneration of the Yellow Emperor as the supreme lineage ancestor and axial alignment practices.

166 Ibid., 26–28.

167 Falkenhausen and Shelach (2013, 44).

168 Pines (2013, 227). See also Pines (2008).

169 Pines (2013, 279).

The peculiar posture, manifested in paleographical inscriptions that present the Emperor Ying Zheng's "self-image," resonates with historical data that reveals Qin rulers to an almost obsessive attention directed toward the preservation of Western Zhou royal precedent in ritual. Rhetoric evinces a merging of Qin and Western Zhou identities to the point of asserting equality with the Zhou king. Lexical patterns reverberate with the discourses of "lineage potency,"[170] Sky mandates, and axial alignment, further linking Ying Zheng's "messianic" posture to the Western Zhou Ritual Reform. These data, and Sima's account, alert us to the existence of a Western Zhou inflection deep within the timbre of Qin state self-representations.

The particular penchant for inscribing royal utterances at locations that demarcate physical boundaries betrays a concern with marking spatial limits with images of sovereignty. The utterances are compositions larded with lexical fragments that scholars have traced directly to the Ritual Reform repertoire.[171] The implicit expectation, on the part of the Qin ruler, that a definite rhetorical effect will be produced by the textual images of royal prerogative recall similar assumptions underlying King Xiao's deployment of rituals as a technique for sociopolitical organization.

This is most clearly demonstrated by the way memory figures in Qin stelae inscriptions. The implication that spatial demarcation is integral to the royal project recalls the heightened sensitivity to spatial context that we have seen is endemic to interdependent mindsets. We are also reminded that the trope of a ruler's spatial delimiting acts dramatizes society's needs to accommodate and adjust to the experience of deviant events, including shameful ones. The bravado of the act of setting boundaries and proclaiming new, irreplaceable standards for royal expression, recalls the acts of King Xiao, whose initiatory reforms ushered in a new concept of sovereignty. The First Emperor's claim for legitimacy as a new leader of a new state may perhaps be seen as an effort to reinstate King Xiao the usurper's legitimacy.

The probability that the Qin are responsible for the preservation of compendia of prescriptive ritual rules, and the fact that their collation is believed to have been generated by a desire to preserve and gloss old religious vocabulary,[172] complement archaeological data that reveals how the "Qin played a role in the transmission of the Zhou ritual standards of the Late Western Zhou Ritual to later Confucian China."[173] The Qin tendency toward implementing radical reforms that effect acute changes in the relationship between state and society, such as those instituted by Duke Xiao of Qin (r. 361-338), echoes the radical changes wrought by the institutionalization of *xiao* reforms.

170 Kern (2000, 148–154).
171 Ibid.
172 Riegel (1993, 293).
173 Von Falkenhausen and Shelach (2013, 46).

The overlap in temple name contains important historical information about the relationship between the ruler who implemented policies that "transformed Qin from a loose aristocratic entity into… a 'ruler-centered' territorial state," and King Xiao.[174] While the scope of Duke Xiao's success in achieving a high level of centralization far exceeds the results of King Xiao's transformative efforts, the comparison emphasizes a genealogical link between King Xiao and Duke Xiao's vision of sovereignty. Both are premised on the ruler's capacity to control the integration of the constituent components of their domain. To cite one example of resonance, King Xiao, Duke Xiao and Ying Zheng all shared a reliance on slogans whose rhetorical objective was to bolster congruent concepts of sovereignty, one that convokes the position of the king at the top of a hierarchical axis, and one that highlighted the king's horizontalizing and alignment tendencies toward integrating broader swaths of society into socio-political circulation.

The reconstruction of concealed patterns that link these historically distinct social movements was facilitated by disinterring an archaic neural substrate that brought to light regressive family and collective histories. The wordless memories of distress experienced during Qin infancy are recoverable once we recognize how they were "locked into somatic representations" and behaviors.[175] The light illuminates the degree to which Qin messianism may be construed as a behavioral response to early social distress in the same way Neolithic alignment behavior functioned to mediate distress caused by Turtle's obsolescence. Messianism mediated the Qin's relationship with an impossible history.

Finally, the Qin quest to unify the seven warring states remaining after the more than one hundred and forty that existed upon the Western Zhou collapse may now be construed as a "gigantomaniacal" effort to retroactively legitimize their spurned claim for social and political legitimacy. The utopian wish for unification reflects a wish that the memory of King Xiao's death and the Qin's resultant social exclusion had not inflicted humiliation and grief.[176] Both the filial complex and Qin messianism reveal themselves as behaviors that bear within them traces of their own missing historical complements.

The conclusion that an act of concealment is a fundamental element of Chinese culture and history suggests that silence may be an unacknowledged historical agent. The evidence to corroborate this lies in the cultural behaviors discussed above, which are similar by virtue of the way they disguised and encoded bits or pieces of texts that were broken off from the same trauma silenced by an ancestor. Each behavior calls upon another to hear and understand that which must remain unspoken. The nonlinear approach into the roots of cultural behavior bring to the fore the precise conditions for secret transmissions. The

174 Pines et al. (2013, 29).
175 Simms (2006, 63).
176 Ibid. 30. Abraham and Torok (1994, 134).

filial complex, and Qin Imperialism, embody how a father and son's existence is culturally defined in terms of the perpetual re-creation of living out others' unspoken stories. My own attempt to listen at the very least puts into focus the processes by which early Chinese society engaged in the activity of self-fashioning.

Cited Sources

Abraham, N., & Torok, M. (1994). Nicholas Rand. Trans. *The shell and the Kernel.* Chicago.

Ames, R. T., & Rosemont Jr, H. (2016). Family reverence (xiao 孝) in the Analects: Confucian role ethics and the dynamics of intergenerational transmission. *Global East Asia, 73.* doi:10.1007/978-94-007-7113-0_7

Bachner, A. (2018). From China to Hong Kong with horror transcultural consumption in Fruit Chan's dumplings. *Interventions, 20*(8), 1137–1152.

Boodberg, P. A. (1937). Some proleptical remarks on the evolution of Archaic Chinese. *Harvard Journal of Asiatic Studies, 2*(3/4), 329–372.

Brashier, K. E. (2011). *Ancestral memory in early China* (Vol. 72). Harvard University Press.

Brown, M. (2012). *The politics of mourning in Early China.* SUNY Press.

Chan, A. (2004). *Filial piety in Chinese thought and history.* Psychology Press.

Chunqiu gongyangzhuan. Shisanjing zhushu edition. China Text Project.

Chunqiu Gongyang jingzhuan jiugu. Sibucongkan chubian edition. Vols. 31-33. Chinese Text Project.

Cook, C. A. (1997). Wealth and the Western Zhou. *Bulletin of the School of Oriental and African Studies, 60*(2), 253–294.

Cook, C. A. (2008). Ancestor worship during the Eastern Zhou. In Lagerwey, J. & Kalinowski, M. (Eds.) *Early Chinese Religion, Part One: Shang through Han (1250 BC–220 AD) . Vol. 1.* (pp. 235–280). Brill.

Csikszentmihalyi, M. (2020). Confucius. In Zaita, E. N. (Ed.) The Stanford Encyclopedia of Philosophy

Csikszentmihalyi, M., & Nylan, M. (2003). Constructing lineages and inventing traditions through exemplary figures in early China. *T'oung Pao, 89*(1), 59–99.

Di Cosmo, N. (2002). *Ancient China and its enemies: The rise of nomadic power in East Asian history.* Cambridge University Press.

Du, Y. (2018). Cong Jing shicaiyikan Xi-Zhou shiqing zhidu de zunxian gongneng. *Journal of Ancient Civilizations. 12*(4), 43–55.

Eno, R. (2003). The background of the Kong family of Lu and the origins of Ruism. *Early China, 28*, 1–41.

Feuchtwang, S. (2000). The avenging ghost: Paradigm of a shameful past. *Anthropology II: Beliefs and Everyday Life, 1*, 29.

Feuchtwant, S. (2003). The avenging ghost: A paradigm of a shameful past. In Lin, M. R. (Ed.) Belief, Ritual and Society. Institute of Ethnology, Academica Sinica, 7–36.

Feuchtwang, S. (2010). *The anthropology of religion, charisma and ghosts: Chinese lessons for adequate theory* (*Vol. 46*). Walter de Gruyter.

Fu, R. X. (2018). Xi- Zhou wangchao' guannian yuanliu kao--jianlun xian Qin "Xi-Zhou" yuci de lishi bianhua. *Lishi jiaoxue, 4*, 25–30, 37.

Gassmann, R. (2009). Two types of ancestors. A note on Xiao in *Eastern Zhou Times*," In Xiaobing Wang-Riese and Thomas O. Hollmann (Eds.), *Time and ritual in Early China*, (pp. 93–114). Harrassowitz-Verlag.

Goldin, P. R. (2008). When Zhong 忠 does not mean "Loyalty." *Dao*, 7(2), 165–174.

Goldin, P. R. (2014). *Confucianism*. Routledge.

Goldin, P. R. (2018). Confucius and his disciples in the Lunyu: The basis for the traditional view. In M. Hunter & M. Kern (Eds.), *Confucius and the Analects Revisited* (pp. 92–115). Brill.

Grundmann, J. P. (2019). Command and commitment: Terms of kingship in Western Zhou bronze inscriptions and in the Book of Documents.

Harbsmeier, C. (2019). The authenticity and nature of the Analects of Confucius. *Journal of Chinese Studies, 68*, 171–233.

Holzman, D. (1988). The place of filial piety in ancient China. *Journal of the American Oriental Society, 118*(2), 185–199.

Hsu, C. Y. (1999). The Spring and Autumn Period. In Loewe, M. & Shaughnessy, E. L. (Eds.). The Cambridge history of ancient China: From the origins of civilization to 221 BC. Cambridge University Press. (pp. 545–586).

Hsu, Y. H. (2013). A critical review of studies on Western Zhou ritual bronzes and inscriptions, from 1990 to the present. *Xin Shixue (New History), 24*(3), 185–216.

Ikezawa, M. (1994). *The philosophy of filiality in ancient China: ideological development of ancestor worship in the Zhanguo period* (Doctoral dissertation, University of British Columbia).

Jin, F. T. (2019). "Mou zhi sun, mou zhi zi"—tan Zhoudai qingtongqi mingwenzhong yzhong teshu de chengwei fangshi. *Guoxue xuekan, 3*, 31–39. *Jizhong Zhoushu*. Sibu congkan edition. Chinese Text Project.

Kaogu yu wenwu bianjibu. (2003). Baoji Mei Xian Yangjiacun jiaocang Shan shi jiazu qingtongqiqun zuotan jiyao. *3*, 13–16.

Kangxi, zidian. (1985).

Kao, K. S. (1985). *Classical Chinese tales of the supernatural and the fantastic*. Indiana University Press.

Kao, K. S. (1986). Rhetoric. In William H. Nienhauser (Ed.), *The Indiana companion to traditional Chinese literature* (pp. 121–137). Indiana University Press.

Karlgren, B. (1957). *Grammatica serica recensa* . Museum of Far Eastern Antiquities.

Kern, M. (2000). *The Stele Inscriptions of Ch'in Shih-huang: Text and Ritual in Early Chinese Imperial Representation*. American Oriental Society.

Kern, M. (2009). Bronze inscriptions, the Shijing and the Shangshu: The evolution of the ancestral sacrifice during the western Zhou. In J. Lagerwey & M. Kalinowski (Eds.), *Early Chinese Religion, Part One: Shang through Han (1250 BC–220 AD)* (2 vols.) (pp. 143–200). Brill.

Khayutina, M. (2002a). Host-guest opposition as a model of geo-political relations in pre-imperial China. *Oriens Extremus, 43*, 77–100.

Khayutina, M. (2002b). Studying the private sphere of the ancient Chinese nobility through the inscriptions on bronze ritual vessels. In McDougall, B. S. & Hansson, A. (Eds). *Chinese concept of privacy*, (pp. 81–94). Brill.

Khayutina, M. (2003). Welcoming guests—constructing corporate privacy? An attempt at a socio-anthropological interpretation of ancestral rituals evolution in ancient China (ca. XI–V cc. BC). *Berliner China-Hefte, 24*, 35–50.

Khayutina, M. (2010a). Royal hospitality and geopolitical constitution of the Western Zhou polity. *T'oung Pao, 96*(1), 1–73.

Khayutina, M., Pines, Y., Linduff, K. M., Cook, C. A., & Zhi, C. (2010b). *Landscape and power in Early China: The crisis and fall of the Western Zhou*, 1045–771 BC. Early China 33/34, Cambridge University Press, 263–286.

Kirkpatrick, A. (1995). Chinese rhetoric: Methods of argument. *Multilingua-Journal of Cross-Cultural and Interlanguage Communication, 14*(3), 271–296.

Knapp, K. N. (2005). *Selfless offspring: Filial children and social order in early medieval China.* University of Hawaii Press.

Knoblock, J. (1988-1994). *Xunzi: A translation and study of the complete works* (*Vol. 3*). Stanford University Press.

Kroll, J. L. (1985). Disputation in ancient Chinese culture. *Early China, 11*, 118–145.

Kutcher, N. (2006). *Mourning in late imperial China: Filial piety and the state.* Cambridge University Press.

Lagerway, J., & Kalinowski, M. (2009). *Early Chinese religion.* Brill.

Lee, C. Y., Chan, A. K., & Tan, S. H. (2004). *Filial piety in Chinese thought and history.* Routledge.

Levi, J. (2009). The rite, the norm and the Dao: Philosophy of sacrifice and transcendence of power in ancient China. In J. Lagerwey & M. Kalinowski (Eds.), *Early Chinese Religion, Part One: Shang through Han (1250 BC–220 AD)* (2 vols.) (pp. 645–748). Brill.

Levi, J. (2018). *Les deux arbres de la voie.* Les Belles lettres.

Lewis, T. J. (2006). Covenant and blood rituals: Understanding Exodus 24: 3-8 in its ancient near eastern context. In S. Gitin, J. E. Wright, & J.P. Dessel (Eds.), *Confronting the past: Archaeological and historical essays on ancient Israel in honor of William G. Dever* (pp. 341–350). Eisenbrauns.

Li, F. (2001). "Offices" in Bronze Inscriptions and Western Zhou government administration. *Early China, 26*, 1–72.

Li, F. (2004). Textual criticism and Western Zhou Bronze Inscriptions: The example of the Mu Gui. *Essays in Honour of An Zhimin*, 26, 1–72.

Li, F. (2006). *Landscape and power in early China: the crisis and fall of the Western Zhou 1045–771 BC.* Cambridge University Press.

Li, F. (2008). *Bureaucracy and the state in early China: governing the western Zhou.* Cambridge University Press.

Li, F. (2013). *Early China: A social and cultural history.* Cambridge University Press.

Li ji zhushu. Shisanjing zhushu edition. Chinese Text Project.

Li, W. Y. (1999). Knowledge and skepticism in ancient Chinese historiography. In C.S. Kraus (Ed.), *The Limits of Historiography* (pp. 27–54). Brill.

Li, W., & Yi L. W. (2005). Review: Foundations of Confucian thought: Intellectual life in the Chunqiu period, 722–453 B.C.E. by Yuri Pines. Honolulu: University of Hawai'i Press. 2002. *Harvard Journal of Asiatic Studies, 65*(2), 506–521.

Li, X. P. (1991). Wangquan yu shenquan. Liaoning jiaoyu.

Li, X. Q. (2003). Mei Xian Yangjiacun xinchu qingtongqi yanjiu. *Wenwu, 6*, 66–73.

Liu, Q. (2003). Filiality versus sociality and individuality: On confucianism as "consanguinitism." *Philosophy East and West, 53*, 234–250.

Liu, Q. (2006). On Confucius' principle of consanguineous affection: A reading of the dialogue about the three-year mourning in the Lunyu. *Asian Philosophy, 16*(3), 173–188.

Liu, Z. J. (1990). Shitong xinjiaozhu. Xinhua.

Loewe, M., & Shaughnessy, E. L. (Eds.). (1999). *The Cambridge history of ancient China: From the origins of civilization to 221 BC*. Cambridge University Press.

Loy, H.C. (2014). Language and ethics in the Analects. In Olberding, A. (Ed.) Dao Companions to Chinese Philosophy, vol 4. (pp. 137–158). Springer, Dordrecht.

Lunyü, Z.. Shisanjing Z. (1990).

Lunyu zhushu. Kanding Siku quanshu edition. Chinese Text Project.

Maoshi, Zhengyi (Shijing). Shisanjing zhushu edition. Chinese Text Project.

Mühlhahn, K., & Klaus, M. (2009)Nowosad,. *Criminal justice in China: A history*. Harvard University Press.

Nowosad, S. (2017). Basic Ethical Terms of Confucianism. Roczniki Teologiczne, *64*(3EV), 49–59.

Olberding, A. (2009). Ascending the hall: "Style and moral improvement in the Analects." *Philosophy East and West, 59*, 503–522.

Olberding, A. (Ed.). (2013). *Dao companion to the analects* (Vol. 4). Springer Science & Business Media.

Pankenier, D. W. (2013). *Astrology and cosmology in early China: conforming earth to heaven*. Cambridge University Press.

Pines, Y. (2000). Disputers of the "Li": Breakthroughs in the concept of ritual in pre-imperial China. *Asia Major, 13*, 1–41.

Pines, Y. (2002a). Changing views of "tianxia" in pre-imperial discourse. *Oriens Extremus, 43*, 101–116.

Pines, Y. (2002b). Lexical changes in Zhanguo texts. *Journal of the American Oriental Society, 122*, 691–705.

Pines, Y. (2002c). *Foundations of Confucian thought: Intellectual life in the Chunqiu period, 722–453 BCE*. University of Hawaii Press.

Pines, Y. (2005). Beasts or humans: Pre-imperial origins of the 'Si no-Barbarian'dichotomy. In Amitai, R. & et Biran, M. (Eds) Mongols, Turks, and others: Eurasian nomads and the sedentary world, *11*, (pp. 59–102). Brill.

Pines, Y. (2008a). *Envisioning eternal empire: Chinese political thought of the Warring States era*. University of Hawaii Press.

Pines, Y. (2008b). A hero terrorist: adoration of Jing Ke revisited. *Asia Major, 21*, 1–34.

Pines, Y. (2009). Chinese History writing between the sacred and the secular. In J. Lagerwey & M. Kalinowski (Eds.), *Early Chinese Religion, Part One: Shang through Han (1250 BC–220 AD)(2 vols.)* (pp. 315–340). Brill.

Pines, Y. (2017). Confucius' Elitism: The Concepts of junziand xiaoren Revisited. In Goldin, P. R. (Ed.). (2017). A Concise Companion to Confucius. (pp.164–184).

Pines, Y., Shelach, G., von Falkenhausen, L., & Yates, R. D. (Eds.). (2013). *Birth of an Empire* (*Vol. 5*). University of California Press.

Porter, D. L. (1996). *From deluge to discourse: Myth, history, and the generation of Chinese fiction*. SUNY Press.

Puett, M. (2005). The offering of food and the creation of order: The practice of sacrifice in early China. In Sterckx, R. (Ed.). Of tripod and palate: food, politics, and religion in traditional China, (pp. 75–95). Springer.

Puett, M. (2019). Life, domesticated and undomesticated: Ghosts, sacrifice, and the efficacy of ritual practice in early China. *HAU: Journal of Ethnographic Theory, 9*(2), 439–460.

Pulleyblank, E. G. (1962). *Chinese Historical Criticism: Liu Chih-chi and Ssu-ma Kuang. The Historical Journal, 26*, 431–446.
Pulleyblank, E. G. (2000). Ji 姬 and Jiang 姜: The role of exogamic clans in the organization of the Zhou polity. *Early China, 25*, 1–27.
Qiang, X., & Lambert, A. (2020). Translating junzi in the Lunyu as gentleman: underlying norms and deviances. *Translation Review, 106*(1), 69–88.
Qiu, X. G. (1990). Hanshi yu gaihuo—Jiezi tuifensi chuanshuo yanciu. *Zhongguo wenhua, 1*, 66–77.
Qiu, Z. L. (1995). Bu xiao zhi xiao-Tang yi lai gegu liaoqin xiansiang de shehuishi chu tan. *Xinshi xue 6*(1), 49–94.
Olberding, A. (2014). Introduction. In Olberding A. (Ed.)Dao Companions to Chinese Philosophy, *vol 4.* (pp. 1–17. Springer, Dordrecht.
Quan, G. Z. (1989). *Liangzhou jinwen. Liang-Zhou jinwen tong jiazi yanjiu.* Xuesheng shuju.
Radice, T., & Goldin, P. R. (2017). Confucius and filial piety. In Paul R. Goldin (Ed.), *A concise companion to confucius* (pp. 185–207). Wiley.
Raphals, L. (2014). Uprightness, indirection, transparency. In A. Olberding (Ed.), *Dao companion to the analects* (pp. 159–170). Springer.
Raphals, L. (2021). Virtue, Body, Mind and Spirit in the Shijing: New Perspectives on Pre-Warring States Conceptions of Personhood and Virtue. *Journal of Chinese Philosophy, 48*(1), 28–39.
Rashkin, E. (1992). *Family secrets and the psychoanalysis of narrative.* Princeton University Press.
Rawson, J. (1985). Late Western Zhou: A break in the Shang bronze tradition. *Early China, 11/12*, 289–296.
Rawson, J. (1990). *Western Zhou ritual bronzes from the Arthur M. Sackler collections.* Arthur M. Sackler Foundation.
Rosemont Jr, H., & Ames, R. T. (2008). Family reverence (xiao) as the source of consummatory conduct (ren). *Dao*, 7. doi:10.1007/s11712-008-9035-3
Rosemont Jr, H., & Ames, R. T. (2016). Confucian role ethics: A moral vision for the 21st century?. In Huang, C. C. (ed.) Global East Asia, *vol. 5.* National Taiwan University Press.
Riegel, J. K. (1993). Li chi 禮記. In M. Loewe (Ed.), *Early Chinese texts: A bibliographical guide* (pp. 293–297). Cambridge University Press.
Riegel, J. (1997). Eros, Introversion, and the Beginnings of Shijing Commentary. *Harvard Journal of Asiatic Studies*, 57(1), 143–177.
Sena, D. M. (2012). Arraying the ancestors in ancient China: Narratives of lineage history in the "Scribe Qiang" and "Qiu" Bronzes. *Asia Major, 25*, 63–81.
Shaanxi sheng kaogu yanjiu suo. (2003). Shaanxi Meixian Yangjiacun Xi Zhou qingtongqi jiaocang fajue jianbao. *Wenwu, 6*, 4–42.
Shaughnessy, E. L. (1992). *Sources of Western Zhou history: inscribed bronze vessels.* University of California Press.
Shaughnessy, E. L. (1999). Western Zhou history. In Michael Loewe and Edward Shaughnessy (Eds.), *The Cambridge history of ancient China: From the origins of civilization to 221 BC* (pp. 292–351).Cambridge.
Shaughnessy, E. L. (2009). Chronologies of ancient China: A critique of the "Xia-Shang-Zhou" chronology project. In Clara Wing-chung Ho (Ed.), *Windows on the Chinese World: Reflections by five historians* (pp. 15–28). Lexington Books.

Shaughnessy, E. L. (2011). History and Inscriptions, China. In A. F. & G. Hardy (Eds.), *The Oxford history of historical writing: Volume 1: Beginnings to AD 600, 371.*

Schuessler, A. (2007). *ABC etymological dictionary of Old Chinese*. University of Hawaii Press.

Sibau, M. F. (2018). Filiality, cannibalism, sanctity: Fleshing out Gegu in a Late Ming tale of a filial girl. *Chinese Literature, Essays, Articles, Reviews, 40*, 51–71.

Silbergeld, J. (1985). In Praise of Government: Chao Yung's Painting, "Noble Steeds," and Late Yüan Politics. *Artibus Asiae, 46*(3), 159–202.

Sima, Q. Shiji. Wuyingdian ershisishi edition. Chinese Text Project.

Simms, N. T. (2006). *Masks in the mirror: Marranism in Jewish experience*. Peter Lang.

Song, Y. W. (2018). *Divination and deviation: The problem of prediction and personal freedom in early China* (Ph.D. dissertation. University of Pennsylvania).

Slingerland, T. (1996). The conception of Ming in Early Confucian thought. *Philosophy East and West, 46*, 567–581.

Teng, M. (2013). From vassal state to empire: An archaeological examination of Qin culture. In Y. Pines, G. Shelach, L.V. Falkenhausen, & R. Yates (Eds.), *Birth of an Empire: The state of Qin revisited* (pp.113–140). University of California Press.

Valmisa, M. (2019). The reification of fate in Early China. *Early China, 42*, 147–199.

Van Ess, H. (2013). Emperor Wu of the Han and the First August Emperor of Qin in Sima Qina's Shiji. In Pines, Y. , Shelach, G. , von Falkenhausen, L. & Yates, R. D. (Eds.). Birth of an Empire, (Vol. 5). 239–25. University of California Press.

Vogt, P. N. (2012). *Between kin and king: Social aspects of Western Zhou ritual* (Doctoral dissertation, Columbia University).

Von Falkenhausen, L. V. (1993). Issues in Western Zhou studies: A review article. *Early China, 18*, 139–226.

Von Falkenhausen, L. V. (1999a). The waning of the Bronze Age: Material culture and social developments, 770–481 BC. In Loewe, M. & Shaughnessy, E. L. (Eds.) *The Cambridge History of Ancient China*, (pp. 450–544). Cambridge University Press.

Von Falkenhausen, L. V. (1999b). Late Western Zhou Taste. *Études chinoises.* 漢學研究, *18*(1), 143–178.

Von Falkenhausen, L. V. (2001). The use and significance of ritual bronzes in the Lingnan region during the eastern Zhou Period. *Journal of East Asian Archaeology, 3*(1), 193–236.

Von Falkenhausen, L. V. (2006a). The inscribed bronzes from Yangjiacun: New evidence on social structure and historical consciousness in Late Western Zhou China (c. 800 bc). In *Proceedings of the British Academy* (*Vol. 139*, p. 239). Oxford University Press.

Von Falkenhausen, L. V. (2006b). *Chinese society in the age of Confucius (1000–250 BC): The archaeological evidence* (*Vol. 2*). ISD LLC.

von Falkenhausen, L. (2011). The royal audience and its reflection in Western Zhou Bronze Inscriptions. In von Falkenhausen, L., Feng, L., & Prager, D. (Eds) Writing and Literacy in Early China: Studies from the Columbia Early China Seminar, Vol. 74, 239.

Von Falkenhausen, L., Feng, L., & Prager, D. (2011). The royal audience and its reflection in western Zhou bronze inscriptions. In L. Feng, & D.P. Branner (Eds.), *Writing and literacy in early China: Studies from the Columbia Early China Seminar* (*Vol. 74*, p. 239). University of Washington Press.

Von Falkenhausen, L., & Shelach, G. (2013). Introduction: Archaeological perspectives on the "unification" of China. In Pines, Y. , Shelach, G. , von Falkenhausen, L. & Yates, R. D. (Eds.) Birth of an Empire, (Vol. *5*). (pp. 37–52).

Wakeman, F. (1977). Rebellion and revolution: The study of popular movements in Chinese history. *Journal of Asian Studies*, 2, 201–237.

Walton, J. (2013, September). The obligatory passage point: abstracting the meaning in tacit knowledge. In *Proceedings of the 14th European Conference on Knowledge Management* (Vol. 2, pp. 769–775). Academic Conferences and Publishing International Limited.

Wang, K. P. (2020). Shehui zhengzhi biandong yu Xi Zhou wanqi de lishi biaoshu. *Shixue yuekan, 4*, 22–31.

Wang, Q. E. (2000). Objectivity, truth, and hermeneutics: Re-reading the Chunqiu. In Ching-I Tu (Ed.), *Classics and interpretations: The hermeneutic traditions in Chinese culture* (pp. 155–172) Routledge.

Wilson, B. R. (1975). *The noble savages: The primitive origins of charisma and its contemporary survival (No. 5).* University of California Press.

Xiaojing zhushu. Kanding siku quanshu edition. Chinese Text Project.

Yang, F.Y. (2017). Qianxi Xi Zhou shi rou wenhua. Huaihai gongxueyuan xuebao, *15*(2), 81–83.

Yang, B. J. (1981). *Chun qiu zuo zhuan zhu.* Zhonghua.

Yu, A. C. (1988). History, fiction and the reading of Chinese narrative. *Chinese Literature: Essays, Articles, Reviews (CLEAR), 10*(1/2), 1–19.

Zhang, X. L. (2006). Xiao zi de zhijian jiegou "Yi" Haidege'r de shijian fenxi. *Beijing daxue xuebao, 1*, 14–24.

Zhao, H. (2013). New explorations of early Qin culture. In Y. Pines, G. Shelach, L.V. Falkenhausen, & R. Yates (Eds.), *Birth of an Empire The State of Qin Revisited* (pp. 53–70). Cambridge University Press.

Zheng, Dong. (2019). Xi Zhou nong zuowu de zhongshou shijie yu wuxing xueshuo. *Nongye kaogu, 6*, 51–62.

Zhou, Z. M. (1984). *Erya jiaojian.* Jiangsu jiaoyu.

INDEX

Note: Page numbers followed by n and number represent endnote and note number.

For Product Safety Concerns and Information please contact our EU
representative GPSR@taylorandfrancis.com
Taylor & Francis Verlag GmbH, Kaufingerstraße 24, 80331 München, Germany

www.ingramcontent.com/pod-product-compliance
Ingram Content Group UK Ltd.
Pitfield, Milton Keynes, MK11 3LW, UK
UKHW020153200926
475702UK00016B/2692
9781032103969